CISTERCIAN STUDIES SERIES: ONE HUNDRED FORTY–THREE

HANDMAIDS OF THE LORD

Contemporary Descriptions of Feminine Asceticism
in the First Six Christian Centuries

Translated and Edited by
† Joan M. Petersen

CISTERCIAN STUDIES SERIES: ONE HUNDRED FORTY–THREE

HANDMAIDS OF THE LORD

Contemporary Descriptions of Feminine Asceticism
in the First Six Christian Centuries

Translated and Edited by
† *Joan M. Petersen*

Cistercian Publications, Inc.

A Cistercian Publications title published by Liturgical Press

Cistercian Publications
Editorial Offices
Abbey of Gethsemani
3642 Monks Road
Trappist, Kentucky 40051
www.cistercianpublications.org

The work of Cistercian Publications is made possible in part
by support from Western Michigan University to
The Institute of Cistercian Studies

ISBN 978-0-87907-743-3

TABLE OF CONTENTS

IN MEMORY OF
MY TEACHER AND FRIEND

AMY K. CLARKE

formerly Senior Classics Mistress

Cheltenham Ladies' College

and

Fellow of Lucy Cavendish College

Cambridge

ABBREVIATIONS

AA SS	Acta Sanctorum
CCSL	Corpus Christianorum Series Latina
CSEL	Corpus Scriptorum Ecclesiasticorum latinorum
DACL	Dictionnaire d'archéologie chrétienne et de liturgie
MGH	Monumenta Germaniae Historica
AA	Auctores antiquissimi
SRM	Scriptores rerum Merovingicarum
PG	Patrologia Graeca, ed. Migne
PL	Patrologia Latina, ed. Migne
PLRE	John R. Martindale. *Prosopography of The Later Roman Empire*. Cambridge: University Press, 1992.
SCh	Sources chrétiennes

TRANSLATOR'S PREFACE

THIS BOOK is intended for the growing number of readers in two areas. First, for those who are interested in the world of classical and late antiquity and in the history of the early Church, but who lack the necessary linguistic equipment for reading the original texts. And then I hope that it will appeal to those who are concerned with the position of women both in the Church and in contemporary society. My aim has been primarily to produce a readable translation, though I have tried to adhere as closely as possible to the original Latin or Greek. The Select Bibliography has been compiled with the needs of these readers in mind.

The choice of material for translation is my own. After consulting with Dr E. Rozanne Elder of Cistercian Publications, Inc., I have tried to cover the ground adequately, but I have deliberately omitted to translate the Rule of Saint Caesarius of Arles for nuns (*Regula sanctarum virginum*), since this has been well translated and annotated by Sister Maria Caritas McCarthy in 1960 and more recently by Père Adalbert de Vogüé in the Sources Chrétiennes series.

Acknowledgements to various individuals have been made in the separate chapters of this book, but my thanks are especially due to SCM Press Ltd for permission to reproduce the translation by the late Professor S. L. Greenslade of Jerome's *Letters* 107 and

108 from *Early Latin Theology*, and to the Community of Christ the Saviour, Little Gidding, Cambridgeshire, for information about the present-day community there.

J. M. P.

PUBLISHER'S NOTE

Joan M. Petersen was educated at Cheltenham Ladies College and St Anne's College, Oxford. For many years she worked as the Church History Editor at S.P.C.K., London, and was well known and highly respected for her discerning eye and her gracious critical judgement. After retirement, she returned to studies at Westfield and King's Colleges of the University of London, and was awarded a Doctorate in Philosophy. Her dissertation, *The Dialogues of Gregory the Great in Their Late Antique Cultural Background* was published by the Pontifical Institute of Mediæval Studies, Toronto, in 1984. Active in her parish church and a keen observer of the ecclesiastical scene, Dr Petersen died in 1994, shortly after reading the first proofs of this volume.

Ancillae tuae, Domine, cum sanctis tuis
dona requiem et gaudium aeternum

FEMININE MONASTICISM IN THE FIRST SIX CHRISTIAN CENTURIES:

AN HISTORICAL INTRODUCTION

FEMININE MONASTICISM IN THE FIRST SIX CHRISTIAN CENTURIES: AN HISTORICAL INTRODUCTION

WE DO NOT KNOW exactly how, where, and when christian monasticism began; it seems likely that the earliest monks and women religious were not formally separated from the world, but lived a life of devotion in their own homes. The author of the *Didache* writes that such people bear the whole yoke of the Lord.[1] There is also a tradition that at the time of the Decian persecutions (*c.* 250), many Christians from the civilized parts of Egypt fled to the deserts. Some of these refugees must surely have been people who had practiced a monastic discipline in their own homes. All this, however, is surmise.

It is not until the fourth century that a clearer picture of early monasticism emerges. The principal sources of our knowledge are the three most easily accessible collections of *Sayings of the Desert Fathers*: the latin subject collection, printed in PL 73 as *De vitis patrum* or *Verba seniorum*; the greek alphabetical collection of *Apophthegmata patrum* in PG 65; the greek anonymous collection, edited by Nau; the life of Antony, by Athanasius; the writings of Evagrius Ponticus; the lives of Paul the Hermit, Hilarion, and Malchus, by Jerome; the *History of the Monks in Egypt*, both in the Greek and in the Latin translation by Rufinus; the *Lausiac History* of Palladius, in the original Greek and in the latin translation known as the *Heraclidis Paradisus*; the first *Dialogue* of Sulpicius Severus; and the *Conferences* and *Institutes* of John Cassian. In addition, there are the lives of various eastern saints, by Cyril of Scythopolis, Leontius of Naples, and other authors.

Our authors do not tell us much about the origins of monasticism. All they can do is look at the phenomenon as they see it and draw their own conclusions. We can only adopt the same procedure, but we are at a disadvantage, because we are one stage further away. We have only the evidence of the writings, whereas they were able to examine the organization of the communities at first hand.

For our purposes perhaps the most valuable and important account of monasticism in the fourth and early fifth centuries is that given by John Cassian. Probably a native of the district at the mouth of the Danube now known as the Dobrudja, he became a monk in Bethlehem, but was able to make an extensive tour of the egyptian desert with his friend Germanus. There is some doubt as to whether Greek or Latin was his native tongue; at any rate he knew both languages, and writing in Latin, became a valuable interpreter of Eastern monasticism and spirituality to the West.[2] Writing in the fifth century, he aimed not so much to make an historical analysis of monasticism as to provide a schematization of what he had seen. He observed the cenobites, who lived in community under an abbot; the anchorites who, having emerged from the cenobites, lived in cells as solitaries; the Sarabaites, feeble characters who made a public cult of *abrenuntiatio*, but did not submit themselves to the will of the *seniores* or Old Men; and the rest, who lived an idiorrhythmic life in private cells, without submitting to discipline.[3] Like most Christians of Late Antiquity, Cassian sought biblical precedents for monasticism and for these divisions: the cenobites live as the whole Church lived in apostolic times, according to the celebrated description in Acts 4:32–35 and 2:44–45. When, with increasing conversions, church discipline became lax, the more zealous spirits broke away to form *coenobia* of their own and became known as μονάξουτες or monks (μοναξειν = to live in solitude and also to be celibate).[4] The anchorites are those who withdraw ἀναχωροῦντες, in order to live a more perfect life. The founders of this form of monasticism were Paul the Hermit and Antony the Great, and its exponents were regarded as imitators of Elijah, Elisha, and John the Baptist.[5] Cassian sees the cenobitic life as prior to the eremitic life, perhaps because this accorded with the practice of his own day. Once monasticism had become institutionalized, it would be more usual for new recruits to the eremitic life to emerge from the *coenobia* which they had joined earlier, rather than to attach themselves to *seniores* for training or to go far into the desert straight from secular life. Contemporary experience of the religious life supports this view. Nowadays solitaries are almost invariably men and women who have lived for some years as members of a religious community and who remain in some kind of relationship with their original house.

There is, however, an alternative tradition regarding the origins of monasticism. According to this it began with individuals who, after living some years as solitaries, became founders of *coenobia*. The principal examples of such individuals are Antony, Martin, and Benedict.

We can only speculate as to the reasons for the widespread flight into the desert—whether actual or metaphorical—in the late fourth century, but there seems no reason to reject the widely-accepted view that the establishment of Christianity as the official religion of the Empire in 315 was ultimately responsible. Cassian's schematization is probably too rigid, but it certainly appears likely that many committed Christians, no doubt sickened by the hypocrisy of new recruits who joined the Church now that it was safe and indeed fashionable to do so, took themselves off to a place where they could live a stricter and simpler life.

It will be convenient for us, in considering the question of feminine monasticism, to retain Cassian's categories of monks, though we will eliminate the worthless Sarabaites. Whatever their origins may be, these categories can be traced throughout the history of the Church, though in the case of women in the earlier periods, it would be a mistake to draw the boundaries too rigidly. We shall also need to consider two sub-categories which were unknown to Cassian: the domestic monastery, which involved male members of the family, and the dual monastery, which housed both sexes.

Perhaps the earliest mention of women leading the religious life is found in the *Catechetical Lectures* of Cyril of Jerusalem, c. 348. He tells us that at that time there were virgins in Jerusalem as well as monks. He especially exhorts them to attend to his teaching on chastity, because they are establishing an angelic life in the world; for them, a great crown is laid up.[6] We know nothing of the circumstances of the lives of these virgins, but from the fact that Cyril lists them as a category among those for whom the Church is to pray—the others are bishops, priests, deacons and solitaries—we surmise that they possessed some kind of official status.[7] Possibly they lived in their own homes, but were recognized by the Church as members of a group committed to a particular way of life.

We are on more certain ground when we come to study the lives of some christian women who lived about forty years later than Cyril, but we have to remember that these lives are not biographies in the modern sense and that they were written with the specific aim of stressing the sanctity of their subjects. The details of daily life, whether in a *coenobium* or in a domestic monastery, would therefore be of lesser interest to the author and his readers and consequently can be gleaned only incidentally.

The first picture of life in a domestic monastery is afforded by the life of Saint Macrina, written by her brother, Gregory, bishop of Nyssa. It is difficult to establish a definite chronology of the lives of Basil, Gregory, and Macrina, but it seems that Macrina decided to lead a life of virginity after the death of her fiancé when she was twelve years old, and to do so without ever leaving her mother.[8] It is interesting that Macrina took these decisions for herself. She was not dedicated to virginity by her parents, but chose a life of virginity of her own free will. At first, she continued alone in this way of life, probably at the family home at Annisa, but it appears that round about 357, on the return of her brother Basil from his studies, Macrina persuaded not only her mother but also the women of the household, both slave and free, to adopt a monastic way of life in common.[9] Their days were devoted to prayer and worship, study and manual work. At that time it was revolutionary for educated women to do humble work with their hands, but Macrina occupied herself not only with spinning wool—which had always been considered a ladylike occupation[10]—but also with baking bread.[11] The education which Gregory of Nyssa describes is an idealized monastic education rather than the education which she in fact received. This is because he was writing for a monastic readership. Gregory of Nyssa's account of his sister's education is an example of the efforts of the early writers of saints' lives to stress the special sanctity of their subjects: he says that Macrina was given a purely christian education because of the indecencies mentioned by pagan writers.[12] This observation is a commonplace among early christian writers; the alleged indecencies of classical authors do not seem to have deterred Christians, whether male or female, from reading them. If we are to believe the treatise *De anima et resurrectione* of Gregory of Nyssa, Macrina was well aware of the doctrines of the pagan philosophers, particularly the Stoics and Epicureans.[13]

The monastic household at Annisa was not an isolated phenomenon. By the end of the fourth century information about the religious life as led in Eastern Christendom had penetrated to the West by various agents, both travellers and exiles. The *Dialogues* of Sulpicius Severus contained a detailed description of the life of the Desert Fathers;[14] Honoratus, the founder of Lérins, had travelled in the Christian East,[15] but the two most important sources of knowledge were Athanasius, who was twice in exile in the West in the 330s and 340s,[16] and Jerome, who had spent a period as a solitary in the Desert of Chalcis in the 370s.[17] Athanasius's life of Antony was available in at least two latin versions in the latter half of the fourth century,[18] and Jerome supplied further information in his three religious romances, the lives of Paul the Hermit, Hilarion, and Malchus.[19]

By the end of the fourth century there may well have been feminine *coenobia* in Spain and Gaul, but the evidence for this is tantalizing rather than solid. The *Peregrinatio Egeriae* (or *Etheriae*), an account of a pilgrimage to the Holy Land made by the author from 381–384, is primarily valuable as a source of information on topographical and liturgical matters, but for our purpose what is significant is that it was written by a woman religious for the benefit of other members of her community, whom she addresses as 'reverend ladies my sisters' and 'loving sisters'.[20] Unfortunately the earlier pages of the sole manuscript of this work, from which we might have obtained information about the community, are missing, but its location was almost certainly in the West. A bishop who met Egeria at Edessa was certainly impressed by the fact that she came from 'the other end of the earth', and there is also a comparison of the nature of the Red Sea with that of 'the Ocean'.[21] Scholars now generally agree that she came from Spain.

We have no idea of the size of this community or of its rule. It may have been a large institution on pachomian lines, but more probably it was a small group of women living together on a domestic basis. All we can infer about its rule is that at least one member of the community was allowed considerable opportunities for travel.

By the time Jerome returned to Italy in 382, the religious life was already established there. As long ago as the second century, Hermas, Justin, and Minucius Felix all praise the conduct of men and women of the roman church who lead continent lives.[22] Evidence for the religious life in Italy in the third century is scanty, but in the fourth century Ambrose knew of the existence of women's communities in Verona and Bologna.[23] We do not know the date of their foundation.

Jerome gives us to understand that 340 was the year of the birth of monasticism in Rome and that Athanasius, who was in exile there between 340 and 346, was the founding father of the movement, but his words, *nulla eo tempore nobilium feminarum noverate Romae propositum monachorum*, 'at that time at Rome no lady of noble birth knew the monks' way of life', have given rise to controversy.[24] In the first place, evidence cited above, and the fact that the sister of Ambrose, Marcellina, took vows of virginity in Saint Peter's in the presence of Pope Liberius in 353, argues that they are not strictly accurate.[25] Secondly, it is possible that there was already a community of virgins in existence in the mid-fourth century at the church of Saint Agnes (in what is now the Via Nomentana), which had been founded by Constantina, daughter of the emperor Constantine, but the evidence for this is not as definite as we should like.[26] Finally, there is the evidence supplied by the ladies of Jerome's circle, to which we will return shortly.

Various attempts have been made to explain away Jerome's statement. It has been suggested that he may be implying that the monastic life was not unknown to ladies who were not *nobles*. This, however, does not account for Marcellina, the sister of Ambrose, unless Jerome was using the word *nobles* only for describing persons descended from such famous and ancient Roman families as the Scipiones or the Anicii. On the whole, it seems best to assume that he was merely writing in a rhetorical and exaggerated fashion, without giving much thought to the historical background.

In Rome Jerome was to find a number of particularly interesting women who were already leading the religious life in their own homes. They withdrew from ordinary social life and though they lived in elegant houses on the Aventine Hill, which was then a very fashionable district, they practiced rigorous fasting, wore coarse and squalid clothing, and renounced baths and hairdressing. Above all, they shunned sex. Most of them were widows or spinsters, and virginity was represented to young girls growing up in these circles as the state of the highest virtue.

The *doyenne* of these ladies was Marcella, a widow, who lived with her mother Albina, who was also a widow. According to Jerome, Marcella learned of the religious life from Athanasius himself, but she was only about twelve years old at the time of his roman exile, commentators have sometimes queried this. However, it is quite likely that when she was a child, she may have met him or heard him preach, and that being of an impressionable age, she took to heart what he said. She probably acquired more solid knowledge when she was older, during the visit of his successor, Peter of Alexandria, to Rome in 373. She was almost certainly in touch with him.[27] One scholar suggests that her rejection of the opportunity to marry the wealthy Cerealis as her second husband in *c.* 358 (at about the same time as Athanasius's life of Antony appeared in Latin) may indicate that she was conscious of a monastic vocation long before she met Jerome.[28]

One of her closest associates was another widow called Lea, a woman of deep humility and sartorial carelessness, who lived confined to her own room.[29] Another of this group was Asella, who was dedicated to virginity when she was a little over ten years old, and lived in a cell, where she fasted and worked with her hands.[30] There are two important points to be noted here. First of all, her dedication to virginity must surely have occurred some time before the arrival of Athanasius in Rome, thus contradicting the controversial statement of Jerome. Secondly, as we have already noted in the case of Macrina, it was a most extraordinary departure from convention for an educated girl or woman in those days to undertake manual work.

Originally Paula had been a member of this group, but by the time of her first meeting with Jerome—fateful for them both—she was the center of an independent circle of ascetics. This included her daughters Blesilla, Paulina, Eustochium, and Rufina. Paula, when Jerome first met her, was a wealthy widow of thirty-five. For religious reasons she had ceased to have intercourse with her husband, Toxotius, once she had borne him a son, but his death a year earlier had been a great blow.[31] Of the daughters, Blesilla and Paulina both married. Blesilla's husband soon died, and she underwent a conversion experience which led her to forsake the smart set of Rome for life in the maternal monastery.[32] Paulina married Pammachius, a very religious man many years older than herself, but predeceased him.[33] Eustochium was the daughter who was the chief source of joy to Jerome, since she freely chose a life of virginity.[34]

In these two domestic monasteries, as in the home of Macrina, intellectual activity had its place. Marcella was clearly an able woman with a down-to-earth outlook. An avid student of the Bible, she demanded and obtained from Jerome lengthy explanations of Hebrew and other words and phrases which baffled her, such as *maranatha*, or *Selah* in the Psalms.[35] Paula, on the other hand, though not lacking in ability, was of a more romantic nature. She and her circle, too, were keen students of the Bible and practiced an ardent, christocentric devotion. She preferred a more allegorical style of biblical exegesis than Marcella; this was a congenial field for Jerome, who was at this time devoting himself to the study of Origen.[36]

We know little of the liturgical practices of these fourth-century feminine monasteries. We gather from the life of Macrina that she recited portions of the Psalter seven times a day: on getting up; on beginning and finishing her work; on taking her meal; on leaving the table; on going to bed; and on getting up for prayer. In the *coenobium* which Paula subsequently founded at Bethlehem, there seem to have been five 'hours' when the Psalter was recited. We may be fairly certain that, whatever the details, the Psalter formed the basis of a round of corporate prayer.[37] There may still have been domestic monasteries in Rome during the next hundred and fifty years, but we have no evidence for them. We next hear of such monasteries there in the sixth century, when the three paternal aunts of Pope Gregory the Great—Tarsilla, Aemiliana and Gordiana—led a monastic life together, though the last named defected by marrying after the deaths of her sisters. Tarsilla was a woman of such devotion that when she died the skin on her knees was found to be hard like that of a camel.[38] On the death of her husband, Gordianus, Gregory's mother, Silvia, adopted the monastic way of life in a house on the Little Aventine, on or near the site of the present-day church of San Saba.[39] It is perhaps no coincidence that Gregory's family lived in the same district of Rome as Paula, where the tradition of domestic monasticism may have lingered on.

Some of these mixed or family monasteries, which have already been mentioned, deserve more attention. Paula's son-in-law, the widower, Pammachius, assumed the monastic habit on his wife's death, for which he was ridiculed by his senatorial colleagues. yet though he was still associated with the group on the Aventine through his family connection, there is no suggestion that he lived as a member of the community.[40] Sulpicius Severus, on the death of his wife withdrew from the world to a country house in the south of France, where he lived with his mother-in-law, Bassula, but how far this establishment can be described as a monastery is hard to determine.[41] A more definitely monastic institution was the colony of ascetics at Nola, presided over by Paulinus,

who subsequently became bishop there. A man of considerable
wealth, Paulinus originally lived in Aquitaine. Later he moved to
Spain, where he married a lady called Therasia, who bore him
a son. This child, whose name was Celsus, lived only eight days
and was touchingly commemorated by his father in one of his
poems.[42] Subsequently Paulinus underwent a conversion, which
caused him to dispose of all his property and to cease to have
sexual intercourse with Therasia. The couple ultimately settled at
Nola, where they founded a monastic community devoted to the
cult of Felix, a martyr who was buried there. Each year his feast
day was commemorated by Paulinus with a poem.[43] It appears
from the writings of Paulinus that he, like the Desert Fathers and
Benedict, laid immense stress on the physical assumption of the
monastic habit.[44] Indeed one wonders whether at first he did
not know more about the outer than the inner characteristics of
monasticism, though he probably acquired knowledge of these
later through his friend, Sulpicius Severus, and his kinswoman,
Melania the Elder.

Melania's grand-daughter, known as Melania the Younger, and
her husband Pinianu provide another example.[45] Melania wished
to become a consecrated virgin, just as Macrina had done, but
was obliged to marry Pinianus at an early age. After the deaths
of their two children, they agreed to live as brother and sister
and to free themselves from their vast possessions, though when
they had done so, the arrival of an unexpected sum of money
from Spain enabled them to create further monastic foundations.
Together they made a journey to Egypt to visit the monasteries and
hermitages in the desert—something that was the ambition of all
would-be ascetics. Then, after the death of her mother, Melania
founded a feminine monastery in Jerusalem, and later after the
death of her husband, a male monastery.

Conditions and discipline must have varied very much in these
domestic monasteries. In the entirely feminine monasteries the
materfamilias, or lady of the house, would be the ruler, with
the guidance of a priest, such as Jerome, on spiritual matters.
In the monasteries centering round a married couple, the *pater-
familias*, such as Paulinus, would take the lead, and the discipline

would be that of an old-fashioned roman family. It would appear that vows had not been strictly formulated. We do not hear of ladies, such as Paula or Melania the Elder, giving away their money or property. Instead they made good use of it to found other monastic houses. Similarly, Pammachius, though he assumed the habit of a monk, continued to attend the Senate and used the money inherited from his wife Paulina to found a *xenodochion* or hospice for pilgrims.[46] The end result might be the same as would have been achieved, had these people given their money away, but the fact remains that they retained control of it. It may well be that Paulinus acted in the same manner by using his personal fortune to erect the very extensive range of church and monastic buildings at Nola, but in his case we know that there was some definite act of *abrenuntiatio*.[47] All the monastic households we have considered certainly took the duty of chastity very seriously. Yet one has a lingering impression that people such as Sulpicius and Bassula saw their monastic life as a disciplined and consecrated version of contemporary country-house life. They perhaps anticipated Nicholas Ferrar and Little Gidding[48] rather than, for example, Benedict or the founders of Lérins.

The development of *coenobia* seems to have run parallel to that of the domestic monasteries, but here again, we find many tantalizing references and only incidental information about internal organization, discipline, and spirituality. The *coenobia* were established through the leadership of outstanding personalities rather than through the coalescing of individuals to form a cooperative. The earliest feminine *coenobia* of which we have any knowledge were all in the eastern Mediterranean area. We know that Antony, before retiring into the desert, for example, gave his sister into the care of a community of women religious, apparently in Alexandria, but details about it are not available.[49]

Paula did not confine her energies and abilities to the administration of a domstic monastery. We left her ruling her establishment on the Aventine under the spiritual direction of Jerome, who was living through what was perhaps the happiest period of his life, enjoying both his own studies and a relationship with women which was perfectly legitimate and satisfied his own emotional cravings. However, these halcyon days came to an end with the death of Pope Damasus in 384. With the powerful protection of the pope now gone, the tongues of Rome began to wag about Jerome's allegedly scandalous relationship with Paula. In great mental distress he fled to Antioch, where he was joined by Paula and her entourage. After an extensive sight-seeing tour of the Holy Land and Egypt, they returned to Palestine to found the two monasteries which were to be their homes for the rest of their lives. Both monasteries flourished. When Eustochium took over the women's monastery at Bethlehem on the death of her mother in 404, it contained consecrated virgins of many nationalities.[50] As we have seen already, they had five prayer 'hours' in the day when they recited the Psalter, and the intervals were filled with Bible study, sewing, and some domestic chores.[51] Paula kept strict discipline and did not encourage too much cleanliness. She herself took a bath only when ill. Jerome was fond of saying that dirty clothes were tokens of a clean mind.[52]

Another powerful mother-foundress was Melania the Elder, a cousin of Paulinus of Nola and, like him, immensely wealthy. This lady had been left a widow at the age of twenty-two and had also lost two of her three sons. In 372 she went to Egypt and visited the Desert Fathers. There she seems to have met Rufinus, who at that time was still the friend of Jerome. In about 381 we hear of her in Jerusalem at the head of a monastery on the Mount of Olives which contained fifty women. She also collaborated with Rufinus in founding a monastery for men in the same locality. Thus her foundations were established shortly before those of Jerome and Paula.[53] Jerome does not mention either of them in his report of his and Paula's arrival in Jerusalem, but this was written after he had quarreled with Rufinus.[54] Yet it seems highly likely that at the time of his visit, before the rift took place, he and Paula would have inspected the monasteries to glean some ideas for those which they planned to establish. Another, still later, foundation on the Mount of Olives was the women's monastery established by Melania the Younger in the 430's, after the death of her mother, but we have no details of its organization. Palladius has left us an interesting description of a women's *coenobium* in the Thebaid, run on the same lines as the men's monasteries founded by Pachomius. It contained four hundred virgins, who lived in the same manner as the men, except that they did not wear the *melota* or sheepskin. From the previous chapter in the *Lausiac History* and from the various lives of Pachomius we know how these monasteries were conducted. The members were grouped in residential communities rather like residence halls in universities today—with this difference, that they were placed together according to their personal characteristics. The pachomian monks—and presumably the women religious also—were allowed to take food and drink in proportion to the work they undertook; that is, those doing heavy work had more to eat and drink than those doing sedentary work. The diet included bread, olives, cheese, and vegetables. Meals were taken by the dormitories in shifts at different times. Work consisted of farm-laboring, gardening, metal-work, work in the bakery, basket-weaving, shoe-making, copying manuscripts, and learning the scriptures by heart. Whether all these occupations were open to the women we do not know.[55]

We have little information about the daily routine in the women's *coenobia* until the sixth century, when we learn that Caesarius, bishop of Arles, founded a women's *coenobium* in that city, under the direction of his sister Caesaria, and drew up a rule for it.[56] This rule was less severe than his rule for the masculine monastery at Arles, but as the sisters were to be in perpetual enclosure, never leaving the premises, its basis seems severe enough. These sisters seem to have been given more opportunity for intellectual development than those in the Pachomian communities. Those who were illiterate were to be taught their letters, and *lectio*, which means meditation and Bible study, was to occupy two hours every day. A book was to be read during meals. For the rest of their time, they were to do whatever the abbess directed, particularly spinning and weaving, and they were to carry out domestic tasks 'without a murmur'. Their clothing was to be neither black nor white, but *lactea*, natural-colored. Bed-clothes and table-linen were to be as plain as possible. No meat was to be eaten, not even at feasts. There were to be no private cells. The position of the abbess is defined. The community is to elect unanimously someone who is holy and spiritual. She is to appoint officers to help her by taking charge of the different departments of the monastery; one is to be in charge of the catering, another of the distribution of wool, and a third, of the porter's lodge. No candidate is to be admitted to the monastery who is less than six or seven years old.

In the mid-sixth century Radegunde founded her religious house at Poitiers. She had been married somewhat reluctantly to the frankish king Chlothar I, but she abandoned him for the cloister after an unknown period of married life. She appears to have consummated her marriage, but to have had no children. Her house was famous for its relic of the True Cross, which had been received from the emperor Justin II and which still exists at the Abbaye de Sainte-Croix de Poitiers at Saint Benoît-sur-Quinçay, a few miles from Poitiers. It was this relic that inspired Venantius Fortunatus, an Italian who became bishop of Poitiers in the late sixth century, to write the magnificent hymns, *Vexilla regis prodeunt*, and *Pange, lingua, gloriosi*, familiar to English-speaking Christians as 'The royal banners forward go' and 'Sing, my tongue, the glorious battle'. They were sung when the relic arrived at Poitiers. The Rule of Saint Caesarius of Arles for nuns was adopted by Radegunde, but almost certainly modified to suit the circumstances of the monastery at Poitiers. Radegunde's sisters lived as an enclosed, contemplative community, guarding the precious relic. Fortunatus clearly regarded the house as an oasis of civilization amid the turmoil of Merovingian Gaul. The amusing poems and acrostics he sent to Radegunde suggest that life here had its lighter side, strict though it was. His touching affection for Radegunde and her spiritual daughter Agnes was a more gentle version of the feelings of Jerome for Paula and Eustochium.

During the same period *coenobia* were to be found in Rome itself. Gregory the Great refers in his *Dialogues* to a number of *sanctaemoniales*, some of whom seem to have been cenobites. Among these was the bearded nun, Galla, who 'having laid aside her secular attire, devoted herself to the service of Almighty God at the monastery of Blessed Peter the Apostle'. The doctors told this unfortunate widow that since she had a fiery complexion, she would grow a beard unless she worked off her sexual energy in a second marriage, but so strong was her sense of her religious vocation that she was prepared to endure this deformity. There are references in the same passage to her colleague, Sister Benedicta, and to the Mother of the whole community. We are given no details about the internal arrangements of this religious house, but we have the impression that the women were occupied principally in prayer and contemplation. Gregory writes that Gallas was dedicated to simplicity of heart and to prayer and that she gave substantial alms to the poor, which suggests that she retained control of her own fortune.[57]

Women were certainly to be found among Cassian's category of anchorites. Our impression so far is that the majority of the women solitaries were to be found in or near towns. We have already noticed Lea and Asella, who were members of the group of ascetic roman ladies led by Marcella, but who lived as recluses, confined to their own rooms. Palladius tells us of other women living under similar conditions in Eastern Christendom: the virgin of Jerusalem who lived as a recluse clad in sackcloth, but later unfortunately fell from grace, for example; and the deaconess of Antioch, Sabiniana, the aunt of John Chrysostom, who lived in communion with God.[58] Melania the Younger lived on two occasions in a hermitage on the Mount of Olives, not too far from the center of Jerusalem. By the mid-sixth century there were certainly women solitaries in Italy: Gregory the Great tells us of the virgin Gregoria, who lived near the church of Saint Mary Major in Rome; she was probably an exile from Spoleto which lay in Lombard territory.[59] He also mentions a consecrated virgin of Spoleto who drove a demon into a pig, but does not indicate her exact status.[60] Some of the virgins in Italy may have lived in groups, rather as the groups of anchorites lived in Egypt: for example Herundo had lived in the hills above Praeneste (the modern Palestrina), where she trained a companion, Redempta, who later settled in Rome with two disciples.[61] The evidence, in fact, suggests that the monastic life for women was organized on a

more informal basis than for men, and that owing to the unsettled
state of the countryside, resulting from the campaigns of Belisar-
ius and the later Lombard wars, it tended to be urban in character.
Thus the individual women religious whom Gregory mentions
are settled in Rome and Spoleto, and the spiritual descendants of
Herundo do not remain at Praeneste, but come down from the
hills into Rome.

A letter from Gregory to the empress Theoctista appears to con-
firm the idea that the women religious had to flee from invaders
and settle in Rome and other cities. Gregory thanks the empress
for a gift of thirty pounds of gold which, he says, will be used to
provide beds for the considerable number of sisters in Rome. The
inference is that they are refugees who have had to flee, leaving
all their belongings behind them. It seems most unlikely that there
were large cenobite institutions of the Pachomian type for women
in Rome at this date.[62]

As we have already noticed, Gregory does not furnish us with
much information about the role of these women in the christian
community, but we form the impression that whether living as
cenobites or anchorites, they were occupied principally in prayer
and contemplation, though Gregoria was quite prepared to indulge in reminiscences of Spoleto with interested visitors.[63] There
is no record of any of them performing any kind of counselling
function. The sole mention by Gregory of 'Works' carried out by
a community of women religious is found in *Dialogue* 3, where
he writes of a little boy living in the care of such a community.[64]

I have purposely left as a separate topic, taken out of chronological order, a very interesting group of women, whom we may call
the Desert Mothers. We find in the greek alphabetical version of
the *Apophthegmata patrum* and also in the latin subject version
a collection of sayings uttered by women bearing the title *Amma*,
the feminine form of *Abba*, the title given to the Desert Fathers.
Who were these women? How did they arrive in the desert? What
was their mode of life there? Above all, is there anything about
their utterances which distinguishes their spirituality from that of
their male colleagues? Their names may afford a slight clue. Sarah
suggests that its bearer was of Jewish descent, whereas Theodora

and Syncletica are names of greek origin. It has sometimes been argued that there cannot have been women living independently in the desert, but there is certainly evidence to the contrary. For example, Palladius tells us of Alexandra, who made her home in a tomb, a practice which recalls Antony.[65] The sayings of these *Ammas* are found in both collections of *Apophthegmata* in exactly the same form as those of the Desert Fathers. Might not these women have been included among the characters in the *Apophthegmata patrum* precisely because they lived in the Desert in the same way as the men?

Theodora was obviously an outstanding character among the resident Desert Mothers. She was capable of consulting Archbishop Theophilus, the great opponent of Origenism, but at the same time, she was herself consulted by many monks about the problems of the monastic life. The keynote of her counsel was the practice of humility. She was a woman who looked problems and difficulties in the face. She pointed out that as soon as living in peace was achieved, the monk or virgin was immediately assailed by evil, which could best be cured by humility.[66]

Amma Sarah was an equally valiant woman. She never prayed for deliverance from the demon of fornication, but only for strength for the battle. She was never one to dwell on her weakness as a woman. One of her sayings was, 'According to nature, I am a woman, but not according to my thoughts'.[67] Amma Syncletica must have been consulted frequently, just as Amma Theodora was. Like some of the Desert Fathers, she uses the imagery of fire to signify the purification of the human spirit. She too believed in facing evil and doing battle and cultivating humility.[68]

It seems unlikely that the Desert Mothers had much time or opportunity for study, if the lives of the Desert Fathers are to serve as a precedent. The desert monks, both the cenobites in the pachomian monasteries and the anchorites, were chiefly local peasants, despite a group of sophisticated intellectuals, such as Arsenius, Evagrius Ponticus, and Macarius of Alexandria. Books were regarded with some displeasure; a monk who sold a copy of the Gospels and gave away the proceeds, was respected and admired.[69] It is, of course, possible that Amma Theodora was the feminine counterpart of the more intellectual Desert Fathers, but of this we have no evidence.

There is about the teaching of the women of the desert the same willingness to face reality, to attack evil vigorously, to make war on sloth and to practice charity and humility that we find among the Desert Fathers. There is nothing in the utterances of these women to suggest that they practiced or preached some kind of spirituality peculiar to women.

In considering the whole subject of early feminine monasticism —or indeed any other historical subject—it is important to see it in relation to the circumstances of its own time. It is useless to try to judge early feminine monasticism in the light of the ideas and attitudes of the late twentieth century, expecting to see in it some early manifestation of the feminist movement of our own day. These women were not out to demonstrate anything except their love of God and their faithfulness to their calling and were prepared to make considerable sacrifices in order to do so, just as many christian women, by the grace of God, are doing today and will continue to do in the future.

NOTES

1. Didache 6.1 (Didache); *La doctrine des douze apôtres*, ed. and trans. W. Rordorf and A. Tuilier, SCh 248 (Paris, 1978) 168–169.

2. For an exposition of the generally accepted view that Cassian was a native of the Dobrudja, with Greek as his mother tongue, see H. I. Marrou, 'Jean Cassien à Marseille,' *Revue du moyen âge latin* 1 (1945) 1–26; 'La patrie de Jean Cassien,' *Orientalia Christiana periodica* 13 (1947) 588–596. This view is questioned by K. Zelzer, 'Cassianus natione Scytha, ein Südgallier,' *Wiener Studien* 104 (1991) 161–168, who makes out a good, but not altogether conclusive, case for the western origins of Cassian.

3. John Cassian, *Collationes* 18.4; *Conférences*. ed. and trans. W. Rordorf and A. Tuilier, SCh 248 (Paris, 1978) 168–169.

4. *Ibid*. 5. SCh 2: 14–16. For a recent and most interesting interpretation of μόναχοι see A. de Vogüé, 'Renoncement et désir: la définition du moine dans le commentaire de Grégoire le Grand sur la premier livre des Rois', *Collectanea Cisterciensia* 48 (1986) 54–70.

5. *Conf* 6; SCh 42: 17–18, and *De institutis coenobiorum* 1.1, *Institutions cénobitiques*, revised text, intr., ed. and trans. J. C. Guy, SCh 109 (Paris, 1965) 36–39.

6. Cyril of Jerusalem, *Catechesis* 4.24; PG 33:485.

7. *Ibid*., 16.22; PG 33:949.

8. Gregory of Nyssa, *Vita S. Macrinnae* 4; *Vie de sainte Macrine*, ed. and trans. P. Maraval, SCh 178 (Paris, 1971) 154–155.

9. *Ibid.*, 5; SCh 178:156–157.

10. Jerome, *Ep.* 107.10; *Epistulae*, ed. I. Hilberg, CSEL 55 (Vienna, 1912) 300.

11. *Vita S. Macrinae* 5; SCh 178:158–159.

12. *Ibid.* 3; SCh 178:148–151.

13. See PG 46:21.

14. Sulpicius Severus, *Dialogues* 1.1–24; *Libri qui supersunt*, ed. C. Halm, CSEL 1 (Vienna, 1866) 152–176.

15. Hilary of Arless, *Vita S. Honorati* 13; *Vie de saint Honorat*, ed. and trans. M. D. Valentin, SCh 235 (Paris, 1977) 102–103.

16. The first exile of Athanasius was at Trier, 335–337 (*contra Arianos* 87; PG 25:408) and the second at Rome, 340–346 (*de synodis* 26; PG 26:72). See also Socrates, *HE* 4.23; PG 67:520; Jerome, *Ep.* 127.5; CSEL 56:149.

17. For Jerome's experiences in the desert, see *Ep.* 22.7–8; CSEL 54:152–153 and pp. 175–6 of this book. See also P. H. Rousseau, *Ascetics, authority and the Church in the age of Jerome and Cassian* (Oxford, 1978) 133; J. N. D. Kelly, *Jerome: his life, writings and controversies* (London, 1975) 170–171.

18. See Athanasius, *Vita S. Antonii: un temoin important du texte de la vie de saint Antoine: la version inédite des archives des chapître de Saint Pierre à Rome*, ed. G. Garitte (Brussels and Rome, 1939) 4–7. H. Hoppenbrouwers, ed., *La plus ancienne version de la vie de saint Antoine, par saint Athanase: étude de critique* (Nijmegen, 1960) supplies a better text.

19. *Vita Pauli primi eremitae*; PL 23:17–30; (*Vita Ilariolnis*) *Vita di Ilarione*, intr. by C. Mohrmann; ed. A. A. R. Bastiaensen; Italian trans. by C. Moreschini, Vite di Santi 4 (Milan, 1975) 73–143; *Vita Malchi monachi captivi*, PL 23:55–62.

20. *Egeria's travels*, ed. and trans. by J. Wilkinson (London, 1971) 3.8 (p. 95), 5.7 (p. 98).

21. *Ibid.*, 19.5 (p. 115); see also p. 207.

22. (Shepherd of Hermas) *Der Hird des Hermas*, Sim. 87.1; ed. M. Whittaker, GCS 48, 48/2 (Berlin, 1967) 84–85.

23. Ambrose, *Ep.* 5; PL 16:929–937; idem, *de virginitate* 1.10.16; PL 16:216.

24. Jerome, *Ep.* 27.5; CSEL 56:149.

25. Paulinus of Milan, (*Vita S. Ambrosii*) *Vita de S. Ambrogio*, intr. by C. Mohrmann; ed. A. A. R. Bastiaensen, Italian trans. by L. Canali, Vite di Santi 3 (Milan, 1975) 58–59.

26. Ambrose, *De virginitate* 1.2.5–9 (PL 16:200). See P. Schmitz, 'La première communauté de vierges à Rome', *Revue Bénédictine* 38 (1926) 189–195; G. D. Gordini, 'Origine e sviluppo del monaschesimo a Roma', *Gregorianum* 37 (1956) 220–260; R. Lorenz, 'Die Anfänge des abendländischen Mönchtums im 4. Jahrhundert', *Zeitschrift für Kirchengeschichte* 77 (1966) 12–18.

27. Jerome, *Ep.* 27.5; CSEL 56:149.
28. See above, note 24.
29. Jerome, *Ep.* 23.2; CSEL 54:213–214.
30. Jerome, *Ep.* 24 (CSEL 54:214–217); Palladius, *Historia Lausiaca* 41.4, ([*Historia Lausiaca*] *La storia Lausiaca*, intr. by C. Mohrmann; ed. G. J. M. Bartelink; Italian trans. by M. Barchesi, Vite di Santi 2 [Milan, 1974] 212–213= *Heraclidis Paradisus* 29, PL 74:315).
31. Jerome, *Ep.* 108.4–5; CSEL 55:309–310.
32. For Blesilla, see *Ep.* 22.15 (CSEL 54:162–163); *Ep.* 39 (293–311).
33. *Ep.* 108.4–5; CSEL 55:309–310.
34. For Jerome's attitude to Eustochium, see *Ep.* 39 (293–311).
35. For the ten Hebrew names of God, see *Ep.* 22; CSEL 54:143–211.
36. E.g., *Ep.* 30; CSEL 54:243–249.
37. Gregory of Nyssa, *Vita S. Macrinae* 3.22–24 (SCh 178:148–151: see also pp. 69–71); Jerome, *Ep.* 108 (CSEL 55:334–336).
38. Gregory the Great, *Dialogues* 4.17 (*Grégoire le Grand: Dialogues*, ed. A. de Vogüé, trans. by P. Antin, 3 vols, SCh 251, 265, 266 [Paris, 1978–1980] SCh 266:68–71); *Homeliae in Evangelia* 38.15 (PL 76:1290–1291). The description of Tarsilla's knees is a *topos*; cf. Jerome, *Ep.* 24.5 (CSEL 54:216–217, Asella); Hegesippus, cited in Eusebius, *HE* 2.23.6 (GCS Eusebius 2 [1], ed. E. Schwartz and Th. Mommsen [Leipzig, 1903] 166–167: St James the Less).
39. John the Deacon, *Vita S. Gregorii Magni* 1.9–10; PL 75:65–66. For Gregory's mother's name, see (The anonymous Monk of Whitby) *The earliest life of Gregory the Great*, ed. and trans. by B. Colgrave (Lawrence, Kansas, 1968).
40. Jerome, *Ep.* 66.6; CSEL 54:654. See also Palladius, HL 62.1, 268–269 (HP 50, PL 74:334).
41. Sulpicius Severus, *Ep.* 3 (CSEL 1:146); Paulinus of Nola, *Ep.* 5.5–7 (CSEL 29:28–29).
42. Paulinus of Nola, *Carmina* 31.607–608; ed. W. von Hartel (Vienna, 1894), CSEL 29.2:329. For the act of *abrenuntiatio*, see Gregory of Tours, *Liber in gloria confessorum* 108; *MGH rerum Merovingicarum* 1.2:367–368.
43. Augustine, *De civitate Dei* 1.10; ed. B. Dombart and A. Kalb, CCSL 47 (Turnholt, 1953) 11–12.
44. Jerome, *Ep.* 66.6; CSEL 54:654. Cf. e.g., Gregory the Great, *Dialogue* 2.1 (SCh 265:142–143); [Rufinus] *Historia monachorum in Aegypto* 9 (PL 21:423); (Pachomius) *Vita latina* 7 (trans. by Dionysius *Exiguus*, ed. H. van Cranenburgh, Subsidia hagiographica 46 [Brussels, 1969] 96–97; *De Vitis patrum* 6.5, (PL 73:994); Cyril of Scythopolis, *Vita S. Iohannis Hesychastis* 4 (*Kyrillos von Skythopolis*, ed. E. Schwartz [Leipzig, 1939] 41.
45. For details of their lives, see Palladius, HL 61:264–269.
46. Jerome 66.11 (CSEL 54:661–662); 118.5 (CSEL 55:441).
47. See note 43 above.
48. See Appendix, page 433.
49. Athanasius, *Vita S. Antonii* 3.1; intr. by C. Mohrmann, ed. G. J. M.

Bartelink; Italian trans. by P. Citati and S. Lilla, Vite di Santi 1 (Milan, 1974) 10–11.

50. Jerome, *Ep.* 108; CSEL 55: 306–351, especially 335–338.

51. For prayers at the monastery, see *ibid.*, pp. 334–336; and for the monastic routine, pp. 326 and 348.

52. On the undesirability of baths, see Jerome, *Ep.* 108.15 (CSEL 55:325–326); 125.7 (CSEL 56:124). Apart from the general feeling of distaste for the body and its functions, which was perhaps derived from the Orient and fostered by the unconscious influence of Manichaeism, there were good grounds for discouraging Christians from attendance at the public baths, where it was normal in both republican and imperial Rome to take the daily bath. Bathing there was mixed and in the nude, and by the fourth century the ablutions themselves were chiefly a pretext for gossip and licentious behavior on premises which were sometimes adorned with wall-paintings and graffiti, such as would embarrass the virtuous and corrupt the young. Various efforts were made, particularly by Christians, to enforce single-sex bathing, either by setting aside rooms for women only or by arranging separate bathing hours for them, but the bad behavior persisted. It seems as though disapproval of bad behavior was somehow transferred to the act of bathing itself. For further information on the subject, see the article *Bain* in the DACL.

53. Palladius, HL 46:224–25 (HP 33; PL 74:319).

54. We might have expected to find a reference to these establishments in Jerome, *Ep.* 108.9 (CSEL 55:14–15), where Jerome describes his and Paula's visit to Jerusalem, but we do not.

55. For the women's monastery, see Palladius, HL 33:160–163 (HP 20; PL 74:298); for the men's monastery, HL 32.2–7; 152–157 (HP 19, PL 74:296–297).

56. For the foundation of the monastery, see Cyprian of Toulon, *Vita Caesarii Arelatensis* 1.35 (MGH rerum Merovingicarum 3:470); ibid., 2.47 (500). For the text of the rule, see *Regula Caesarii*, ed. G. Morin, Florilegium patristicum (Bonn, 1933). A useful translation of the Rule is provided by M. C. McCarthy, *The Rule for Nuns of Saint Caesarius of Arles*: Translation with a critical Introduction (Washington, DC, 1960).

57. Gregory the Great, *Dialogues* 3.14; SCh 260; 302–303.

58. For the virgin of Jerusalem, HL 28, 142–144 (HP 16; PL 74:293); for Sabiniana, HL 41, 210–211 (HP 29; PL 74:315).

59. Gregory the Great, *Dialogues* 3.14; SCh 260:302–303.

60. *Ibid.*, 3.21 (352–355).

61. *Ibid.*, 4.16; SCh 265:62–69.

62. Gregory the Great, *Registrum* 7.23; ed. D. Norberg, CCSL 140 (Turnholt, 1984) 477.

63. See note 58 above.

64. *Dialogues* 3.21; SCh 260:352–353.

65. Palladius, HL 5, 28–31 (HP 1; PL 74:255).

66. For Sarah, see *Apophthegmata patrum Graecorum* (PG 65:420–421). *de Vitis patrum*, 5.10 (PL 73:876); 7.19 (896–897); 10.73–74; *ibid.*, 925.

67. For Theodora, see *Apophthegmata patrum Graecorum*, PG 65:201–204.

68. For Syncletica, see *Ibid* (PG 65:421–428); *De Vitis patrum* 5.3.16 (PL 73:862); 41–43, (870); 6.13, (890–891); 7.15–18 (895–896); 8.19–20 (909); 10.70–72 (924–925); 11.32–34, (937–938); 14.9 (949–950); 6.1.2 (993).

69. This story is told of at least two of the Desert Fathers. See *Apophthegmata patrum Graecorum* (PG 65:188); *De Vitis patrum* 5.6.6 (PL 73:889: Theodore of *Pherme*); 3.70 (*Ibid*. 772–773: Serapion).

MACRINA

A DOMESTIC
MONASTERY
IN
CAPPADOCIA

INTRODUCTION

THE CHARMING *Vita S. Macrinae* of Gregory of Nyssa was first translated into English by the late Dr W. K. Lowther Clarke, a former General Secretary of the Society for Promoting Christian Knowledge. His little book was published by that house in 1916. Owing to wartime publishing difficulties, the edition was small and the work consequently did not have as wide a circulation as it deserved. It has long been out of print and in the interval, much work has been done in the field of textual criticism and hagiography which has provided the occasion for further editions and translations, notably those of Dr Virginia Woods Callahan (*St Gregory of Nyssa: Ascetical Works*, Fathers of the Church 58 [Washington, 1967] pp. 159–191) by Kevin Corrigan (Peregrina Press: Saskatoon-Toronto, 1987), and of M. Pierre Maraval (*Vie de sainte Macrine*, SCh 178 [Paris, 1971]). It seems, however, that there is room for another translation, which would set the work in its context as a record of life among women in the fourth-century Church and an account of early monasticism. I have used Pierre Maraval's text throughout. My debt to this scholar as regards the notes and commentary to my translation is immense, and I acknowledge here with grateful thanks the help that his work has afforded me.

THE SETTING OF THE WORK

The scene of the life and work of Macrina is set in what was then called Asia Minor, but which is now part of modern Turkey. We do not know where Macrina was born, but the chief part of her life was passed in her family home at Annisa, not far from the shores of the Black Sea. Her background was aristocratic. We learn from Gregory of Nyssa's narrative that her father, the elder Basil, had been an able local leader, but that he was not much known outside his own district. Her mother, Emmelia, was apparently also of good family: Gregory tells us that Macrina persuaded her to abandon 'the manners of a woman of the world' when their home was converted into a monastery. The family had long been Christian; indeed some of their forebears had suffered for their faith. Their financial circumstances in the late fourth century were certainly very comfortable, though they do not appear to have possessed the vast wealth of other Christians of the same era, such as Melania the Younger or Paulinus of Nola.

In all probability Emmelia bore nine children, though the number of her family has been disputed. Three of them became famous: Macrina herself, who was the eldest, Basil, who became bishop of Caesaraea and is regarded as the father of monasticism in the Eastern Church; and Gregory, bishop of Nyssa, a theologian, and the author of this work. Another great theologian, Gregory of Nazianzus, was a close friend of Basil and must have formed part of the family circle. In fact this household is an early example of a phenomenon which is attractive both in literature and in life, the extended christian family, where there is deep affection between relatives and a few intimate friends and where strong common interests are to be found.

We do not know the exact site of the family home, but we may conjecture that it was a large house built round a courtyard, similar in ground plan to those remains of roman villas that are still to be found in Europe and the Middle East in the former Roman Empire. The chapel, in which Emmelia had deposited the relics of the Forty Martyrs of Sebaste,[1] and where she and her husband and Macrina were to be buried, was eight stades from the house. From

Gregory's narrative, we can distinguish two monastic buildings, one for men and one for women, which were apparently close to one another, and a hermitage on the river bank, where Basil and by inference, Naucratios lived, but unless and until archaeological excavations are carried out in the district, we cannot determine the layout or extent of the monastic settlement.

Just as we do not know where Macrina was born, we do not know the exact date of her birth, but it is probable that it occurred in 327 and that Basil was born a year or two later. In that case, Macrina's decision to lead a celibate life must have been made in 339 or 340, and the return of Basil from his studies and the adoption of the fully monastic life by Emmelia must have occurred in 357. The death of Emmelia may have taken place between the great famine of 368/9 and the consecration of Basil as bishop in 370, as Gregory's narrative suggests, but in all probability, he was grouping events in their logical rather than their chronological order. Basil in *Ep.* 30, which can be dated to 371, writes of his mother's death as though it were quite a recent event. This suggests 370 or 371 as its probable date.

The whole of Gregory's narrative is full of chronological difficulties, although it is not necessary to trouble the general reader with the details. We need constantly to remember that he was neither an historian nor a biographer in the modern sense., but was concerned with remembering the deeds of a holy woman for the benefit of his contemporaries and posterity. According to the evidence relating to the death of Basil and the Council of Antioch, which Chapter Fifteen of the *Life* supplies, the death of Macrina must have occurred either late in 379 or early in 380, but this conflicts with Gregory's description of his rest in the arbor. The district of Pontus is notorious for its severe winters, so it is unlikely that Macrina should have sent him out of doors if her illness occurred during December or January. One suggestion is that Gregory is here introducing a *topos* known as the *locus amoenus*: the lovely place. There is evidence elsewhere in his writings that he was a lover of natural beauty, and the arrangments he describes, of vines climbing up trees to form a kind of tunnel, are common in the district to this day. It would be natural for someone familiar with Annisa to employ this *topos*. In support of this view it is also urged that the commemoration of Saint Macrina is assigned to 19 July in all the menologies and synaxaria of the Eastern Orthodox Church, but those who compiled them may simply be following Gregory's *topos*. For those who are interested, Pierre Maraval sets out the various hypotheses in his introduction to his edition of the *Vita*.[2] Perhaps the most reasonable interpretation is that of Bollandus.[3] We know that in the Eastern Mediterranean area the New Year did not begin on 1 January. If we take the year of the Council of Antioch as beginning in September/October 379, then 19 July 380 would be a reasonable date for the death of Macrina. It would accord with Gregory's desire to see his sister, after the ending of the Council, but before a year had passed.[4]

THE LITERARY FORM OF THE *VITA S. MACRINAE*

The *Life of Saint Macrina* contains a high proportion of material relating to the death and burial of its subject, but it is neither a funeral oration nor a eulogy. The composition of both these literary forms was based on certain strict rules of which Gregory of Nyssa was well aware, but he makes no attempt to follow them here. He himself explains in his introduction that his writing is in the form of a letter, but because he has so much to say, it exceeds a normal letter in length and has taken on the character of a piece of historical writing.

As we have already seen, however, this work is not a history or a biography in the modern sense of the terms. There is no attempt to collect and sift evidence in order to arrive at the truth or to provide exact dates or indeed to arrange the material in chronological order. We know well that historians existed in classical times, in Late Antiquity, and in the early Middle Ages, who were perfectly capable of doing any of these periods was not to provide a factual record in his *Life*, or to draw conclusions from his evidence, but to instruct and edify his readers with spiritual and moral reflections. The *Vita S. Macrinae* appears to have two literary ancestors: the greek philosophical biography and the legends of the martyrs, from which the whole genre of late antique and early medieval hagiography is derived.

The earliest philosophical biography written in Greek was perhaps the life of Heracles, by Antisthenes of Athens, who lived *c.* 449 bc. Later examples are the life of Aollonius of Tyana, by the second-century writer Philostratus, which contains accounts of miracles that may have been intended to counteract the influence of the miracle stories in the Gospels, and various lives of Pythagoras. The life of Antony by Athanasius may be cited as a christian counterpart of these works, written in Gregory's own day. *The Vita S. Macrinae* possesses a certain philosophical content, related to Platonism and Stoicism, particularly in its stress on the government of the passions by reason and on the virtue of impassibility, but it differs from other philosophical biographies in that it does not use as its ground-plan the various stages in Macrina's spiritual development, but simply tells the reader that as time went on, her life became more and more detached from earthly things and acquired an angelic quality.

The *Vita S. Macrinae* may be regarded as an example of a hagiography—that is, of a class of writing about holy men and women—which in its christian guise began in Late Antiquity and came to its full development in the Middle Ages, but which has affinities with the celebrated *Parallel Lives* of noble Greeks and Romans by Plutarch (*c.* ad 50–120), and with the early accounts of the martyrs, such as the *Passio S. Perpetuae* in the early third century. In the early days of the Christian Church martyrdom was held up to the faithful as the highest good; after the Peace of the Church, when opportunities for martyrdom were much less frequent, if not altogether non-existent, some substitute for it had to be found to encourage church people to strive for the highest. The principal substitute for it was monastic life. In the life of Saint Macrina, Gregory of Nyssa makes a definite effort to equate his subject, the leader of a religious community, with the martyrs. He professes to recognize in his dying sister 'the relics of a holy martyr, who lay dead to sin, but shone with the grace of the Holy Spirit'. The aim of the hagiographer was to paint the portrait of a holy person for the edification of the reader, but on the whole, Gregory sits lightly upon the accepted structures. Apart from linking Macrina with the martyrs, his writing is free from moral conclusions; he lets Macrina's beauty of character speak for itself. Yet it would be extraordinary if his writing did not bear the marks of the culture of his age, and we certainly find a few of them in the *Vita*. In hagiographical writings the role of the father of the holy man or woman is generally played down, as it is here, but in this case, he may be a shadowy figure simply because Gregory of Nyssa had been only a small boy when his father, the elder Basil, died. The hagiographers always lay great stress on the importance of the pious widowed mother in the upbringing of the saint, but though this aspect of the matter is not neglected by Gregory of Nyssa, the work is unusual in that we find *two* mother figures: Emmelia in relation to Macrina, and Macrina, in relation to her younger brothers and to the women in her community. Various *topoi* or commonplaces occur: Macrina's physical beauty; her aptitude for learning; her determination to ward off potential suitors in order to lead a life of celibacy; her ability to perform miracles. I have tried to draw attention to these points in the notes. The existence of such *topoi* inevitably affects the value of a saint's life as an historical source, but once one is aware of their nature, it is possible to look beyond them to see how far the writer has succeeded in both conveying useful information and in painting a portrait of a real person.

The *Vita S. Macrinae* is a unique historical, social and spiritual document. Though it may contain some of the *topoi* of a hagiography, it does not altogether conform to the conventional structure of either a philosophic life or the life of a late antique or medieval saint. It possesses its own distinct framework, from which, however, Gregory makes a number of digressions. The reason for its freshness, liveliness, and lack of rigid conformity with accepted norms of composition is that it is written in the form of a family chronicle by someone who was an eyewitness of many of the events that it described and who was actuated by motives of family affection and a desire to honor the dead.

The work falls into six sections:

THE VALUE OF THE VITA S. MACRINAE

In spite of the very different circumstances of our lives, the *Vita S. Macrinae* has a devotional value for us today. Gregory's beautiful account of his sister's life still has power to move us. When once we have cleared away the traces of conventional hagiography, the portrait of a capable woman of strong character who, though clearly a person of intellectual ability, was willing to perform lowly household tasks and was devout, loving, patient, and humble, emerges. It is evident that Macrina was a person who inspired deep affection in others and that she had a considerable influence on those around her, particularly her mother and brothers. She indeed lives up to Basil's description of her in *Ep.* 19,[5] where he compares her to a strong tower,[6] a shield[7] and a strong city.[8] He also stresses the quality of motherliness, which we can see that Macrina showed towards Basil when she helped him to shed his youthful conceit on his return from his studies,[9] and towards Gregory himself, when as she lay dying, she made arrangements for his comfort after a long and tiring journey and gave him wise advice.[10]

In an age when death, not sex, is the forbidden subject, Macrina shows us how to die. Early in her life, when she refused to marry after the death of her fiancé, Macrina proclaimed her faith in the resurrection and the life of the world to come. The same faith is evident in Gregory's description of her death. Macrina has no regrets; detached from worldly possessions, she is not only free from fear herself, but she strives to raise the spirits of those around her deathbed. There is nothing morbid about the scene. The only note of gloom is struck by the community of virgins and the general congregation at the funeral service, which Gregory himself does his best to check. This work is of immense importance for the study of certain aspects of early monasticism and of the early liturgy. Unfortunately we do not know to whom the letter is addressed, but we have the impression that it is intended for a reader who was acquainted with the monastery as it was at the time of Macrina's death, but knew rather less about its origins. Gregory therefore describes the circumstances of Macrina's early life in so far as they affect the establishment of the monastery and brings out its revolutionary character by emphasizing the fact that Macrina engaged in manual labor and that she and her mother regarded the women servants as their equals. On the other hand, we are not told very much about the daily routine of the monastery, such as the times and nature of the chapel services or the hours of meals or the way in which the manual work was divided among the members of the community. We learn of the times of day at which Macrina recited the Psalter,[11] but we do not know how it was divided into portions. These times appear to correspond to what Basil describes in a letter[12] which he wrote in 358 from Annisa to his friend Gregory of Nazianzus, inviting him to share his solitary life. The only service mentioned by Gregory of Nyssa is the evening office of thanksgiving at the time the lamps were lit.[13] This was presumably an office performed by the whole community, since Macrina's solitary recital of it on her deathbed is evidently regarded as something exceptional. There is no direct reference to the Eucharist, but it is mentioned obliquely when we are told that Macrina made the bread for it with her own hands.[14] We are not told how often or at what time it was celebrated, because this would presumably be familiar to Gregory's readers.

THE DEATH AND BURIAL OF MACRINA

Gregory is less reticent about Macrina's death and burial than he is about the services in the monastery chapel, probably for two reasons. In the first place, he was an eye-witness of the events and would naturally want to do full justice to the last rites for a beloved sister; secondly, he was conscious of the need to preserve for posterity an account of the words and behavior of so holy a woman when she was at the point of death and to set down the details of such a remarkable funeral service.

Some of the burial customs which Gregory describes were common to the pagans as well as to the Christians; others were peculiar to the Christians. Among the former was the practice of closing the eyes and mouth immediately after death, which is described, for example, in the *Phaedo* of Plato,[15] where Crito closes the eyes and mouth of Socrates. Another such custom was the carrying of candles in the funeral procession. Among the latter customs was the practice of burying the dead facing towards the East, which is attested by numerous writers and by archaeological evidence.

The dressing of Macrina's body for burial presented certain problems, since she had not followed the accepted custom of preparing grave-clothes in advance for herself. Gregory was compelled to produce some that he was holding in reserve for himself. In the end she was attired as a bride, which was the normal practice for women who were betrothed but who died before marriage. This would mean that she would be clad in white with a wreath of flowers on her head and that her face would be covered with a veil, a practice well attested by other christian writers in the East, such as Gregory of Nazianzus and John Chrysostom. This last would account for the cry of one of the virgins[16] that she would see her face no longer. The dark cloak, with which Macrina's body was covered, ostensibly to spare the virgins the sight of their leader in bridal attire, which might come as a shock to them, has a special significance. In monastic circles it was customary to bury the dead in a garment which had belonged to some deceased holy man or woman. We remember the request of Paul the Hermit to Antony that he might be buried in the cloak that he had received from Athanasius,[17] and we shall meet the custom again in the case of Melania the Younger.[18]

After the preparation of the body, there followed a vigil, which took place in church, as was usual in monastic circles, but we do not know definitely whether such a vigil was held for Macrina. The vigil included the singing of psalms and hymns, which were intended to take the place of the dirges sung at pagan funerals. John Chrysostom tells us that these included Psalms 114 (113), 22 (21) and 31 (30), which are all psalms of hope. Gregory tells us that he and Araxios, the bishop of the region, and two senior clerics carried the bier. This carrying of the bier by bishops and priests was a mark of respect; we know that it was accorded to Paula, the disciple of Jerome, and to Saturus, the brother of Ambrose. In death, as in life, Macrina was granted the honor that she so richly deserved.

NOTES

1. See Gregory of Nyssa, *In XL martyres*; PG 46:784.
2. Pp. 57–66.
3. AA SS 1 January:589.
4. See below, p. 63.
5. *Gregoire de Nyssa's Lettres*, ed. and tr. by P. Meraval, SCh 363 (Paris: Cerf, 1990) pp. 243/4–256/7.
6. Ps 60:4 (61:3).
7. Ps 5:13.
8. See below, pp. 67–9.
9. Below, p. 56.
10. Below, pp. 67–9.
11. Below, p. 53.
12. *Ep.* 2; PG 32:224–233.
13. Below, p. 72.
14. Below, p. 55 at n. 10.
15. 118.
16. Below, p. 79.
17. Jerome, *Vita S. Pauli Eremitae* 12.16; PL 23:26–28.
18. See pp. 350, 357 below.

A LETTER FROM GREGORY, BISHOP OF NYSSA ON THE LIFE OF SAINT MACRINA

UST AS ITS TITLE INDICATES, the form of my writing appears to be that of a letter, but the greater part of it exceeds the limits of a letter, as it is extended to the length of a piece of historical writing. However, the subject on which you have directed me to write is larger than can be confined within the normal proportions of a letter. Indeed you have not quite forgotten our meeting, when I was intending to go to Jerusalem in accordance with my vow, in order to see the remains of our Lord's stay in those regions. Then I came to meet you near the city of Antioch, when all kinds of questions were exercising our minds (for it was not likely that our meeting took place in silence, when Your Intelligence[1] was bringing up many points as a basis for discussion), such as often happens on these occasions, when conversation flows and the life of some distinguished person is called to mind. A woman was the starting-point of our story, if indeed one may call her a woman, for I do not know whether it is appropriate to call someone a woman who was by nature a woman, but who, in fact, was far above nature. Our story inspires belief not from its dependence upon what we have heard from others, but from its exact report of what we have learned from our own experience. Our report will go over these matters with accuracy, without offering as evidence anything that we have merely heard from other people. The virgin whom we recall was not a stranger to our family (for if she had been, we should of

51

necessity have had to learn her wonderful history from others), but was born of the same parents as ourselves; she was a shoot springing up in our mother's womb, as a pledge of the fruit to come. In order, therefore, that such a life should not be unnoticed in the future and that the virgin who had raised herself to the highest peak of human virtue through the pursuit of philosophy, should not remain concealed as a result of our silence, I thought that it would be good both to obey you and to tell her life-story as shortly as I could and in a simple and unadorned style.[2]

Macrina's Birth and Family Background

The virgin's name was Macrina. Long ago there was another Macrina in our family, who enjoyed a high reputation. She was our father's mother; at the time of the persecutions she took part in the struggle by confessing Christ on more than one occasion.[3] The child was named after her by her parents. This was her public name, by which she was called by people who knew her, but she was granted another, secret name. As a result of a vision, she was called by it before she passed through the pangs of birth to the light of day. Indeed her mother was of such virtuous character that she let herself be guided everywhere by the divine will. She adhered with remarkable eagerness to a pure and spotless way of life, so that she did not choose marriage of her own free will; but since, on the one hand, she was bereft of both her parents, and on the other, was in the physical bloom of youth and the fame of her beauty attracted many suitors, there was the danger that unless she willingly entered into a union with someone, she would undergo some involuntary suffering as the result of cruel treatment, for men who were aware of her beauty were planning to carry her off by force.[4] She therefore chose a man who was well-known for his dignified way of life and was of good reputation, so as to acquire a guardian of her own personal life. Soon afterwards, in her first pregnancy, she became the mother of this virgin. When the moment of her delivery was approaching, which would naturally and inevitably bring the pains of childbirth to an end, she fell asleep. It seemed to her then that she was carrying in her arms the child who was still within her womb, and that a being of greater magnificence in form and appearance than a mortal man addressed the child whom she was carrying as Thecla, the name of that Thecla whose fame is great among the virgins. After he had done this three times, he withdrew himself from her sight, and granted her ease in giving birth, so that the mother woke up in the same place and beheld what she had dreamed. Thecla, therefore, was Macrina's secret name. The visionary being seemed to me to proclaim this name not so much to guide the mother in the choice of name as to foretell what the life of the virgin would be and to show, through the identical character of the name, that she would choose the same way of life as Thecla did.[5]

Macrina's Upbringing and Education

The baby grew, and though she had her own nurse, she was often cared for in her mother's arms. When she had passed the age of infancy, she easily learned the things which children are usually taught and shone at whatever subject her parents decided she should study.[6] It was her mother's object not to bring her up in the ordinary secular culture, which in the early years of study is for the most part conveyed through the works of the poets; for she thought it degrading and altogether improper that either the passions of tragedy—or the indecencies of comedy or the causes of the misfortunes at Troy should be expounded to a girl whose character was gentle and easily influenced and would in some way be polluted by these ignoble stories about women. On the contrary, the subjects of the child's study consisted of all the material contained in the Scriptures which are inspired of God that seemed capable of being grasped in her earliest years, especially the Wisdom of Solomon, and for preference, as much of the subject matter of that book as would make a contribution to her moral life.[7] Neither was she in any way ignorant of the Psalter; she recited each of its parts at appropriate times: on getting out of bed, when beginning serious work and when resting from it, when coming to meals and when rising from the table, on going to bed and on getting up for prayer—everywhere she kept the Psalter as a good companion who did not waste a single moment.[8]

The Prospect of Marriage

Having grown up amid these and similar pursuits, especially in working with her hands at spinning, she reached her twelfth year, in which the flower of youth begins to blossom in particular splendor. Here it is appropriate for us to wonder whether or not the beauty of the young girl, though it had been kept hidden, would escape notice. Indeed there did not seem anything so marvelous throughout the whole of that region that it could be compared with her beauty and charm.[9] The hands of painters could not do justice to her in her bloom.

Although the art of the painter is altogether ingenious and dares to confront the greatest subjects, so as to create by means of imitation images of the sun and planets themselves, it was unable to represent accurately the harmonious beauty of her form. A swarm of suitors besieged her parents on account of her beauty, but her father (a man of prudence and good judgement) chose out from the rest a well-born young man from those of his own kin, who was remarkable for his good character and had only recently completed his education. It was to him that he decided to betroth his daughter, when she had reached the appropriate age. In the meantime, the young man showed promise for the future and brought to Macrina's father, as a joyful wedding gift, a character which equalled his reputation. In the law-courts he displayed his power of speech on behalf of those who had been wronged. Yet envy cut off these promising hopes by snatching him from life at an age to arouse our pity.

Macrina's Decision to Adopt a Life of Virginity

The young girl was not unaware of her father's decision, but when the plans that had been made for her were destroyed by the death of the young man, she came to regard the marriage which her father had arranged for her as though it had actually taken place. She made up her mind to live the rest of her life on her own, and her decision was firmer than might have been expected at her age. Her parents often brought up the subject of marriage with her, because there were many men wishing to be her suitors on account of the fame of her beauty. To them she replied that it was absurd and contrary to law and custom for them not to be satisfied with the marriage which had been concluded for her by her father once and for all, but to require her to look to marriage to another; for marriage was by its nature unique, just as birth and death are unique. She strongly maintained that the man to whom she was united in accordance with the decision of her parents had not died; her judgement was that he was 'living in God' through hope of the resurrection and that he had 'gone away' and was not a corpse. It was absurd, in her opinion, not to keep faith with a bridegroom who was on a journey.

Repelling by such arguments those who tried to overrule her, she decided that the only way of safeguarding her noble resolve was never to be separated from her mother, not even for a single moment, so that her mother used to say that she carried her other children for the normal length of time, but that she carried Macrina everywhere within herself, always enclosed, so to speak, within her heart. However, living in common with her daughter was by no means burdensome or lacking in advantage for the mother, for the loving service that her daughter bestowed upon her replaced the work of several maids. There was a fruitful exchange between them: the mother cared for her daughter's soul and the daughter, her mother's body. Macrina fulfilled the service required of her in every other department; she even frequently prepared bread for her mother with her own hands.[10] This, however, was not the principal activity in which she displayed her zeal; after she had used her hands for liturgical purposes, she then provided food for her mother by her own labors in the time that she had left, as she thought this appropriate to her way of life.[11] Not only did she do this, but she also shared with her mother full responsibility in running the household, for her mother had four sons and five daughters[12] and paid taxes to three rulers, because her property was scattered over as many provinces. For this reason, Macrina shared in her mother's varied concerns, for her father was already dead. In all these affairs she was the partner of her mother's labors, sharing her burdens and lightening the weight of her grief. At the same time she both retained her own purity of life through her mother's training—that life which was throughout directed and witnessed by her mother—and provided her mother with a similiar ideal—I mean the ideal of philosophy—by means of her own example, drawing her gradually towards a more simple way of life, detached from material things.

Macrina's Influence Over Her Brother Basil

At the time when her mother was suitably occupied in regulating the affairs of Macrina's sisters, according to what seemed to her right for each of them,[13] the great Basil returned home. He was the brother of the aforesaid Macrina, and during all this long period, he had been receiving training in rhetoric in the schools.[14] Macrina found that he had become excessively exalted by the idea of his own gift of oratory. He despised all those who held public office and was puffed up with pride, regarding himself as a man above the notabilities of the province. She therefore drew him too towards the ideal of philosophy, so rapidly that he renounced worldly fame. He despised the admiration which he had won through his eloquence and became, as it were, a deserter to a hard life of manual labor. Through his complete detachment from material possessions he prepared for himself a way of life in which he would be unhindered in his pursuit of virtue. However, his life and his subsequent practices, through which he became known in every country under the sun and overshadowed all those who were distinguished for their virtue with his reputation, would need a lengthy narrative and plenty of time. Let my story return once more to its point.

The Conversion of the Family Home Into a Monastery

As the pretext for every kind of materialistic life had already been taken away from them, Macrina persuaded her mother to abandon the conventions of social life and the manners of a woman of the world, to give up the services of her maids, which she had been accustomed to receive up to that time, and to regard herself as being of the same rank as the mass of the people, involving herself in her personal life with all the virgins she had with her, by sharing their pursuits and making sisters and equals out of slave-women and servants. Here I should prefer to make a slight digression in my narrative; I do not wish to let the following story, through which the high ideals of the virgin are better revealed, remain unrecorded.

The Life of Her Brother Naucratios

The second of her four brothers, who came after the great Basil, was called Naucratios. He was superior to the others in his happy disposition, his physical beauty, his strength, and swiftness and his all-round ability. When he had reached his twenty-second year, he displayed examples of his own work at a public gathering, with the result that the whole audience was overwhelmed by him. But by some divine providence, he came to despise all the gifts that he had in his hands, and by a sudden inspired thought, he turned away towards a solitary life of poverty, taking with him nothing except himself. One of his servants, Chrysaphios by name, followed him on account of both his affection for Nucratios and his own choice of the same way of life. Naucratios lived therefore on his own, having taken possession of a remote place by the river Iris. The Iris is a river flowing through the middle of Pontus. Its source is in Armenia itself. It flows through our provinces and discharges into the Euxine Sea. Near this river the young man found a place covered with dense woodlands and hidden in a hollow of the cliff at the top of the mountain. There he lived, far from the troubles of the city, the activities of the military, and the rhetoric of the law-courts. Once he had thus liberated himself from all those cares which encompass human life, he looked after some old men who were living together in poverty and ill-health; he considered that it was appropriate to his way of life to devote his attention to such a task. Owing to his skill in all forms of hunting, he occupied himself with this activity and provided the aged men with food, while at the same time working off his youthful energy by such labors. However, he also governed his life by eagerly conforming to his mother's wishes, if ever she gave him any commands, adopting, as it were, a double life: by his labors, he joined the mastery of his youthful high spirits, and by his serious attitude with regard to his mother, he was eagerly guided towards God through the divine commands.

The Death of Naucratios

Thus he passed five years in the pursuit of philosophy and made his mother happy by his personal life. At one and the same time he both regulated his own life through his self-control and directed all his energy to the fulfillment of the wishes of the being who had brought him into the world. Then his mother chanced to undergo a grievous and tragic experience—due, in my opinion, to the plotting of our Adversary—which sufficed to plunge the whole family into misfortune and sorrow.[15] For Naucratios was suddenly snatched from this life, without having any illness to prepare him for what he was to suffer and without encountering any of the habitual and normal events, such as cause a young man to die. He set out in the pursuit of game, by which he furnished provisions for the old men for whom he cared, but he was brought back as a corpse; so also was Chrysaphios, his companion in his way of life. His mother was far from the scene of these events; she was three days' march away from the disaster, when a messenger arrived to inform her of what had happened. She had attained perfection in every kind of virtue, but even she was overcome by nature like other people; for her soul was cut down, and she was immediately deprived of breath and the power of speech. Her sorrow overcame her reason. There she lay, prostrated by the shock of the terrible news, like a well-trained athlete who is laid low by an unexpected blow.

How Macrina Supported Her Mother in This Time of Trial

In this situation the great Macrina revealed the nobility of her character. One saw how by overcoming her sorrow with her reason, she bore herself without flinching; she became the support of her mother in her weakness and aroused her again from her depths of grief. Through her own unyielding firmness, she trained her mother to be stout-hearted. Thus her mother was not carried away by her sorrow, nor did she give way to any base or womanish sentiment,[16] such as crying aloud against her misfortune or tearing her tunic or lamenting over what had happened or encouraging the singing of dirges with mournful tunes.[17] On the contrary, though she endured the onslaughts of her human nature, she thrust them from herself through her own thoughts and those suggested to her by her daughter, to bring healing to her soul. Then it was that the sublime and exalted spiritual character of the virgin was revealed, for she too was personally undergoing the same experience of her human nature; after all, it was her brother, indeed the best-loved of her brothers, who had been snatched from her by such a death. Nevertheless she rose above her human nature, and by means of her own reflections, caused her mother to rise too. She helped her to overcome her sorrow and taught her by her own example to be steadfast and brave. Moreover, her own life, which was always rising to greater heights of excellence, provided her mother with an opportunity not so much for grieving over the son and brother who had left them as for rejoicing in the goodness which she could see.

The Monastic Way of Life at Annisa

When the mother no longer had to think about the upbringing of her children and the care of their education and their establishment in life was at an end, the greater part of her material resources was divided among her children. Then, as has already been stated, the virgin's life became her mother's guide to this philosophical and non-materialistic life-style. Macrina, who had already renounced all the conventionalities, brought her mother to her own state of humility. She induced her to place herself on an equal footing with the whole group of virgins, so that she shared with them in equality the same table, the same kind of bed and all the same necessities of life. All differences of rank were removed from their way of life. Indeed, such was the ordering of their lives and so sublime their philosophy and so noble the principles underlying their way of living, both by night and by day, that no words can describe them. Just as souls, when released from bodies by death, are at the same time freed from the cares of this life, so was their life similarly liberated. It was lived apart from all worldly trivialities and was brought into harmony with the life of the angels. For neither anger nor envy nor hatred nor pride nor anything else of that kind was ever seen in them; the desire for earthly vanities, honor, glory, pride, and everything of that kind had been banished. Their delight was in self-control; their glory was to be unknown; their wealth was to possess nothing, having shaken off all material superfluity from their bodies as though it were dust. Their work, except incidentally, was unconnected with the tasks about which people busy themselves in this life. It consisted only of attention to the things of God, prayer without ceasing, and the uninterrupted chanting of the Psalms, which was extended equally in time through night and day, so that for the virgins it was both work and rest from work.

What human words could bring before our eyes a picture of such a way of life, lived as it was by beings whose life was bounded by both human and incorporeal nature? On the one hand, the liberation of their nature from human passions was something which made them superhuman; on the other, their appearance in a body, their confinement within a human form and their existence as beings equipped with the organs of perception made them into beings lower than those whose nature is angelic and incorporeal. Perhaps one might dare to say that the difference between them and the angels was rather slight, because though living in the flesh, the virgins resembled the incorporeal powers and were not weighed down by the burden of the body. On the contrary, their life was elevated above the earth, and they walked on high with the heavenly beings. They led this kind of life for a long time, and as time passed, their good qualities increased. Their philosophy advanced ceaselessly towards greater purity with the help of the good gifts which they had discovered.

Peter of Sebaste

Macrina had a brother, born of the same mother, whose name was Peter and who gave her much help in the pursuit of her high ideal of life. After his arrival, our mother never again suffered birth-pangs; for he was the last child of his parents and received the names of son and orphan together, since at the same time as he saw the light, his father departed this life. But scarcely had he been weaned when his eldest sister, she with whom this narrative deals, immediately snatched him from his wet-nurse and looked after him herself. She introduced him to all the higher forms of culture and, from his childhood, so trained him in the sacred branches of learning as not to provide leisure for his soul to incline itself to any kind of vanity.[18] She became everything for the little boy: father, teacher, tutor, mother, counsellor in all that was good; thus, even before he left the age of childhood, he flourished with the gentle charm of an adolescent boy and was being raised up towards the high goal of philosophy. By some fortunate gift of nature, he displayed an aptitude for all kinds of manual work, so that, without the help of anyone who could give him exact teaching, he acquired all those practical skills for which the majority of people need time and effort. He despised the pursuit of secular studies, holding that nature was an adequate teacher of all sound knowledge. He looked always to his sister, and making her his ideal in all that was good, he arrived at such a degree of virtue that he was not held in less respect than the great Basil as regards his supremacy in all that concerns excellent conduct. These things belong to the period of his life subsequent to these events, but from this moment, he was everything to his mother and sister and worked with them towards the goal of the angelic life. Once when there was a cruel food-shortage and many people, on account of the family's reputation for kindness and generosity, were streaming in from all directions to the remote place where they lived, he procured such an abundance of provisions through his planning that the crowd of visitors made the desert look like a city.[19]

The Death of the Mother

At this time, their mother, who had comfortably advanced to old age, departed to God; she left this life in the arms of both her children.[20] It is appropriate to her to relate the words of blessing which she pronounced over her children. As was proper, she remembered each one who was absent, so that no one should be deprived of her blessing; she also specially commended to God in prayer those who were present. These two children sat beside her on either side of her bed, and she took each of them firmly by the hand. In her last words she addressed God in the following way:

> To you, O Lord, I offer the first-fruits and the tithe of my labor in child-birth.[21] My first-fruits are my first-born daughter and my tithe is my last-born son. Both have been consecrated by your law and are your votive offerings. May your sanctification come upon these, my first-fruits, and this, my tithe.

She indicated by these words that she meant her daughter and her son. When she had finished giving her blessing, she ceased to live, having directed her children to lay her body in the tomb of their father.

When they had carried out her instructions, they held to a higher form of philosophy; they battled fiercely and ceaselessly against their personal inclinations and eclipsed by stages their early achievements.

The Consecration of Basil as Bishop and the Ordination of Peter as Priest: the Death of Basil

At this time, Basil, who was a man of importance among the saints, was chosen as head of the great church of Caesaraea.[22] He brought his brother into the fellowship of those holding office as priests, having consecrated him at his own holy service. Owing to this, their lives again advanced towards greater reverence and greater holiness, as their philosophy had been enlarged through Peter's priesthood. Over eight years later, Basil, who was a man of universal renown, left humankind to dwell with God.[23] He became a cause for grief which was common to both his native country and the world at large.[24] When Macrina, who was living far away, received news of this disaster, she suffered inwardly in her soul at so great a loss (for how would the suffering leave even her untouched, when even the enemies of truth were aware of it?). They say that the testing of gold takes place in different furnaces, so that if any impurity escapes the first smelting, it is separated in the second, and once more in the final smelting, when the substance is purged of every impurity that is mixed with it. The most accurate proof that gold has been properly tested is that it throws up no further impurity after it has been through every melting-pot. What happened to Macrina was of similar character. The lofty nature of her thought was tried from every direction by successive blows of fortune, but she displayed purity and steadfastness of soul first on the death of her other brother, Naucratios, secondly, on the separation from her mother, and thirdly, when Basil, the glory common to all our family, departed from human life. Then she remained firm, like an athlete who could not be defeated, and never flinched at the blows of fortune.

Gregory's Decision to Visit Macrina and
His Premonitory Dream

Nine months—or perhaps a little longer—after this experience, a synod of bishops gathered at the city of Antioch,[25] in which we also took part. When we were once more at liberty to return, each to his own home, I, Gregory, experienced a desire, before a year had passed, to go to my sister's.[26] For in the meantime, there had been a long period, in which the circumstances of the persecutions prevented me from visiting her.[27] I was driven into exile from my native land by the leaders of the heresy and endured these conditions everywhere. When I was calculating the length of the period in which the persecutions prevented me from meeting Macrina face to face, the interval seemed far from short; it was eight years or perhaps a little less. When I had completed the greater part of my journey and I was only one day's travel from home, a vision appeared to me in a dream, which filled me with foreboding. It seemed that I was carrying the relics of a martyr in my hands and that a ray of light was coming from them, such as occurs when a clear mirror is held against the sun, so that my eyes were dimmed by the flash off its rays. That same night the same visitor appeared to me three times. I could not clearly grasp the hidden meaning of the dream, but foreseeing that my soul would meet with some sorrow, I watched for subsequent developments, in order to judge its significance. When I arrived near to the remote place where Macrina happily lived her angelic and heavenly life, I first of all asked one of my brother's servants if he were at home. He replied that he had set out three days earlier to meet me, from which I concluded that he had taken a different route from mine. Then I learned news of the great Macrina. When he told me that she was suffering from an illness, I set out with greater eagerness and speed to accomplish what remained of my journey, for some premonition of the future crept over me and filled me with fear.

Gregory's Arrival at Annisa

When I arrived at the place itself and the news of my presence was announced to the community, the whole assemblage of men from the male side of the monastery prepared itself to meet me; for it is their custom to honor those whom they wish to welcome by going to meet them.[28] The choir of virgins from the women's side of the monastery was drawn up at the church in good order and awaited our entry. When the prayer and the blessing had finally been given, and those who had respectfully bowed their heads to receive the blessing[29] had retired to their own quarters, not one of them was left among us. From that I concluded that the lady who directed them was not with them. Someone took me to the house where the great Macrina was and opened the door. Then I found myself in that holy place. Macrina was already seriously ill; nevertheless she was resting not on a bed nor on a mattress, but on the ground, on a board covered with a sack. Another board supported her head; its function was to serve as a pillow for her head, maintaining her muscles in a slanting position and comfortably holding up her neck.

Gregory's First Meeting With Macrina

When she saw me close to the door, she raised herself by pressing on her elbow, but she was unable to run towards me, because her strength had already been sapped by the fever. However, she placed her hands firmly on the ground and fulfilled the office of coming to meet me by raising herself up from her couch as far as she could.[30] I ran to her and took her face, which was bowed down towards the ground, between my hands. I straightened her out and restored her to her customary supine position. She stretched out her hand to God and said:

You have filled me with this grace, O God, and you have not deprived me of the fulfillment of my wish, because you have moved your servant to visit your handmaid.

In order not to bring distress to my soul, she moderated her groaning and, as far as she could, she concealed her pain in breathing. By every possible means, she created a more cheerful atmosphere, by confining her conversation to pleasant topics and giving us the opportunity to do the same through her questioning. However, the memory of the great Basil crept into our conversation. My heart trembled, my gaze turned downwards, and tears poured from my eyes, but so far was she from yielding to share our suffering with us that she made the memory of the saint a point of departure for a higher flight of philosophy and developed such subjects—enquiring into the nature of humankind, revealing in her discourse the divine providence that has been concealed by sad events, and relating what concerns the future life, as if she had been inspired by the Holy Spirit—that my soul seemed to be freed—or almost freed—from its human nature, to have been elevated by her words and to have been set down within the inner sanctuary of heaven through the guidance of her discourse.

Comparison of Macrina With Job

We hear in the story of Job how this man's whole body was wasting away from the septic discharge from his wounds spreading on all sides; yet by his right thinking he did not allow his sensitive feelings to degenerate into grief; on the one hand, he suffered bodily pain, but on the other he neither let his energy become blunted nor did he cut short his speeches, which dealt with lofty themes. I saw the great Macrina behaving in a similar manner. Though the fever was consuming all her powers and was drawing her towards death, she refreshed her body with, as it were, a kind of dew; thus she kept her intellect clear for the contemplation of high matters and unaffected by so serious an illness. If my narrative could be boundless, I should set down in good order everything that she said, and describe how exalted she was in her own speech, both by giving us a philosophical discourse about the soul and in explaining in detail the origin of our life in the flesh: why it happens that man is mortal and how it is that death is finally a release from this world into life. On all these topics she spoke clearly and consistently, as if inspired by the power of the Holy Spirit; her speech flowed with complete ease, just as water from a spring, if it does not meet with any obstacle, is carried downhill.

Gregory's Rest in the Garden

When she had finished speaking, she remarked, 'Brother, it is time that you gave your body a little rest, for you must be very tired after your journey', but indeed it was a great and genuine relaxation for me just to look at her and to hear her noble words. However, since this gave her pleasure and was a cherished scheme of hers, I went into one of the little gardens nearby and finding a delightful resting place that had been prepared for me, I took my repose in the shade of the arbor formed by the climbing vines,[31] in order that I might be seen to be obedient to her, my teacher, in every respect. Yet it was not possible for me to find any pleasure in my agreeable surroundings, when my soul was in a state of inward turmoil in expectation of sad events in the future. For what I saw seemed to reveal the mystery of my dream through what was happening. What I saw lying before me was really the remains of a holy martyr, who lay dead to sin, but shone with the grace of the Holy Spirit. I explained this to one of the people who had earlier heard me describing my dream. When, as was natural, we felt depressed in anticipation of the sorrows that were to come, Macrina, by what means I do not know, grasped what state of mind we were in and conveyed to us news of a more cheerful character. She exhorted us to be of good courage and to maintain a more hopeful attitude on her behalf, she herself felt that she had taken a turn for the better. She did not speak in this way in order to deceive us; her words sprang from the very truth, even if we ourselves at that moment did not recognize their significance. The situation was in fact similar to that of a runner when he has already passed his opponent and has already reached the end of the stadium. He draws near to the prize for the race and seeing the victor's crown, inwardly rejoices as if he had already won the prize and announces his victory to those of the spectators who are better disposed towards him. In the same way, Macrina, actuated by the same feelings as the runner, gave us to hope for a happier fate for herself; she was already looking towards 'the prize of her high calling', since almost applying to herself the words of the Apostle, she said, 'There is stored up for me the crown of righteousness, which the righteous Judge shall offer me',[32] and then, 'I have fought the good fight and I have finished my course and I have kept the faith'.[33] We therefore took heart at her good news and began to taste the meal which had been prepared for our enjoyment; the dishes were varied and much pleasure had gone into their preparation; the great Macrina had given thought even to such details.

Gregory's Second Meeting With Macrina

When we were once again in her presence—for she would not let us spend our unoccupied time alone—she recalled the memories of her life from her youth onwards; she went through everything in order, like a history book. She described as much of the event of the lives of our parents as she could remember and also the events which occurred before my birth, and her subsequent life. The purpose of her recital was to give thanks to God. She showed that the lives of our parents were not so much honored and admired in the eyes of their contemporaries on account of their wealth as they were rendered significant because of their divinely inspired philanthropy. Our father's parents had been deprived of their property on account of their having confessed Christ; an ancestor on our mother's side had been put to death as the result of having provoked the emperor and all his property had been distributed to other masters. Nevertheless the property of our family was increased so much through their faith that it was not possible, at this period, to name anyone who surpassed them in wealth. Subsequently, when our parents' estate had been divided into nine portions, according to the number of their children, each child's share was increased by divine blessing in such a way that the wealth of each of the individual children surpassed the prosperity of their parents. Macrina, however, did not keep for herself the property that had been allotted to her when the estate was shared out equally between the brothers and sisters, but caused it to be administered at the hands of the priest, in accordance with the divine command. Through the riches of God's grace, her life was such that her hands never ceased working to carry out the commandments of God; she never relied upon a man nor did the wherewithal for an honorable life come to her through the kindness of men. On the contrary, she sought to turn away neither beggars nor benefactors, for God secretly caused the small resources that she obtained from her work to multiply through his blessing, just as if they were seeds.

Macrina's Advice to Gregory

On my side, I described to her the personal difficulties in which I found myself, first of all, when the emperor Valens drove me into exile on account of my faith, and afterwards, when owing to the confusion prevailing in the local churches, I was summoned to distressing disputes.[34] 'Will you not give up your hardheartedness towards God's good gifts?' she asked, 'Will you not heal the wound of ingratitude that is in your soul? Will you not compare your situation with that of your parents? Indeed from a worldly point of view, at any rate, we could take pride in this fact, that we appear as people of good birth, sprung from a noble family. Our father,' she continued, 'was highly thought of in his time on account of his culture, but his reputation extended only as far as the local law-courts. His subsequent fame did not reach beyond Pontus, although he was ahead of other people of his age through his skill in rhetoric, but he was satisfied with being well-known in his native country, You, on the other hand,' she continued, 'are a celebrated man in the cities, in the provinces and among the peoples. It is you whom some churches send and others summon, to bring help and achieve reform. Do you not see the grace that is given you? Do you not see the cause of such blessings? Is it not the prayers of your parents that have raised you to these heights, when you yourself have little or no predisposition for such things?'[35]

The Last Day of Macrina's Life

While Macrina was expounding these matters, I longed to make the day last longer, that she might continue to charm our ears with her words, but the voices of the choir summoned us to the service of thanksgiving held at the lighting of the lamps.[36] The great Macrina, having dispatched me to church, again withdrew herself into God's presence through her prayers. Night fell during these exercises. When day broke, it became clear to me from what I saw that the day which was dawning would be the limit of her life in the flesh, for the fever had consumed all the natural force that was in her. She noticed the feeble character of our thoughts and continued to distract us from our gloomy expectations; once again she dispersed the grief that was in our hearts through her beautiful words, but now she did so with a slightly troubled sigh. It was at that moment especially that my soul was torn by varied feelings over what was happening. One part of me was weighed down by depression, as was natural, because I foresaw that I should never again hear such words and I was expecting that this amazing person, the glory common to all our family, would soon pass from our human life; the other part of me, however, was carried away with emotion at what was happening and was secretly thinking that she had transcended our common human nature. She had made up her mind from the very beginning to experience, when breathing her last, not feelings of strangeness at the prospect of removal to a different place nor to fear leaving this life, but on the contrary, to engage with sublime thought in philosophical meditation right until the very end. This attitude seemed to me to be no longer characteristic of a breathing human being. It was as if an angel had assumed human shape in the household—an angel who had no relationship with the life of the flesh nor in any way adapted to it, and whose thought remained, in a perfectly natural way, in a state of impassibility, since the flesh did not attract her to her own feelings. For this reason, it seemed to me that she revealed to those around her that pure love for the unseen Bridegroom which she cherished, hidden in the secret places of her soul, and made public the inclination of her heart to hasten to him for whom she longed, so that, once freed from the fetters of her body, she might be with him as soon as possible. In fact it was to her lover that her course was directed. No other of the sweets of life distracted her gaze from him.

Macrina's Last Moments

The greater part of the day was already over and the sun was beginning to set. Her zeal, however, was undiminished, but as the time of her departure approached, so much the more did she contemplate the beauty of the Bridegroom and so much the greater was her haste to go to him for whom she longed. She no longer spoke (as she had done) to us who were present, but to him, upon whom she gazed directly. Her bed had been turned towards the East;[37] she gave up talking to us and thence-forward addressed God in prayer. She stretched out her hands to him in supplication and spoke in a gentle undertone, so that we could scarcely hear her words. Her prayer follows. I quote it, so that there may be no doubt that she was in the presence of God and that he was listening to her.

Macrina's Prayer[38]

It is you, O Lord, who have freed us from the fear of death.[39] You have made our life here the beginning of our true life. You grant our bodies to rest in sleep for a season and you rouse our bodies *again at the last trumpet*.[40]

You have given in trust to the earth our earthly bodies, which you have formed with your own hands, and you have restored what you have given, by transforming our mortality and ugliness by your immortality and your grace.[41]

You have delivered us from the curse of the law and from sin, by being made both on our behalf.[42] You have *broken the dragon's head*—that dragon who had seized man by the throat and dragged him through the yawning gulf of disobedience.[43] You have opened for us the way of the resurrection, after breaking the gates of hell, and have destroyed him that had the power of death.[44]

You have given as a token to those who fear you the image of the holy cross, to destroy the adversary and to bring stability to our lives.[45]

Eternal God, for whom I was snatched from my mothers womb,[46] whom my soul loved with all its strength, to whom I consecrated my flesh from my youth until now,[47] entrust to me an angel of light, who will lead me by the hand to the place of refreshment, where the 'water of repose' is, in the bosom of the holy patriarchs.[48]

May you, who cut through the fire of the flaming sword and assigned to paradise him who was crucified with you and entrusted to your pity,[49] remember me too in your kingdom, because I too have been crucified with you; from fear of you I have nailed down my flesh and have been in fear of your judgements.[50]

May the terrible gulf not separate me from those whom you have chosen,[51] nor may the malignant Enemy set himself across my path, nor may my sin be discovered in your sight, if having error through the weakness of our human nature, I have committed any sin in word or in deed.

May you who have power on earth to forgive sins,[52] forgive me, that I may draw breath[53] and that I be found in your presence, 'having shed my body and without spot or wrinkle'[54] in the form of my soul, and that my soul may be innocent and spotless and may be received into your hands *like incense in your presence*.[55]

The Death of Macrina

While she was thus speaking, she made the sign of the cross on her eyes, on her face and on her heart. Gradually, her tongue, which was dried up by the fever, could no longer pronounce words distinctly; her voice faltered, and only by the parting of her lips and the movement of her hands could we recognize that she was engaged in prayer. In the meantime, evening fell, and when the lamp was brought in, Macrina suddenly opened her eyes and gazed at the light. By this she showed clearly that she too wished to recite the evening office of thanksgiving. But her voice failed her, and it was only in her heart and through the gestures of her hands that she fulfilled her desire; the movement of her lips synchronized with her inner activity. When she had completed the office and had indicated, by putting her hand to her face in making the sign of the cross, that she was reaching the end of her prayers, she gave a great, deep sigh and ended her life and her prayers at the same moment.[56] When she finally ceased to breath and lay still, I recalled her directions, which she had given me at our first interview. She had said that she wished me to close her eyes with my hands and to carry out the customary treatment of her body. As the result of what I had just been through, my hand was numb, but I brought it to her holy face, so that as far as possible, I might not seem to have neglected her directions. Her eyes did not need to be attended to, for they were gracefully covered by her eye-lids, just as in natural sleep. In the same way, her lips were properly closed, and her hands folded on her breast. Her whole body had, of its own accord, assumed an harmonious posture and did not need any hand to lay it out.[57]

The Distress of the Virgins

As for myself, my soul was paralysed in two respects: on the one hand, by what I saw and on the other by the sound of the mournful lament which the virgins were pouring forth around me. Until then they had borne themselves calmly and bravely, keeping their sorrow to themselves, and had restrained themselves from bursting into tears on account of their fear of Macrina, as if they were in awe of her reproachful looks—even when she was already in the silence of death. They were afraid lest somewhere a cry should escape from them which would be contrary to the instruction that had been given them, and that their teacher would consequently be grieved at what had happened. They could no longer conceal their suffering, which was like a fire smoldering within their hearts. Suddenly a bitter and irrepressible cry broke out. It was such that I could no longer be controlled by my reason;

indeed I was carried away by the current of my distress, as if I were submerged by a torrent which had been swollen by winter rain, and I neglected the tasks that lay to hand, because I had become completely involved in lamentation. Yet in its origin the virgins' distress seemed to me to be somehow right and worthy of approval; they did not mourn the loss of an intimacy or an attachment according to the flesh or any misfortune such as afflicts humankind, but wept as if they had been separated from their hope in God and from the salvation of their souls. Thus they complained in their laments, saying: 'The light of our eyes has been extinguished. The lantern which guided our souls has been destroyed. The stability of our lives has gone. The seal of our immortality has been snatched away. That which bound us together in concord has been torn asunder. We have been deprived of that which gave us firmness in our feebleness. Her loving care for the weak has been taken away. When we were with her, night was equally as bright as day, because of the purity of her life. Now day itself is turned to darkness.'

Some, calling her nurse and mother, expressed their feelings more vigorously than others. They were the women whom she had received at the time of the famine, when they were wandering about the roads, and whom she had cared for and brought up and directed towards a pure and incorrupt life.

Gregory Restores Calm

When I had somehow brought my soul back from the abyss, I looked intently at Macrina's holy person, and as if I had been reproached for the disorderly behavior of the virgins, who caused trouble through their funerary lamentations, I called out to them in a loud voice, 'Look at her and remember her teachings, through which she trained you in what was always and everywhere proper and fitting. This holy soul prescribed for you a single time for tears, by bidding you weep in your prayer time. It is possible for you to do this now, at this moment, by exchanging your groaning and lamentation for the singing of psalms together.' I shouted these words in a louder tone, in order to be heard above the noise of the lamentation. Then I ordered them to retire into the adjacent building, while some of those whose care she used willingly to accept in her lifetime stayed behind.

Conversation With Vetiana

Among this group was a lady of wealth and good family, who was remarkable in her youth for both her her physical beauty and her general distinction. She had been married to a man in the higher ranks of society and had lived with him for a short time, but their union was broken, and since that time, she had made the great Macrina the watch and ward of her widowhood. She lived chiefly with the virgins and learned from them the way of life conducive to virtue. This lady's name was Vetiana, and her father Araxios was a member of the Senate. I told her that now, at any rate, we need not reproach ourselves for dressing Macrina's body in more cheerful clothing and adorning her pure and spotless flesh with bright garments. Vetiana, however, said that we must discover what the saint herself believed to be right where such matters were concerned, for it would not be proper for us on our side to go against her wishes. But certainly that which would be completely pleasing to God would be pleasing to her too.

Conversation With Lampadion

Now there was a lady there called Lampadion, who was in charge of the choir of virgins and who held the rank of deaconess. She said that she knew exactly what Macrina had decided about her burial. When I questioned her on the subject—for she was present at our consultation—she replied with tears in her eyes, 'The adornment for which the saint was most anxious was that of a pure life. This is both the pride and glory of her life and the shroud for her death. As for all those things that serve to adorn the body, she neither possessed them in her lifetime nor stored them up for the present eventuality, with the result that even if we wished it, there would be nothing more for the purpose than what Macrina was at present wearing.' 'But is it not possible,' I asked, 'for us to find something among her stores to enable us to adorn her for her funeral procession?'

'What stores?' asked Lampadion, 'You have all her store in your hands. Here are her tunic, her veil, and the shabby sandals on her feet. This is her wealth; these are her riches. Nothing—beyond what you see—is stored up in secret chests or protected in inner rooms., She knew only one place for her private wealth; it was stored up as treasure in heaven. Everything was stored there and nothing was left on earth.'

'In that case,' I said, 'would it be going against any wish of hers, if I myself were to offer her something from the things which I have prepared for my own burial?'

Lampadion replied that, in her opinion, Macrina would not have disapproved of this idea. 'When she was still alive, she would have accepted this honor from you for two reasons: on account of your priesthood, which she always venerated, and on account of your kinship. She would not have looked upon something belonging to her brother as the property of a stranger. That is why she asked that her body should be laid out by your hands.'

Macrina's Cross and Ring

When this decision had been reached and we had also made up our minds to clothe her holy body in fine linen, we divided the work between us, one person doing one task and one, another. I ordered one of my servants to bring the clothing. Vetiana, whom I mentioned just now, adorned Macrina's holy person with her own hands. Putting her hand on Macrina's neck and looking at me, she said, 'Do you see what kind of ornament the saint wore round her neck?' As she spoke, she unfastened the clasp at the back, held out her hand to me, and showed me an iron cross and a ring of the same material. They both hung from a fine cord and lay always over her heart. I said to Vetiana, 'Let us hold this property in common. You must be custodian of the cross; the ring will be a sufficient legacy for me'. A cross was engraved on the signet. The lady looked at me and said, 'You did not make a bad choice in taking possession of this, for the hoop surrounding the seal is hollow, and a fragment of the Tree of Life lies hidden in it. Thus the engraving on the outside of the seal indicates by its design what lies within'.

A Miracle Performed by Macrina

When the time came to dress the chaste body of Macrina in the linen clothes, this duty devolved upon me, in accordance with the great Macrina's directions. The lady who shared that important legacy with me was present when I performed this task and took part in it with me.

'Do not leave untold,' she said, 'the story of the greatest of the miracles performed by this holy woman.'

'What is it?' I asked.

She bared part of Macrina's breast and replied, 'Do you see this slight, almost imperceptible scar under Macrina's skin? It is like the mark left by a fine needle.' As she said this, she brought the lamp nearer to the place which she had shown me.

'What is miraculous," I remarked, 'about her body being marked in this place by an almost imperceptible prick?'

'This mark,' she replied, 'is left on her body as a reminder of the great help given her by God. One day a malignant growth developed in this part of her body. It was equally dangerous either to cut out the tumor or to let the malignancy develop so as to become completely incurable, should it extend to the area round the heart. Her mother,' she continued, 'often begged and implored her to receive the attention of a surgeon, as he too had received his skill from God for the saving of men, but Macrina judged that it would be even more painful than the illness to reveal part of her naked body to the eyes of another person. One evening, after she had finished carrying out those services which she was accustomed to render to her mother with her own hands, she went into the sanctuary and prostrated herself all night before God the healer. She spread the water that fell from her eyes over the earth and used the mud formed by her tears as a remedy for her illness. Her mother lost heart and once again begged her to put herself into the hands of the surgeon, but she said that if her mother would make the sign of the cross on the place with her own hands, that would be enough to bring about a cure. When her mother had placed her hand on her breast to make the sign of the cross on the affected part, the sign was efficacious and the illness disappeared. 'But this little mark,' she continued, 'could be seen from that day forward, instead of the terrible lump, and lasted until the end of her life, in order that it might be a reminder, as I see it, of a divine visitation, to form a source and a reason for unceasing thankfulness to God.'

Macrina's Beauty in Death

When we had completed our task and had adorned the corpse from what lay to our hands, the deaconess again said that it was not suitable that the virgins should look upon Macrina adorned as a bride. 'But I have a cloak,' she said, 'which I have kept and which was your mother's.[58] I think that it would be as well to spread it over her, so that the beauty and holiness of her character should not shine in splendor through the accidental adornment of her clothing.'

This advice prevailed, and the cloak was laid over her, but even under this dark covering, she was radiant; the divine power, I think, added this further grace to her body, so that her beautiful form seemed to throw out rays of light, exactly as I had seen in the vision which occurred in my dream.

The Chanting of the Psalms

While we were engaged in these matters and the virgins' chanting of the Psalms, mingled with their lamentations, echoed and re-echoed round the place, the report of Macrina's death—by what means I do not know—began suddenly to circulate everywhere in the surrounding countryside, and all the people living in the locality poured in in such numbers in the face of this tragedy that the vestibule of the house was not large enough to hold them. They passed the whole night around her, singing hymns just as they would have done for the feasts of the martyrs. At daybreak, the crowd of both men and women who had flocked in together from the surrounding district, disturbed the chanting of the Psalms with their groaning. As for me, although my soul was in a turmoil owing to this sad event, I nevertheless made up my mind that as far as our resources permitted, nothing that was appropriate to such a funeral should be left out. I divided the crowd up according to sex; I joined the throng of women to the chorus of virgins and the men to the group of monks and organized the chanting so that the rhythm and harmony were the same on both sides, just as in a choir, and were completely synchronous, thanks to the tune which was common to both. When the day was a little further advanced, and the whole of the surrounding area was not large enough to hold the mass of people who thronged in, the bishop of those regions, who was called Araxios, (he was present with all his clergy), proposed that the body should proceed slowly, for the distance that we had to go was considerable and the crowd was an obstacle to rapid movement. At the same time as he addressed us in this way, he told his priests to join him in carrying the body themselves.

The Funeral Procession

When these decisions had been taken, we proceeded to carry them out. I put myself at the head of the bier and invited Araxios to stand on my other side, while two respected members of the clergy took the hind part. I began to walk forward slowly, as is the custom, and we gradually moved forward. The people pressed closely round the bier, and not one of all of them failed to feast his eyes as fully as he could on that holy spectacle—so much so that it was not easy for us to make headway. On either side of the corpse, a considerable number of deacons and men in minor orders advanced in procession, one behind the other, each holding a wax candle in his hand. It became a kind of liturgical procession, for from its beginning to its end, the psalms were chanted with one voice, as in the Song of the Three Holy Children.[59] It was seven or eight stades from this remote spot to the Church of the Holy Martyrs, in which the bodies of our parents also lay. We made our way there with difficulty, and the journey took us all day, for the crowd which accompanied us grew bigger and bigger and thus did not permit us to make the progress that we should have liked. Once we were inside the doors of the church, we halted and putting down the bier, at once turned to prayer as our first duty. Our prayer, however, afforded the people a pretext for lamentation. At a moment when the psalm-singers were silent, the virgins turned their gaze upon that holy face. The tomb of our parents, in which it had been decided to lay her, was already uncovered, when one of them cried out in a disorderly way that from now onwards, we should no longer see this divine countenance. Thereupon the other virgins joined her in crying out in the same way. Indiscipline and confusion broke out, which destroyed the good order and the sacred character of the chanting. Everyone burst into tears at hearing the lamentations of the virgins. With difficulty, we made signs to ask for silence. The cantor called us to prayer, and as he intoned the words that are customary in church, the people returned to the characteristic form of prayer.

The Burial

When the prayer had been appropriately concluded, I was suddenly stricken with the fear of breaking the divine commandment which forbids a man to uncover the nakedness of his parents.[60] 'How shall I escape this kind of condemnation,' I said to myself, 'when I see in the bodies of my parents that nakedness which is common to all humanity? As is normal, their bodies will have fallen into decay and will have been changed into something ugly, unpleasant and shapeless.' But when I was thinking about these matters and about the fear which I had of the wrath of Noah against his son being extended to me also,[61] it was from the story of Noah that I derived advice as to what I must do.[62] Before they came before our eyes, the bodies were covered by a new grave-cloth from one end of the sarcophagus to the other, at the moment when the lid was raised. When the bodies had been thus concealed by the grave-cloth, both I myself and the bishop of the region, whom I have already mentioned, lifted Macrina's holy body from the bier and laid it beside that of her mother. Thus we fulfilled their common prayer; for both of them, throughout their lives, had asked God with one voice that their bodies might be reunited to each other after death and that the fellowship which they had enjoyed in life might not be broken, even in death.

An Interesting Encounter on Gregory's Return Journey

When we had performed all the customary funeral rites, I had to go back. I threw myself on the ground before the tomb and kissed the dust. Then I set out on my return journey, broken and in tears at the thought of all the goodness which had now gone out of my life. On my way, a man of high military rank, who was in command of the garrison in a small town in Pontus called Sebastopolis and was living there with his troops, came courteously to meet me when I arrived there. When he had heard about my troubles, he took them really to heart (for he was connected with our family through ties of kinship and friendship) and gave me an account of a miracle which Macrina had performed. I shall add it to my narrative only when I have finished my own story. 'Listen to me,' he said, 'and I will tell you how much good comes from withdrawing from the life of men'. Saying these words, he began to tell me the following story.

A Visit to the Monastery

'One day my wife and I experienced a great desire to make our way to the "School of Virtue". For that, I think, is what we must call the place where that blessed soul, Macrina, passed her life. We had with us our little daughter, who was having trouble with her eye as the result of an infectious illness. She was a hideous and pitiful sight, because the cornea of her eye had become swollen round the pupil and had taken on a livid hue as the result of the disease. Once we had entered this holy dwelling,we were separated—my wife and I—according to sex, for our visits to the people who were leading the life of philosophy there. I was in the men's quarters, of which your brother Peter was in charge, while my wife went into the virgins' house and met the saint there. After a certain interval, we decided that it was time to leave this place of retreat, and we were already on the point of departing when a proof of friendship came to us from both sides. Your brother told me to stay and to share the meal of the philosophers, and the holy woman would not let my wife go, but taking my little girl on her lap, refused to let them leave before she had set a meal before them and offered them the riches of philosophy. As was natural, she caressed the child; as she put her lips to her eyes, she noticed that the pupils were diseased. "If you grant us the favor of sharing our common table," she said, "I will give you a reward which is not unworthy of such a mark of honor on your side". The child's mother asked what this reward would be. "I have a remedy," replied the great Macrina, "which is powerful for healing eye-diseases." When I had received a message from the women's monastery to inform me of this promise, we stayed on with pleasure, without worrying about the necessity which was obliging us to be on our way.'

Macrina Works a Miracle

'When the meal was over, our hearts were full, for the great Peter had entertained us with his own hands and had encouraged us, and the saint Macrina had taken leave of my wife with all the courtesy that was appropriate. We set out cheerfully and joyfully on our return journey and passed the time in telling each other of our experiences. For my part I described all that I had seen and heard in the men's monastery, while my wife went over each incident, one by one, as in an historical narrative. She thought that she should leave nothing out, even down to the smallest detail. As she described everything in sequence, just as in a history book, she came to the part where the promise of a remedy for the eye-disease had been given. She cut short her account, saying, "What have we done? How could we forget the promise which has been given us, the promise of a lotion as a remedy?" I was most distressed at our carelessness and was ordering one of our servants to run back quickly for the remedy, when the child, who was in her nurse's arms, happened to look at her mother, who fixed her eyes on the child. "Stop worrying over your carelessness," she said in a loud voice, filled with both joy and surprise, "Look, we lack nothing that has been promised us. The true remedy for healing her illness is treatment by prayer; that she has been given, and it has already had its effect. No trace of the eye-trouble is left, as the eye has been made clean by the saint's remedy."

'At the same time as she made these observations, my wife picked up the child and put her into my arms. As for me, I recalled the unbelievable miracles in the Gospels and said, "What is there surprising about sight being given to the blind through the hand of God, when his handmaid brings about these healings by her own faith and achieves something which is only a little less than these miracles?" '

As he said these words, his voice was choked by his sobs and his tears poured down while he described what had happened. This is what I learned from the soldier.

Epilogue

We heard many such stories from those who had lived with Macrina and knew all about her in detail, but I do not think it appropriate to add them to my narrative. The majority of people judge the truth of what has been said by measuring it against their own experience; whatever is beyond the hearer's power to grasp, they insultingly conjecture to be beyond the bounds of truth. That is why I pass over the unbelievable care shown at the time of the famine, when the corn supply was distributed according to people's necessities, but never showed any sign of growing less; on the contrary, it appeared the same in bulk both before and after it had been given to those who needed it. I shall also pass over all the other things that are even more surprising than these: the cures of illnesses, the castings out of devils, and the prophecies of the future which came true. The people who know about these happenings in detail believe them to be true, even if they are beyond belief; but they are unacceptable to those who are more carnal and those who do not know that the distribution of graces is made 'in proportion to our faith.'[63]

It is small for those who have little faith and great for those who provide within themselves a large room for faith. In order that those with little faith in the gifts of God may come to no harm, I have for this reason refrained from listing in succession the more noble of Macrina's miracles, thinking that those which I have already related are enough to complete her history.

NOTES

1. This is simply a polite formula of a kind often found in correspondence in Late Antiquity.

2. This sentence contains a number of commonplaces often found in the literature of Late Antiquity and the early Middle Ages, when the writer protests, as a matter of routine, that he is unworthy to deal with the subject and that his style is rustic and inelegant.

3. Gregory of Nazianzus, in dealing with these persecutions in his *In Lauden sancti Basille*, 5–8 (PG 36:500–504), mentions seven years of exile in the forests of Pontus (6.2); this period is generally believed to have been between 306 and August 312, during the persecutions of the emperor Maximin.

4. Gregory of Nyssa does not supply the name of their mother, which we know from Gregory of Nazianzus, *Epitaphia* 120 (PG 38:75–76) to have been Emmelia. It appears from Basil's letters that cases of rape of this type were not uncommon at this period; an edict of Constantine, dated 520, laid down extremely severe penalties for this crime. See *Codex Theodosianus* 9.24, *The Theodosian Code and Novels and the Sirmondian Constitution* tr. with commentary by Clyde Pharr *et al.*, Princeton, 1952, p. 22.

5. There are numerous other examples in Late Antiquity and the early Middle Ages of pregnant women who had remarkable dreams and visions. F. L:anzoni has collected many of them in 'il sogno presago della madre incinta nella letteratura medievale e antica,' *Analecta Bollandiana* 45 (1927) 225–261. The cult of Saint Thecla was very popular in Asia Minor in the fourth century, as many writers of the period testify.

6. The saint's high intellectual ability and love of study is a *topos* in hagiography.

7. The works of the poets referred to here are the writings of Homer and the Greek dramatists. 'The ignoble stories about women' are those relating to the heroines of greek tragedy, such as Clytemnestra, Medea, and Phaedra, but there are, of course, greek tragic figures, such as Antigone, Alcestis, and Iphigeneia, who might afford finer examples to a young girl. It is likely that the programme of religious education set out here relates to an ideal education and not to the education which Macrina actually received. See p. 53. We may compare with this the education which Jerome proposed for the young Paula (Lr. 107.4, 12; CSEL 55:302, and pp. 257ff. of this book).

8. For a similar methodical use of the Psalter, see Jerome's programme for Paula (Lr 107.9; CSEL 55; 300, and p. 264 of this book) and Eustochium (Lr 22.37; CSEL 54:201 and pp. 147f. of this book. Cf. also Ambrose, *De virginibus* 3.4.18; PL 16:237.

9. The physical beauty of the young saint, whether man or woman, is a *topos* in hagiographical literature. References to it are also often found in inscriptions.

10. It is difficult for us to realize what a revolutionary development it was for educated women and girls to undertake manual labour. Spinning and weaving had always been considered ladylike occupations but cooking and housework were looked upon as tasks fit only for slaves.

11. There is some difficulty over the meaning of this passage, owing to

variant readings in the manuscripts. Some of them contain a greek word which means *anoint*; if this reading is adopted, the sentences means that Macrina's hands were anointed through her receiving of the Host in them. In other manuscripts, however, we find a word (very simlar in the Greek) which means 'used'. This reading, in my opinion, makes better sense. The interpretation then is that Macrina used her hands first to make the bread for the Eucharist, and afterwards for preparing food for her mother.

12. The number of children in the family has been much disputed. Nine are mentioned in this chapter, but in chapter 13.2, Peter is described as the tenth child. For a discussion of this matter, see J. F. Pfister, 'The brothers and sisters of St Gregory of Nyssa,' *Vigiliae Christianae* 18 (1964) 108–113. See also n 21 on p. 62 of this book.

13. Presumably this means that she found husbands for them all. It is highly unlikely that Macrina would have been the sole daughter present at her mother's funeral, had any of her sisters been living as members of the monastic community.

14. Basil's return from his studies in the schools of Athens took place in 355.

15. We learn from an epitaph to Naucratios, composed by Gregory of Nazianzus, that he died as the result of an accident while he was fishing. His net became entangled with a rock at the bottom of the river, where there was a dangerous whirlpool, and he was sucked down in his efforts to free it. (*Epitaphia* 1–4; Pg 38:112).

16. Chapter Ten develops the stoic theme of the opposition of reason to passion. In equating baseness with femininity, Gregory of Nyssa is following a line of thought which was very common in the Greek Fathers and which was probably derived from the teachings of the Alexandrian Jew, Philo (*c*. 20 BC–AD 30). It occurs frequently in the writings of Origen and in other works by Gregory of Nyssa.

17. Ostentatious forms of mourning were common in the Mediterranean area in late Antiquity—as they still are today—but were frequently denounced by the Fathers, particularly by Basil, John Chrysostom, and Jerome, as well as by Gregory of Nyssa.

18. Peter was probably born between 341 and 345 and must have lived at Annisa until 380, when he was elected bishop of Sebaste in the place of his brother Gregory. Unlike his elder brothers and his sister Macrina, he appears to have received an entirely religious education.

19. This famine, to which there are several references in Basil's letters, occurred in 368/369.

20. The death of Emmelia appears to have occurred in 371, according to Basil, *Epistola* 30; PG 32:313.

21. Probably Gregory of Nyssa wished to stress not only that Peter and Macrina were present at Emmelia's death, but also that Christians should give alms methodically and in accordance with biblical teaching. The jewish custom of offering the first-fruits (Exod 13:2) was retained by the early Church, as references in the Didache (13.7) and in the

writings of Origen testify. The practice of giving the tithe appears to have become more widespread among Christinas in the fourth century. It is possible that Peter is described here as the tenth child, because his mother described him as her 'tithe', whereas he was in reality the ninth.

22. Basil was elected bishop of Caesaraea in 370 (see PG 29, p. lvii).

23. Basil died in 379.

24. The idea of universal mourning for a holy man is a *topos* which is found, for example, in at least two other places in the writings of Gregory of Nyssa and also in those of Gregory of Nazianzus.

25. The Council of Antioch took place in 379 or 380.

26. We know from one of Gergory's letters that while he was staying in Cappadocia on his way back from the Council, he recieved news of his sister's illness. This would account for his sudden decision to visit her. (See *Epistolae* 19.10; PG 46:1076).

27. This is presumably a reference to the persecutions carried out by the Arians. See n. 34 below.

28. The custom of members of religious communities, both male and female, going out to meet distinguished visitors is attested by many christian writers in early times. (See, for example, *Egeria's Travels* 3.4, Ed. J. Wilkinson, London, 1971, p. 94; *The Lives of the Desert Fathers* 20, 6, Ed. B. Ward, tr. N. Russell, London, Oxford and Kalamazoo, 1980, p. 105. Cf also the military governor of the city going out to meet Gregory of Nyssa, p. 80 below).

29. This is another monastic custom, for which there is plenty of evidence. (See, for example, *Egeria's Travels* 3.6; p. 94; 11.1, p. 106.

30. This is a reference to the custom mentioned in n. 28 above.

31. See p. 43 above.

32. 2 Tm 4:8.

33. 2 Tm 4:7.

34. Gregory was deposed from the bishopric of Nyssa in 375 on a trumped-up charge by a synod of Arian bishops, which met on the instructions of the emperor's representative, Demosthenes. He did not return to Nyssa until after the death of the emperor Valens in 378.

35. The words which Gregory puts into Macrina's mouth appear to refer to both the past and the future: (a) to the mission to Arabia, which was entrusted to Gregory by the Council of Antioch in 379; (b) to the important part which he was to play at the council of Contstantinople in 381 and to the influence of his writings. The speech is an example of a well-known *topos* of hagiography, the ability of the holy man or woman to foretell future events.

36. After the time of Saint Benedict (*c*. 480–*c*. 540), this ancient evening office came in the West to be known as Vespers. It included a hymn to be sung at the lighting of the lamps, which is familiar to english-speaking Christians as 'Hail, gladdening light'. The service in the Anglican Church known as Evensong is a blend of this office and the late evening service of Compline.

37. Gregory of Nyssa was following a custom which was widespread,

if not universal, among the early Christians. Since it was believed that paradise lay in the East (see Gen 2:8), that Christ ascended into heaven in the East, and that at his second coming, he would return from the East (see Ps 67(68):34, Acts 1:11), it was normal to turn the dying—and sometimes even the dead—to face East.

38. It is unlikely that Macrina was in a state to enable her to recite this beautiful prayer, which is a mosaic of scriptural passages, probably compiled by Gregory himself. It is, however, possible that she may have uttered single verses, particularly from the Psalms, as 'arrow prayers', and that these passages formed the basis for Gregory's composition.

39. Cf. Heb 2:15.

40. 1 Cor 15:52.

41. Cf. 1 Cor 15:53.

42. Cf. Gal 3:13; 2 Cor 5:21.

43. Ps 74 (73):14.

44. Ps 107 (106):16; Mt 16:18; Heb 2:14.

45. Ps 60 (59):6.

46. Ps 22 (21):11.

47. Sg 1:7 *et passim*.

48. Ps 23 (22):2; cf. Lk 16:26.

49. Gen 3:24; cf. Lk 23:42.

50. Lk 23:42; cf. Gal 2:20; Ps 119 (118):120.

51. Cf. Lk 16:26.

52. Mt 9:6; Mk 2:10.

53. Ps 39 (38):14.

54. Col 2:11; Eph. 5:27.

55. Ps 141 (140):2.

56. The coincidence of the ending of a prayer with the ending of a life is a commonplace in accounts of christian deaths in Late Antiquity. Gregory of Nazianzus furnishes us with several examples, such as *Oratio* 18.15 (PG 35:1036); *Epitaphia* 52 (PG 38:110–111).

57. This too is a commonplace, cf. Gerontius, *Vita S. Melaniae Iunioris* 68; SCh 90: pp. 268–269, and p. 357 of this book.

58. For further comment on the practice of dressing a corpse in preparation for burial, see p. 158 of this book.

59. Dan 3:51.

60. Lev 18:7.

61. Gen 9:25.

62. Gen 9:23.

63. Rom 12:6.

ANCILLAE
DOMINI

ASCETIC WOMEN
IN THE
ROMAN EMPIRE
IN THE
LETTERS OF
SAINT JEROME

HISTORICAL INTRODUCTION

The recollection that the late Professor S. L. Greenslade had provided an excellent translation of a selection of Jerome's letters in his Early Latin Theology, published by SCM Press Ltd in 1956, prompted me to suggest to Cistercian Publications, Inc., that they should ask them for permission to reproduce his general introduction and his versions of Letters 107 and 108. I should like to thank SCM Press for generously granting this permission and to record my personal pleasure at thus being able to revive the work of a scholar and friend who helped and encouraged me at an earlier stage of my career. Like Professor Greenslade, I owe much to the spirited and imaginative translation by the late Dean Fremantle, published in the Library of Nicene and Post Nicene Fathers (series 2, vol. 4) but the changes in English usage since 1893, combined with the publication of Hilberg's edition in the CSEL in 1910–18, render it unsuitable for reproduction as it stands. In general I have based my translation on Hilberg's text, but have indicated where I have adopted an alternative reading. In my own translations I have used the forms 'you' and 'your', as elsewhere in this book, but in the case of Letters 107 and 108, the text of which is still in copyright, I have retained the archaic forms employed by Professor Greenslade.

Since Professor Greenslade's general introduction gives a most useful summary of Jerome's life and writings, it has been retained, but the reader should remember that the letters in Early Latin

Theology *were chosen with the primary object of setting out the general development of Jerome's theological thought, whereas my own selection was made in order to illustrate his teaching on asceticism for women dedicated to the religious life.* Père Adalbert *de* Vogüé's Histoire Littéraire du mouvement monastique dans l'antiquité, *volume 1,* appeared too late for me to make as much use of it as I should have liked, but I gratefully acknowledge it for the help which his valuable analysis of Letter 22 has afforded me.*

J. M. P.

EUSEBIUS HIERONYMUS was born about AD 347 at Stridon near Aquileia, of a prosperous middle-class family. 'I was born a Christian, of Christian parents,' Jerome said, and 'From my cradle I have been nourished with catholic milk.' When he was about twelve years old he was sent to Rome, together with his friend Bonosus, to continue his education. For four years he studied 'grammar' (that is, literature), having as his master the famous Aelius Donatus, the commentator on Terrence and Virgil, whose elementary grammars were standard works in the Middle Ages. After this Jerome went on to another four years' study of 'rhetoric' and philosophy. He was an ardent student of literature and a lover of books, always eager to build up his library. His moral life was far from blameless—of course the later ascetic may exaggerate his youthful sins—but he never strayed far from his Christianity and was baptized in Rome near the end of his studies, very probably at Easter, AD 366.

Soon afterwards Jerome and Bonosus paid a visit to the court of Valentinian at Augusta Treverorum (Trier), probably in the hope of obtaining employment in the imperial service. The outcome was something very different, for in this distant western city they came upon evidences of the anchoritic life. Athanasius had been there and made known the practices of the Egyptian desert. His life of St. Antony was read in Trier, and some had tried to follow the hermit's example, as we know from Augustine's *Confessions*. The young men vowed to do the same one day. Bonosus found himself able to do this quite soon, and without going far from home, but Jerome was more restless. For a time he associated with the brilliant group of clergy at Aquileia—the choir of the blessed, as he called them—which included Chromatius, later bishop, and Rufinus, and through which he became known to Evagrius, the Antiochene presbyter and friend of Eusebius of Vercellae. Eventually, however, he decided to break away and go to the East, the true home of the ascetic life. In 373 or 374[1] he arrived at Antioch, where he was entertained and assisted by Evagrius. There he was visited by his friend Heliodorus of Altinum, who had left the army with the intention of adopting the monastic life in some form and was on a pilgrimage to the Holy Places. Jerome tried vainly to persuade him to share with him the life of a hermit in the desert. Heliodorus went back to Italy, and in 374 or 375, Jerome set out for the desert of Chalcis.

It was either at Antioch or in the desert that he had his famous dream, related in one of his letters (22.20). 'Suddenly I was caught up in the spirit and brought before the Judgement-seat. I was asked my condition, and said that I was a Christian. 'Thou liest', said the Judge. 'Thou art a Ciceronian, not a Christian. For where thy treasure is, there will thy heart be also.' . . . I took an oath, calling upon his name, and said, 'Lord, if ever I possess worldly books or read them, I have denied thee' . . . Henceforth I read God's books with greater zeal than I had ever read men's books.' If he did not keep his promise literally, he kept it in spirit, and the first fruit of his new biblical studies was a commentary on Obadiah, a work which caused him some rueful amusement in later days. He had tried to expound an allegorical interpretation of the prophet before he had understood the literal sense. He had read that to faith all things are possible, and had not understood that there are diversities of gifts, and that his knowledge of profane letters would not unlock the secrets of a sealed book. He hoped his youthful essay might lie hidden in some corner of a library. If it does, no one has yet found it. About this time, too, he wrote the first of his romances of the desert, the *Life of Paul the Hermit*.

By 377 at latest he had returned to Antioch, still under thirty and altogether unaware of the venerable figure he would cut in the art of many centuries to come.

In Antioch Jerome was ordained presbyter by Paulinus, whom the West recognized as bishop of the city, and soon afterwards he went to Constantinople, where he studied theology and the Bible under Gregory of Nazianzus, who (it may fairly be presumed) made him conscious of the riches of Origien's biblical commentaries. He was in Constantinople for the Council of ad 381 and came to know Gregory of Nyssa. In the next year, owing partly to the continued disputes about the episcopal succession at Antioch, Jerome accompanied Paulinus to Rome, where he stayed for three years, eminent both as a scholar and as a spiritual director dedicated to the promotion of the ascetic life. As a scholar, he was secretary to Pope Damasus, who commissioned him to revise the current Latin versions of the Bible and produce a standard text. While at Rome he revised the Gospels and some of the remainder of the New Testament, at any rate the Pauline Epistles. This he did, of course, from the Greek original. He also revised the Psalms, but only from the Greek text of the Septuagint, without recourse to the Hebrew. This is the *Psalterium Romanum*.[2] As an ascetic teacher and spiritual director, Jerome had a great following among Roman ladies of high birth and ample fortune, many of whom figure largely in his correspondence. Some of them lived lives of abstinence and charity at home, others went in time to the monasteries of Jerusalem and Bethlehem. The impulse to this domestic asceticism had been given by Athanasius when he was in Rome in ad 340 attended by two Egyptian monks. Entertained by the rich widow Albina in her house on the Aventine, Athanasius had so much impressed her daughter Marcella that, becoming a widow within a few months of marriage, she devoted herself to a life of piety and renunciation in her mother's home, which became a center for others of like mind. Marcellina, Ambrose's sister, joined them after her own mother's death. Marcella was one of Jerome's most frequent correspondents. Another of the circle was Paula, who became head of Jerome's convent at Bethlehem and was succeeded in this office by her daughter Eustochium. Another great lady, Melania the Elder, founded a convent on the Mount of Olives, working there with Rufinus.[3]

In Rome Jerome could not escape controversy. He wrote against the Luciferians, followers of Lucifer of Cagliari who would not communicate with the bishops who had 'lapsed' in the Arian controversy, particularly at Ariminum in 359, even when they were reconciled with the Church in general. This book is moderate in tone, for Jerome, and may have been written earlier. Certainly of this period is his attack on Helvidius, an opponent of asceticism, whose teaching was taken up a little later by Jovinian.

When Damasus died in December, 384, there were rumors that Jerome might succeed him. 'In the opinion of most people,' said Jerome himself, 'I was fit for the *summum sacerdotium*.' And although in other circumstances, *summum sacerdotium* might mean no more than a bishopric, it is pretty clear that in its context it means the bishopric of Rome. We must conclude that he was a disappointed man. There was opposition to his unfamiliar text of the bible, and even greater opposition to his extreme ascetic teaching, and probably to his biting tongue and pen. If it is true that he had hoped for the Chair of Peter, he might not be altogether welcome to the new Pope, Siricus. Be that as it may, he left Rome for the East in August, 385, and made Palestine his home for the rest of his life.

Jerome sailed with his brother Paulinian and the Roman presbyter Vincent to Cyprus, where he was entertained by Epiphanius, Bishop of Salamis, and so to Antioch, where he again consorted with Paulinus and Evagrius. Meanwhile Paul and Eustochium had also left Rome. They joined Jerome's party at Salamis and Antioch, from which they all started on a long pilgrimage to the biblical sites of Palestine, reaching Jerusalem in mid-winter and continuing to Bethlehem and then back into Galilee. After that they all went to Egypt, the classic home of monasticism. At Alexandria Jerome met the theologian Didymus the Blind, whom he counted among his revered masters. When they returned to Bethlehem in the summer of 386, Jerome and Paula set about establishing monasteries there. The story of this pilgrimage is told in his Letter 108. The buildings, constructed by means of Paula's money and credit, were not ready until 389. There were separate monasteries for men and women and a hospice for pilgrims. These monasteries were organized as distinct communities, the men under Jerome, the women under Paula, but both groups met for worship on Sundays in the Church of the Nativity. A similar pair of monasteries had been established some years previously by Rufinnus of Aquileia and Melania on the Mount of Olives, and at this time John, Bishop of Jerusalem, was on friendly terms with the whole Latin community in his diocese.

Established once and for all in his monastery, Jerome devoted himself to study and writing. Lives of Malchus and Hilarion continued the romantic descriptions of famous hermits. He translated Didymus's *On the Holy Spirit*, wrote many biblical commentaries, and, now equipped with a knowledge of Hebrew, tackled the translation of the Old Testament, which he did not complete until ad 405. Unfortunately the peace which he needed for the work which called out his best qualities was broken by a dispute which simulated his worst. The Origenistic controversy is much too involved to be related here.[4] Up to ad 392 Jerome, proud to call himself the pupil of Gregory of Nazianzus and Didymus of Alexandria, and familiar with the library at Caesarea, was a devoted student of Origen, translated his works, accepted his principles of exegesis, and introduced the substance of his commentaries into his own. At Bethlehem he had translated Origen's *Homilies on Saint Luke*, and the notice of him in the *De Viris Illustribus* (written *c.* 392) is still full of praise. But in 393 a certain Atarbius, otherwise unknown, arrived in Palestine and began to go round the monasteries, calling on the monks to denounce Origen as a heretic. Jerome was disturbed, but Rufinus shut the door on the intruder. This herald was soon followed by his principal, Epiphanius of Salamis, a man of holy life but a narrow-minded and pedantic heresy-hunter. Rufinus held out for Origen, and John of Jerusalem was not disposed to denounce his teaching, especially when urged to do so by a bishop who showed no regard for his colleague's jurisdiction. But Jerome was not only anxious to be strictly orthodox, but also had the deepest respect for Epiphanius as a man of ascetic life. So he took his side. Soon Epiphanius ordained Jerome's brother, Paulinian, against his will and against all canonical propriety, in another bishop's diocese. Consequently relations between Jerusalem and Bethlehem were strained almost to breaking-point. In 395, when threat of invasion by the Huns caused a panic in Palestine, Jerome thought of returning to the West. Some of his company did go, but Jerome stayed. It was not long before John of Jerusalem tried to make sure of his departure by getting an imperial order for his expulsion, but it was not put into effect; possibly it lapsed through the fall and death of the great minister, Rufinus, in November 395. In autumn 396 Jerome wrote a virulent pamphlet against John, but in 397, by the mediation of Theophilus of Alexandria (who had not yet come out against Origen), a reconciliation was effected between Jerome and his old friend Rufinus, which pacified John as well.

The reconciliation with Rufinus was brief, for he returned to the West as a champion of Origen against all adversaries. His translation of the *Apology for Origen* composed by the martyr Pamphilus with the help of the scholar Eusebius of Caesarea, was a clever move. When he followed it with a version—with improvements!—of Origen's *De Principiis*, the fat was in the fire. Jerome pursued him relentlessly, even for some years after Rufinus had refused to enter into any further controversy with him. When Theophilus turned against Origen, Jerome supported him in his campaign against John Chrysostom, Bishop of Constantinople. To a large extent, John of Jerusalem stood aloof from the conflict after the reconciliation of 397, though he wrote to Pope Anastasius in favor of Rufinus.

The unhappy controversy did not occupy Jerome's whole attention. He continued with his Old Testament translation until its completion in 405, and wrote more commentaries. His controversy with the opponents of asceticism went on. To the work against Helvidius he had added a bitter refutation of Jovinian in 393, which was followed in 406 by the *Contra Vigilantium*. From 394 or 395 he was corresponding with Augustine (mostly in 404), discussing among other things the advisability of making biblical versions from the Hebrew, which might upset people used to translations made from the Septuagint, and the possibility that Peter and Paul, in the story told in Galatians, might have exercised a little expedient dissimulation, a notion of Jerome's which horrified Augustine. The correspondence was sometimes friendly, sometimes distinctly cool. But when Jerome was drawn into the Pelagian controversy he was entirely on Augustine's side, and wrote against the heretic. No doubt he could do this *ex animo*, but we may suspect that his zeal was not diminished by the fact that John of Jerusalem had received Pelagius kindly.

As Jerome grew old, he had to suffer from the loss of his friends. Paula died in 404, Marcella in 411, soon after the sack of Rome by the Goths, Eustochium, who had succeeded her mother at Bethlehem, at the turn of 418–19. Jerome himself died in September 419 or 420.[5]

Jerome's writings are numerous and bulky. First, he translated the whole of the Old Testament from the Hebrew into Latin, besides making two versions of the Psalms and one of Job from Greek; and he translated the New Testament books from the Greek. Secondly, he wrote commentaries, some of them substantial, on each of the prophets, the Psalms, Ecclesiastes, Matthew, Galatians, Ephesians, Philemon, and Titus. These vary considerably in nature and value, the later ones tending to be more literal and historical than the earlier, showing a revulsion from the influence of Origen. Some of them are composed mainly of extracts from Greek commentators. With these we may group the translations of Origen's *Homilies* on Isaiah, Jeremiah, Ezekiel, Canticles, and Luke. There are also a book on difficult passages in Genesis, the handbooks on Hebrew names and place-names, largely taken from Eusebius, and some notes and sermons on the Psalms and on Mark.

The controversial works include the group against opponents of asceticism (Helvidius, Jovinian, and Vigilantius), the treatises against the Luciferians and the Pelagians, and the anti-Origenist works, that is, the three books against Rufinus and the pamphlet against John of Jerusalem.

Purporting to be historical, but perhaps without intent to deceive, are the lives of the hermits, Paul, Malchus, and Hilarion. The truly historical works are the translation of Eusebius' *Chronicon* and its continuation to AD 378, and the very valuable collection of Christian bio-bibliographers called *De Viris Illustribus*. Unfortunately Jerome did not carry out his project of writing a history of his own time. The 154 letters are, of course, full of the most important historical materials; some of them are really treatises, like the famous Lr 22 to Eustochium on *Virginity* or Lr 52 to Nepotian on the *Duties of the Clergy*. Jerome also translated the *De Spiritu Sancto* of Didymus and the *Rule* of Pachomius. Some of his translations have not survived, including that of the *De Principiis* of Origen, which he made to show up how Rufinus had doctored his own version in the interest of Origen's orthodoxy.

Jerome's faults of character are obvious enough. He lacked breadth of mind, and would rarely try to understand the other point of view. He nursed his animosities and grievances, and only too often let his clever and satirical pen run away with him. With this want of restraint and judgement he would, humanly speaking, have made a poor bishop and an impossible pope. It is not difficult to gather a highly unfavorable impression of his personality from his letters and certain other works. Yet he had high qualities, even apart from his scholarship. He was capable of the warmest human affections, he schooled himself to endure hardship, and he worked with almost incredible assiduity.

No doubt judgement on his ascetic teaching will vary with the judge, for here the whole course of Christian history is involved, and any attempt to strike a balance can only be very tentative. There are imponderables which elude us. On the one hand, he tramples on natural affections and social duties in a way which no Christian society can accept as normative, even if it is ever proper in particular cases; and he proclaims a double standard of morality, with a tariff of rewards, which is insidiously demoralizing and false to the Gospel. Not that he invented all this, and he shared this outlook, alas, with such great men as Athanasius and Ambrose; but it has to be remembered that his writings ranked high among the clerical studies of the Middle Ages. On the other hand, the strong challenge to self-sacrifice and simplicity of life was of enormous value as the Church emerged from the shadows of unpopularity and persecution to a place in the sun, tempted every moment to compromise with the world. Jerome's teaching and example led many to dedicate themselves to a life of charity and piety and prayer.

Though he was no philosopher and not really a constructive, certainly not an original, theologian, he was the outstanding scholar of his time—and it is seldom that one can thus single a man out with such confidence. If in many respects his scholarship was superficial and unreliable, and if this was sometimes the result of a more or less culpable haste and impatience, it was more often due to the absence of those tools of systematic learning which have slowly accumulated in subsequent centuries and to which he himself contributed not a little. He had the instincts of a scholar. Without him our picture of his age would be much poorer and much less vivid. As an exegete he had much more concern than was usual in his day for textural and historical matters, and he shared with Ambrose and Hilary of Poitiers the merit of revealing the riches of Greek biblical scholarship to the churches of the latin West.

Then there is the Vulgate, his chief claim upon the gratitude of the Church. In the first place, he provided a standard text for all those who wanted to read the Bible in Latin, and that in itself was no small benefit at a time when a welter of widely different translations—as many versions as manuscripts—was confusing the Christian reader. Secondly, he established, against much opposition, the principles that, where possible, Scripture should be studied in the original tongues, and that translations, above all when they are intended for common use in the Church, should be made from the original. Finally, the version which he produced was, with all its faults, a very good one, far more reliable than anything available up to his own time, and not to be superseded in the West for many centuries. It is still of cardinal importance to the student of the text of the Scriptures, and still the official Bible of a great multitude of Christians.[6]

S. L. Greenslade

NOTES

* Paris: Cerf, 1991—an english translation is in preparation—ed.

1. 373 is on the whole the more likely date, but the chronology of this period of Jerome's life is full of difficulty. For a detailed explanation of the situation, see S. L. Greenslade, *Early Latin Theology* (London, 1956) pp. 302–306, which form the introduction to his translation of Letter 15.

2. The *Psalterium Romanum* or Roman Psalter has traditionally been identified with the latin translation of the psalms, which Jerome says that he made on the basis of the LXX, but this has been disputed. It was used in italian churches until the reign of Pius V (1566–1572), when it was replaced by the so-called Gallican Psalter. It is still used in Saint Peter's, Rome.

3. See pp. 283ff.

4. See Letter 127, p. 114.

5. Jerome's horrifying description of old age in his *Commentary on Zechariah* 8.6 (CCSL 76A: 841) suggests what his condition at the end of his long life may have been. He probably died in 420.

6. This introduction was written in 1956, before the changes brought about by Vatican II.

MARCELLA,
LEA, ASELLA, AND PRINCIPIA:
WIDOWS AND VIRGINS IN ROME

MARCELLA was one of the first women to establish a domestic religious community in Rome. Jerome tells us that she was influenced in this by Athanasius and by his successor Peter, who was in Rome in 373 (Letter 127.5). She as an avid student of the Bible, and the first sentence of Letter 23 is an example of the detailed, literal biblical exegesis which she particularly enjoyed. We learn in Letter 127 that she died as a result of being beaten by a band of gothic soldiers who had broken into the house during the conquest of Rome.

LETTER 23 is a letter of condolence from Jerome to Marcella on the death of her friend Lea, who, like herself, has been the head of a domestic monastery. Her distress was caused, not by doubt about Lea's fate in the next world, but by regret that she herself had not been able to perform the last offices for her. While the sentiments expressed in Letter 23 are admirable, Jerome's uncharitable confidence that the deceased consul Praetextatus would burn in hell for having remained a pagan somewhat mars the modern reader's appreciation of his sentiments. Lea, like Marcella, was a widow, as we gather from Letter 24. Jerome's phrase, 'mother of virgins', may therefore refer to her as a mother of biological daughters as well as the head of a religious community of women. She practiced the kind of life style commended by Jerome, but was not ostentatious in her austerities for fear of being praised for them by others. In Jerome's opinion, the lesson to be drawn from her life is that Christians in this world should hold on to what is eternal and should remember their own mortality.

LETTER 24 on Asella, the virgin sister of Marcella, was written at Rome in 384, two days after Letter 23. Jerome felt that he had erred in writing a letter in praise of a widow, who, after all, belonged only to the second order of chastity, while saying nothing of a virgin, who is a member of the first order. Letter 24 is unusual in several ways. First, it is a eulogy of a living person. Moreover, Asella appears to have been a solitary, confined to her own cell, whereas Marcella and Lea were cenobites. Jerome says that this letter is not to be read to Asella, as this would cause her embarrassment, but it is to be shown to the young girls of Marcella's acquaintance, to provide them with a model.

Asella, Jerome tells us, was a child oblate, as were the younger Paula (Letter 107) and Pacatula (Letter 128). After the age of twelve, she assumed personal responsibility for the promises which had been made on her behalf and, as an outward sign of her dedication, gave away her jewelry and adopted distinctive dark clothing to make her situation clear to her family. Her life style was extremely austere and involved great fasting and solitude, though she sometimes slipped out to worship unrecognized at the shrines of the martyrs, a practice to which Jerome refers in his letter praising Marcella after her death (Letter 127). Jerome praises Asella for creating a place of stillness and peace amid the hurly-burly of Rome and says that priests (*sacerdos*—which can mean either a priest or a bishop) should look up to her.

LETTER 127, like Letter 23, falls into the category of obituaries or memoirs. Its recipient, Principia, was a member of Marcella's religious community and her closest friend and companion. Principia had evidently been distressed at receiving no word of sympathy from Jerome on the death of Marcella, but he justified a two-year silence by saying that his deep sorrow had made it impossible for him to praise Marcella's virtue in adequate language. The date of this letter must surely be 412, since the fall of Rome in 410 was the immediate cause of Marcella's death.

A great deal of valuable information can be learned from the letter. (1) Paragraphs 1–8 describe Marcella's character and the origins of feminine monasticism in Rome. (2) Paragraphs 7–11 provide details of the outbreak of the Origenist dispute in Rome and a vigorous part Marcella played in helping Jerome combat it there. (3) Paragraphs 12–14 give a graphic description of the sack of Rome by Alaric and the Goths in 410 and of Marcella's death. Since Jerome was resident in Palestine at the time, this description must be based on what he had heard from people who had been present in Rome at the time.

Although Letter 127 is the product of careful thought and writing some time after the events it describes, it is nevertheless a moving document, perhaps because it is comparatively brief and is free of mannerisms and stylistic elaboration.

J. M. P.

To Marcella (*Letter 23*)

TODAY, about the third hour, just as I was beginning to read with you the seventy-second[1] psalm—the first, that is, of the third book—and to explain that its title belonged partly to the second book and partly to the beginning of the third book— namely that the words, 'The prayers of David the son of Jesse are ended', belong to the previous book and 'A psalm of Asaph' to the beginning of the next—and just as I had come upon the passage in which the righteous man declares, *I was saying, 'If I shall speak thus, behold! I have sinned against the generation of your sons*[2] —a verse which is differently rendered in our latin manuscripts[3] —suddenly the news arrived that our very saintly friend Lea had departed from the body. I saw you turn deathly pale, as there are few, if any, people who do not burst into tears of sadness, when the earthen vessel is broken.[4] You were grieving not because you were uncertain of her future, but simply because you had not rendered to her the last sad offices which are due the dead. At length, in the middle of our conversation, we received the further news that her remains had already been conveyed to Ostia.

You may ask, What is the point of repeating all this? I will answer you in the Apostle's words, *Much in every way.*[5] First, my repetition shows that everyone must hail with joy the release of a soul which has trampled Satan underfoot and won for itself at last a crown of tranquillity. Secondly, it gives me an opportunity of briefly describing her life. Thirdly, we are able to explain, as we disparage our present age, that the consul-elect[6] is now in hell.[7]

Indeed, who can praise our dear Lea's way of life highly enough? So complete was her conversion to the Lord that she became the head of a monastic community and the mother of virgins, that instead of her own soft raiment she clothed her limbs in sackcloth, that she passed sleepless nights in prayer and taught her companions more by her example than by her words. So great was the depth of her humility that she who had once been the ruler of many was regarded as the servant of a man; but the more she was thought to be the servant of Christ, the less was she thought to be the ruler of men. Her dress was careless, her food was coarse, and her hair was neglected, but in all that she did, she shunned any display of individual peculiarities, in order that she might not receive her reward in this world.[8]

Now therefore Lea enjoys everlasting bliss in return for her brief toil. She is welcomed by choirs of angels; she is comforted in Abraham's bosom. As once the poor man Lazarus saw the rich man, clad in purple,[9] she sees the consul not robed in his tunic embroidered with palms, but doomed to destruction, ask for a drop of water from her little finger. What a change of circumstances! A few days ago, all the highest dignitaries of the city preceded him, as he mounted the citadel of the Capitol as if he were triumphing over a defeated enemy. The people of Rome leaped up to applaud him and at the news of his death, the whole city was moved. Now he is desolate and naked, a prisoner in foul darkness and not, as his unhappy wife[10] falsely asserts, a dweller in the royal palace of the Milky Way.[11] On the other hand, Lea—whom the secrecy of her one little room protected as with a rampart, who seemed poor and weak, whose life was thought to be madness—[12] now follows Christ and sings, *As we have heard, so have we seen in the city of our God.*[13]

On account of all this I exhort you and call you to witness, with tears and groans, that as long as we run our race in this world we do not clothe ourselves with two coats, that is, with a faith looking in two directions, or burden ourselves with leather shoes, that is, with dead works;[14] we do not allow money-filled purses to weigh us down, or lean upon the staff or worldly power.[15] We must not seek to possess both Christ and the world. No, things eternal must take the place of things transitory.[16] And since, physically speaking, we daily anticipate death, if we wish for immortality, we must realize that we are only mortal.

To Marcella (*Letter 24*)

LET NO ONE blame my letters for the eulogies and censures which are contained in them. To draw public attention to sinners is to reprove other sinners, and to praise the virtuous is to quicken the zeal of those who wish to do right. The day before yesterday I spoke to you about Lea of blessed memory,[17] and I had hardly done so when I was pricked in my conscience. It would be wrong for me, I thought, to be silent about a virgin, after speaking of one who, as a widow, held a place in the second order of chastity. Accordingly, in my present letter, I mean to give you a brief sketch of the life of our dear Asella. Please do not read it to her, for she is made uncomfortable by other people's praise of her. Show it rather to the young girls of your acquaintance, that they may guide themselves by her example and may take her behavior as the pattern of a perfect life.

I pass over the facts that, before her birth, she was blessed while still in her mother's womb, and that, virgin-like, she was in a dream delivered to her father in a bowl of shining glass, brighter than a mirror, and that while she was still a baby wrapped in swaddling clothes, hardly more than ten years old, she was consecrated in the office of future blessedness. For all that comes before works should be counted of grace,[18] although, doubtless God had foreknowledge of the future, when he sanctified Jeremiah, as yet unborn,[19] when he made John leap in his other's womb,[20] and when, before the foundation of the world, he set Paul apart to preach the gospel of his Son.[21]

I come now to the life which after her twelfth year she, by her own exertion, chose, laid hold of, held fast to, entered upon, and fulfilled. Enclosed in the narrow confines of a single cell, she enjoyed the wide pastures of paradise. The same patch of earth existed as her place both of prayer and of rest. Fasting was her recreation and hunger her refreshment. If she took food, it was not from love of eating but from human exhaustion, and the bread, salt, and cold water to which she restricted herself sharpened more than appeased her appetite.

But I have almost forgotten to mention what I should have spoken of first. When her resolution was still fresh, she took her gold necklace, made in what is commonly called the lamprey pattern—because bars of metal are linked together to form a flexible chain—and sold it without her parents' knowledge. Then putting on a dark dress, for which she was not able to ask her mother, and adorning herself with her holy intention and purpose, she consecrated herself immediately to the Lord. In this way, she showed her relatives that they need hope to wring no further concessions from someone who, by her very dress, had condemned the world.

To go on with my story, her ways were quiet and she lived in great privacy. She never appeared in public or spoke to a man. More wonderful still, much as she loved her virgin sister,[22] she did not care to see her. She worked with her own hands, for she knew that it was written, *If anyone will not work, neither shall he eat.*[23]

To the Bridegroom she spoke constantly in prayer and psalmody. She hurried to the martyrs' shrines unnoticed. Such visits gave her pleasure, and the more so because she was never recognized. All the year round she observed a continual fast, remaining without food for two or three days at a time; but when Lent came, she hoisted—if I may so speak—every stitch of her canvas and fasted almost from week's end to week's end with *a cheerful countenance.*[24] What would perhaps be incredible, were it not that *with God all things are possible,*[25] is that she lived this life until her fiftieth year without weakening her digestion or bringing stomach pains on herself. Lying on the dry ground did not affect her limbs, and the rough sackcloth she wore failed to make her skin either evil-smelling or rough. With a sound body and a still sounder soul,[26] she sought all her delight in solitude and found for herself a monastic hermitage amidst the hurly-burly of the city.

You are better acquainted with all this than I am, and the few details I have given I learned from you. In that holy little body you have seen with your own eyes the hardness of the knees that have become calloused like those of a camel, through the frequency of her prayers.[27] For our part, we set forth what we have been able to learn. She is equally pleasant in her serious moods and serious in her pleasant moods. She is equally solemn in her laughter and charming in her sadness. Her face is pale enough to indicate continence but not ostentatiously to display austerity. Her speech is silence and her silence speech. Her walk is neither fast nor slow. Her appearance is always the same. She neglects neatness and her dress is untidy; when she attends to it, she takes no trouble. So deserving of merit has she been for the consistent quality of her life that in this city of vain show, debauchery, and luxury, where it is regarded as poor-spirited to be humble, good people praise her and bad people do not dare to defame her character. Let our widows and virgins imitate her, let our married women reverence her and let our priests[28] look up to her.

To Principia (Letter 127)

YOU HAVE PLEADED with me often and earnestly, Principia,[29] virgin of Christ, to dedicate a letter to the memory of that holy woman Marcella,[30] and to describe her goodness, which we have long enjoyed, so that others may know and imitate it. I myself am so anxious to do justice to her merits that it grieves me that you should spur me on and fancy that your entreaties are needed, when I do not yield even to you in affection for her. In putting her immense virtues on record, I shall receive far more benefit myself than I can possibly confer on others. If I have hitherto remained silent and have allowed two years to pass by without saying a word about her, this has been due not, as you wrongly suppose, to a desire to ignore her, but to an incredible sorrow which so overcame my mind that I judged it better to remain silent in the present circumstances than to praise her virtues in language unworthy of them. Neither will I now follow the rules of rhetoric in eulogizing someone so dear to both of us and to all holy persons, Marcella, the glory of her own city, Rome. I will not set forth her illustrious family and exalted lineage, nor will I trace her pedigree through a line of consuls and praetorian prefects. I will praise her for nothing but the virtue which is her own and which is the more noble because, in forsaking both wealth and rank, she has sought the true nobility of poverty and lowliness.

Bereft of her father by death, she was also deprived of her husband in the seventh month after their marriage. Then, as she was young and highborn as well as remarkable for her beauty— something which always attracts men—and for her self-control, a distinguished man of consular rank named Cerealis courted her assiduously. As he was an old man, he offered to make over his fortune to her, not so much to a wife as to a daughter. Her mother, Albina, went out of her way to secure for the young widow so exalted a protector, but Marcella answered, 'Had I a wish to marry and not rather to dedicate myself to perpetual chastity, I should look for a husband and not for an inheritance'. When Ceralis argued that sometimes old men live long, while young men die early, she cleverly retorted, 'A young man may indeed die early, but an old man cannot live long'. This decided rejection of Cerealis convinced others that they had no hope of winning her hand.

In the Gospel according to Luke, we read the following passage: *There was Anna prophetess, the daughter of Phanuel, of the tribe of Aser. She as of a great age and had lived with a husband seven years from her virginity; and she was a widow aged eighty-four, who never left the temple, but served God with fasting and prayer night and day.*[31] It was no marvel that she was worthy to see the Saviour whom she sought so earnestly, let us then compare Anna and Marcella: the seven years with the seven months; the hope for Christ and the possession of Christ; the confession of the Christ-child at his birth and the belief in the crucified Christ; the non-denial of the child and the rejoicing in the full-grown man as King. I do not draw distinctions between holy women, a thing which some persons are foolishly in the habit of doing in the case of holy men and church leaders. The conclusion towards which I tend is that those who have the same task should have the same reward.

In a slander-loving community like Rome, filled as it formerly[32] was with people from all parts of the world and bearing the palm of wickedness of all kinds, the characters of honorable men were defamed and indeed even the pure and clean were defiled. In such an atmosphere it is hard to escape the breath of calumny. A stainless reputation is difficult, indeed almost impossible, to attain; the prophet yearns for it but hardly hopes to win it: *Blessed, he says, are the undefiled in the way who walk in the law of the Lord.*[33] The undefiled in the way of this world are those, whose fair fame no breath of scandal has ever sullied, and who have earned no reproach at the hands of the neighbors. This is what makes the Saviour say in the Gospel, *Agree with*, or, be well-disposed to, *your enemy while you are on the road with him*.[34] Who ever heard a slander of Marcella that deserved the slightest credit? Or who ever credited such a thing without making himself guilty of malice and defamation? No, she put the Gentiles to confusion by showing them the nature of that Christian widowhood which her conscience and appearance alike set forth. Women of the world are accustomed to paint their faces with rouge and white-lead, to be resplendent in robes of silk, to pierce their ears and hang in them the costliest pearls of the Red Sea,[35] and to blaze, so to speak, with the scent of musk,[36] so that in the end they rejoice that they lack the domination of their husbands and seek others, not to obey them as God wills,[37] but to rule over them.

With this object in view, they select poor men so contented with the mere name of husbands that they are more than ready to put up with rivals, knowing that if they so much as murmur, they will immediately be thrown out. Our widow used her clothes to keep out the cold and not to show off her figure. Of gold she would not wear so much as a signet-ring, choosing to store her money in the stomachs of the poor rather than keep it in her purse. She went nowhere without her mother and would never see without witnesses such monks and clergy as the needs of a large house required her to interview. She was always accompanied by virgins and widows, and these were women of staid and serious character. For as she well knew, people pass judgement on the habits of the mistress of the household as the result of the loose behavior of its young girls, and when they see how she is led astray by associating with such a society as they comprise.[38]

Her delight in the divine Scriptures was incredible. She was for ever singing, *Your words have I hidden in my heart that I might not sin against you*,[39] as well as the words which describe the perfect man, *His delight is in the law of the Lord; and in his law will he meditate day and night*.[40] She did not regard this meditation as being on the written words, as the jewish Pharisees think, but understood it as relating to action in accordance with that saying of the Apostle, *Whether you eat or whether you drink or whether you perform some action, do everything to the glory of God.*[41] She remembered also the prophet's words, *Through your precepts I get understanding,*[42] and felt sure that only when she had fulfilled all these would she be permitted to understand the Scriptures. In this sense we read elsewhere that *Jesus began both to do and to teach.*[43] For teaching is put to the blush when a person's conscience rebukes him, and it is in vain that his tongue preaches poverty or teaches almsgiving if he is rolling in the riches of Coresus and if, in spite of his threadbare cloak, he has silken robes at home, to save them from the moth.

Marcella practised fasting, but in moderation. She abstained from eating flesh, and she knew rather the scent of wine than its taste, touching it only for her stomach's sake[44] She seldom appeared in public and especially avoided the houses of married ladies of noble birth, that she might not be forced to look at what she had once and for all renounced. She frequented the basilicas of apostles and martyrs that she might escape the crowd and give herself up to private prayer. So obedient was she to her mother that sometimes she did things of which she herself disapproved. For example, when her mother, careless of her own offspring, was for transferring all her property from her children and grandchildren to her brother's children, Marcella wanted the money to be given to the poor instead, and yet could not bring herself to thwart her parent. Therefore she made over her jewels and other effects to persons who were already rich; she was willing to throw away her money rather than to sadden her mother's heart.

In those days no highborn lady in Rome had made profession of the monastic life or had ventured—so strange and degrading did it then seem—publicly to call herself a nun.[45] It was from some priests of Alexandria and from bishop Athanasius, and subsequently from Peter[46] —who, to escape the persecution of the Arian heretics had all fled for refuge to Rome as the safest haven in which they could find communion—it was from these that Marcella heard of the life of the blessed Antony, then still alive,[47] and of the monasteries in the Thebaid founded by Pachomius,[48] and of the discipline laid down for virgins and widows. Nor was she ashamed to profess a life which she had thus learned was pleasing to Christ. Many years later her example was followed first by Sophronia[49] and then by others, of whom it may be well said in the words of Ennius, 'Would that not in Pelion's grove . . . .'[50] My revered friend Paula enjoyed Marcella's friendship, and it was in Marcella's cell that Eustochium, that paragon of virgins, was brought up, so it is easy to evaluate the quality of a mistress who had such pupils.

The unbelieving reader may perhaps laugh at me for dwelling so long on the praises of mere women. Yet if he remembers those holy women who accompanied our Lord and Saviour and ministered to him of their substance,[51] the three Marys who stood before the cross[52] and especially Mary Magdalene, who was called the Tower[53] on account of the earnestness and glowing enthusiasm of her faith and who was deemed worthy to be the first to see the risen Christ, before the apostles, he will convince himself of pride rather than me of folly, for I judge people's virtues not by their gender but by their character. Jesus loved John the Evangelist most of all the disciples, for John, who was known to the High Priest on account of the nobility of his family,[54] had so little fear of the plots of the Jews that he introduced Peter into the courtyard of the High Priest's palace and alone of the apostles stood at the cross and received the Mother of our Saviour into his home. Thus the virgin son[55] received the virgin mother as a legacy from the Lord.

Marcella lived out her life span in this manner for so many years, that she found herself an old woman before she recollected that she had been a young girl. She used to quote with approval Plato's saying that philosophy is meditation on death.[56] Our Apostle too says, *For your salvation I die daily,*[57] and indeed, according to the old copies, our Lord himself says, *Unless a person carries his cross daily and follows me, he cannot be my disciple.*[58] Long ago the Holy Spirit said through the prophet, *For your sake we are killed all day long; we are counted as sheep for the slaughter.*[59] Many generations later the words were spoken *Always remember the day of your death and you will never sin.*[60] Then there is what the satirist eloquently teaches, 'Live with death in mind; time flies.

This saying of mine is so much taken from it.'[61] Well then, as I was beginning to say, she passed her days and lived her life as one who always believed she ws going to die. She dressed in such a way that she was reminded of the tomb and offered herself as a living sacrifice, reasonable and pleasing to God.[62]

Then, when the needs of the Church had brought me to Rome in the company of the holy bishops Paulinus and Epiphanius, of whom the one ruled the Church of Antioch in Syria and the other, of Salamis in Cyprus, and I was modestly avoiding the eyes of highborn ladies,[63] she worked on me *in season and out of season*, as the Apostle says,[64] in such a way that her perseverance overcame my shyness. As in those days I was looked on as a person of some reputation in the study of the Scriptures, she never met me without asking me some question relating to the Scriptures. Nor did she immediately agree with my explanations, but to the contrary she would dispute them, not for the sake of argument, but in order to learn by her questions the answers to the objections which, she grasped might be raised to them. How much virtue, ability, sanctity, and purity I found in her I am afraid to say, lest I should exceed the bounds of belief and should increase your sorrow as you recall how much goodness you have lost. I will say only this, that whatever had been assembled together in me through long study and had, as it were, been transformed into my nature through daily meditation, this she tasted, learned, and made her own. The result of this was that after my departure, if a dispute arose concerning some testimony of the Scriptures, it was brought to her as judge. Since she was very wise and understood what the philosophers call πρέπον (that is, what is fitting), as you do, when she was asked questions, she voiced her opinion not as if it were hers, but as if it were mine or someone else's, thus admitting that what she taught she had learned as a disciple. For she knew what had been said by the Apostle, *I do not allow a woman to teach*,[65] and she would not seem to inflict any injury upon the male sex and the priests, who sometimes asked her about obscure and doubtful points.

I have heard that my place with her was immediately taken by you and that, as the saying goes, you never let even a hair's breadth[66] come between her and you. You had both retired into the same house and had occupied the same room, indeed the same bed, so that it became known to everyone in our most famous city that you had found a mother and she a daughter. On the outskirts[67] of Rome you found for yourselves a monastic retreat, and you chose the country instead of the town because of its isolation. For a long time you lived together and as many ladies modelled their lives on your example, I rejoiced to see Rome become another Jerusalem. Monastic establishments for virgins became numerous, and there was a countless throng of monks. As a result, owing to the large number of servants of God, monasticism, which had previously been a term of reproach, subsequently became one of honor. In the meantime we comforted one another for our absence by words of mutual encouragement and discharged in the spirit the debt which we could not pay in the flesh. We always went to meet each other's letters, tried to outdo each other in attentions and anticipated each other in courteous enquiries. We did not lose much, since we were linked to one another in constant correspondence.

In this time of tranquillity and the Lord's service there arose in the provinces a tornado of heresy which threw everything into confusion. It lashed itself into such a storm of madness that it spared neither itself nor anything that was good.[68] As if it were too little to have disturbed everything here, it brought a ship full of blasphemies into the port of Rome. The dish soon found itself a cover,[69] and the muddy feet of heretics soon fouled the clear spring water of Rome's faith. No wonder that in the streets and market-places a false soothsayer can slap fools on the buttocks or, taking up his cudgel, shatter the teeth of those who sting him, when such venomous and filthy doctrine as this has found at Rome people whom it can lead astray. Next came the scandalous translation of the books *On First Principles*,[70] and that disciple, by name 'Fortunate', who would indeed have been fortunate, had he not fallen in with such a master.[71] Next followed the confutation by my supporters, and the sect of Pharisees was thrown into confusion. It was then that the holy Marcella, who had long been allied to me, in order not to be believed to be acting from party spirit, publicly threw herself into the breach, preferring to please God rather than men. This was after she became conscious that the faith of Rome, once praised by the Apostle,[72] was now being violated in many quarters, that the heresy was attracting priests and some monks and especially members of the laity to assent to it and was impinging on the bishop,[73] who thought that other people were as guileless as he was himself.

In the Gospel the Saviour commends the unjust steward because, although he defrauded his master, he acted wisely in his own interests.[74] The heretics, seeing that a very great fire was being aroused from a small spark, and that the flame which they had applied to the foundations had by this time reached the housetops, and that the deception which they had practiced on many people could no longer be concealed, asked for and obtained letters from the Church,[75] in order to appear to take their departure in communion with the Church. Shortly afterwards, the distinguished man, Anastasius, succeeded to the pontificate, but he was soon taken away. Rome was not fit to hold him for long,[76] lest the head of the world be struck off under the rule of such a bishop.[77] No doubt he was snatched up and carried off elsewhere, that he might not attempt by his prayers to turn away the sentence of God passed once and for all. For the Lord said to Jeremiah, *Do not pray for this people or intercede for their good, for if they fast, I will not hear their prayers, and if they offer burnt offerings and victims, I will not accept them; for I will consume them by sword, famine and plague.*[78] You may say to me, 'What has this to do with the praises of Marcella?' I reply: She it was who originated the condemnation of the heretics. She it was who produced witnesses who had first been taught by them and had then been cured of their heretical error. She it was who showed how large a number had been deceived by them and who brought up against them the impious books *On First Principles*, which were being displayed after being 'improved' by the hand of the scorpion.[79] She it was, lastly, who called on the heretics in frequent letters to defend themselves. They indeed did not dare to come, for they were so conscience-stricken that they preferred to be condemned in their absence than to be convicted of their guilt in person. This great victory owes its origin to Marcella, and you, the source and cause of this great blessing, know I speak the truth. You know too that out of many incidents I mention only a few, lest vexatious repetition weary the reader, and I appear in the eyes of malevolent persons to be giving vent to my own rancor under the pretext of praising another.

The whirlwind[80] passed from the West to the East and threatened in its passage to shipwreck many vessels. Then were the words of Jesus fulfilled, *When the Son of Man comes, shall he find faith on earth?*[81] The love of many people grew cold, but the few who still loved the true faith rallied to my side. Men openly sought to take their lives and all possible resources were employed against them, so that *Barnabas also was carried away by their dissimulation*[82], indeed he committed open parricide, if not by physical violence, then at least in his will.[83] Then behold God blew, and the tempest passed away; the prediction of the prophet was fulfilled, *You shall take away their breath, they shall die and return to dust.*[84] *In that very day his thoughts perish,*[85] as also the gospel-saying, *You fool, this night your soul shall be taken away from you: then whose shall those things be, which you have provided?*[86]

While these things were happening in Jebus,[87] a dreadful rumor came from the West that Rome was being besieged, that the safety of its citizens was purchased with gold, and that having been thus despoiled, they were once more surrounded, so that they lost not only their substance but also their lives.[88] My voice sticks in my throat and sobbing chokes my words as I dictate. The city which had taken the whole world was itself taken; indeed it perished more by famine than by the sword and only a few citizens were left to be captured.[89] In their frenzy the starving people had recourse to unmentionable food and tore at each other's limbs, while the mother did not spare the infant at her breast and received into her belly what she had a little earlier brought forth from it. *By night was Moab taken, by night her wall fell down.*[90] *O God, the pagans have come into your inheritance; they have defiled your holy temple; they have made Jerusalem the guardian of an orchard.*[91] *They have put out the dead bodies of your servants to*

be food for the birds of heaven and the flesh of your saints for the
beasts of the earth. They have shed their blood like water round
about Jerusalem; and there was no one to bury them.[92]

> Who can set forth the carnage of that night?
> What tears are equal to its agony?
> Of ancient date a sovereign city falls;
> And lifeless in its streets and houses lie
> Unnumbered bodies of its citizens.
> In many a ghastly shape doth death appear.[93]

Meantime, as was natural in a scene of such confusion, one of the blood-stained victors found his way into Marcella's house. Now is it my duty to say what I have heard, indeed to relate what holy men have seen, for there were some of them present and they say that you too were with her in the hour of danger. When the soldiers entered, she is said to have received them without any look of alarm, and when they asked her for gold, she pointed to her coarse tunic to show them she had no buried treasure. However, they would not believe her self-chosen poverty, but scourged her and beat her with cudgels. She is said to have felt no pain but to have thrown herself at their feet and to have pleaded with tears for you, that you not be taken from her, or, in your youth, have to endure what she as an old woman had no occasion to fear. Christ softened their hard hearts and even among their blood-stained swords, filial affection asserted its rights. The barbarians conveyed both you and her to the basilica of the apostle Paul, that you might find there a place of safety or, if not that, at least a tomb. Here Marcella is said to have burst into great joy and to have thanked God for having kept you unharmed in answer to her prayer. She said that she was thankful, too, that the sack of the city had found her poor, not made her so, that she was now in want of daily bread, but that filled with Christ, she no longer felt hunger, that she was able to say in word and in deed, *Naked I came out of my mother's womb and naked I shall return to it: the Lord gave and the Lord has taken away; blessed be the name of the Lord.*[94]

After a few months, while in good health, with unimpaired powers and with bodily vigor, she fell asleep in the Lord. She made you the heir of her poverty, or rather she made the poor her heirs through you. When she closed her eyes, it was in your arms. When she breathed her last, your lips received it. You shed tears, but she smiled, conscious of having led a good life and hoping for her reward hereafter.

In one short night I have dictated this letter in honor of you, revered Marcella, and of you, my daughter Principia; not to show off my own eloquence, but to express my heartfelt gratitude to you both; my one desire has been to please both God and my readers.

NOTES

1. Hebrew:seventy-third.
2. Ps 72 (73):20.
3. 'Our Latin' refers to the latin translation of the Bible, generally known as the Vetus Italica, which preceded the Vulgate.
4. Cf. 2 Cor 4:7.
5. Rm 3:2.
6. Vettius Agarius Praetextatus (*c.* 310–384), one of the most distinguished men of his day, had been Prefect of Rome and was consul-elect when he died. In Jerome's opinion, he was assuredly in hell, because he had been a zealous pagan. He had ironically informed Jerome's friend, Pope Damasus, that if he could be assured of the papacy, he would at once embrace Christianity (*Against John of Jerusalem*, 28; PL 23:355–396; for translation, see Fremantle, p. 428). There is some doubt about the text here; I have followed Hilberg's reading, *detrahentes in suis saeculis*.
7. The latin words *in tataro* used here recall the greek word ταρταρίξειν used by the author of 2 Peter of God casting the angels down to hell (2:4).
8. Mt 6:2.
9. Lk 16:23.
10. Paulina, the chief priestess of Ceres.
11. In roman mythology the Milky Way was the abode of gods and heroes.
12. Ws 5:4.
13. Ps 47 (48):8.
14. Cf. Letter 22, p. 185.
15. Mt 10:10.
16. 2 Cor 4:13.
17. Letter 23, above.
18. Rm 11:6.
19. Jr 1:5.
20. Lk 1:41.

21. Eph 1:4.
22. Probably Marcella before she was married.
23. 2 Th 3:20.
24. Mt 6:17.
25. Mt 19:26.
26. Cf. Juvenal, *Sat.* 10, 356, for the famous tag, *Mens sana in corpore sano.*
27. This is a *topos*, probably derived from Hegesippus, the second-century church historian, whose works are no longer extant. He is quoted in Eusebius, *Historia Ecclesiastica* 2.23.6 (translated by Rufinus), who attributes the same quality to Saint James the Less. Gregory the Great reports that his aunt Tarsilla was said to have the same characteristics; see *Dialogues* 4.17.3.
28. The Latin word here, *sacerdos*, may be used for either priest or bishop. Since Jerome's strictures about the behavior and appearance of the clergy are directed towards priests, the former seems to be the more appropriate rendering.
29. This roman lady, Principia, like her friend Marcella, was a keen student of the Bible. In Letter Sixty five (not included in this selection and Fremantle provides only a summary, p. 134) Jerome expounds Ps 64 (65) to her at some length, after a brief introduction defending his practice of writing for women.
30. See Letter 23.
31. Lk 2:36–7.
32. I.e., before the sack of Rome by Alaric in 410.
33. Ps 118 (119):1.
34. Mt 5:25.
35. I.e., the Indian Ocean. The latin word used here for 'pearl' is *granum*, which literally means a globule.
36. The text is difficult here: I have adopted Hilberg's reading (vol. 3, p. 147), *flagrare mire*, as being more vivid than *fragrare* (=scent themselves), the reading adopted by Fremantle.
37. Eph 5:22.
38. Cf Letter 79.9ff (not included in this selection; for translation, see Fremantle, pp. 163–168) for Jerome's cautions on the behavior of widows.
39. Ps 118 (119):11.
40. Ps 1.2.
41. 1 Cor 10:31.
42. Ps 118 (119):104.
43. Ac 1:1.
44. 1 Tm 5:23.
45. This sentence has given rise to controversy. For a full discussion of the situation described in this chapter, see Historical Introduction, pp. 92ff.
46. Athanasius (c. 296–373) was succeeded as bishop of Alexandria by Peter.

47. Saint Antony the Great of Egypt (c. 251–356), whose life was written by Athanasius.

48. Saint Pachomius (c. 292–346).

49. Otherwise unknown.

50. A fragment of the *Medea* (now lost) by the roman poet Ennius (b. 239); it does not seem particularly apt here.

51. Lk 8:3.

52. Mt 27:55; Jn 19:25.

53. I can find no grounds for the derivation of the name Magdala as meaning a tower.

54. There appears to be no grounds for the often-made assertion that John was of noble birth.

55. Tertullian goes so far as to call him John 'Christ's eunuch' (*De monogamia* 17).

56. Marcella was probably acquainted with the saying, derived from the *Phaedo* of Plato, through the writings of Cicero (*Tusculanae Disputationes* 1.30.74).

57. 1 Cor 15:31.

58. Lk 14:27; cf. 9:23.

59. Ps 43 (44):22; Rm 8:36.

60. Si 7:36.

61. Persius, *Satiricon*. 5, 133.

62. Rm 12:1.

63. Jerome had been attending the Council of Constantinople, the Second Ecumenical Council of the church, in 381. At this Council the supremacy of the Nicene faith was reaffirmed, and Constantinople, as the New Rome, was exalted to the position of the second See of Christendom. In the summer of 382, when the Council was over, Jerome went to Rome with the two bishops, Paulinus of Antioch and Epiphanius of Salamis (now Famagusta) in Cyprus, on urgent business regarding certain dissensions between the churches (see also Letter 108.6, p. 129). Ambrose, bishop of Milan, had become exasperated by the behavior of the bishops in the East and in particular, by the recognition as their spokesman of the schismatic bishop of Antioch, Meletius, thus brushing aside the claims of Paulinus, who held orthodox opinions. Ambrose succeeded in persuading the Emperor Gratian to summon a General Council, but this was a failure, as only three bishops from the East attended. However, it recognized the status of Paulinus as bishop of Antioch and excommunicated Flavian, who had succeeded to the schismatic bishopric on the death of Meletius. In the meantime, Jerome had become confidential adviser to Pope Damasus and therefore did not return with his friends to the East.

64. 2 Tm 4:2.

65. 1 Tm 2:12.

66. Literally, 'the thickness of a nail'.

67. The phrase used by Jerome literally means 'in suburban territory', but this would give a misleading impression to the modern English-speaking reader.

68. The Origenist disputes erupted in 393 and were to lead to a breach between Jerome and his friend Rufinus. See S. L. Greenslade, pp. 94–5 above, and for further details, J. N. D. Kelly, *Jerome: His Life, Writings and Controversies* (London, 1975), esp. pp. 195–210, 227–258.

69. The same proverb is found in Letter 7.5 (not included in this collection). For a translation, see Fremantle, p. 10.

70. The translation of *Peri Hermineas* was the work of Rufinus, now Jerome's enemy because he held Origenist views.

71. This is a play upon the name of Macarius (=blessed or fortunate), a roman Christian who, according to Rufinus himself, insistently entreated him to enlighten him about Origen's opinions on the problems of divine providence, a subject upon which he subsequently wrote a treatise. See Rufinus, *Apologia contra Hieronymum* 1.11.

72. Rm 1:8.

73. Pope Siricius, who succeeded Damasus in 384 and died in 399. He had complete confidence in Rufinus and disregarded the anti-Origenist coterie in Rome.

74. Lk 16:8.

75. Rufinus obtained such letters from Pope Siricius, when he left Rome for Aquileia in 373. See his *Apologia c. Hier.* 3.31.

76. Anastasius I (399–402) was more kindly disposed to the ascetic movement and was at once set upon by Marcella to have the writings of Origen proscribed. Aided and abetted by Principia, the recipient of this letter, she produced evidence of Christians who had been corrupted by them. Anastasius had little grasp of the theological implications of the dispute, and while he was trying to sort out his ideas, the monk Theodore, who had been having sessions with Jerome on the subject, arrived in Rome in 400 with the news of the condemnation of Origen's writings in Egypt. The Synod, which Anastasius subsequently convoked, anathematized Origen's alleged blasphemies—a moment of triumph for Jerome. This was the reason for his proclaiming here that Anastasius was too good for this wicked world.

77. Jerome means the capture of Rome by Alaric in 410.

78. Jr 14:11–12.

79. The scorpion is, of course, Rufinus, whom Jerome accused of suppressing the more controversial statements of Origen, in order to make the more subtle heresies acceptable.

80. I.e., the Origenist movement.

81. Mt 24:12.

82. Cf. Gal 12:13.

83. 'Barnabas' may be taken to stand either for Bishop John of Jerusalem, who held Origenist views and was therefore the friend of Rufinus and the enemy of Jerome, or for St John Chrysostom. The former seems the more likely interpretation.

84. Ps 103 (104):9.

85. Ps 145 (146):4.

86. Lk 12:20.

87. The Canaanite name for Jerusalem. It occurs in the Bible only in

the form of Jebusite(s), the inhabitants of Jerusalem (Gn 10:16, 2 Sm 24:16, Jdg 1:21).

88. In 408, the Goths, led by Alaric, undertook to depart on receipt of 5,000 pounds of gold, 30,000 of silver, 4,000 silk tunics, 3,000 scarlet-dyed skins and 3,000 pounds of pepper. As the treasury was empty and the contributions of the citizens fell short of the required amount of gold and silver, ornaments were stripped from the images of the gods, and gold and silver statues were melted down.

89. Alaric captured and sacked Rome in 410. Because Rome was dependent on imports of grain from North Africa, which were stored at Portus, Alaric was able to blockade the city. It is unlikely that the citizens were actually reduced to the dire situation described by Jerome, but another writer, Zosimus the historian, reported that someone in the circus, 'Put a price on human flesh'.

90. Is 5:1.

91. Ps 78 (79):1.

92. Ps 78 (79):2–3.

93. Vergil, *Aeneid* 2.361.

94. Jb 1.21.

PAULA THE ELDER:
AN ASCETIC PILGRIM TO
ROME AND BETHLEHEM

PAULA came of a patrician family in Rome, and was born in ad 347, the daughter of Rogatus and Blesilla. She was a member of the group of christian ladies who frequented the house of Marcella, and when her husband, Toxotius, died, she gave herself to the life of religion. This was in 379 or 380, before Jerome was in Rome. She had borne four daughters, Blesilla, Paulina, Eustochium, and Rufina, and one son, Toxotius, still a baby. Jerome affords us an unusual glimpse of the unofficial side of ecclesiastical assemblies when he relates how she 'put up' Epiphanius, bishop of Salamis, during the Council of Rome in 382. Jerome, who also went to Rome for the council, did not meet her at once, for he says that he was well known in the city before he became acquainted with her family (Letter 453). But they soon became such intimate friends that he had eventually to defend himself from the slander and make a calumniator retract his words. Paula was an enthusiastic student of the Bible, eager for a mystical interpretation of it, while her friend Marcella had a taste for textual and historical studies. During these years in Rome, Jerome addressed to her Letter 30, on the alphabetical psalms and the mystical significance of the hebrew alphabet; Letter 33, which contains an important catalogue of the writings of Origen; and Letter 39, on the death of her eldest daughter, Blesilla. There is also a note thanking the girl Eustochium for her Saint Peter's day presents to Jerome. Blesilla had married, only to lose her husband

123

after seven months of marriage. Very soon afterwards she was 'converted' to the ascetic life, but died three months later. Jerome, though genuinely sympathetic, found it necessary to chide Paula for giving way to excessive grief. But was there something of a bad conscience in this excess? For it was rumored that Blesilla had died of fasting, and her death seems to have been one of the incidents which helped to drive Jerome out of the capital. 'When shall we drive these detestable monks out of Rome? Why not throw them into the Tiber?'

Jerome left the city in 385, and Paula soon followed him, taking Eustochium with her. Their journey to Antioch, with a visit to Epiphanius on the way, and their pilgrimages in the Holy Land and in Egypt, are told at some length in the present letter. By autumn 386 they had settled in Bethlehem, where Paula spent the rest of her life as head of the monastery for women which she founded. Again, many of the details of her life in it are related in this letter. Bible studies still held her attention, and besides what the letter has to say, there is something to be gleaned from the numerous prefaces to the translations and commentaries on the books of the Bible. It was at Paula's request that Jerome revised his first psalter, producing the so-called Gallican Psalter, and that he translated Origen's *Homilies on Saint Luke's Gospel*. Paula and Eustochium received the dedication of a good many of his biblical works, and it was to them that the celebrated 'Helmeted' Preface to the Books of Kings was addressed, with its brief introduction to the Hebrew Bible and its rejection of the Apocrypha from the Canon. Paula supervised the Bethlehem convent until her death on 26 January 404, at the age of fifty-six. She was succeeded by her daughter, Eustochium, to whom Jerome dedicated several of his later works. Eustochium was succeeded by the younger Paula, daughter of the Toxotius whom his mother, some twenty years before her death, had left 'stretching forth his hand in entreaty' on the shore at Ostia.

Jerome's description of the pilgrimage is of special interest, not so much philologically and topographically as psychologically and spiritually. It has not been found practicable to annotate it adequately in this volume, or even to give the hundred and more biblical references which these sections alone require. They can all be found in Hilberg's edition in the Vienna *Corpus*, or through the full-scale concordances and dictionaries of the Bible. To a large extent Jerome's comments on the places are taken from his own translation of a work of Eusebius of Caesarea on the place-names of Palestine, the references to which are also given by Hilberg. The derivations are frequently fanciful, but the topographical information is of some value, at least for the pilgrim routes. With Paula's pilgrimage one should compare that of Egeria, dating from much the same time. Her travel journey has come down in a mutilated form, beginning at her visit to Sinai and ending with a detailed account of the rites of Holy Week at Jerusalem. Translations of both these pilgrimages and of other early ones will be found in the first volume of the Palestine Pilgrims Text Society.

There is another part of this letter which calls for special notice. It is the digression against heresy, a digression curious in itself and in the circumstances in very poor taste. The heresy is, of course, Origenism, and even in a letter of consolation Jerome cannot restrain himself from snatching at an opportunity to attack it and to exhibit his own cleverness. To affirm Paula's orthodoxy the detail is quite unnecessary; as so often, he lets his impetuous pen run away with him. We are not told who the 'cunning knave' was who approached Paula with his awkward questions, some of which might have been put by any Origenist. There are points of detail, however, which appear also in Jerome's tract against John of Jerusalem, written in ad 396. It is perhaps unlikely that the bishop is being directly attacked here; that would have been in execrable taste, for he attended Paula's funeral, as Jerome himself records. More probably it was one of his circle. Jerome's principal onslaught upon the Originists, the three books against Rufinus, had also been written before the death of Paula. In the present passage he is able to appeal to the letter of Scripture and to everyday orthodox beliefs, but, though he makes some sound points, he reveals no sympathy whatsoever for those who struggle with profound and difficult problems, nor does he say positively what he thought Paul meant by a spiritual body.

S. L. G.

To Eustochium (*Letter 108*)

IF ALL THE MEMBERS of my body were to be converted into tongues, and if each of my limbs were to be gifted with a human voice, I could still do no justice to the virtues of the holy and venerable Paula. Noble in family, she was nobler still in holiness; rich formerly in this world's goods, she is now more distinguished by the poverty that she has embraced for Christ. Of the stock of the Gracchi and descended from the Scipios, the heir and representative of that Paulus whose name she bore, the true and legitimate daughter of that Maecia Papiria who was mother to Africanus, she yet preferred Bethlehem to Rome, and left her palace glittering with gold to dwell in a mud cabin. We do not grieve that we have lost this perfect woman; rather we thank God that we have had her, nay that we have her still. For all live unto God, and they who are given back to the Lord are still to be reckoned members of the family. We have lost her, it is true, but the heavenly mansions have gained her; for as long as she was in the body she was absent from the Lord, and would constantly complain with tears: *Woe is me that my sojourning is prolonged; I have dwelt with the inhabitants of Kedar; my soul has been this long time a sojourner.*[1] It was no wonder that she sobbed out that she was in darkness (for this is the meaning of the word Kedar) seeing that *the world lies in the evil one*[2] and that, *as its darkness is, so is its light;*[3] and that *the light shines in the darkness and the darkness apprehended it not.*[4] Therefore she would frequently exclaim: 'I am a stranger with thee and a sojourner as all my fathers were',[5] and again, I desire *to depart and to be with Christ.*[6] As often too as she was troubled with bodily weakness (brought on by incredible abstinence and by redoubled fastings), she would be heard to say: *I keep under my body and bring it into subjection; lest, when I have preached to others, I myself should be found a castaway,*[7] and: *It is good neither to eat flesh nor to drink wine,*[8] and: *I humbled my soul with fasting,*[9] and: *You have turned my bed in my sickness,*[10] and *I am turned in my anguish, while the thorn is fastened upon me.*[11] And when the pain which she bore with such wonderful patience darted

through her, as if she saw the heavens opened she would say:
*Oh that I had wings like a dove! for then would I fly away and be
at rest*.[12]

I call Jesus and his holy angels, yes and the particular angel
who was the guardian and the companion of this admirable
woman, to bear witness that these are no words of adulation
and flattery but sworn testimony, every one of them, borne to
her character. They are, indeed, inadequate to the virtues of one
whose praises are sung by the whole world, who is admired by
bishops, regretted by bands of virgins, and wept for by crowds
of monks and poor. Would you know all her virtues, reader, in
short? She has left those dependent on her poor, but not so poor
as she was herself. In dealing thus with her relatives and the men
and women of her small household—her brothers and sisters
rather than her servants—she has done nothing strange; for she
has left her daughter Eustochium—a virgin consecrated to Christ,
for whose comfort this sketch is made—far from her noble family
and rich only in faith and grace.

Let me then begin my narrative. Others may go back a long way
even to Paula's cradle and, if I may say so, to her rattle, and may
speak of her mother Blesilla and her father Rogatus. Of these the
former was a descendant of the Scipios and the Gracchi, whilst
the latter came of a line wealthy and distinguished throughout
Greece down to the present day. He is said there to have in his
veins the blood of Agamemnon who destroyed Troy after a ten
years' siege. But I shall praise only what belongs to herself, what
wells forth from the pure spring of her holy mind. When in the
Gospel the apostles ask their Lord and Saviour what he will give
to those who have left all for his sake, he tells them that they shall
receive an hundredfold now in this time and in the world to come
eternal life.[13]

From which we see that is not the possession of riches that is
praiseworthy but the rejection of them for Christ's sake; that, instead of glorying in our privileges, we should make them of small
account as compared with faith in the Lord. Truly the Saviour has
now in this present time made good his promise to his servants
and handmaidens. For one who despised the glory of a single

city is today famous throughout the world; and one who while she lived at Rome was known by no one outside it, has by hiding herself at Bethlehem become the admiration of all lands roman and barbarian. For what race of men is there which does not send pilgrims to the holy places? And who could find there a greater marvel than Paula? As among many jewels the most precious shines most brightly, and as the sun with its beams obscures and puts out the paler fires of the stars, so by her lowliness she surpassed all others in virtue and influence and, while she was least among all, was greater than all. The more she cast herself down, the more she was lifted up by Christ. She was hidden and yet she was not hidden. By shunning glory she earned glory; for glory follows virtue as its shadow; and deserting those who seek it, it seeks those who despise it.[14] But I must not neglect to proceed with my narrative or dwell too long on a single point, forgetful of the rules of writing.

Being then of such parentage, Paula married Toxotius in whose veins ran the noble blood of Aeneas and the Julii. Accordingly his daughter, Christ's virgin Eustochium, is called Julia, as he Julius, 'A name from great Iulus handed down.'[15]

I speak of these things not as of importance to those who have them, but as worthy of remark in those who despise them. Men of the world look up to persons who are rich in such privileges. We, on the other hand, praise those who for the Saviour's sake despise them; and strangely depreciating all who keep them, we eulogize those who are unwilling to do so. Thus nobly born, Paula through her fruitfulness and her chastity alike won approval from all, from her husband first, then from her relatives, and lastly from the whole city. She bore five children: Blesilla, for whose death I consoled her while at Rome;[16] Paulina, who has left the reverend and admirable Pammachius to inherit both her vows and property, to whom also I addressed a little book on her death,[17] Eustochium, who is now in the holy places, a precious necklace of virginity and of the Church;[18] Rufina, whose untimely end overcame the affectionate heart of her mother; and Toxotius, after whom she had no more children. You can thus see that it was not her wish to continue to fulfill a wife's duty, but that she only complied with her husband's longing to have male offspring.

When he died, her grief was so great that she nearly died herself; yet so completely did she then give herself to the service of the Lord, that it might have seemed that she had desired his death. In what terms shall I speak of her distinguished and noble and formerly wealthy house, almost all the riches of which she spent on the poor? How can I describe the great consideration she showed to all and her far-reaching kindness even to those whom she had never seen? What poor man, as he lay dying, was not wrapped in blankets given by her? What bedridden person was not supported with money from her purse? She would seek out such with the greatest diligence throughout the city, and would think it her loss were any hungry or sick person to be supported by another's food. She robbed her children; and, when her relatives remonstrated with her for doing so, she declared that she was leaving to them a better inheritance in the mercy of Christ.

Nor was she long able to endure the visits and crowded receptions which her high position in the world and her exalted family entailed upon her. She received the homage paid to her sadly, and made all the speed she could to shun and to escape those who wished to pay her compliments. It so happened that at that time the bishops of the East and West had been summoned to Rome by letter from the emperors to deal with certain dissensions between the churches, and in this way she saw two most admirable men and christian prelates, Paulinus, bishop of Antioch, and Epiphanius, bishop of Salamis (or, as it is now called, Constantia) in Cyprus.[19] Epiphanius, indeed, she received as her guest; and, although Paulinus was staying in another person's house, in the warmth of her heart she treated him as if he too were lodged with her. Inflamed by their virtues, she thought every moment of forsaking her country. Disregarding her home, her children, her servants, her property, and in a word everything connected with the world, she was eager—alone and unaccompanied (if ever it could be said that she was so)—to go to the desert made famous by its Pauls and by its Antony.[20] And at last when the winter was over and the sea was open, and when the bishops were returning to their churches, she also sailed with them in her prayers and desires. Not to prolong the story, she went down to the harbor accompanied by her brother, her kinsfolk and, above all, her own children [eager by their demonstrations of affection to overcome their loving mother[21]] At last the sails were set and the strokes of the oars carried the vessel into the deep. On the shore the little Toxotius stretched forth his hands in entreaty, while Rufina, now grown up,[22] with silent sobs besought her mother to wait till she should be married. But still Paula's eyes were dry as she turned them heavenwards; and she overcame her love for her children by her love for God. She knew herself no more as a mother, that she might prove herself a handmaid of Christ. Yet her heart was rent within her, and she wrestled with her grief, as though she were being torn away from part of herself. The greatness of the affection she had to overcome made everyone admire her victory the more. Among the cruel hardships which attend prisoners of war in the hands of their enemies, there is none severer than the separation of parents from their children. Though it is against the laws of nature, she endured this trial with unabated faith; nay more she sought it with a joyful heart; and spurning her love for her children by her greater love for God, she concentrated herself quietly on Eustochium alone, the partner alike of her vows and of her voyage. Meantime the vessel ploughed onwards and all her fellow-passengers looked back to the shore. But she turned her eyes that she might not see what she could not behold without agony. No mother, it must be confessed, ever loved her children so dearly. Before setting out she gave them all that she had, disinheriting herself upon earth that she might find an inheritance in heaven.

The vessel touched at the island of Pontia, ennobled long since as the place of exile of the illustrious lady Flavia Domitilla,[23] who under the Emperor Domitian was banished because she confessed herself a Christian. And Paula, when she saw the cells in which this lady passed the years of her martyrdom, longed to take wing and see Jerusalem and the holy places. The strongest winds seemed weak and the greatest speed slow. After passing between

Scylla and Charybdis she committed herself to the Adriatic sea and had a calm passage to Methone. Stopping here for a short time to recruit her wearied frame,

> She stretched her dripping limbs upon the shore;
> Then sailed past Malea and Cytera's isle,
> The scattered Cyclades, and all the lands
> That narrow in the seas on every side.[24]

Then leaving Rhodes and Lycia behind her, she at last came in sight of Cyprus, where falling at the feet of the holy and venerable Epiphanius, she was by him detained ten days; though this was not, as he supposed, to restore her strength but, as the facts proved, that she might do God's work.[25] For she visited all the monasteries in the island, and left, so far as her means allowed, substantial relief for the brothers whom love of the holy man had brought thither from all parts of the world. Then crossing the narrow sea she landed at Seleucia, and going up thence to Antioch allowed herself to be detained for a little time by the affection of the reverend confessor Paulinus. Then, such as the ardor of her faith that she, a noble lady who had always previously been carried by eunuchs, went her way—and that in midwinter—riding on an ass.

I say nothing of her journey through Coele-Syria and Phoenicia (for it is not my purpose to give you a complete itinerary of her wanderings). I shall name only such places as are mentioned in the sacred books. After leaving the roman colony of Berytus and the ancient city of Zidon she entered Elijah's little tower on the shore at Zarephath and therein adored her Lord and Saviour. Next passing over the sands of Tyre, on which Paul had once knelt,[26] she came to Jaccho or, as it is now called, Ptolemais,[27] rode over the plains of Megiddo which had once witnessed the slaying of Josiah,[28] and entered the land of the Philistines. Here she wondered at the ruins of Dor, once a very powerful city; and Strato's Tower, which though at one time insignificant was rebuilt by Herod, King of Judaea, and named Caesarea in honor of Caesar Augustus.[29] Here she saw the house of Cornelius[30] now turned into a christian church, and the humble abode of Philip, and the chamber of his daughters, the four virgins 'which did prophesy'.[31] She arrived next at Antipatris, a small town half in ruins, named by Herod after his father Antipater, and at Lydda, now become Diospolis, a place made famous by the raising again of Dorcas[32] and the restoration to health of Aeneas.[33] Not far from this are Arimathaea, the village of Joseph who buried the Lord,[34] and Nob, once a city of priests but now the tomb in which their slain bodies rest.[35] Joppa too is hard by, the port of Jonah's flight;[36] which also—if I may introduce a poetic fable—saw Andromeda bound to the rock. Again resuming her journey, she came to Nicopolis, once called Emmaus, where the Lord became known in the breaking of bread;[37] an action by which he dedicated the house of Cleopas as a church. Starting thence she made her way up lower and higher Bethhoron, cities founded by Solomon but subsequently destroyed by several devastating wars;[38] seeing on her right Ajalon and Gibeon, where Joshua, the son of Nun, when fighting against the five kings, gave commandments to the sun and moon,[39] where also he condemned the Gibeonites (who by a crafty stratagem had obtained a treaty) to be hewers of wood and drawers of water.[40] At Gibeah also, now a complete ruin, she stopped for a little while remembering its sin, and the cutting of the concubine into pieces and how twice three hundred men of the tribe of Benjamin were saved,[41] that in after days Paul might be called a Benjamite.

To make a long story short, leaving on her left the mausoleum of Helena, Queen of Adiabene,[42] who in time of famine had sent corn to the Jewish people, she entered Jerusalem, Jebus, or Salem, that city of three names which, after it had sunk to ashes and decay, was by Aelius Hadrianus restored as Aelia. And although the proconsul of Palestine, who was an intimate friend of her house, sent forward his apparitors and gave orders to have his official residence placed at her disposal, she chose a humble cell in preference to it.

Moreover, in visiting the holy places, so great was the passion and the enthusiasm she exhibited for each, that she could never have been torn away from one had she not been eager to visit the rest. Before the Cross she threw herself down in adoration as though she beheld the Lord hanging upon it; and when she entered the tomb which was the scene of the Resurrection, she kissed the stone which the angel had rolled away from the door of the sepulchre.[43] Indeed so ardent was her faith that she even licked with her mouth the very spot on which the Lord's body had lain, like one athirst for the river which he had longed for.[44] What tears she shed there, what groans she uttered, and what grief she poured forth, all Jerusalem knows; the Lord also, to whom she prayed, knows it well. Going out thence she made the ascent of Zion, a name which signifies either 'citadel' or 'watch-tower'. This formed the city which David formerly stormed and afterwards rebuilt.[45] Of its storming it is written: *Woe to you, Ariel*—that is, God's lion, (and indeed in those days it was extremely strong)— *the city which David stormed.*[46] And of its building it is said: *His foundation is in the holy mountains: the Lord loves the gates of Zion more than all the dwellings of Jacob.*[47] He does not mean the gates which we see today in dust and ashes; the gates he means are those against which hell prevails not, and through which the multitude of those who believe enter in to Christ. There was shown to her, upholding the portico of a church, the blood-stained column to which our Lord is said to have been bound when he suffered his scourging.[48] There was shown to her also the spot where the Holy Spirit came down upon one hundred and twenty souls, thus fulfilling the prophecy of Joel.[49]

Then, after distributing money to the poor and her fellow-servants so far as her small means allowed, she proceeded to Bethlehem stopping on the right side of the road to visit Rachel's tomb. (Here it was that she gave birth to her son, destined to be not what his dying mother called him, Benoni, that is the 'Son of my pangs' but, as his Father in the spirit prophetically named him, Benjamin, that is 'the Son of the right hand').[50] After this she entered into the cave where the Saviour was born. Here, when she looked upon the inn made sacred by the virgin and the stall where *the ox knew his owner and the ass his master's crib*,[51] that the words of the same prophet might be fulfilled: *Blessed is he who sowes upon the waters where the ox and the ass trample*[52] —when she looked on these things, I say, she protested in my hearing that she could behold with the eyes of faith the infant Lord wrapped in swaddling clothes and crying in the manger,[53] the wise men worshipping God, the star shining overhead, thè virgin mother, the attentive foster-father, the shepherds coming by night to see *the word that was come to pass*[54] and thus even then to consecrate those opening phrases of the evangelist John: *In the beginning was the word* and *the word was made flesh.*[55] She declared that she could see the slaughtered innocents, the raging Herod, Joseph and Mary fleeing into Egypt; and with a mixture of tears and joy she cried: 'Hail Bethlehem, house of bread, wherein was born that Bread that came down from heaven. Hail Ephratah, land of fruitfulness and fertility, whose fruit is God himself. Concerning thee has Michah prophesied of old, *Thou, Bethlehem, house of Ephratah, are you not the least among the thousands of Judah? Out of thee shall come forth to me he who is to be ruler in Israel; whose goings forth are from the beginning, from days everlasting. Therefore wilt thou give them up, until the time of her who is in travail. She shall bring forth, and the remnant of his brethren shall turn unto the children of Israel.*[56] For in you was born the prince begotten before Lucifer, whose birth from the Father is before all time; and the cradle of David's race continued in you, until the virgin brought forth her son and the remnant of the people that believed in Christ turned unto the children of Israel and preached freely to them: *It was necessary that the word of God should first have been spoken to you; but seeing you put it from you and judged yourselves unworthy of everlasting life, we turn to the Gentiles.*[57] For the Lord had said: *I am not come but unto the lost sheep of the house of Israel.*[58] At that time also the words of Jacob were fulfilled concerning him: *A prince shall not fail from Judah nor a ruler from his thighs, until he come for whom it is laid up, and he shall be the expectation of the nations.*[59] Well did David swear, well did he make a vow saying: *Surely I will not come into the tabernacle of my house nor climb up into my bed: I will not give sleep to my eyes, or slumber to my eyelids, or rest to the temples of my head, until I find out a place for the Lord, an habitation for the God of Jacob.*[60] And immediately he explained the object of his desire, seeing with prophetic eyes that he would come whom we now believe to have come. *Lo we heard of him at Ephratah: we found him in the fields of the wood.*[61] The Hebrew word *zoth*, as I have learned from your lessons,[62] means not Grk alut'hn (her), that is Mary the Lord's mother, but αὐτόν, himself. Therefore he says boldly: *We will go into his tabernacle: we will adore in the place where his feet stood.*[63] I too, miserable sinner though I am, have been accounted worthy to kiss the manger in which the Lord cried as a babe, and to pray in the cave in which the travailing virgin gave birth to the infant Lord. *This is my rest*[64] for it is my Lord's native place; *here will I dwell*[65] for this spot has my Saviour chosen. *I have prepared a lamp for my Christ.*[66] *My soul shall live unto him and my seed shall serve him.*[67]

After this Paula went a short distance down the hill to the tower of Edar, that is *of the flock*,[68] near which Jacob fed his flocks, and where the shepherds keeping watch by night were privileged to hear the words: *Glory to God in the highest and on earth peace to men of goodwill.*[69] While they were keeping their sheep they found the lamb of God; whose bright and clean fleece was made wet with the dew of heaven when it was dry upon all the earth beside, and whose blood, when sprinkled on the doorposts, drove off the destroyer of Egypt and took away the sins of the world.

Then immediately quickening her pace she began to move along the old road which leads to Gaza, that is to the 'power' or 'wealth' of God, silently meditating on that type of the Gentiles, the Ethiopian eunuch, who did change his skin,[70] and whilst he read the Old Testament, found the fountain of the Gospel.[71] Next turning to the right she passed from Bethzur to Eshcol which means 'a cluster of grapes'.[72] It was hence that the spies brought back that marvelous cluster which was the proof of the fertility of the land and a type of him who says of himself: *I have trodden the wine press alone; and of the people there was none with me.*[73] Shortly afterwards she entered the humble home of Sarah and beheld the cradle of Isaac and the traces of Abraham's oak,[74] under which he saw Christ's day and was glad.[75] And rising up from thence, she went up to Hebron, that is Kirjath-Arba, or 'the City of the Four Men'. These are Abraham, Isaac, Jacob, and the great Adam whom the Hebrews suppose (from the book of

Joshua)[76] to be buried there.[77] But many are of opinion that Caleb is the fourth, and a monument at one side is pointed out as his. After seeing these places she did not care to go on to Kirjath-sepher, that is 'the village of letters', because, despising the letter that killeth, she had found the spirit that giveth life.[78] She admired more the upper springs and the nether springs which Othniel, the son of Kenaz, the son of Jephunneh, received for his south land and his waterless possession, and by the conducting of which he watered the dry fields of the old covenant.[79] For thus did he typify the redemption which the sinner finds for his old sins in the waters of baptism. On the next day, soon after sunrise, she stood upon the brow of Caphar-barucha, that is, 'the town of blessing', the point to which Abraham accompanied the Lord.[80] And here, as she looked down upon the wide solitude and upon the country once belonging to Sodom and Gomorrah, to Admah and Zeboim,[81] she beheld the balsam vines of Engedi[82] and Segor, the 'heifer of three years old' which was formerly called Bela and in Syriac is rendered Zoar, that is 'little'.[83] She called to mind Lot's cave, and with tears in her eyes warned the virgins, her companions, to beware of *wine wherein is excess*;[84] for it was to this that the Moabites and Ammonites owe their origin.

I linger long in the land of the midday sun, for it was there and then that the spouse found her bridegroom at rest and Joseph drank wine with his brothers once more.[85] I will return to Jerusalem and, passing by Tekoa and Amos,[86] I will look upon the glistening cross of Mount Olivet, from which the Saviour made his ascension to the Father. Here year by year a red heifer was burned as a holocaust to the Lord, and its ashes were used to purify the children of Israel.[87] Here also, according to Ezekiel, the Cherubim, after leaving the temple, founded the church of the Lord.[88]

After this she visited the tomb of Lazarus and beheld the home of Mary and Martha, as well as Bethphage, 'the town of the priestly jaws'. Here it was that a restive foal, typical of the Gentiles, received the bridle of the Lord, and, covered with the garments of the apostles, offered its easy back for him to sit on.[89] From this she went straight on down the hill to Jericho, thinking of the wounded man in the Gospel, of the savagery of the priests and levites who passed him by, and of the kindness of the Samaritan,[90] that is, the guardian, who placed the half-dead man upon his own beast and brought him down to the inn of the Church.[91] She noticed the place called Adomim or 'the Place of Blood', so-called because much blood was shed there in the frequent incursions of marauders. She beheld also the sycamore tree of Zacchaeus,[92] by which is signified the good works of repentance whereby he trod underfoot his former sins of bloodshed and rapine, and from which he saw the Most High as from a pinnacle of virtue. She was shown too the spot by the wayside where the blind men sat who, receiving their sight from the Lord, became types of the two peoples who should believe in him. Then entering Jericho she saw the city which Hiel founded in Abiram his firstborn, and of which he set up the gates in his youngest son Segub.[93] She looked upon the camp of Gilgal and the mound of the foreskins suggestive of the mystery of the second circumcision;[94] and the twelve stones brought thither out of the bed of Jordan,[95] which established the foundations of the twelve apostles.[96] She saw also that fountain of the Law once most bitter and barren, which the true Elisha seasoned with his wisdom, changing it into a well sweet and fertilizing.[97] Scarcely had the night passed away, when, in burning heat, she hastened to the Jordan, stood by the brink of the river, and as the sun rose recalled to mind the rising of the sun of righteousness; how the priests' feet stood dry in the middle of the river-bed; how afterwards at the command of Elijah and Elisha the waters were divided hither and thither and made way for them to pass;[98] and again how the Lord had cleansed by his baptism waters which the deluge had polluted and the destruction of humankind had defiled.

It would be tedious were I to tell of the valley of Achor,[99] that is, of 'trouble and crowds', where theft and covetousness were condemned; and of Bethel, 'the house of God', where Jacob poor and destitute slept upon the bare ground.[100] Here it was that, having set beneath his head a stone, which in Zechariah is described as having seven eyes[101] and in Isaiah is spoken of as a cornerstone,[102] he beheld a ladder reaching up to heaven;[103]

yes, and the Lord standing high above it, holding out his hand to such as were ascending and hurling from on high such as were careless. Also when she was in Mount Ephraim she made pilgrimages to the tombs of Joshua, the son of Nun, and of Eleazar, the son of Aaron the priest, exactly opposite the one to the other: that of Joshua being built at Timnath-serah *on the north side of the hill of Gaash,*[104] and that of Eleazar *in Gabaath that pertained to Phinehas his son.*[105] She was somewhat surprised to find that he who had had the distribution of the land in his own hands had selected for himself portions uneven and rocky. What shall I say about Shiloh, where a ruined altar is still shown today, and where the tribe of Benjamin anticipated Romulus in the rape of the Sabine women?[106] Passing by Shechem (not Sychar as many wrongly read) or as it is now called Neapolis, she entered the church built upon the side of Mount Gerizim around Jacob's well—that well where the Lord was sitting when, hungry and thirsty, he was refreshed by the faith of the woman of Samaria.[107] Forsaking her five husbands, by whom are intended the five books of Moses, and that sixth, not a husband, of whom she boasted, to wit the false teacher Dositheus,[108] she found the true Messiah and the true Saviour.

Turning away thence she saw in the tombs of the twelve patriarchs, and Samaria which, in honor of Augustus, Herod renamed Augusta or in Greek Sebaste. There lie the prophets Elisha and Obadiah and he than whom there is not a greater among those that are born of women, John the Baptist.[109] And here she was filled with terror by the marvels she beheld; for she saw demons screaming under different tortures and men howling like wolves before the tombs of the saints, baying like dogs, roaring like lions, hissing like serpents and bellowing like bulls. They twisted their heads and bent them backwards until they touched the ground; women too were suspended by the feet and their clothes did not fall to their faces.[110] She pitied them all, and shedding tears over them, prayed Christ to have mercy on them. And weak as she was, she climbed the mountain on foot; for in two of its caves Obadiah, in a time of persecution and famine, had fed a hundred prophets with bread and water.[111] Then she passed quickly through Nazareth, the nursery of the Lord; Cana and Capernaum, familiar with the signs wrought by him;[112] the lake of Tiberias, sanctified by his voyages upon it;[113] the wilderness where countless Gentiles were satisfied with a few loaves, while the twelve baskets of the tribes of Israel were filled with the fragments left by them that had eaten.[114] She made the ascent of Mount Tabor, whereon the Lord was transfigured.[115] In the distance she beheld the range of Hermon; and the wide stretching plains of Galilee, where Sisera and all his host had once been overcome by Barak;[116] and the torrent Kishon separating the level ground into two parts. Hard by also the town of Nain was pointed out to her, where the widow's son was raised.[117] Time would fail me sooner than speech were I to recount all the places to which the revered Paula was carried by her incredible faith.

I will now pass on to Egypt, pausing for a while on the way at Socoh, and at Samson's well which he drew out from the great tooth in the jaw.[118] Here I will lave my parched lips and refresh myself before visiting Moresheth; in old days famed for the tomb of the prophet Micah,[119] and now for its church. Then skirting the country of the Horites and Gittites, Mareshah, Edom, and Lachish, and traversing the lonely wastes of the desert where the tracks of the traveller are lost in the yielding sand, I will come to the river of Egypt called Sihor, that is 'the muddy river', and go through the five cities of Egypt which speak the language of Canaan, and through the land of Goshen and the plains of Zoan, on which God wrought his marvelous works.[120] And I will visit the city of No, which has since become Alexandria; and Nitria, the town of the Lord, where day by day the filth of multitudes is washed away with the pure niter of virtue. No sooner did she come in sight of it than there came to meet her the reverend and estimable bishop, the confessor Isidore, accompanied by countless multitudes of monks, many of whom were dignified by priestly or levitical rank. On seeing these she rejoiced to behold the glory of the Lord, but protested that she had no claim to be received with such honor. Need I speak of the Macarii, Arsetes, Serapions, or other pillars of Christ?[121] Was there any cell she did not enter? Or any man at whose feet she did not throw herself? In each of his

saints she believed that she saw Christ himself; and whatever she
bestowed upon them, she rejoiced to feel that she had bestowed
on the Lord. Her enthusiasm was wonderful and her endurance
scarcely credible in a woman. Forgetful of her sex and of her
weakness, she even desired to make her abode, together with the
girls who accompanied her, among these thousands of monks.
And, as they were all willing to welcome her, she might perhaps
have sought and obtained permission to do so, had she not been
drawn away by a still greater passion for the holy places. Coming
by sea from Pelusium to Maiuma on account of the great heat,
she returned so rapidly that you would have thought her a bird.
Not long afterwards, making up her mind to dwell permanently
in holy Bethlehem, she took up her abode for three years[122] in
a miserable hostelry till she could build the requisite cells and
monastic buildings, to say nothing of a guest house for passing
travellers, where they might find the welcome which Mary and
Joseph had missed.[123] At this point I conclude my narrative of the
journeys that she made, accompanied by her daughter and many
other virgins.

I am now free to describe at greater length the virtue which
was her peculiar charm; and in setting this forth I call God to
witness that I am no flatterer. I add nothing. I exaggerate nothing.
On the contrary I tone down much, that I may not appear to
relate incredibilities. My carping critics, for ever biting me as
hard as they can, need not insinuate that I am drawing on my
imagination or decking Paula, like Aesop's crow, with the fine
feathers of other birds. Humility is the first of christian graces, and
hers was so pronounced that one who had never seen her, and
who on account of her celebrity had desired to see her, would
have believed that he saw not her but the lowest of her maids.
When she was surrounded by companies of virgins she was
always the least remarkable in dress, in speech, in gesture, and in
gait. From the time her husband died until she fell asleep herself,
she never sat at meat with a man, even though she might know
him to be holy and standing on the pinnacle of the episcopate.
She never entered a bath except when dangerously ill. Even in the
severest fever she rested not on an ordinary soft bed but on the

hard ground, covered only with a mat of goat's hair—if that can be called rest which made day and night alike a time of almost unbroken prayer. Well did she fulfill the words of the psalter: *Every night I shall wash my bed; I shall water my couch with my tears.*[124] Her tears welled forth as it were from foundations, and she lamented her slightest faults as if they were sins of the deepest dyad. Constantly did I warn her to spare her eyes and to keep them for reading the gospel, but she only said: 'I must disfigure that face which, contrary to God's commandment, I have painted with rouge, white lead, and antimony. I must mortify that body which has been given up to many pleasures. I must make up for my long laughter by constant weeping. I must exchange my soft linen and costly silks for rough goat's hair. I who have pleased my husband and the world, desire now to please Christ.' Were I, among her great and signal virtues, to select her chastity as a subject of praise, my words would seem superfluous; for, even when she was still in the world, she set an example to all the matrons of Rome, and bore herself so admirably that the most slanderous never ventured to couple scandal with her name. No mind could be more considerate than hers, or none kinder towards the lowly. She did not court the powerful; at the same time she did not turn from them with a proud and vainglorious disdain. If she saw a poor man, she supported him: and if she saw a rich one, she urged him to do good. Her liberality alone knew no bounds. Indeed, so anxious was she to turn no applicant away that she borrowed money at interest and often contracted new loans to pay off old ones. I was wrong, I admit; but when I saw her so profuse in giving, I reproved her, alleging the Apostle's words: *I mean not that other men be eased and ye burthened; but by an equality that now at this time your abundance may be a supply for their want, that their abundance also may be a supply for your want.*[125] I quoted from the Gospel the Saviour's words: *He that hath two coats, let him impart one of them to him that hath none,*[126] and I warned her that she might not always have means to do as she would wish. Other arguments I adduced to the same purpose, but with admirable modesty and brevity she overruled them all. 'God is my witness,' she said, 'that what I do I do for his sake. My prayer is that I may die a beggar, not leaving a penny to my daughter and be indebted to strangers for my winding-sheet.' She then concluded with these words: 'I, if I beg, shall find many to give to me; but if this beggar does not obtain help from me who by borrowing can give it to him, and dies, of whom will his soul be required?' I wished to be more careful in managing our concerns, but she, with a faith more glowing than mine, clung to the Saviour with her whole heart, and, poor in spirit, followed the Lord in his poverty, giving back to him what she had received and becoming poor for his sake. She obtained her wish at last and died leaving her daughter overwhelmed with a mass of debt. This she still owes and indeed cannot hope to pay off by her own exertions, but only by the faith and mercy of Christ.

Many ladies like to confer their gifts upon those who will blow their trumpet for them, and while they are extremely profuse to a few, withhold help from the many. From this fault Paula was altogether free. She gave her money to each according as each had need, not ministering to self-indulgence, but relieving want. No poor person went away from her empty-handed. And all this she was enabled to do not by the greatness of her wealth but by her careful management of it. She constantly had on her lips such phrases as these: *Blessed are the merciful, for they shall obtain mercy*:[127] and *As water quenches a fire, so alms quench sins*;[128] and *Make to yourselves friends of the mammon of unrighteousness that they may receive you into everlasting habitations*;[129] and *Give alms, and behold all things are clean*;[130] and Daniel's words to King Nebuchadnezzar in which he admonished him to redeem his sins by almsgiving.[131] She wished to spend her money not on these stones, that shall pass away with the earth and this age, but on those living stones which roll over the earth;[132] of which, in the Apocalypse of John, the city of the great king is built; of which also the scripture tells us that they shall be changed into sapphire and emerald and jasper and other gems.[133]

But these qualities she may well share with not a few others, and the devil knows that it is not in these that the highest virtue consists. For, when Job has lost his substance and when his house has been overthrown and his children destroyed, Satan says to the

Lord: *Skin for skin, all that a man has will he give for his life. But put forth your hand and touch his bone and his flesh, and he will curse you to your face.*[134] We know that many persons, while they have given alms, have yet given nothing which touches their bodily comfort, and while they have held out a helping hand to those in need, are themselves overcome with sensual indulgences. They whitewash the outside, but within they are *full of dead men's bones.*[135] Paula was not one of these. Her self-restraint was so great as to be immoderate; and her fasts and labors were so severe as to weaken her constitution. Except on feast days she would scarcely ever take oil with her food—a fact from which may be judged what she thought of wine, sauce, fish, honey, milk, eggs, and other things agreeable to the palate. Some persons believe that in taking these they are extremely frugal; and, even if they surfeit themselves with them, they still fancy their chastity safe.

Envy always follows in the track of virtue; 'It is not surprising that I declare this of men, when the jealousy of the pharisees succeeded in crucifying our Lord himself. All the saints have had ill-wishers, and even paradise was not free from the serpent, through whose envy death came into the world.[136] So the Lord stirred up against Paula Hadad the Edomite,[137] to buffet her that she might not exalt herself, and warned her frequently by the thorn in her flesh not to be elated by the greatness of her own virtues or to fancy that, compared with the faults of other women, she had attained the summit of perfection.[138] For my part I used to say that it was best to give in to rancor and to retire before madness. So Jacob dealt with his brother Esau;[139] so David met the unrelenting persecution of Saul.[140] I reminded her how the first of these fled into Mesopotamia; and how the second surrendered himself to men of another race, and chose to submit to foreign foes rather than to enmity at home. She, however, replied as follows: 'Your suggestion would be a wise one if the devil did not everywhere fight against God's servants and handmaidens, and did he not always precede the fugitives to their chosen refuges. Moreover, I am deterred from accepting it by my love for the holy places; and I cannot find another Bethlehem anywhere else in the world. Why may I not by my patience conquer this rancor? Why may I not by my humility break down this pride, and when I am smitten on the one cheek offer to the smiter the other?[141] Surely the apostle Paul says *Overcome evil with good*.[142] Did not the apostles glory when they suffered reproach for the Lord's sake? Did not even the Saviour humble himself, taking the form of a servant and being made obedient to the Father unto death, even the death of the cross,[143] that he might save us by his passion? If Job had not fought the battle and won the victory, he would never have received the crown of righteousness, or have heard the Lord say: *Do you think that I have spoken to you for aught else than this, that you might appear righteous?*[144] In the gospel those only are said to be blessed who suffer persecution for righteousness' sake.[145] If conscience is at rest, and we know that it is not from any fault of our own that we are suffering, affliction in this world is a ground for reward'.

When the enemy was more than usually forward and ventured to strive with her in argument, she used to chant the words of the Psalter: *While the sinner stood against me, I was dumb and humbled myself; I kept silence even from good words;*[146] and again, *I, as a deaf man, heard not; and I was as a dumb man that openeth not his mouth;*[147] and *I was as a man who hears not, and in whose mouth are no reproofs*.[148] When she felt herself tempted, she dwelt upon the words in Deuteronomy: *The Lord your God tests you, to know whether you love the Lord your God with all your heart and with all your soul*.[149] In tribulations and afflictions she turned to the splendid language of Isaiah: *You that are weaned from the milk and drawn away from the breasts, look for tribulation upon tribulation, for hope upon hope: here a little, there a little, must these things be by reason of the malice of the lips and by reason of a strange tongue*.[150] This passage of Scripture she explained for her own consolation as meaning that the weaned, that is, those who have come to full age, must endure tribulation upon tribulation, that they may be accounted worthy to receive hope upon hope, *knowing that tribulation works patience, and patience probation, and probation hope: and hope makes not ashamed*[151] and *though our outward man perish, yet the inward man is renewed;*[152] and *our light affliction which is but for a moment works in us an eternal weight of glory; while we look not at the things which are seen but at the things which are not seen: for the things which are seen are temporal but the things which are not seen are eternal.* She used to say that, although to human impatience the time might seem slow in coming, yet that it would not be long but that presently help would come from God who says: *In an acceptable time have I heard you, and in a day of salvation have I helped you.*[153] We ought not, she declared, to dread the deceitful lips and tongues of the wicked, for we rejoice in the aid of the Lord and we ought to listen to his warning [of his prophet: *Fear not the reproach of men, neither be afraid of their revilings; for the moth shall eat them up like a garment, and the worm shall eat them like wool*][154] *In your patience ye shall win your souls:*[155] and *the sufferings of this present time are not worthy to be compared with the glory which shall be revealed in us;*[156] and in another place, that we may be patient in all things that befall us, *he that is patient is of great understanding: but he that is little of spirit exalts folly.*[157]

In her frequent sicknesses and infirmities she used to say: *When I am weak, then am I strong;*[158] *We have this treasure in earthen vessels*[159] until *this corruptible shall have put on incorruption and this mortal shall have put on immortality;*[160] and again: *as the sufferings of Christ abound in us, so our consolation also abounds by Christ;*[161] and then *as you are partakers of the sufferings, so shall you be also of the consolation.*[162] In sorrow she used to sing: *Why are you cast down, O my soul? and why are you disquieted within me? Hope in God, for I shall yet praise him, who is the health of my countenance and my God.*[163] In the hour of danger she used to say: *If any man will come after me, let him deny himself and take up his cross and follow me;*[164] and again: *Whosoever will save his life shall lose it;*[165] and *whosoever will lose his life for my sake, shall save it.*[166] When the exhaustion of her substance and the ruin of her property were announced to her, she said: *What is a man profited, if he shall gain the whole world and lose his own soul? or what shall a man give in exchange for his soul?*[167] and *Naked came I out of my mother's womb, and naked shall I return thither. As it pleased the Lord, so has it come to pass;*

blessed be the name of the Lord;[168] and these words: *Love not the world neither the things that are in the world. For all that is in the world is the desire of the flesh and the lust of the eyes and the pride of this life, which is not of the Father, but is of the world. And the world passes away and the lust thereof.*[169] I know that when word was sent to her of the serious illnesses of her children and particularly of Toxotius whom she very dearly loved, she first by her self-control fulfilled the saying: *I was troubled and I did not speak,*[170] and then cried out in these words: *Anyone who loves son or daughter more than me is not worthy of me.*[171] And she prayed to the Lord and said: *Possess the children of those who have been put to death*[172] who for thy sake every day put their own bodies to death. I am aware that a talebearer—a class of persons who do a great deal of harm—once told her as a kindness that, owing to her great fervor in virtue, some people thought her mad and declared that something should be done for her head. She replied: *We are made a spectacle to the world and to angels and to men; we are fools for Christ's sake*, but *the foolishness of God is wiser than men.*[173] It is for this reason that even the Saviour says to the Father: *Thou knowest my foolishness,*[174] and again *I am as a wonder unto many, but thou art my strong refuge.*[175] *I was as a beast before thee; nevertheless I am continually with thee.*[176] In the gospel we read that even his kinfolk desired to bind him as one of weak mind. His opponents also reviled him saying: *He has a devil and is a Samaritan,*[177] and *He casts out devils by Beelzebub the chief of the devils.*[178] But let us listen to the exhortation of the Apostle: *Our rejoicing is this, the testimony of our conscience that in holiness and sincerity and by the grace of God, we have had our conversation in the world.*[179] And let us hear the Lord when he says to his apostles: *Because you are not of the world, therefore the world hates you; if you were of the world the world would love its own.*[180] And then she turned her words to the Lord himself, saying: *Thou knowest the secrets of the heart,*[181] and *all this is come upon us; yet have we not forgotten thee, neither have we dealt falsely against thy covenant; our heart is not turned back. For thy sake are we killed all the day long; we are counted as sheep for the slaughter.*[182] But *the Lord is on my side: I will not fear what man does to me.*[183] For I have read: *My son, honor the Lord, and you shall be made strong; and beside him fear no man.*[184] These passages and others like them she used as Christ's armor against all vices in general, and particularly to defend herself against the furious onslaughts of envy. And thus, patiently enduring wrongs, she stilled the fury of a heart ready to burst. Down to the very day of her death two things were conspicuous in her life, one, her own great patience and the other, the jealousy which was manifested towards her. Now jealousy gnaws the heart of him who harbors it: and while it strives to injure its rival, raves with all the force of its fury against itself.

I shall now describe the order of her monastery and the method by which she turned the continence of saintly souls to her own profit. She sowed carnal things that she might reap spiritual things;[185] she gave earthly things that she might receive heavenly things; she forewent things temporal that she might in their stead obtain things eternal. Besides establishing a monastery for men, the charge of which she left to men, she divided into three companies and monasteries the numerous virgins whom she had gathered out of different provinces, some of whom are of noble birth while others belonged to the middle or lower classes.[186] But, although they worked and had their meals separately from each other, these three companies met together for psalm-singing and prayer. After the chanting of the Alleluia—the signal by which they were summoned to the Collect[187] —no one was permitted to remain behind. But coming either first or among the first, she used to await the arrival of the rest, urging them to diligence rather by her own modest example than by motives of fear. At dawn, at the third, sixth, and ninth hours, at evening, and at midnight they recited the Psalter each in turn.[188] No sister was allowed to be ignorant of the psalms, and all had every day to learn a certain portion of the holy Scriptures. On the Lord's day only, they proceeded to the church beside which they lived,[189] each company following its own mother-superior. Returning home in the same order, they then devoted themselves to their allotted tasks, and made garments either for themselves or else for others. If any was of noble birth, she was not allowed to have an attendant from home lest her maid, having her mind full of the doings of old days and of the licence of childhood, might by constant converse open old wounds and renew former errors. All the sisters were clothed alike. Linen was not used except for drying the hands. So strictly did she separate them from men that she would not allow even eunuchs to approach them, lest she should give any occasion to slanderous tongues, always ready to cavil at the religious, to console themselves for their own misdeeds. When anyone was backward in coming to the recitation of the psalms or showed herself remiss in her work, she used to approach her in different ways. Was she quick-tempered? Paula coaxed her. Was she phlegmatic? Paula chided her, copying the example of the Apostle who said: *What do you want? Shall I come to you with a rod or in the spirit of gentleness and meekness?*[190] Apart from food and raiment she allowed no one to have anything she could call her own, for Paul had said: *Having food and raiment we are content.*[191] She was afraid lest the custom of having more should breed covetousness in them—an appetite which no wealth can satisfy, for the more it has, the more it requires, and neither opulence or indigence is able to diminish it. When the sisters quarrelled one with another, she reconciled them with soothing words. If the young girls were troubled with fleshly desires, she broke their force by imposing frequent and redoubled fasts; for she wished them to be ill in body rather than to suffer in soul. If she chanced to notice any sister too attentive to her dress, she reproved her for her error with knitted brows and severe looks, saying: 'A clean body and a clean dress mean an unclean soul; a virgin's lips should never utter an improper or an impure word, for such indicate a lascivious mind, and by the outward man the faults of the inward are made manifest.' When she saw a sister verbose and talkative or forward and taking pleasure in quarrels, and when she found after frequent admonitions that the offender showed no signs of improvement, she placed her among the lowest of the sisters and outside their society, ordering her to pray at the door of the refectory and take her food by herself, in the hope that where rebuke had failed, shame might bring about a reformation. The sin of theft she loathed as if it were sacrilege; and that which among men of the world is counted little or nothing, she declared to be a crime of the deepest dye in a monastery. How shall I describe her kindness and attention towards the sick or the wonderful care and devotion with which she nursed them? Yet, although when others were sick she freely gave them every indulgence, and even allowed them to eat meat, whenever she fell ill herself, she made no concessions to her own weakness, and seemed unfair in this respect, that in her own case she exchanged for harshness the kindness which she was always ready to show to others.

No young girl of sound and vigorous constitution ever delivered herself up to a regimen so rigid as that imposed upon herself by Paula, whose physical powers age had impaired and enfeebled. I admit that in this she was too determined, refusing to spare herself or to listen to advice. I will relate something in my own experience.

In the extreme heat of the month of July she was once attacked by a violent fever, and we despaired of her life. Yet by God's mercy she rallied and the doctors urged on her the necessity of taking a little light wine to accelerate her recovery, saying that if she continued to drink water they feared that she might become dropsical. I secretly appealed to the blessed pope Epiphanius[192] to admonish, nay even to compel her, to take the wine. But she, with her usual sagacity and quickness, at once perceived the stratagem, and with a smile told him that his advice came from me. Not to waste more words, the blessed prelate after many exhortations left her chamber; and, when I asked him what he had accomplished, replied: 'Only that, old as I am, I have been almost persuaded to drink no more wine.' I relate this story not because I approve of persons rashly taking upon themselves burdens beyond their strength (for does not the Scripture say: *Burden not thyself?*[193] but because I wish, from this quality of perseverance in her, to show the passion of her mind and the yearning of her believing soul, as she says: *My soul thirsteth for thee, and my flesh, in how many ways!*[194] Difficult as it is always to avoid extremes, the philosophers are quite right in their opinion that virtue is a mean and vice an excess,[195] or as we may express it in one short sentence 'In nothing too much.'[196] While thus unyielding in her contempt for food, she was easily moved to sorrow and felt crushed by the deaths of her kinsfolk, especially those of her children. When, one after another, her husband and her daughters fell asleep, on each occasion the shock of their loss endangered her life. And although she signed her mouth and her breast with the sign of the cross, and endeavoured thus to alleviate a mother's grief, her feelings overpowered her, and her maternal instincts were too much for her confiding mind. Thus while her intellect retained its mastery, she was overcome by sheer physical weakness. For when sickness once seized her, it clung to her so long that it brought anxiety to us and danger to herself. Yet even then she was full of joy and repeated every moment: *O wretched being that I am! who shall deliver me from the body of this death?*[197] The careful reader may say that my words are an invective rather than a eulogy. I call that Jesus whom she served and whom I desire to serve to be my witness, that so far from unduly eulogizing her or depreciating her, I tell the truth about her as one Christian writing of another; that I am writing a memoir and not a panegyric, and that what were faults in her might well be virtues in others less saintly. I speak thus of her faults to satisfy my own feelings and the passionate regret of us her brothers and sisters, who all of us love her still and all of us deplore her loss.

Yet, she has finished her course, she has kept the faith, and now she enjoys the crown of righteousness.[198] She follows the lamb whithersoever he goes.[199] She is filled now because once she was hungry.[200] With joy does she sing: *As we have heard, so have we seen in the city of the Lord of hosts, in the city of our God.* O blessed change! Once she wept but now laughs for evermore. Once she despised the broken cisterns;[201] but now she has found the Lord a fountain.[202] [Once she wore haircloth but now she is clothed in white raiment, and can say: *Thou hast cut off my sackcloth, and girded me with gladness.*[203] Once she ate ashes like bread[204] and mingled her drink with weeping; saying: *My tears have been my meat day and night;*[205] but now for all time she eats the bread of angels[206] and sings: *O taste and see that the Lord is gracious;*[207] *and my heart hath uttered a good*

word; I speak the things which I have made for the king.[208] She
sees fulfilled in herself Isaiah's words, or rather those of the Lord
speaking through Isaiah: *Behold, my servants shall eat, but ye
shall be hungry: behold, my servants shall drink, but ye shall be
thirsty: behold, my servants shall rejoice, but ye shall be ashamed:
behold, my servants shall sing for joy, but ye shall cry for sorrow
of heart, and shall howl for vexation of spirit.*[209] I have said that
she always shunned the broken cisterns; she did so that she
might find the Lord a fountain,[210] and that she might rejoice
and sing: *As the hart desireth the waterbrooks, so longeth my
soul after thee, O God. My soul is athirst for the strong God, the
living God. When shall I come and appear before the presence
of God?*[211]

I must briefly mention the manner in which she avoided the
foul cisterns of the heretics whom she regarded as no better
than heathen. A certain cunning knave, in his own estimation
both learned and clever, began without my knowledge to put to
her such questions as these: 'What sin has an infant committed
that it should be seized by the devil? Shall we be young or old
when we rise again? If we die young and rise young, we shall
after the resurrection need to have nurses. If, however, we die
young and rise old, the dead will not rise again at all: they will
be transformed into new beings. Will there be a distinction of
sexes in the next world? Or will there be no such distinction?
If the distinction continues, there will be wedlock and sexual
intercourse and procreation of the children. If it does not continue,
the bodies that rise again will not be the same.' For, he argued:
*the earthy tabernacle weighs down the mind that muses on many
things,*[212] but the bodies that we shall have in heaven will be subtle
and spiritual according to the words of the Apostle: *It is sown a
natural body: it is raised a spiritual body.*[213] From all of which
considerations he sought to prove that rational creatures have
through their faults and previous sins fallen to bodily conditions;
and that according to the nature and guilt of their transgression,
they are born in this or that state of life. Some, he said, rejoice
in sound bodies and wealthy and noble parents; others have for
their portion diseased frames and poverty-stricken homes, and by

imprisonment in the present world and in bodies pay the penalty of their former sins.

She listened and reported what she heard to me, at the same time pointing out the man. Thus on me was laid the task of opposing this utterly noxious viper and deadly pest. It is of such that the psalmist speaks when he writes: *Deliver not the soul that confesseth thee unto the wild beasts*,[214] and *Rebuke, Lord, the wild beast of the reeds*,[215] creatures who write iniquity and speak lies against the Lord[216] and lift up their mouths against the most High.[217] As the fellow had to deceive Paula, I went to him at her request, and by asking him a few questions involved him in a dilemma. 'Do you believe', said I, 'that there will be a resurrection of the dead or not?' He replied, 'I believe'. I went on: 'Will the bodies that rise again be the same or different?' He said, 'The same'. Then I asked: 'What of their sex? Will that remain unaltered or will it be changed?' At this question he became silent and swayed his head this way and that as a serpent does to avoid being struck. Accordingly I continued, 'As you have nothing to say I will answer for you and will draw the conclusion from your premises. If the woman shall not rise again as a woman nor the man as a man, there will be no resurrection of the dead. For sex has its members, and the members make up the whole body. But if there shall be no sex and no members, what will become of the resurrection of the body, which cannot exist without sex and members? And if there shall be no resurrection of the body, there can be no resurrection of the dead. But as to your objection taken from marriage, that, if the members shall remain the same, marriage follows, that is disposed of by the Saviour's words: *You err, not knowing the Scriptures or the power of God. For in the resurrection of the dead they shall neither marry nor be given in marriage, but are as the angels.*[218] When it is said that they neither marry nor are given in marriage, the distinction of sex is shown to persist. For no one says of things which have no capacity for marriage, such as a stick or a stone, that they neither marry nor are given in marriage; but this may well be said of those who, while they can marry, yet abstain from doing so by their own virtue and by the grace of Christ. But if you will cavil at this and say, how shall we in that case be like the angels with whom there is neither male nor female, hear my answer in brief as follows. What the Lord promises to us is not the nature of angels, but their mode of life and their bliss. And therefore John the Baptist was called an angel,[219] even before he was beheaded, and all God's holy men and virgins manifest in themselves, even in this world, the life of angels. When it is said: *You shall be like the angels*,[220] likeness only is promised and not a change of nature.

'And now do you in your turn answer me these questions. How do you explain the fact that Thomas felt the hands of the risen Lord and beheld his side pierced by the spear?[221] And the fact that Peter saw the Lord standing on the shore and eating a piece of a roasted fish and a honeycomb.[222] If he stood, he must certainly have had feet. If he pointed to his wounded side, he must have also had chest and belly, for to these the sides are attached and without them they cannot be. If he spoke, he must have used a tongue and palate and teeth. For as the blow strikes the strings, so does the tongue come in contact with the teeth to produce vocal sounds. If his hands were felt, it follows that he must have had arms as well. Since therefore it is admitted that he had all the members which go to make up the body, he must have also had the whole body formed of them, and that not a woman's, but a man's; that is to say, it rose again in the sex in which it died. And if you cavil further and say: "We shall eat then, I suppose, after the resurrection?" or, "How can a solid and material body enter in, contrary to its nature, though closed doors?" you shall receive this reply. Do not for this matter of food find fault with belief in the resurrection. For our Lord, after raising the daughter of the ruler of the synagogue, commanded food to be given her;[223] and Lazarus, who had been dead four days, is described as sitting at meat with him,[224] the object in both cases to show that the resurrection was not merely apparent. And if from his entering in through closed doors[225] you strive to prove that his body was spiritual and ethereal, he must have had a spiritual body even before he suffered, since—contrary to the nature of heavy bodies—he was able to walk upon the sea.[226] The apostle Peter also must be believed to have had a spiritual body, for he also walked upon the waters with hesitant step.[227] The true explanation is that when anything is done against nature, it is a manifestation of God's might and power. And to show plainly that in these great signs our attention is asked not to a change in nature but to the almighty power of God, he who by faith had walked on water, began to sink for the want of faith, and would have done so, had not the hand of the Lord lifted him up with the words: *O you of little faith, why did you doubt?*[228] I wonder that you can display such effrontery when the Lord said: *Reach out your finger, and behold my hands; and reach out your hand and thrust it into my side: and be not faithless but believing,*[229] and in another place: *Behold my hands and my feet that it is I myself. Handle me and see; for a spirit has not flesh and bones as you see me have. And when he had thus spoken he showed them his hands and his feet.*[230] You hear him speak of bones and flesh, of feet and hands; and yet you want to palm off on me the bubbles and airy nothings of which the Stoics rave![231]

'Moreover, if you ask how it is that a mere infant which has never sinned is seized by the devil, or at what age we shall rise again seeing that we die at different ages; my only answer— an unwelcome one, I fancy—will be in the words of Scripture: *The judgments of the Lord are a great deep,*[232] and *O the depth of the riches both of the wisdom and knowledge of God! How unsearchable are his judgments, and his ways past finding out! For who has known the mind of the Lord? or who has been his counsellor?*[233] No difference of age can affect the reality of the body. Although our frames are in a perpetual flux and lose or gain daily, these changes do not make of us different individuals every day. I was not one person at ten years old, another at thirty and another at fifty; nor am I another now when all my head is grey. According to the traditions of the churches and the teaching of the apostle Paul, the answer must be this: that we shall rise as perfect men in the measure of the age of the fullness of Christ.[234] At this age the Jews suppose Adam to have been created, and at this age we read that the Lord and Saviour rose again.' Many other arguments did I adduce from both testaments to stifle the outcry of this heretic.

From that day forward so profoundly did she commence to loathe the man—and all who agreed with him in his doctrine—that she publicly proclaimed them as enemies of the Lord. I have related this incident less with the design of confuting in a few words a heresy which would require volumes to confute it, than with the object of showing the great faith of this saintly woman who preferred to subject herself to perpetual hostility from men, rather than by friendships hurtful to herself to provoke or to offend God.

To revert then to that description of her character which I began a little time ago; no mind was ever more docile than hers. She was slow to speak and swift to hear,[235] remembering the precept: *Keep silence and hearken, O Israel.*[236] The holy Scriptures she knew by heart, and said of the history contained in them that it was the foundation of the truth. But, though she loved even this, she still preferred to seek for the underlying spiritual meaning and made this the keystone of the spiritual building raised within her soul. She asked leave that she and her daughter might read through the Old and New Testaments under my guidance. Out of modesty I at first refused compliance, but as she persisted in her demand and frequently urged me to consent to it, I at last did so and taught her what I had learned, not from myself—self-confidence is the worst of teachers—but from the Church's most famous writers. Wherever I stuck fast and honestly confessed myself at fault, she would by no means rest content, but would force me by fresh questions to point out to her which of many possible solutions seemed to me the most probable. I will mention here another fact which to those who are envious may well seem incredible. While I myself, beginning as a young man, have with much toil and effort partially acquired the Hebrew tongue, and study it now unceasingly lest if I leave it, it also may leave me, Paula, making up her mind that she too would learn it, succeeded so well that she could chant the psalms in Hebrew and could speak the language without a trace of the pronunciation peculiar to Latin. The same accomplishment can be seen to this day in her daughter Eustochium, who always kept close to her mother's side, obeyed all her commands, never slept apart from her, never walked abroad or took a meal without her, never had a penny that she could call her own, rejoiced when her mother gave to the poor her little patrimony, and fully believed that in filial affection she had the best heritage and the truest riches.

I must not pass over in silence the joy which she felt when she heard her granddaughter, Paula, the child of Laeta and Toxotius—who was born, and I may even say conceived, in answer to a vow of her parents, dedicating her to virginity—when, I say, she heard the little one in her cradle, still playing with a rattle, still stammering, sing 'alleluia' and falter out the words 'grandmother' and 'aunt'.[237] One wish alone made her long to see her native land again: that she might know her son and his wife and child to have renounced the world and to be serving Christ. And it has been granted to her in part. For while her granddaughter is destined to take the veil, her daughter-in-law has vowed herself to perpetual chastity, and by faith and alms emulates the example that her mother has set her. She strives to exhibit at Rome the virtues which Paula set forth in all their fullness at Jerusalem.

What ails you, my soul? Why do you shudder to approach her death? I have already made my treatise longer than it should be; dreading to come to the end and vainly supposing that by saying nothing of it and by occupying myself with her praises, I could postpone the evil day. Hitherto the wind has been all in my favor and my kneel has smoothly ploughed through the heaving waves. But now my speech is running on the rocks, the billows are mountain high, and imminent shipwreck awaits both monasteries.[238] We must needs cry out: *Master, save us, we perish*;[239] and *awake, why are you sleeping, O Lord?*[240] For who could tell the tale of Paula's dying with dry eyes?

She fell into a very serious illness, and thus gained what she most desired, to leave us and to be joined more fully to the Lord. Eustochium's affection for her mother, always true and tried, in this time of sickness approved itself still more to all. She sat by her bedside, she fanned her, she supported her head, she arranged her pillows, she chafed her feet, she rubbed her stomach, she smoothed down the bedclothes, she heated hot water, she brought towels. In fact she anticipated the servants in all their duties, and when one of them did anything, she regarded it as so much taken away from her own gain. How unceasingly she prayed, how copiously she wept, how constantly she ran to and fro between her prostrate mother and the cave of the Lord, imploring God that she might not be deprived of a companion so dear, that if Paula was to die she might herself no longer live, and that one bier might carry them both to burial! Alas for the frailty and perishableness of human nature! Except that our belief in Christ raises us up to heaven and promises eternity to our souls, the physical conditions of life are the same for us as for the brutes. *There is one event to the righteous and to the wicked; to the good and to the evil; to the clean and to the unclean; to someone who sacrifices and to someone who sacrifices not: as is the good, so is the sinner; and he who swears as he who fears an oath.*[241] Man and beast alike are dissolved into dust and ashes.

Why do I still linger, and prolong my suffering by postponing it? Paula's intelligence showed her that her death was near. Her body and limbs grew cold, and only in her holy breast did the warm beat of the living soul continue. Yet, as though she were leaving strangers to go home to her own people, she whispered the verses of the psalmist: *Lord, I have loved the beauty of thy house and the place where thine honor dwelleth,*[242] and *How amiable are thy tabernacles, O Lord of hosts! My soul longeth, yea, even fainteth, for the courts of the Lord,*[243] and *I had rather be an outcast in the house of my God than to dwell in the tents of the wicked.*[244] When I asked her why she remained silent, refusing to answer my call, whether she was in pain, she replied in Greek that she had no suffering and that all things were to her eyes calm and tranquil. After this she said no more, but closed her eyes as though she already despised all mortal things; she kept repeating the same verses down to the moment she breathed out her soul, but in a tone so low that I could scarcely hear what she said. Raising her finger also to her mouth, she made the sign of the cross upon her lips. Then her breath failed her and she gasped for death; yet even when her soul was eager to break free, she turned the death-rattle (which comes at last to all) into the praise of the Lord. The bishop of Jerusalem and some from other cities were present, also a great number of the lower clergy, both priests and levites.[245] The entire monastery was filled with companies of virgins and monks. As soon as she heard the bridegroom say: *Rise up, my love, my fair one, my dove, and come away: for, lo, the winter is past, the rain is over and gone,*[246] she answered joyfully *'The flowers appear on the earth; the time to cut them has come*[247] and *I believe that I shall see the good things of the Lord in the land of the living.'*[248]

No weeping or lamentation followed her death, such as are the custom of the world; the swarms of monks united in chanting the psalms in their several tongues. The bishops lifted the dead woman up with their own hands, and some of them put their shoulders to the bier, carried her to the church in the cave of the Saviour, and laid her down in the centre of it. Other bishops meantime carried torches and tapers in the procession, and yet others led the singing of the choirs. The whole population of the cities of Palestine came to her funeral. Not a single monk lurked in the desert or lingered in his cell. Not a single virgin remained shut up in the seclusion of her chamber. To each and all it would have seemed sacrilege to have withheld the last tokens of respect from a woman so saintly. As in the case of Dorcas,[249] the widows and the poor showed the garments Paula had given them; while the destitute cried aloud that they had lost in her a mother and a nurse. Strange to say, the paleness of death had not altered her expression, but a certain solemnity and seriousness had spread over her features. You would have thought her not dead but asleep.

One after another they chanted the psalms, now in Greek, now in Latin, now in Syriac— and this not merely for the three days which elapsed before she was buried beneath the church and close to the cave of the Lord, but throughout the remainder of the week. All who were assembled felt that it was their own funeral, and shed tears as if for themselves. Her daughter, the revered virgin Eustochium, *as a child weaned from its mother*[250] could not be torn away from her parent. She kissed her eyes, pressed her lips on her brow, embraced her frame, and wanted to be buried with her mother.

Jesus is witness that Paula has left not a single penny to her daughter, but, as I said before, a large mass of debt; and, worse even than this, a crowd of brothers and sisters[251] whom it is hard for her to support, but whom it would be undutiful to cast off. Could there be a more admirable instance of virtue than that of this noble lady who in the fervor of her faith gave away so much of her great wealth that she reduced herself to well-nigh the last degree of poverty? Others may boast, if they will, of money spent in charity, of large sums heaped upon God's treasury,[252] of votive offerings hung up with cords of gold. None of them has given more to the poor than she, for she kept nothing for herself. But now she enjoys the true riches and those good things *which eye has not seen nor ear heard, neither have they entered into the heart of man.*[253] If we mourn, it is for ourselves and not for her; yet even so, if we persist in weeping for one who reigns with Christ, we shall seem to envy her her glory.

Be not anxious, Eustochium: you are endowed with a splendid heritage. The Lord is your portion;[254] and, to increase your joy, your mother has now after a long martyrdom won her crown. It is not only the shedding of blood that is accounted a confession; the spotless service of a devout mind is itself a daily martyrdom. Both alike are crowned; with rose and violets in the one case, with lilies in the other. Thus in the Song of Songs it is written: *My cousin is white and ruddy,*[255] for whether the victory be won in peace or war, God gives the same guerdon to those who win it. Like Abraham, your mother heard the words: *Get thee out of thy country, and from thy kindred, and come unto a land that I will show thee;*[256] and the Lord's command given through Jeremiah: *Flee out of the midst of Babylon, and save your souls.*[257] To the day of her death she never returned to Chaldaea, or regretted the fleshpots of Egypt[258] and its savory meats. Accompanied by her virgin bands, she became a fellow-citizen of the Saviour: and now that she has ascended from her little Bethlehem to the heavenly realms, she can say to the true Naomi: *Thy people shall be my people and thy God my god.*[259]

I have spent the labor of two nights in dictating for you this treatise; and in doing so I have felt a grief as deep as your own. I say in 'dictating' for I have not been able to write it myself. As often as I have taken up my pen and have tried to fulfil my promise, my fingers have stiffened, my hand has fallen, and my power over it has vanished. The rudeness of the diction, devoid as it is of all elegance or charm, bears witness only to the wishes of the writer.

And now, Paula, farewell, and aid with your prayers the old age of your votary. Your faith and your works unite you to Christ; thus standing in his presence you will the more readily gain what you ask. 'I have built a monument more lasting than bronze,'[260] which no lapse of time will be able to destroy. And I have cut an inscription on your tomb, which I here subjoin; that, wherever my narrative may go, the reader may learn that you are buried at Bethlehem and not uncommemorated there.

THE INSCRIPTION ON THE TOMB

Within this tomb a child of Scipio lies,
A daughter of the far-framed Pauline house,
A scion of the Gracchi, of the stock
Of Agamemnon's self, illustrious:
Here rests the lady Paul, well-beloved
Of both her parents, with Eustochium
For daughter; she the first of roman dames
Who hardship chose and Bethlehem for Christ.

In front of the cavern there is another inscription as follows:

Seest thou here hollowed in the rock a grave?
'Tis Paula's tomb; high heaven has her soul.
Who Rome and friends, riches and home, forsook,
Here in this lonely spot to find her rest.
For here Christ's manger was, and here the kings
To him, both God and man, their offerings made.

The holy and blessed Paula fell asleep on the 26th of January on the third day of the week, after the sun had set. She was buried on the 28th of January, in the sixth consulship of the Emperor Honorius and the first of Aristraenetus.[261] She lived in the vows of religion five years at Rome and twenty years at Bethlehem. The whole duration of her life was fifty-six years, eight months, and twenty-one days.

NOTES

1. Ps 119 (120):5, 6.
2. 1 Jn 5:19.
3. Ps 138 (139):12.
4. Jn 1;5.
5. Ps 38:13 (39:12).
6. Ph 1:23.
7. 1 Cor 9:27.
8. Rm 14:21.
9. Ps 34 (35):13.
10. Ps 40 (41):4.
11. Ps 31 (32):4.
12. Ps 54:7 (55:6).
13. Mk 4:28–30.
14. Cicero, *Tusculan disputation* 1.109; Seneca, *Epistola* 79.13; Pliny, *Ep.* 1.8,14.
15. Vergil, *Aeneid* 1.288.
16. Letter 39.
17. Letter 66.
18. Letter 22, p. 171.
19. The Council of Rome, ad 382, met to consider the Western attitude to the Council of Constantinople, ad 381. Paulinus was accepted in the West as the true bishop of Antioch.
20. Paul, the supposed first hermit, whose 'life' was written by Jerome; Antony, the real leader of anchoritic monasticism, whose life was written by Athanasius.
21. Hilberg excludes this clause; but it hardly seems to be an invention.
22. *nubilis*, i.e., marriageable.
23. Wife of Flavius Clemens and niece of Domitian. According to Dio Cassius (67, 14) he was executed and she banished to Pandateria for atheism. Pontia is twenty-five miles from Pandateria. Eusebius (*Historia Ecclesiastica* 3.18) who believed that she was a Christian, also gives Pontia. Her Christianity is not quite proved, but her connection with the Catacomb of Domitilla adds to the probability.
24. Vergil, *Aeneid* 1.173 and 3.126–127.
25. The friendship between Epiphanius and Paula played its part in the Origenistic controversy.
26. Ac 21:5.
27. Cf. Ac 21:7.
28. 4 (2) Kgs 23:29.

29. At that time Caesarea was the civil and ecclesiastical metropolis of Palestine. The bishop of Jerusalem was a suffragan of its bishop until the Council of Ephesus, ad 431, which assigned a small patriarchate to Jerusalem.

30. Ac 10:1.,
31. Ac 21:9.
32. Ac 9:39–41.
33. Ac 9:32–34.
34. Jn 19:38.
35. 1 Kgs (1 Sm) 22:19.
36. Jon 1:3.
37. Lk 24:35.
38. 3 (1) Kgs 9:17.
39. Jos 10:12–13.
40. Jos 9:27.
41. Jdg 19–20.
42. Josephus, *Antiquitates Iudaicae (Jewish Antiquities) 20.2, 6.*
43. Mt 28:2.

44. Reading *fide et ore* or *fidei ore*. With Hilberg's *fide, ore* the meaning will presumably be 'which faith longed for,' with perhaps a reference to John 4, as in paragraph 13.

45. 2 Kgs (2 Sm) 5:6–10.
46. Is 29:1.
47. Ps 86 (87):1–2.
48. Mt 27:26.
49. Ac 2:16–17, Jl 2:28ff.
50. Gn 35:18–20.
51. Is 1:3.
52. Is 32:20.
53. Lk 2:7.
54. Jn 1:1.
55. Jn 1:1, 14.

56. Micah 5:2–3. Jerome translates the very awkward text of the LXX literally.

57. Ac 13:46.
58. Mt 15:24.
59. Gn 49:10.
60. Ps 131 (130):3–5.
61. Ps 131 (132):6.
62. Paula is still speaking. Jerome taught her Hebrew.
63. Ps 131 (132):7.
64. Is 28:12.
65. Ps 131 (132):14.
66. Ps 131 (132) 17.
67. Ps 21 (22):31.
68. Gn 35:21.
69. Lk 2:14.

70. Jer 13:23.
71. Ac 8:27–39.
72. Num 13:34.
73. Is 63:3.
74. Gn 18.
75. Jn 8:56.
76. Josh 14:15.
77. Josh 14:15, with a confusion between Adam as a proper name and as 'man'.
78. 2 Cor 3:6.
79. Jdg 1:13–15.
80. Gn 18:16.
81. Gn 29:23.
82. Sg 1:14.
83. Cf Gn 14:3, 8.
84. Eph 5:18.
85. Am 1:1.
86. Am 1:1.
87. Gn 19.
88. Ezk 11:22–25.
89. Mt 21:5.
90. Lk 10.
91. The inn is taken allegorically to mean the Church. Spiritual exegesis of all the details of this parable is common in the Fathers. The Good Samaritan is Christ.
92. Lk 19:4.
93. 3 (1) Kgs 16:24.
94. Cf. Josh 5.
95. Josh 4:1–9.
96. Rv 21:14; cf. Eph 2:30.
97. 4 (2) Kgs 2:19ff.
98. 4 (2) Kgs 2:8.
99. Josh 7:24.
100. Gn 28:11ff.
101. Zach 3:9.
102. Is 28:16.
103. Gn 28:12–13.
104. Josh 24:30.
105. Josh 24:33.
106. Jdg 21:23.
107. Jn 4:5–42.
108. A Samaritan, pre-christian, heretic mentioned by Hippolytus and Eusebius.
109. Mt 11:11.
110. Cf. Hilary, *In Constantium* 8; ed. A. Rocher, SCh 334 (Paris, 1987) 183, 31.
111. 3 (1) Kgs 18:4.

112. Lk 4:16, Jn 2.
113. Mt 8:23.
114. Mt 14:20.
115. Mt 17.
116. Jdg 4.
117. Lk 7:11-17.
118. Jdg 15:19.
119. Mi 1:1.
120. Ps 77 (78): 12, 43.
121. Cf. Palladius, *Lausiac History* 46, where Melania 'went to the mountain of Nitria, where she met ... Arsisius, Sarapion the great ... Isidore, the confessor, bishop of Hermopolis.' Three hermits named Macarius, two of them eminent, are described by Palladius (15, 17, 18).
122. ad 386-389.
123. Lk 2:9.
124. Ps 6:6.
125. 2 Cor 8:13-14.
126. Lk 3:11, reading *alteram*, one of the two, only.
127. Mt 5:7.
128. Si 3:30.
129. Lk 16:9.
130. Lk 11:41.
131. Dn 4:27.
132. Zch 9:16.
133. Rv 21:14, 19-21.
134. Jb 2:4.
135. Mt 23:27.
136. Wis 2:24.
137. 3 (1) Kgs 11:14.
138. What Hadad, Solomon's adversary, stands for is unclear. Thorn: cf. 2 Cor 12:7.
139. Gn 27:41ff.
140. 1 Kgs (Sam) 21:10.
141. Cf. Mt 5:39.
142. Rm 12:21.
143. Ph 2:7-8.
144. Jb 40:3.
145. Mt 5:10.
146. Ps 38:2-3 (39:1-2).
147. Ps 37 (38):12.
148. Ps 37 (38):13-14.
149. Dt 13:3.
150. 1 S 28:9-11.
151. Rm 5:3-5.
152. 2 Cor 4:16.
153. 1 Is 49:8.
154. Is 5:7-8. This passage was rejected by Hilberg.

155. Lk 21:19.
156. Rm 8:18.
157. Pr 14:29.
158. 2 Cor 12:10.
159. 2 Cor 4:7l.
160. 1 Cor 15:54.
161. 2 Cor 1:5.
162. 2 Cor 1:7.
163. Ps 41:12 (42:11).
164. Lk 9:23.
165. Lk 9:24.
166. Mt 16:26.
167. Mt 16:26.
168. Jb 1:21.
169. 1 Jn 2:15–17.
170. Ps 76:5 (77:4).
171. Mt 10:37.
172. Ps 78 (79):11.
173. 1 Cor 4:9–10, 1:25.
174. Ps 68:6 (69:5).
175. Ps 70 (71):7.
176. Ps 72 (73):22–23.
177. Jn 8:40.
178. Lk 11:15.
179. 2 Cor 1:12.
180. Jn 15:18–19.
181. Ps 43 (42):21.
182. Ps 43 (42) 17–18, 22.
183. Ps 117 (118):6.
184. Pr 7:1a (LXX).
185. 1 Cor 9:11.
186. The Latin does not say quite unambiguously that the three companies were determined by social status, but that is what it seems to mean.
187. *Collecta*, assembly; cf. 51.1.
188. See note 43 to Letter 107 (pp. 263, 268).
189. The Church of the Nativity at Bethlehem.
190. 1 Cor 4:21.
191. 1 Tm 6:8.
192. Epiphanius, bishop of Salamis (Paragraphs 6–7), who was in Palestine on his campaign against Origenism. Bishops were often called *papa*.
193. Si 13:2.
194. Ps 62 (63):1.
195. Jerome gives the terms in Greek; cf. Aristotle, *Nicomachaean Ethics* 2.6.
196. *Ne quid nimis*, Terence, *Andria* 61, from a greek proverb.

197. Rm 7:24.
198. 2 Tm 4:7–8.
199. Rv 14:4.
200. Lk 6:21.
201. Jr 2:13.
202. Jn 4:14.
203. Ps 29:12 (30:11).
204. Ps 101 (102):9.
205. Ps 40 (41):3.
206. Wis 16:20.
207. Ps 33 (34):8.
208. Ps 44:2 (45:1).
209. Is 65:13–14.
210. The bracket passage is marked by Hilberg as being the addition of some learned reader. The repetition of the last words is certainly awkward.
211. Ps 41 (42):1. For background, see the literature on Origenism and Jerome's Letter against John of Jerusalem, especially cc. 7, 16, 23–36.
212. Ws 9:15.
213. 1 Cor 15:44.
214. Ps 73 (74):19.
215. Ps 67 (68):30.
216. Hos 7:13.
217. Ps 72 (73):9.
218. Mt 22:29–30.
219. Lk 7:27. The greek word *angelos* ἄγγελος means messenger.
220. Mt 22:30.
221. Jn 20:27.
222. Lk 24:42, Jn 21:9.
223. Mk 5:43.
224. Jn 11:44, 12:2.
225. Jn 20:19.
226. Mt 14:25.
227. Mt 14:29.
228. Mt 14:31.
229. Jn 20:27.
230. Lk 24:39–40.
231. *Globos Stoicorum atque aeria quaedam deliramenta.* The Stoic Chrysippus said that souls are spherical after their separation from the body (Arnim, *Fragmenta veterum Stoicorum* [Leipzig, 1676] 815). Since to the Stoic, soul is a substance (*corpus*), however tenuous, it must have shape, and, being soul, the perfect shape. See Plato, *Timaeus* 33b, 63a, for the sphere. Again, it must have color, and so that of the pure air (cf. Tertullian, *De anima* 9). I leave the version 'airy nothings' as a familiar phrase. Strictly, the shape and color are necessary because they are 'somethings'. On stoic and early christian notions of the soul, J. H. Waszink's commentary on Tertullian, *De anima*, is of very great value. For

the origenistic notion of the spherical resurrection body, see *Alexandrian Christianity*, Library of Christian Classics 2:191, 232, 381–382.

232. Ps 35 (36):6.
233. Rm 11:33–34.
234. Eph 4:13.
235. Jm 1:19.
236. Dt 27:9.
237. See Letter 107.
238. Not *nostrum*, both of us, as Fremantle's text read, but *monasterii* (Hilberg), the two monasteries for men and women at Bethlehem.
239. Lk 8:24.
240. Ps 43 (44):23.
241. Si 9:2.
242. Ps 25 (26): 8.
243. Ps 83 (84):1–2.
244. Ps 83 (84):11.
245. Priests and Levites are presbyters and deacons.
246. Sg 2:10–11.
247. Sg 2:12.
248. Ps 26 (27):13.
249. Ac 9:39.
250. Ps 130 (131):2.
251. Brothers and sisters means monks and nuns.
252. *In corban Dei*; cf. Mt 27:6, Mk 7:11.
253. 1 Cor 2:9.
254. Lm 3:24.
255. Sg 5:10, with *fratuelis*, cousin, following the Septuagint. In the Vulgate, Jerome has the familiar 'beloved'.
257. Jr 51:6.
258. Gn 16:3.
259. Ruth 1:16.
260. Horace, *Odes* 3.30, 1.
261. AD 404.

EUSTOCHIUM
THE THEOLOGY OF
FEMININE ASCETICISM

USTOCHIUM WAS THE DAUGHTER of Paula the Elder, the leader of the aristocratic ladies living on the Aventine Hill in Rome and leading the religious life. Jerome acted as their spiritual director (see Historical Introduction, p. 92 above). Letter 22 to Eustochium, completed in the spring of 384 at the latest, while cast in the form of a letter, is actually a sizable treatise on asceticism. In it Jerome analyzes the motives of those who devote themselves to a life of virginity and lays down the rules by which they ought to govern their daily lives. Indeed Jerome himself, some thirty years later, refers to it (in Letter 13) as 'a treatise'.

Jerome's attitude strikes the modern reader as harsh, and it is not immediately apparent why such an obviously conscientious and responsible disciple as Eustochium should have been in need of such stern exhortation. In fact, during the years 383–384, Jerome, with the approval of Pope Damasus, was carrying on a campaign in favor of asceticism, not only among devout upper-class ladies, but also in roman society in general, and this letter formed part of it. Jerome likely intended it to be read by others besides Eustochium. The vivid descriptions of roman society in this letter and elsewhere suggest that there was a real need to such a campaign, particularly among the clergy.

The letter, though not completely lacking in structure, is somewhat diffuse in its arrangement and includes a digression on the categories of monks to be found in Egypt. Its principal message is: (1) Virginity is superior to marriage, which is valuable only as a means of producing a further supply of virgins; (2) Fasting is all-important and the minimum of very simple food should be taken; (3). Dress should be unobtrusive, neither fashionable nor ostentatiously shabby; (4) The companions of the virgin should be widows or spinsters of blameless life, for she would shun the society of frivolous young people of either sex and of married women.

This letter is important not only for its teaching about asceticism, but also for its vivid portrayal of roman society in the late fourth century, the state of which gave particular scope for Jerome's satirical tongue and pen. It is therefore of value to the social historian as well as to the reader interested in theology and spirituality.

J. M. P.

To Eustochium (Letter 22)

LISTEN, O DAUGHTER, and see, and incline your ear; and forget your people and your father's house and the king shall desire your beauty.[1] In this forty-fourth[2] psalm, God speaks to the human soul, saying that, following the example of Abraham,[3] it should go out from its own land and from its kindred and should leave the Chaldeans, that is, the demons, and should dwell in the country of the living, for which elsewhere the prophet sighs, *I believe that I shall see the good things of the Lord in the land of the living.*[4] But it is not enough for you to go out from your own land, unless you forget your people and your father's house; unless you scorn the flesh and cling to the Bridegroom in a close embrace. *Do not look behind you,* he says, *or remain in the entire region; take refuge on the mountain, lest by chance you be consumed.*[5] Anyone who has grasped the plough must not look behind him or return home from the field, or, having Christ's tunic, descend from the roof to fetch another garment.[6] What a marvelous thing, that a father charges his daughter to remember her father. *You are of your father the-devil, and it is your will to do the lusts of your father.*[7] So it was said of the Jews—and, in another place, *Someone who commits sin is of the devil.*[8] Born, in the first instance, of such parentage, we are naturally black, and even when we have repented, so long as we have not scaled the heights of virtue, we may still say, *I am black and beautiful, daughter of Jerusalem.*[9] But you will say to me, 'I have left the home of my childhood; I have forgotten my father, I am born again in Christ. What reward do I receive for this?' The context shows: *The king shall desire your beauty.* This, then, is the great mystery. *For this a man shall leave his father and mother and shall cling to his wife, and they two shall be,* not as is said there *of one flesh,* but of 'one spirit'.[10] Your bridegroom is not haughty or disdainful; he has *married an Ethiopian woman.* When once you desire the wisdom of the true Solomon and come to him, he will avow all his knowledge to you. He will lead you into his chamber with his royal hand. He will miraculously change your complexion, so that it shall be said of you, *Who is this who goes up and has been made white?.*[11] I write to you thus, my lady

Eustochium (I am bound to call my Lord's bride 'my lady'), to show you by my opening words that my object is not to praise the virginity which you follow and of which you have proved the value, or yet to recount the drawbacks of marriage—the swelling of the womb, of a baby, the torments of a mistress, the cares of household management and all those fancied blessings which death at last cuts short; indeed married women have their own status, that is, honorable matrimony and an undefiled marriage bed.[12] My purpose is to show you that you are fleeing from Sodom and should take warning by Lot's wife.[13] There is no flattery, I can tell you, in these pages. A flatterer's words are fair, but for all that, he is an enemy. You need expect no rhetorical flourishes setting you among the angels and, while they extol virginity as blessed, putting the world at your feet.

I would have you draw from your monastic vow not pride but fear.[14] You walk laden with gold; you must keep out of the robber's way. To us human beings this life is a race-course; we contend here, we are downed elsewhere. No one can lay fear aside while serpents and scorpions beset his path. The Lord says, *My sword has drunk deep in heaven,*[15] and do you expect to find peace on the earth? No, the earth yields only thorns and thistles, and its dust is food for the serpent.[16] *For our wrestling is not against flesh and blood, but against the principalities and powers of this world and of this darkness, against the spirits of wickedness in the heavenly places*[17]. We are hemmed in by hosts of foes; our enemies are on every side. The weak flesh will soon be ashes; one against many, it fights against tremendous odds. Not till it has been dissolved, not till the prince of this world has come and found nothing in it,[18] not till then may you safely listen to the prophet's words, *You shall not fear the terror by night or the arrow which flies by day or the activity that surrounds you in darkness or the demon and his attacks at noon day. A thousand shall fall at your side and ten thousand at your right hand, but the terror will not come near you.*[19] When the hosts of the enemy distress you, when you begin to be aroused to separate attacks of temptation to do wrong, when you say in your heart, 'What shall we do?', Elisha's words will supply your answer, *Do not be afraid, for there are more on our side than on theirs.*[20] He shall pray, 'Lord, open the eyes of your handmaid, that she may see,' and then, when your eyes have been opened, you will see a fiery chariot like Elijah's, waiting to carry you to heaven.[21] Then you will joyfully sing, *Our soul has been snatched like a sparrow from the snare of the fowlers; the snare is broken and we have been set free.*[22]

So long as we are held down by this frail body so long as we have our treasure in earthen vessels,[23] so long as the flesh lusts against the spirit and the spirit against the flesh,[24] there can be no sure victory. *Our adversary the devil goes about like a roaring lion, seeking something to devour*[25] . . . *you have placed the darkness and night has been created, when all the beasts of the forest prowl around. The lion cubs roar after their prey and seek their food from God.*[26] The devil does not look for unbelievers, for those outsiders whose flesh the Assyrian king roasted in the furnace.[27] It is the Church of Christ that he *makes haste to spoil.*[28] According to Habbakuk, *his food is of the choicest.*[29] He desires to overthrow Job, and having devoured Judas, he seeks power to sift the [other] apostles.[30] The Saviour came not to send peace on the earth but a sword.[31] Lucifer fell, Lucifer who used to rise at dawn, and he who was bred up in a paradise of delight had the well-earned sentence passed upon him, *If you are borne on high like the eagle, I shall bring you down, says the Lord.*[32] For he had said in his heart, *I will set my throne above the stars of heaven,* and *I will be like the Most High.*[33] Therefore God says every day to the angels, as they descend the ladder that Jacob saw in his dream,[34] *I have said, you are gods and all of you are children of the Most High. But you shall die like men and fall like one of the princes.*[35] The devil fell first, and since *God stands in the congregation of the gods and judges among the gods,*[36] the Apostle[37] writes to those who cease to be gods, *When there is jealousy and rivalry among you, are you not carnal and do you not live according to human standards?*[38]

If then the Apostle, who was a chosen vessel and prepared for the gospel of Christ,[39] keeps his body in subjection, on account of the pricks of the flesh and the attractions of vice, lest while preaching to others, he may himself be found to be a fraud,[40] and yet, for all that, sees another law in his members warring against the law of his mind and bringing him into captivity to the law of sin;[41] if after nakedness, fasting, hunger, imprisonment, scourging and other torments, he turns back to himself and cries, *O wretched man that I am, who shall deliver me from the body of this death?*[42] do you think that you are safe? Take care, I beg you, that God does not say of you someday, *The virgin of Israel is fallen and there is no one to raise her up.*[43] I will say it boldly, that though God can do all things, he cannot raise up a virgin once she has fallen. He may indeed relieve someone defiled from the penalty of her sin but he will not give her a crown. Let us fear lest in us too the prophecy will be fulfilled, *Even good virgins shall fail,*[44] because there are also bad virgins. *The man who looks on a woman to lust after her*, says the Lord, *is already an adulterer in his heart.*[45] Virginity, then, may be lost even by a thought. The virgins who are bad are those who are virgins in the flesh, not in the spirit, the foolish virgins, who having no oil, are shut out by the bridegroom.[46]

But if even real virgins, when they have other failings, are not saved by their physical virginity, what shall become of those who have prostituted the members of Christ and have changed the temple of the Holy Spirit into a brothel? They will immediately hear the words, *Come down, O virgin daughter of Babylon, sit on the ground. There is no throne for a daughter of the Chaldaeans; you shall no longer be soft and delicate. Receive the millstone, grind the flour, uncover your head, bare your legs, cross the rivers, and your shame will be uncovered and your dishonor will stand revealed.*[47] And will she come to this, after the bridal chamber of the Song of God, after the kisses of him who is to her both kinsman and spouse?[48] Yes, she of whom the prophecy once sang, *At your right hand stood the queen in a vestment of gold, shot through with varied colors,*[49] shall be made naked and the hind parts of her skirts shall be placed over her face. She shall sit by the waters of loneliness, her pitcher laid aside, and shall stretch out her legs to every passerby, and shall be polluted to the crown of her head.[50] It would have been better for her to have submitted to the yoke of marriage and to have walked in level places, rather than having aspired to loftier heights only to fall like this into the depth of hell. I pray you, do not let Zion, the faithful city, become a harlot:[51] do not let it be, where the Trinity has lodged, there demons shall dance and serpents make nests and hyenas build.[52] Let us not loose the band that binds the beast. When lust tickles the sense and the soft fire of sensual pleasure sheds its pleasing glow over us, let us immediately break forth and cry, *The Lord is my helper; I shall not fear what the flesh can do to me.*[53] When, for a little while, the inner person shows signs of wavering between vice and virtue, say, *Why are you sad, O my soul, and why do you distress me? Hope in God, since I shall confess to him that he is the health of my countenance and my God.*[54] You must never let suggestions of evil grow in you or a babel of disorder gain strength in your breast. Slay the enemy while he is small. And to avoid having a crop of weeds, nip evil in the bud. Bear in mind the warning words of the Psalmist, *Unhappy daughter of Babylon, happy shall he be who shall reward you as you have been rewarded. Happy shall he be who shall hold your little children and dash them against the stones.*[55] Because natural heat inevitably kindles sensual passion in a man, he is praised and accounted happy who, when foul suggestions arise in his mind, gives them no quarter, but dashes them instantly against the rock. *Now the rock is Christ.*[56]

How often, when I was living in the desert, in the vast solitude which, parched by the blazing heat of the sun, gives the hermits a savage dwelling place, did I imagine myself among the pleasures of Rome![57] I used to sit alone because I was filled with bitterness. I presented a disgusting sight: my filthy skin conveyed the impression of the blackness of an Ethiopian's flesh; tears and groans were my daily portion, and if ever sleep assailed me, though I struggled against it, I beat against the ground my bare bones which scarcely held together. Of my food and drink I say nothing; for even in sickness, the solitaries have nothing but cold water, and to eat one's food cooked is looked on as self-indulgence. Now, although in my fear of hell I had consigned myself to this prison, where I had no companions but scorpions and wild beasts, I often found myself amongst bevies of girls. My lips were pale and my frame chilled with fasting, yet my mind was burning with desire, and the fires of lust kept bubbling up before me when my flesh was a good as dead. Helpless, I cast myself at the feet of Jesus. I watered them with my tears, I wiped them with my hair and then I subdued my rebellious body with weeks of abstinence. I do not blush to avow my abject misery. Rather I lament that I am not now what once I was. I remember how I often cried aloud all night until the break of day and did not stop beating my breast until tranquillity returned at the Lord's chiding. I used to dread my very cell as though it knew my thoughts, and, stern and angry with myself, I used to make my way alone into the desert. Wherever I saw hollow valleys, craggy mountains, steep cliffs, there I made my oratory, there the house of correction for my unhappy flesh. There also the Lord himself is my witness when I had shed copious tears and strained my eyes towards heaven, I sometimes felt myself among angelic hosts, and for joy and gladness sang, *For the scent of your good ointments we will run after you.*[58]

Now, if these are the temptations of men who have only evil thoughts to fear, since their bodies are emaciated with fasting, how must it fare with a girl whose surroundings are those of luxury and ease? Surely, to use the Apostle's words, *She is dead while she is alive.*[59] Therefore, if experience gives me a right to advise or makes my words credible, I urge, first of all, as a most solemn warning that the Bride of Christ shun wine as if it were poison. For wine is the first weapon used by demons against young people. Greed does not shake nor pride puff up nor ambition infatuate as much as this. Other vices we easily escape, but this enemy is shut up within us, and wherever we go, we carry him with us. Wine and youth between them kindle the fire of sensual pleasure. Why do we throw oil on the flame? Why do we add fresh fuel to a miserable body which is already ablaze? Paul, it is true, says to Timothy, *Do not drink water, but use a little wine for the sake of your stomach and your frequent slight indispositions.*[60] But notice the reasons for which the permission is given, to cure an aching stomach and a frequent slight indisposition; and lest we overindulge ourselves on the score of our ailments, he commands that only a little be taken. He advises more as a physician than as an apostle (though, indeed, an apostle is a spiritual physician). He evidently feared that Timothy might succumb to this weakness and might prove unequal to the constant moving to and fro involved in preaching the gospel. Besides, he remembered that he had spoken of *wine wherein is lust*[61] and had said, *It is not good for a person either to eat meat or to drink wine.*[62] Noah drank wine and became intoxicated in that primitive age after the flood, when the vine was first planted. Perhaps he did not know its power of inebriation. And to let you understand the sacramental significance of Scripture in every respect—for the Word of God is indeed a pearl and can be pierced on every side—after his drunkenness came the uncovering of his thighs and lust was joined to riotous living.[63] First came the needs of his belly and the rest immediately followed. For the people ate and drank and *arose to play.*[64] Lot, the friend of God who was saved on the mountain and was found to be the only righteous man out of many thousands of people, was made drunk by his daughters. And although they may have acted as they did more from a desire for children than from love of sinful pleasure—for the human race seemed in danger of extinction—yet they were well aware that the righteous man would not abet their plan unless intoxicated. In fact, he did not know what he was doing, and his sin was not wilful. Still his error was a grave one, for it made him the father of Moab and Ammon,[65] Israel's enemies, of whom it is said, Even to the fourteenth generation they shall not enter into the community of the Lord for ever.[66]

When Elijah, in his flight from Jezebel, lay weary and desolate beneath the oak tree, an angel came and aroused him and said to him, '*Arise and eat*', *and he looked and behold, there was a scone and a vessel of water at his head.*[67] Had God willed it, might he not have sent his prophet spiced wine and food flavored with olive oil and meat which had been tenderized by beating? When Elisha invited the sons of the prophets to dinner, he gave them wild herbs to eat. Then he heard a racket coming from all the diners shouting together, 'Man of God, there is death in the pot'. He did not storm at the cooks—for he was not accustomed to sumptuous meals—but throwing flour into the pot, he sweetened the bitterness of the food.[68] With spiritual strength, as Moses had once sweetened the waters of Marah.[69] Again, when men sent to arrest the prophet were smitten with physical and mental blindness, that he might bring them without their own knowledge to Samaria, notice the food with which Elisha ordered them to be refreshed. *'Set before them bread and water,'* he said, *'that they may eat and drink and be sent back to their master'.*[70] Quite a rich meal, too, could have been brought over to Daniel from the king's table, but he preferred the mowers' lunch brought to him by Habakkuk, which, I think, was country food.[71] He was called *a man of desires*, because he would not eat the bread of desire or drink the wine of concupiscence.[72]

There are in the Scriptures countless divine answers condemning gluttony and approving simple food, but as fasting is not my present theme and an adequate discussion of it would require a treatise to itself, these few observations, of the many which the subject suggests, must suffice. By them you will understand why the first man, obeying his belly and not God, was cast down from paradise into this vale of tears,[73] and why Satan used hunger to tempt the Lord himself in the wilderness;[74] why the Apostle cries, *Food for the belly and the belly for food, but God shall destroy both it and them,*[75] and why he speaks of the self-indulgent as men *whose God is their belly.* For people invariably worship what they like best. Care must be taken, therefore, that abstinence may bring back to paradise those whom satiety once drove out.

You will tell me, perhaps, that, high-born as you are, reared in luxury and always sleeping on a soft bed, you cannot do without wine and gourmet food and would find a stricter rule of life unendurable. I can only say, 'Live by your own rule, then, since God's rule is too hard for you'. Not that the Creator and Lord of all takes pleasure in the rumbling of our intestines and the emptiness of our stomachs and a burning fever in our lungs. But there are no other means by which our chastity can be preserved. Job was dear to God and in his eyes a man of unblemished simplicity, but hear what he says about the devil: *His strength is in the loins and his force is in the navel.*[76]

For the sake of decency the names have been changed, but the reproductive organs of the two sexes are meant. Thus, the descendant of David who, according to the promise, is to sit upon his throne, is said to come from his loins,[77] and the seventy-five souls descended from Jacob who entered Egypt are said to come out of his thigh.[78] So also when his thigh shrank after the Lord had wrestled with him,[79] he ceased to beget children. Again, the Israelites are told to celebrate the passover with their loins girded and mortified.[80] God says to Job, *Gird up your loins like a man.*[81] John wears a leathern girdle.[82] The apostles must gird their loins to carry the lamps of the gospel.[83] When Ezekiel tells us how Jerusalem is found in the plain of wandering, covered with blood, he uses the words, *Your umbilical cord has not been cut.*[84] In his assaults on men, therefore, the devil's strength is in the loins; in his attacks on women his force is in the navel.

Do you want proof of my assertions? Take examples. Samson was braver than a lion and tougher than a rock. Alone and unprotected he pursued a thousand armed men, and yet in Delilah's embrace, his resolution melted away.[85] David was a man after God's own heart and his lips had often sung of the Holy One, the future Christ. And yet, as he walked on his housetop, he was fascinated by Bathsheba's nakedness and added murder to adultery.[86] Notice here how a man cannot use his eyes without danger even in his own house. Then, repenting, he says to the Lord, *Against you alone have I sinned and done this evil in your sight.*[87] Being a king, he feared no one else. So, too, with Solomon. Wisdom used him to sing her praise, and he treated of all plants *from the cedar tree that is in Lebanon to the hyssop that springs out of the wall.*[88,89] Yet he withdrew from God because he was a lover of women.[90] And as if to show that near relationship is no safeguard, Amnon burned with illicit passion for his sister Tamar.[91]

I cannot bring myself to speak of the many virgins who daily fail and are lost to the bosom of the Church, their mother: stars over which the proud foe sets up his throne,[92] and rocks hollowed by the serpent that he may dwell in the fissures. You may see many women dressed as widows before they have married, who try to conceal their miserable fall by adopting a deceitful way of dressing. Unless they are betrayed by swelling wombs or by the crying of their babies, they walk abroad with tripping feet and heads in the air. Some go so far as to take potions to ensure barrenness, and thus murder human beings almost before their conception. Some, when they find themselves pregnant through their sin, use drugs to procure an abortion, and when (as often happens) they die with their offspring, they enter the lower world, laden with the guilt not only of adultery against Christ, but also of suicide and child murder. Yet these are the ones who say, *To the pure all things are pure.*[93] My conscience is guide enough for me. A pure heart is what God looks for. Why should I abstain from food which God has created to be used?' And when they want to appear agreeable and entertaining, they first drench themselves with wine and then, joining the grossest profanity to intoxication, they say, 'Far be it from me to abstain from the blood of Christ'. When they see another woman looking pale and sad, they call her a 'wretch' or a 'Manichaean',[94] quite logically in fact, for by their principles, fasting involves heresy. When they go out, they do their best to attract notice and, with nods and winks, encourage troops of young men to follow them. To each and all of them the prophet's words apply: *You have a whore's face; you refuse to be ashamed.*[95] Their robes have only a narrow purple stripe,[96] it is true; and their heads are bound somewhat loosely, to leave the hair flowing. Their slippers are cheap and little capes flutter over their shoulders. Narrow sleeves cling to their arms, and they walk in a mincing manner, with bent knees. This is the extent of their virginity. Let them have their own admirers of this type and let them perish for a higher price under the pretext of their virginity. To virgins such as these I prefer to be displeasing. I am ashamed to speak of it—it is so shocking—but it is true. How comes this plague of the *agapetae* to be in the Church?[97] Whence come these unwedded wives, this new race of concubines, these women who are harlots though they cling to a single partner? They and their partners occupy the same house, the same bedroom, and often the same bed—and then they call us suspicious, if we believe something is wrong. A brother leaves his virgin sister; a virgin despises her bachelor brother and seeks a brother in a stranger; but though they both pretend to have the same intention, namely to seek spiritual consolation from people not related to them, their real aim is to have sexual intercourse. It is on people of this kind whom God in the book of the Proverbs of Solomon pours his reproaches, saying, *Who will bind fire to his bosom and not set his clothes on fire? Or who will walk on coals of fire and not burn his feet?*[98]

We cast out therefore and banish from our sight those who wish only to seem and not be virgins. Hereafter, all my speech is directed towards you. Just as it is your fate to be the first virgin of noble birth in the city of Rome, so must you labor the more diligently, in order not to lack both the good things of the present day and the good things to come. You have learned at any rate, from the example of your own family, about the troubles of wedded life and the uncertainty of marriage. Your sister Blesilla, more advanced in age than you but less advanced in her vow, has become a widow in the seventh month after taking a husband. O how unhappy is our human condition, ignorant of what is to come! She has lost both the crown of virginity and the pleasure of marriage. Although the second degree of chastity is still hers as a widow, can you imagine her bearing her continual crosses, moment by moment, when every day she sees in her sister what she herself has lost, and finds it more difficult [than you] to be without the pleasure of marriage, having experienced it, and yet to receive a lesser reward for her present continence? Let her nevertheless feel secure and full of joy. The fruit which is an hundredfold and the fruit which is sixtyfold both spring from the same seed, which is chastity.[99]

I do not want you to associate with married women. I do not want you to visit the houses of the nobility. I do not want you to see frequently the things which you spurned in desiring to be a virgin. What if silly little women are in the habit of priding themselves on the fact that their husbands are judges and occupy positions of some dignity, if an eager crowd of visitors collects at the door of the Emperor's wife? Why do you, the bride of God, hurry to visit the wife of a mere human being? Learn in this respect a holy pride. Know that you are better than they. I want you not only to avoid social intercourse with those women, who are puffed up by their husbands' honors, who are hedged in by troops of eunuchs, and are clad in robes delicately worked with metallic threads, but also to flee from those who are widows. It is not that they ought to have desired the death of their husbands, but that, their husbands having died, they have not gladly seized the opportunity for continence. As it is, they have only changed their clothes; their former ambition remains unchanged. A row of eunuchs walks in front of their enclosed litters, their cheeks are ruddy and their skin is stretched over such well-nourished flesh that you would think they had not lost husbands, but were looking for them. Their houses are full of flatterers and full of guests. Even the clergy, who ought to be held in authority and respect, kiss their patronesses on the forehead and, putting out their hands in such a way that you would think if you did not know otherwise, that they wanted to confer a blessing, accept fees for their visits. In the meantime, the women, seeing that the priests cannot manage without their protection, are lifted up with pride, and because, having experienced the domination of marriage, they prefer the freedom of widowhood, they are called chaste women and nuns, and, after a dubious dinner, they fall asleep to dream of the apostles.[100]

Let your companions be women who, as you see for yourself, are thin from fasting, whose faces are pale, whose worth is proved by their age and conduct, who daily sing in their hearts, *Where do you feed your flock and where do you bring it to rest at noon?*,[101] and who say with real earnestness, *I desire to be released and to be with Christ.*[102] Be subject to your parents; imitate your Bridegroom. Let your outings be rare, and let the aid of the martyrs be sought in your own room.[103] You will never need a pretext for going out if you always go out when it is necessary. Your food should be moderate in quantity and your belly should never be over-full. Indeed very many women, while temperate with wine, are intemperate with food. When you rise at night to pray, let your breath be that of an empty and not of an over-laden stomach. Read often and learn as much as you can. Let sleep steal over you as you hold the book and let the holy page catch your head as it falls. Let fasting be a daily occurrence and avoid satiety in your refreshment. It is unprofitable to put up with an empty stomach if, in two or three days' time, the fast is to be compensated for by eating your fill. When clogged, the mind immediately grows sluggish, and when the ground is watered, it puts up thorns of lust. If you feel the outward man sighing for the flower of youth and if, as you lie on your couch after a meal, you are excited by an alluring train of sexual desires, then seize the shield of faith, for it alone can quench the fiery darts of the devil.[104] *They are all adulterers*, says the prophet, *Their hearts are like an oven*.[105] But you, keep close to the footsteps of Christ, and intent upon his words,say, *Did not our heart burn within us on the road, while Jesus opened the Scriptures to us?*,[106] and again, *Your word is ablaze and your servant loves it*.[107] It is hard for the human soul to avoid loving something, and our mind must necessarily yield to affection of one kind or another. The love of the flesh is overcome by the love of the spirit. Desire is quenched by desire. What is taken from the one increases the other. Therefore, as you lie on your couch, say again and again, *On my bed by night have I sought him, whom my soul loves*.[108] *Mortify your members on earth*, says the Apostle.[109] Because he himself did so, he could afterwards say with confidence, *I live, yet not I , but Christ, lives in me*.[110] Someone who mortifies his members and feels he is walking in a vain show[111] is not afraid to say, *I have become like a wineskin in the frost*.[112] Whatever there was in me of the moisture of lust has been dried out of me, and again, *My knees are weak through fasting; I have forgotten to eat my bread. By reason off the voice of my groaning my bones cleave to my flesh*.[113]

Be like the grasshopper at night.[114] Wash your bed every night and water your couch with your tears.[115] Watch and be like the sparrow in your solitude.[116] Sing with the spirit and sing with the understanding,[117] too, the psalm, *Bless the Lord, O my soul; and do not forget all his benefits. He forgives all your iniquities, he heals all your infirmities; and redeems your life from destruction*.[118] Can we, any of us, honestly make his words our own, *I have eaten ashes like bread and mixed my drink with my tears?*[119] Yet should I not weep and groan when the serpent again invites me to eat forbidden food? when, after ejecting me from the paradise of virginity, he wishes to clothe me with the tunics of skins which Elijah, on his return to paradise, cast down behind him on earth?[120] What have I to do with sensual pleasures which soon come. What have I to do with the sweet but deadly song of the sirens? I want you not to submit to that sentence, whereby condemnation is brought upon humankind: '*In pain and sorrow, woman, shall you bear children*—say to yourself, 'That is not my law—or its continuation, *and your yearning shall be for your husband.*[121] Let yearning for her husband belong to the woman who has not Christ for her spouse. When at the least God says, *You shall die,*[122] that is the end of the union: say to yourself, 'My purpose is to be without sex. Let those who are wives keep their own time and status. For me, virginity is consecrated in the persons of Mary and Christ.'

Someone may say, 'Do you dare detract from wedlock, which is a state blessed by the Lord?' I do detract from wedlock when I set virginity before it. No one compares a bad thing with a good. Married women are to be congratulated for coming next after virgins. *Increase*, says God, *and multiply and replenish the earth.*[123] Anyone who wants to replenish the earth may increase and multiply if he wishes, but the marching column to which you belong is not on earth, but in heaven. The command to increase and multiply first finds fulfillment after the expulsion from paradise, after the nakedness and the fig-leaves, which betoken sexual passion. Let marry and be given in marriage the person who eats his bread in the sweat of his brow, whose land produces figs and thistles,[124] and whose crops are choked with briars. My seed produces fruit a hundredfold. *Not everyone can receive the word of God, but only those to whom it is given.*[125] Some people may be eunuchs from necessity; I am one by free will.[126] *There is a time to embrace and a time to withdraw the hands from the embrace. There is a time to cast away stones and a time to gather stones together.*[127] Now that God has raised up children from Abraham out of the hard stones of the Gentiles,[128] they begin to be *holy stones rolling on the earth.*[129] They pass through the world's whirlwinds and roll on in God's chariot on rapid wheels. Let people stitch coats for themselves who have lost the coat woven from the top throughout,[130] who delight in the cries of infants who, as soon as they see the light, lament that they were born. In paradise Eve was a virgin, and it was only after the coats of skins that she began her married life. Now, paradise is your home, too. Keep your birthright therefore and say, *Return to your rest, O my soul*[131]. To show that virginity is natural, while wedlock only follows guilt, what is born of wedlock is virgin flesh, and it gives back in fruit what in root it has lost. *There shall come forth a rod out of the root of Jesse and a flower shall arise from the root.*[132] The rod is the Lord's mother—simple, pure, unsullied, drawing no germ of life from outside herself, but fruitful in singleness, like God himself. The flower of the rod is Christ, who says of himself, *I am the flower of the field and the lily of the valley*[133]. In another place he is foretold to be *a stone cut out of the mountain without hands,*[134] a figure by which the prophet signifies that he is to be born a virgin of a virgin. For the hands here are a figure of wedlock, as in the passage, *His left hand is under my head and his right hand embraces me.*[135] This agrees, too, with the interpretation that unclean animals were led into Noah's ark in Pairs, while of the clean an uneven number were taken.[136] Similarly, that Moses and Joshua were ordered to enter on holy ground in their bare feet, whereas the disciples were appointed to preach the gospel unburdened by sandals or leather shoe-laces, and also that the soldiers, after Jesus' clothing had been distributed by lot, found no boots they could take away.[137] For the Lord could not himself possess what he had forbidden his servants to possess.

I praise wedlock, I praise marriage, but only because they produce virgins for me. I gather the rose from the thorns, the gold from the earth, the pearl from the shell. *Does the ploughman plough all day to sow?*[138] Shall he not also enjoy the fruit of his labor? Wedlock is more honored, when what is born of it is more loved. Why, mother, do you envy your daughter? She has been nourished with your milk, she has been brought forth from your womb, and she has grown up at your bosom. Your watchful religious faith has kept her a virgin. Are you angry with her because she wishes to be the wife not of a soldier, but of a king? She has conferred a great benefit on you; you now begin to be the mother-in-law of God. *Concerning virgins*, says the Apostle, *I have no commandment from the Lord.*[139] Why was this? Because his own virginity was due, not to a command, but to his free choice. Those people who claim that he had a wife should not be listened to, since when he is discussing continence and commending perpetual chastity, he uses the words, *I wish that all men were as I am*, and farther on, *I say, therefore, to the unmarried and the widowed: 'It is good for them if they remain just as I am'*,[140] and in another place, *Have we no right to be accompanied by a wife, as are the rest of the apostles?*[141] Why then has he no commandment from the Lord concerning virginity? Because what is freely offered is worth more than what is extorted by force, and to command virginity would have been to abrogate wedlock. It would have been a hard enactment to compel opposition to nature and to extort the angelic life; and not only that, it would have been to condemn what is a divine ordinance.

The old law had a different ideal of blessedness. There it is said, *Blessed is he who has seed in Zion and a household in Jerusalem*[142], and *Cursed is the barren woman who does not bear children*,[143] and *Your children shall be like olive-shoots round about your table*.[144] Riches too are promised to the faithful and we are told that *there was not one feeble person among their tribes*.[145] But now it is said, *Do not say, behold I am a dry tree*,[146] for instead of sons and daughters, you have a place for ever in heaven. Now the poor are blessed, now Lazarus is set before Dives in purple.[147] Now a weak person is counted as strong. But in those days the world was still unpeopled: accordingly, to pass over instances of childlessness meant only to serve as types, only those who could boast of children were considered happy. It was for this reason that Abraham in his old age married Keturah,[148] that Leah hired Jacob with her son's mandrakes,[149,150] and that the beautiful Rachel—a type of the Church—complained of the closing of her womb.[151] But gradually the crop grew up and then the reaper was sent forth with this sickle. Elijah lived a virgin life, as did Elisha and many of the sons of the prophets.[152] To Jeremiah came the command, *Do not take a wife*.[153] He had been sanctified in his mother's womb,[154] and was forbidden to take a wife because the captivity was near. The Apostle gives the

same advice in different words, *I think that it is good on account
of the present distress, namely, that it is good for a man to remain
has he is.*[155] What is this distress which does away with the joys
of wedlock? The Apostle tells us in a later verse, *The time is short.
From now on even those who have wives should be as though
they had not.*[156] Nebuchadnezzar is close by. *The lion is stirring
from his lair.*[157] What good will marriage be to me if it ends in
slavery to the haughtiest of kings? What good will little ones be
to me, if their lot is to be that which the prophet sadly describes:
*The tongue of the sucking child clings to the roof of its mouth in
thirst; the young children asked for bread and there was no one
to break it for them.*[158] In those days, as I have said, the virtue of
continence was found only in men; Eve continued to give birth in
pain. But now that a virgin has conceived in her womb[159] and has
borne to us a child of whom the prophet says, *The government
shall be upon his shoulder, and his name shall be the mighty God,
the everlasting Father,*[160] the chain of the curse is broken. Death
came through Eve, but life has come through Mary. Thus the gift
of virginity has been very richly bestowed on women, in that it
had its beginning from a woman. As soon as the Son of God set
foot on the earth, he formed a new household for himself there,
so that, as he was adored by angels in heaven, angels might serve
him also on earth. Then chaste Judith once more cut off the head
of Holofernes.[161] Then Haman—whose name means iniquity—
was once more burned in a fire of his own kindling.[162] Then
James and John forsook father and net and ship and followed the
Saviour, abandoning ties of kinship, bonds of secular life, and the
care of their homes. Then were heard the words; *Let the person
who chooses to come after me deny himself, take up his cross
and follow me.*[163] No soldier goes to battle with a wife. When a
disciple wanted to bury his father, the Lord forbade it, and said,
*Foxes have holes and the birds of heaven have nests, but the Son
of Man has nowhere to lay his head.*[164] So you must not complain
if you are lodged in cramped quarters. *The man who is without
a wife cares for the things that belong to the Lord and how he
may please the Lord; but the married man cares for the things
that are of this world and how he may please his wife. There is*

the difference also between a wife and a virgin. The unmarried woman cares for the things of the Lord, that she may be holy both in body and in spirit; but the married woman cares for the things of this world and how she may please her husband.[165]

What great inconveniences are involved in wedlock and how many anxieties encompass it I have, I think, described briefly in my treatise—published against Helvidius—on the perpetual virginity of blessed Mary.[166] It would be tedious to go over the same ground now, and anyone who pleases may draw that fountain. But lest I seem wholly to have passed over the matter, I will say now simply that the Apostle bids us pray without ceasing,[167] and that someone in the married state who gives his wife her due[168] cannot so pray. Either we pray always and are virgins, or we cease to pray to fulfil the claims of marriage. Still he says, *If a virgin marries, she has not sinned. Nevertheless she will have trouble of this kind in her flesh.*[169] At the outset I promised that I should say little or nothing of the embarrassments of wedlock, and now I give you notice to the same effect. If you want to know how many vexations a virgin is free of and how many a wife is fettered by, you should read Tertullian, 'To a Philosophic Friend,'[170] and his other treatises on virginity, the blessed Cyprian's noble volume, the writings of Pope Damascus in prose and verse,[171] and the treatises recently written for his sister by our own Ambrose.[172] In these he has poured forth his soul in such a flood of eloquence that he has sought out, set forth, and put in order everything that bears on the praise of virgins.

We must proceed by a different path, for our purpose is not to exalt virginity, but to preserve it. To know that it is a good thing is not enough; when we have chosen it, we must guard it with jealous care. The first requires only judgement, and this we share with many; the second calls for toil, and few compete with us in it. *The person who perseveres to the end shall be saved,*[173] and *Many are called, but few chosen.*[174] Therefore I entreat you, before God and Jesus Christ and his chosen angels, so to guard what you have received, not readily exposing to the public gaze the vessels of the Lord's temple (which only the priests are by right allowed to see), that no profane person may look upon God's sanctuary.

Uzzah, when he touched the ark, which it was not lawful to touch, was suddenly struck down by death,[175] and assuredly no gold or silver vessel was ever so dear to God as is the temple of a virgin's body. The shadow went before, but now the reality is come. You may indeed speak in all simplicity, and from motives of amiability may treat even strangers with courtesy, but unchaste eyes see nothing aright. They fail to appreciate the beauty of the soul and value only that of the body. Hezekiah showed God's treasure to the Assyrians,[176] who ought never to have seen what they were sure to covet. The consequence was that Judaea was ravaged by continual wars, and that the very first things carried away to Babylon were these same vessels of the Lord. We find Belshazzar at his feast and among his concubines drinking out of these sacred cups[177] —vice always glories in defiling what is noble.

Never incline your ear to words of mischief. Men often say an improper word to try a virgin's steadfastness, to see if she hears it with pleasure, and if she is ready to unbend at every silly joke. Such persons applaud whatever you affirm and deny whatever you deny; they speak of you as, not only holy but, accomplished, and say that in you there is no guile. 'Behold a true handmaid of Christ,' they say. 'Behold her complete singleness of heart. She is not like that uncouth, ill-bred country bumpkin of frightful appearance, who perhaps for that reason could not find a husband.' Led by our sinful nature, we readily favor those who flatter us; and although we reply that we are unworthy, and a warm blush suffuses our cheeks, nevertheless our inmost heart rejoices at our own praise.

Like the ark of the covenant, Christ's spouse should be overlaid with gold within and without.[178] She should be the guardian of the law of the Lord. Just as the ark contained nothing but the tables of the covenant,[179] so in you there should be no thought of anything that is outside. The Lord wishes to sit on this mercy-seat—your thoughts—as on the cherubim. He sends his disciples so that they may loose you from worldly cares, as they loosed the colt, the foal of an ass, in order that you may leave the bricks and straw of Egypt, follow Moses into the wilderness, and enter the promised land.[180] Let no one forbid you to do this not your mother nor your sister nor your kinswoman nor your brother. The Lord needs you.[181] If they want to hinder you, let them fear the scourges which fell upon Pharaoh who, because he would not allow the people of God to depart to worship Him, suffered those things which are written in the Scriptures.[182] Jesus entering into the temple cast out everything which did not belong in the temple.[183] God is jealous and will not allow the father's house to be made into a robbers' den.[184] Moreover, where money is counted, where doves are sold, where simplicity is stifled, where, that is, a virgin's breast glows with the cares of this world, the veil of the temple is immediately rent,[185] and the Bridegroom rises in anger, saying, *Your house shall be left desolate*.[186] Read the Gospel and see how Mary, sitting at the feet of the Lord, is preferred to the zealous Martha. In her eagerness to be hospitable, Martha was preparing a meal for the Lord and his disciples; yet Jesus said to her, *Martha, Martha, you are worried and distressed about many things, but few things, or one, are necessary. Mary has chosen the good part, which shall not be taken away from her*[187]. Be like Mary, then. Prefer spiritual knowledge to bodily food. Leave it t o your sisters to run to and fro and to seek how they may receive Christ as their guest. Having once and for all flung away the burden of the world, sit at the Lord's feet and say, *I have found him for whom my soul was seeking; I will hold him and I will not let him go*.[188] And he will reply, *My dove, my perfect one is my only one; she is the only one of her mother, the chosen one of her who bore her, that is, the heavenly Jerusalem*.[189] Always let the privacy of your bedroom keep guard over you, always let your Bridegroom disport himself with you within it.[190] You pray, you speak to him there and you read there. There he speaks to you and, when sleep assails you, he will come behind the wall and put his hand through an opening and will touch your belly. You will arise, trembling, and will say, *I am wounded by love*.[191] *My sister, my betrothed, is a garden enclosed, a fountain sealed*.[192]

Be careful not to leave your home and do not wish to see the daughters of a foreign country when you have the patriarchs for your brothers and rejoice in Israel as your father. Dinah went out and was corrupted.[193] I do not want you to search for your

Bridegroom in the thoroughfares or to go around the nooks and crannies of the city. For though you may say, *I will rise and walk around in the city, in the market-place and in the main streets, and search for him whom my soul loves*, and you may enquire, *Have you seen him whom my soul loves?*,[194] no one will condescend to answer you. The Bridegroom cannot be found in the streets. *Strait and narrow is the way that leads to life.*[195] Then there follows [in the Song of Songs], *I have sought him and I have not found him; I have called him and he has not responded to my call.*[196] If only failure to find him were all! You will be wounded, you will be stripped naked and you will groan, as you relate, *The watchmen who patrol the city found me; they struck me; they wounded me; they took my cloak away from me.*[197] Now if someone who could say, *I am asleep, but my heart is awake,*[198] and *My brother is a bunch of myrrh for me; he shall remain all night between my breasts,*[199] if someone who could say such things suffered so much when she went out from her house, what will happen to us, who are still young girls, and who still remain outside, when the bride goes in with the Bridegroom? Jesus is jealous. He does not want your face to be seen by others. Although you may make excuses and say, 'I have covered my face closely with a veil and have sought you and have said to you, *Tell me, you whom my soul loves, where you feed your flock, where you sleep at mid-day, lest I may ever become as one covered with a veil in the presence of the flocks of your companions;*[200] he will be angry and will swell with rage and will say, *If you do not know yourself, fairest of women, go forth in the steps of my flocks and feed your goats in the shepherds' tents.*[201] *You may be fair and of all faces yours maybe the dearest to the Bridegroom.* Yet, unless you know yourself and keep your heart with utmost diligence,[202] unless also you avoid the eyes of young men, you will be turned out of my bride-chamber to feed the goats, which shall be set on the left hand'.[203]

These things being so, my Eustochium, daughter, lady, fellow-servant, sister—these names refer, the first to your age, the second to your rank, the third to your religious vocation, the last to the place you hold in my affection—hear the words of Isaiah, *My people, enter into your bedrooms and shut your doors; hide yourself for a brief moment, until the anger of the Lord has passed over.*[204] Let foolish virgins stray outside; you be indoors with your Bridegroom, because if you shut your door and, in accordance with the precept of the Gospel,[205] pray to your Father in secret, he will come and knock and say, *Behold, I stand at the door and knock. If anyone will open it to me, I will enter and dine with him and he with me.*[206] Then at once you will eagerly reply, 'It is the voice of my kinsman, who knocks: open the door to me, my sisters, my nearest and dearest, my dove, my perfect one'. It is impossible that you should refuse and say, *I have taken off my tunic; how shall I put it on? I have washed my feet; how shall I defile them?*[207] Get up at once and open the door. Otherwise he may pass on as you linger, and you may have mournfully to say, *I opened the door to my kinsman, but my kinsman has passed by.*[208] Why do the doors of your heart need to be closed to the Bridegroom? Let them be open to Christ, but closed to the devil, according to the saying, *If the spirit of him who has power rises up against you, do not leave your place.*[209] Daniel, in that upper room to which he withdrew when he could no longer continue below, had its windows open towards Jerusalem.[210] Keep your windows open, too, but only on the side where light may enter and from which you may see the city of God. Do not open those other windows, of which the prophet says, *Death has entered through our windows.*[211]

You must also take care to avoid being seized with a passion for vainglory. *How*, says Jesus, *can you believe, when you receive glory from men?*[212] See how evil a thing it is, when the person who possesses it cannot believe. Instead, let us say, *You are my glory,*[213] and *Let anyone who glories, glory in the Lord*[214], and *If I still pleased people, I should not be the servant of Christ.*[215] *Far be it from me to glory, save in the cross of my Lord Jesus Christ, through whom the world has been crucified to me and I to the world*, and finally, *In you we boast all the day long; my soul shall make her boast in the Lord.*[216] When you give alms, let God alone see you. When you fast, let your face be cheerful.[217] Let your dress be neither overly neat nor overly careless. Neither let it be so remarkable as to draw the attention of passers-by, and to make people point their fingers at you. Is a brother dead? Has the body of a sister to be carried to burial? Take care lest while you perform these offices, you yourself die. Do not wish to seem very devout or more humble than need be, lest you seek glory by shunning it. Many who screen their poverty, charity and fasting from public view want to excite admiration by their very disdain of it, and strangely look for praise while they profess to keep out of its way. From the other disturbing influences which make people rejoice, despond, hope, and fear, I find many free, but this is a defect which few are without and he is best, whose character, like a beautiful body, is spotted with only very rare disfigurements and blemishes. I do not think it necessary to warn you against boasting of your riches, or against priding yourself on your birth or against setting yourself up as superior to others. I know your humility; I know that you can say with sincerity, *Lord, I am not haughty nor do my eyes gaze proudly.*[218] I know that in your case, as in your mother's, the pride through which the devil fell has no place in the depths of your being. It would be a waste of time to write to you about it, for there is no greater folly than to teach a pupil what he already knows. But now that you have despised the boastfulness of the world, do not let the fact inspire you with new boastfulness. Do not harbor the secret thought that, having ceased to court attention in garments of gold, you may begin to do so in mean attire. And when you come into a room full of brothers and sisters, do not sit in too low a place or plead that you are unworthy of a footstool. Do not deliberately lower your voice, as though worn out with fasting; or, leaning on the shoulder of another, mimic the tottering gait of someone who is faint. Some women, it is true, disfigure their faces that they may appear unto men to fast.[219] As soon as they catch sight of anyone, they groan and look down; they cover up their faces, except for one eye, which they keep free to see with. Their dress is somber, their belts are made of sackcloth, their hands and feet are dirty; only their stomachs—which cannot be seen—are hot with food. Of these the psalm is sung daily, *God has scattered the bones of men who please themselves.*[220] Others change their clothes and assume the appearance of men, being ashamed of being what they were born to be—women. They cut off their hair and shamelessly set themselves up to look like eunuchs. Some clothe themselves in goat's hair and shamelessly set themselves up to look like eunuchs. Some clothe themselves in goat's hair and, putting on hoods so they may return to their childhood, make themselves look like night-owls and horned-owls.

But I want to discuss not only women. Shun men also, when you see them loaded with chains and wearing their hair long like women, contrary to the Apostle's precept,[221] not to mention beards like those of goats, black cloaks, and bare feet braving the cold. All these things are tokens of the devil.[222] Such were Antimus, over whom Rome groaned some time ago, and Sophronius more recently. Such persons, when they have once gained admission to the houses of the nobility and have deceived *silly little women laden with sins, always learning and never arriving at knowledge of the truth,*[223] assume a gloomy appearance and pretend to undertake long fasts, whereas at night, they feast in secret. Shame forbids me to say more, for my language might appear more like invective than admonition. There are others—I speak those of my own order—who seek the priesthood and the diaconate simply to be able to see women with less restraint. Such men think of nothing but their clothing. They use perfumes freely and see that there are no creases in their leather shoes. Their curly hair shows traces of the tongs; their fingers glisten with rings; they walk on tiptoe across a damp road to avoid splashing their feet. When you see men acting this way, think of them as bridegrooms rather than as clergy. Certain persons have devoted the whole of their energies and life to the single object of knowing the names, houses, and characters of married ladies. I will here briefly and cursorily describe someone who is at the head of this profession, that from the master's portrait you may more easily recognize his disciples. He rises and goes forth with the sun. The order of his visits is arranged; he seeks the shortest routes and importunately forces his way almost into the bedrooms of ladies while they are still asleep. If he sees a pillow or an elegant tablecloth or some article of domestic furniture, he praises it, admires it, takes it into his hand, and complaining that he lacks such a thing himself, not so much requests as extorts it from its owner, because each and every woman [he visits] is afraid to offend the news-carrier of the city. Chastity and fasting are alike distasteful to him. For lunch a plump bird with a savoury smell—a crane, commonly called a 'cheeper'—meets with his approval. He changes his horses every hour, and they are so sleek and spirited that you would take him for a brother of the Thracian king.[224]

Many are the stratagems which the wily enemy employs against us. The serpent was wiser than all the beasts which the Lord God had made upon earth.[225] Then the Apostle says, *We are not ignorant of his devices.*[226] Neither an affected shabbiness nor a stylish smartness becomes a Christian. If there is anything of which you are ignorant, if you have any doubt about the Scriptures, ask someone whose life commends him, whose age places him above suspicion, whose reputation does not belie him and who can say, *I have espoused you to one husband, to present you as a chaste virgin to Christ*[227] Or if there is no one like this, who can explain things, it is better to be safe but ignorant than to expose yourself to danger in learning. Remember that you walk in the midst of snares, and that many virgins of long-standing and of a chastity never called into question, have on the very threshold of death let their crowns fall from their hands.

If any of your handmaids share your purpose, do not set yourself against them or pride yourself because you are their mistress. You have all chosen the same Bridegroom. You sing psalms to Christ at the same time; you receive his Body at the same time. Why then should there be a different table for them?[228] Let others, too, receive the challenge. Let the office of virgin be an invitation to the rest. If you find one of them weak in the faith, be attentive to her, comfort her, caress her, and make her chastity your treasure. But if a girl pretends to have a vocation because she wants to escape from service, read aloud to her the words of the Apostle, *It is better to marry than to burn.*[229]

Shun like the plague those women, whether virgins or widows, who go from house to house calling on married women from idle curiosity, and who display an unblushing effrontery like that of a parasite on the stage. For *evil communications corrupt good manners,*[230] and women like this care for nothing but their bellies and what is nearest to their bellies. They will often exhort you this way, saying, 'My pet, make the best of your advantages and live while you are alive,' and 'Surely you are not laying up money for your children'. Given to wine and wantonness, they instil all kinds of evil and induce stern minds to indulge in soft pleasures, and 'when they have begun to run riot against Christ, they wish to marry and incur damnation, because they have rejected their original pledge'.[231]

Do not seek to appear overly eloquent or to trifle with verse or to amuse yourself with lyric songs. And do not, from affectation, follow the feeble taste of married ladies, who now clenching their teeth together, now keeping their lips wide apart, speak with a lisp and purposely clip their words, thinking that anything natural is a sign of rusticity. Therefore an adultery of the tongue is what pleases them. For *What have light and darkness in common? And what agreement is there between Christ and Belial?*[232] How can Horace go with the psalter, Vergil with the Gospels, Cicero with the Apostle?[233] Is not a brother made to stumble if he sees you reclining at table in an idol's temple? Although *To the pure all things are pure*[234] and *Nothing is to be refused, which is received with thanksgiving,*[235] still we ought not to drink the cup of Christ and, at the same time, the cup of devils. I will tell you the story of my own unhappy experience.

Many years ago, when, for the kingdom of heaven's sake, I had cut myself off from my home, my parents, my sister, my relatives, and—still more difficult than this—from the exquisite food to which I had been accustomed, and when I was on my way to Jerusalem to wage my warfare, I still could not bring myself to forego the library which I had collected with great care and toil for myself at Rome. Miserable man that I was, I used to fast for the purpose of reading Cicero. After frequent nightly vigils, after tears which the recollection of my past sins brought forth from the depths of my heart, I took Plautus in my hands. If ever I returned to my right mind and began to read a prophet, his uncultivated style caused me to shrink from him with horror. Because I failed to see the light with my blinded eyes, I attributed the fault not to them but to the sun. While the old serpent was playing with me this way, about the middle of Lent a deep-seated fever attacked my body, which was worn out and totally lacked rest. It is almost incredible to say this, but it so wasted my unhappy limbs that my flesh scarcely clung to my bones. As preparations for my funeral were going on, my body gradually grew colder and the warmth of life lingered only in my throbbing breast. Suddenly I was caught up in the spirit and dragged before the tribunal of the Judge. And here the light was so bright, and those who stood around were so radiant, that I threw myself to the ground and did not dare to look up. Asked who and what I was, I replied, 'I am a Christian'. But he who was sitting there said, 'You lie; you are a follower of Cicero and not of Christ. For *Where your treasure is, there will your heart be also.*[236] Instantly I became dumb, and amid the strokes of the lash—for he had ordered me to be scourged—I was tortured still more severely by the fire of conscience, considering within myself that verse, *In the grave who shall give you thanks?*[237] Yet for all that, I began to cry and *to bewail myself,* saying, 'Have mercy upon me, O Lord: have mercy upon me'. Amid the sound of the scourges this cry still made itself heard. At last the people who were standing by fell down before the knees of him who presided and prayed that he would have pity on my youth and would give me space to repent of my error. He might still, they urged, inflict torture on me, should I ever again read pagan literature. By the stress of that awful moment, I should have been ready to make still larger promises than these. Accordingly, I swore an oath and called upon his name, saying, 'Lord, if ever again I possess worldly books, or if ever again I read them, I have denied you'. Dismissed, on taking this oath, then, I returned to the upper world, and to everyone's surprise, I opened on them eyes so drenched with tears that my distress served to convince even the incredulous; and that this was no sleep or idle dream, such as those by which we are often mocked, I call to witness the tribunal before which I lay and the judgement which I feared. May it never be my lot to fall under such an inquisition! I profess that my shoulders were bruised, that I felt the bruises long after I awoke from my sleep and that thereafter I read the holy books with an enthusiasm greater than I had previously given to human writings.

You must also avoid the sin of covetousness, not only by not seizing what belongs to others—for that is punished by the laws of the state—but also by not keeping your own property, which has now become no longer yours. *If you have not been faithful regarding the property of another*, says the Lord, *who will give you your own property?*[238] 'The property of another' is a quantity of gold or silver, while our own property is the spiritual heritage, of which it is said elsewhere, *The ransom of a man's life is his riches*[239] . . . *No one can serve two masters, for either he will hate the one and love the other; or else he will hate the one and love the other; or else he will bear with one and despise the other. You cannot serve God and Mammon*—[240] riches, that is; for in the pagan tongue of the Syrians, riches are called Mammon. The *thorns* which choke our faith are *taking thought for our life;*[241] the root of covetousness is *care for what the Gentiles seek.*[242]

'But', you will say, 'I am a girl who has been delicately nurtured and I cannot work with my hands. If I live to old age and then fall sick, who will take pity on me?' Hear Jesus speaking to the apostles, *Do not ponder in your heart over what you will eat; nor yet over what clothes you will put on your body. Is not the soul more than food and the body more than clothes? Look at the birds in the sky; for they do not sow or reap or gather food into barns; yet your heavenly Father feeds them.* Should you lack clothing, set the lilies before your eyes. Should hunger seize you, think of the words in which the poor and hungry are blessed.[243] Should pain afflict you, read, *Therefore I take pleasure in my infirmities,*[244] and *There has been given me a thorn in my flesh, a messenger of Satan, to buffet me, lest I should become proud.*[245] Rejoice in all God's judgments. Does not the psalmist say, *The daughters of Judah rejoiced in all your judgments, O Lord.*[246] Let these words be always sounding on your lips, *I came naked out of my mother's womb, and naked shall I return to it,*[247] and *We brought nothing into this world and we shall carry nothing out of it.*[248]

Nowadays you see a number of women cramming their cupboards with clothes and changing their tunics daily, but still unable to conquer the moths. A woman who is more scrupulous may wear out one dress; yet she is in rags while her chests are full.

Parchments are tinted purple, liquid gold is poured out for letter-
ing, and manuscripts are decked with jewels; and yet the naked
Christ perishes on their doorsteps. When they stretch out their
hands [to give alms], they sound a trumpet;[249] when they summon guests to a love-feast,[250] a town-crier is employed. I recently
saw the noblest of roman ladies—I suppress her name, for fear
you should think I am being satirical—with eunuchs preceding
her into the basilica of Saint Peter, distributing a penny apiece
to the poor with her own hand, so that she might be thought
more religious. While this was happening, as is quite a familiar
occurrence, an old woman, *full of years and rags*, ran forward to
receive a second coin, but when her turn came, she received not a
coin but a blow from a fist, and guilty blood flowed from her veins.

Covetousness is the root of all evil,[251] and the Apostle speaks
of it as idolatry.[252] Seek first the kingdom of God and all these
things will be added to you.[253] The Lord will not slay the soul of
a righteous man by hunger. I was young, says the psalmist, and
now I am old, and I have never seen the righteous man forsaken
or his seed begging bread.[254] Elijah was fed by the ministering
ravens.[255] The widow of Sarepta, who with her sons expected to
die the same night, went without food herself so she could feed
the prophet. He who had come to be fed then turned feeder, for
by a miracle, he filled the empty barrel.[256] The apostle Peter says,
Silver and gold have I none, but what I have I give you. In the name
of Jesus Christ get up and walk.[257] But many, though they do not
say it in words, do so in deeds: 'Faith and pity I have none, but
what I have, gold and silver, I do not give you. As we have food and
clothing, we are content with these.' Hear what Jacob asks in his
prayers: If the Lord God will be with me and preserve me on this
road by which I am travelling, and will give me bread to eat and
clothing to wear, [then shall the Lord be my God].[258] He prayed
only for what was necessary; yet twenty years later, he returned
to the land of Canaan a rich master and richer still as a father.[259]
Innumerable examples are available from the Scriptures, which
also teach us to shun covetousness.[260]

But since something is now being said on covetousness as
a side-issue—and it will be treated in a book to itself, if Christ

permits—I will relate what took place at Nitria[261] and not very many years ago. A brother, who was thrifty rather than covetous and was unaware that the Lord had been sold for thirty pieces of silver,[262] left behind him a hundred pieces of money which he had earned by weaving flax. The monks took counsel together— there were about five thousand of them living at the same place in as many separate cells—as to what they ought to do. Some said that the coins should be distributed to the poor, others that they should be given to the Church, and yet others that they should be sent back to the relatives of the dead monk. Macarius, Pambo, Isidore and the rest,[263] whom they call Fathers, at the prompting of the Holy Spirit speaking within them, decided, however, that they should be buried with their owner, with the words, *May your money go with you to perdition.*[264] Nor was each monk to think harshly of what had been done; so great a fear has assailed all monks throughout Egypt that it is now a crime to leave behind oneself a single *solidus.*

Since we have made mention of the monks and I know that you like to hear about what is holy, lend an ear to me for a few moments.

There are in Egypt three classes of monks. First, there are the cenobites,[265] whom in their pagan language they call *Sauses,*[266] but whom we can call men living in community. Secondly, there are the anchorites,[267] who live in the desert, each man by himself, and are so-called because they have withdrawn *anachorein* from human society. Thirdly, there is the class called *Remnuoth,*[268] a very inferior and little regarded type, though in my own province this is the main, if not the only, sort.[269] These live together in twos and threes, but seldom in larger numbers, and are bound by no rule but do exactly as they choose. A portion of their earnings they contribute to a common fund, out of which food is provided for all. In most cases they reside in cities and strongholds, and as if it were their skill which is holy and not their life, everything they sell is extremely dear. There are often quarrels among them, because, living as they do on their own food, they do not allow themselves to be subordinate to another. It is true that they vie with one another in their fasting, and they make what should be secret an occasion for boasting. Everything about them is affected: their sleeves are loose, their boots bulge, and their clothing is very coarse. They sigh frequently, they pay visits to virgins, they run down the secular clergy, and whenever a feast day occurs, they eat until they are sick.

Having therefore rid ourselves of these people as though they were so many pests, let us come to that more numerous sort who live together and who are called, as we have said, cenobites. Among these, the first principle of agreement is to obey the elders and to do whatever they command. They are divided into groups, by tens and by hundreds, so that every tenth man is in authority over nine others, and the hundredth man in turn has ten officers placed under him. They live separately, but their cells adjoin one another in groups. Until the ninth hour[270] there is, as it were, a cessation of business. No one may disturb another, except those whom we call deans, so that anyone troubled by wandering thoughts may receive comfort through speaking with them. After the ninth hour they meet together, psalms ring out and the Scriptures are read according to custom. When prayers are finished and everyone has sat down, the person whom they call their Father stands up among them and begins to expound the reading. While he is speaking, the silence is so profound that no one dares to look at another or to cough. The speaker's praise is in the weeping of his hearers.[271] Silently their tears roll down their cheeks but their sorrow does not break out in sobs. Yet when he begins to speak of the kingdom of Christ, of future bliss, and of the glory that is to come, you see all of them sigh gently and, lifting their eyes heavenward, say among themselves, *Who will give me wings like a dove, and I shall fly away and be at rest?*[272] After this the meeting breaks up, and each company of ten goes with its father to its own table. This they take in turns to serve, each for a week at a time. No noise is made over the food; no one talks while eating. They live on bread, beans, and greens, which are seasoned with salt and oil. Only the old men receive wine. (For them and for children there is often a meal prepared to sustain the weary old age of the one group and to save the others from premature decay.) When the meal is over, they all rise together and, having recited a hymn, return to their own huts. There each one of them talks until evening with his friends and say, 'Do you see so-and-so? How much grace he has! How silent he is! How soberly he walks! If they see someone weak, they comfort him. If they see someone fervent in his love for God, they exhort him to further devotion. And because at night, besides the public prayers, each man keeps vigil in his own sleeping-quarters, they go round the cells, one by one, and listening intently to them, carefully ascertain what the occupants are doing. If they find that a man is slothful, they do not scold him, but pretending that they do not know, they visit him more frequently and at first exhort him rather than compel him to pray more. A task is allotted for each day, and when this has been given to the dean, he takes it to the steward. The latter, once a month, returns an accurate account to the father of all the monks in fear and trembling. He also tastes the food after it has been prepared, and as no one is allowed to say, 'I have no tunic or blanket or bed of woven rushes,' he arranges that no one need ask for or go without what he needs. If a monk falls ill, he is moved to more spacious quarters and there so attentively nursed by the old men that he seeks neither the pleasures of city-life nor the affection of a mother. Every Sunday they devote a great deal of time to prayer and reading; indeed once they have finished their small tasks, they do this all the time. Every day they learn a portion of the Scriptures by heart. They keep the same fasts all year round, with the exception of Lent, in which alone they are allowed to live more strictly. At Pentecost they exchange their evening meal for a mid-day meal, in order both to satisfy the tradition of the Church and not to burden their stomachs with a double supply of food.

A similar description of the Essenes is given by Philo, the imitator of Plato's discourse, and also by Josephus, the Greek Livy, in his narrative of the Jewish captivity.[273]

As my present subject is virgins, I have said almost too much about monks. I will now come to the third class, whom they call anchorites and who go from monastic communities into the desert and take nothing with them except bread and salt. Paul was the originator of this way of life,[274] Antony made it famous,[275] and, if I may go back farther still, John the Baptist was its pioneer.

Jeremiah the prophet describes such a person when he says, *It is good for a man, when he shall have borne the yoke from his youth. He will sit alone and will keep silence, because he has borne the yoke upon himself. He will offer his cheek to the man who smites him; he will be filled with reproaches, since the Lord will not cast him away for ever.*[276] The struggle of these men and their way of life, in the flesh and yet not in the flesh, I will, if you wish, explain to you some other time. Now let me return to my subject, covetousness, because it was while I was discussing it that I came to the monks. Setting their example before your eyes, you will despise, I will not say gold and silver and other forms of wealth, but the earth itself and heaven. United to Christ, you will sing, *The Lord is my portion.*[277]

Furthermore, although the Apostle bids us to pray without ceasing,[278] and although to the saints their very sleep is prayer, we ought nevertheless to have fixed hours of prayer, so that if we happen to be detained by some piece of work, the time may remind us of our duty. There is no one who does not know that we should pray at the third, sixth, and ninth hours, and daybreak and at evening.[279] Take no meal unless it is preceded by prayer, and never depart from the table, without returning to the Creator. At night we should get up two or three times and go over the parts of Scripture we know by heart. Let prayer be our amor as we leave the home that shelters us, and when we return from the street, let prayer be said before we sit down, and do not let the puny body rest before the soul is fed. In every act we perform, in every step we take, let our hand trace the cross. Speak against nobody and do not slander your mother's son.[280] *Who are you to judge the servant of another? He stands or falls for his own master; indeed he shall stand, for God has the power to make him stand.*[281] If you have fasted two or three days, do not think yourself better than others who do not fast. You fast and are angry; another eats and wears a smiling face. You work off your irritation and hunger in quarrels; he uses food in moderation and gives God thanks. Daily Isaiah cries, '*Is this the sort of fast I have chosen?' says the Lord,*[282] and again, *In the day of your fast you find your own pleasure and goad all those over whom you have power. If you fast in courts and litigation and strike the lowly man with your fist, what kind of a fast do you perform for me?*[283] What kind of fast can his be, whose wrath is so great that, not only does the night go down upon it, but even the phases of the moon leave it unchanged? Look to yourself and glory in your own success and not in other peoples' failure.

Do not set before yourself the example of those women who take care of the flesh and reckon up their income and daily expenditure. Nor were the eleven apostles crushed by the treachery of Judas, nor, when Phygelus and Alexander made shipwreck,[284] did the rest stop running in the race of faith. Do not say, 'So-and-so enjoys her own property; she is honored by everyone her brothers and sisters come to see her; does she then cease to be a virgin?' In the first place, it is doubtful whether such a woman as she is a virgin. For *God does not see as human beings see. Man looks upon the outward appearance, but God looks into the heart.*[285] Again, even if she is a virgin in body, I do not know whether she is a virgin in spirit. The Apostle himself defines a virgin this way: *That she may be holy both in body and in spirit.*[286] Lastly, let her glory in her own way. Let her override Paul's opinion and live in enjoyment of her good things. But you and I must follow better examples.

Set before yourself the blessed Mary, whose surpassing purity made her worthy to be the mother of the Lord. When the angel Gabriel came down to her in the form of a man and said, 'Hail, lady full of grace, the Lord is with you',[287] she was terror-stricken and unable to reply, for she had never been greeted by a man. But when she learned that he was a messenger, she spoke to him, and she, who had feared a man, conversed fearlessly with an angel. You, too, can be the Lord's mother. *Take to yourself a great book, a new book, and write swiftly in it with the pen of a man who destroys the spoils;*[288] and when you have approached the prophetess[289] and have conceived in the womb and have brought forth a son,[290] say, *Lord, we have conceived a child by your fear, we have been in pain and we have given birth; the spirit of your salvation have we created upon earth.*[291] Then shall your Son replay, *Behold my mother and my brothers.*[292] And he whose name you have a short while earlier inscribed on the amplitude[293] of your heart and have written with flying pen on its renewed surface, he—after he has captured the spoil from the enemy and has laid bare principalities and powers, nailing them to his cross— he, having been conceived, grows to manhood, and as he grows older, he regards you no longer as his mother but as his bride. It is a great struggle, but it is also a great prize, to be as the martyrs or the apostles or as Christ. Indeed all these things are profitable if they are done within the Church, if we celebrate the passover in the same house, if we enter the ark with Noah, if Rahab, once pardoned, holds us while Jericho falls.[294] Such virgins, however, as are said to be among the various sects of heretics and at the side of the infamous Manes,[295] must be regarded as prostitutes, not virgins. For if the devil is the originator of the body [as they claim], how can they honor what their enemy has fashioned? No, it is because they know that the word virgin has a glorious meaning that they go about as wolves in sheep's clothing. As Antichrist claims falsely to be Christ, so they clothe the baseness of their lives with an honorable, but falsely assumed, name. Rejoice, my sister, rejoice, my daughter, rejoice, my virgin, because you begin really to be what other women pretend to be.

All the things we have gone through here one by one will seem hard to a person who does not love Christ. Yet someone who has come to regard all the splendor of the secular world as off-scourings and thinks that everything under the sun is vain,[296] if he may win Christ,[297] someone who has died and risen again with his Lord and has crucified the flesh with its affections and lusts,[298] will boldly cry out, *Who shall separate us from the love of Christ? Shall tribulation or poverty or persecution or hunger or nakedness or danger of the sword?* and again, *I am sure that neither death nor life nor an angel nor principalities nor powers nor the present nor the future nor courage*[299] *nor height nor* depth nor any other created thing can separate us from the love of God, which is in Christ Jesus our Lord,[300] the Son of God, who was made Son of Man for our salvation.[301] For ten months[302] he waits in the womb to be born; he endures revolting conditions, he comes forth covered in blood, he is swathed in rags and covered with caresses. He who shuts the world up in his fist is contained within the narrow limits of a manger.[303] I say nothing of the thirty years during which he lives in obscurity, satisfied with the poverty of his parents.[304] When he is scourged, he holds his peace. When he is crucified, he prays for his crucifiers. *What shall I give to the Lord for all the rewards he bestows upon me? I will receive the cup of salvation and call upon the name of the Lord. Precious in the sight of the Lord is the death of his saints.*[305] The only fitting return we can make to him is to give blood for blood, and, as having been redeemed by the blood of Christ, gladly to lay down our lives for our Redeemer. What saint has ever won his crown without first contending for it? The righteous Abel is murdered.[306] Abraham is in danger of losing his wife,[307] and as I must not turn my book into a large volume, look up [other passages] for yourself, and you will find that all holy men have suffered adversity. Only Solomon lived in luxury and that is perhaps why he fell.[308] For *whom the Lord loves, he snatches up, and he punishes every son whom he receives.*[309] Is it not better to do battle for a short time, to carry stakes for the palisades, to bear arms and rations, to grow weary under breastplates and later to rejoice as a victor, than to be slaves for ever because we cannot endure for a single hour?[310]

Nothing is hard for those who love, no task is difficult for the enthusiast. See how much Jacob bore for Rachel, the wife who had been promised to him. *Jacob*, the Scripture says, *served seven years for Rachel. And they were like a few days in his sight, because he loved her.*[311] Afterwards he himself tells us what he had to undergo. *By day I was burned by the heat and by night by the frost.*[312] So we must love Christ and always seek his embraces. Then everything difficult will seem easy; everything long we shall account short; and smitten with his arrows,[313] we shall say every moment, *Woe is me, because my pilgrimage has been prolonged.*[314] For *the sufferings of this present time are not worthy to be compared with the future glory which will be revealed in us.*[315] For *tribulation bestows patience, patience experience, and experience hope; and hope does not throw us into confusion.*[316] When your lot seems hard to bear, read Paul's Second Epistle to the Corinthians: *In toil most abundant, in blows beyond measure, in prison frequently, often near death. Five times I was beaten thirty-nine times by the Jews; three times I was beaten with rods; once I was stoned; three times I suffered shipwreck, a night and a day I have been in the depths of the sea. I have often been on journeys, in danger from rivers, in danger from robbers, in danger from my own countrymen, in danger from pagans, in danger in the city, in danger in the wilderness, in danger on the sea, in danger among false brethren, in toil and misery, in frequent vigils, in hunger and thirst, in frequent fasting, in cold and nakedness.*[317] Which of us can claim the merest fraction of the virtues here enumerated? Yet it was these which afterwards made him bold to say, *I have finished my course, I have kept the faith. There will be stored up for me a crown of righteousness, which the Lord will give me.*[318] If our food is somewhat insipid, we get gloomy and think we are doing God a favor; if we drink watered-down wine, the cup is smashed, the table overturned, the sound of scourging is heard and the over-warm water is paid for with blood. *The kingdom of heaven endures violence and violent men take it by force.*[319] Still, unless you use force, you will never seize the kingdom of heaven. Unless you knock importunately,[320] you will never receive the sacramental bread. Does it not seem to you typical of a violent man that the flesh yearns to be what God is and to ascend to the place from which angels have fallen, for the purpose of judging angels?

Go forth, I beg you, for a little while from your body and picture before your eyes the reward of your present toil, a reward which *neither the eye has seen nor the ear heard, nor the human heart conceived.*[321] What will be the glory of that day when Mary, the mother of the Lord, will come to meet you, accompanied by choirs of virgins; when Miriam, after the passage through the Red Sea and the drowning of Pharaoh with his army, holding her tambourine, will chant to the answering women, *Sing to the Lord, for he has triumphed gloriously; the horse and its rider has he thrown into the sea.*[322] Then shall Thecla fly with joy to embrace you.[323] Then shall your Spouse himself come forward to meet you and say, *Rise, my nearest and dearest, my fair one, my dove, for, behold! the winter is over, for you the rain has gone away.*[324] Then will the angels say with wonder, *Who is she who looks forth like the dawn, fair as the moon, choice as the sun?*[325] . . . *The maidens shall see you and bless you; the queens shall proclaim you and the concubines praise you.*[326] Then yet another chorus of chaste women shall come to meet you: Sarah will come with the matrons and Anna, the daughter of Phanuel, with the widows.[327] There, as in different groups, will be your physical mother and your spiritual mother.[328] The one will rejoice because she bore you, the other will exult because she taught you. Then truly will the Lord ride on his she-ass[329] and enter the heavenly Jerusalem. Then the little children—of whom the Saviour says in Isaiah, *Look! here I am with the boys whom the Lord has given me*[330] —shall lift up palms of victory and chant with a single voice, *Hosanna in the highest; blessed is he that comes in the name of the Lord; hosanna in the highest.*[331] Then shall the hundred and forty four thousand hold their harps before the throne and before the elders and they shall sing a new song, and no one shall be able to recognize that song save those for whom it is appointed. *These are they who have not contaminated themselves with women; for they are virgins. These are they who follow the Lamb wherever he goes.*[332] As often as this life's idle show tries to charm you, as often as you see in the world some vain pomp, transport yourself in your mind to Paradise. Try to be now what you will be hereafter, and you will hear from your Spouse, *Set me as a seal upon your heart, as a seal on your arm.*[333] Then, strengthened in both body and mind, you will cry out and say, *Many waters cannot quench love, neither can the floods drown it.*[334]

NOTES

1. Ps 44 (45):11.
2. Hebrew enumeration: forty-fifth.
3. Gn 11:31, 12:1.
4. Ps 26 (27):13.
5. Gn 19:17.
6. Mt 24:17–18.
7. Jn 8:44.
8. 1 Jn 3:8.
9. Sg 1:5.

10. Mt 19:5.
11. Sg 8:5.
12. Hb 13:4.
13. Gn 19:26.
14. Rm 11:20.
15. Is 34:5.
16. Cf. Gn 3:18.
17. Eph 6:12.
18. Cf. Jn 14:30.
19. Ps 90 (91):5–7.
20. 2 Kgs 6:16.
21. 2 (4) Kgs 2:11, 6:17.
22. Ps 123 (124):7.
23. 2 Cor 4:7.
24. Gal 5:17.
25. 1 Pt 5:8.
26. Ps 103 (104):20–21.
27. Jer 29:21–22.
28. Is 8:1.
29. Hab 1:16.
30. Cf. Lk 22:31.
31. Mt 10:34.
32. Ob 4.
33. Is 13–14.
34. Gn 27:12.
35. Ps 81 (82):6–7.
36. Ps 81 (82):1.
37. 'The Apostle' here as in subsequent letters refers to Saint Paul.
38. 1 Cor 3:3.
39. Gal 1:15.
40. 1 Cor 9:27.
41. Rm 7:23.
42. Rm 7:24.
43. Am 5:2.
44. Am 8:13.
45. Mt 5:28.
46. Mt 25:3, 10.
47. Is 47:1–3.
48. Cf. Sg 5:2.
49. Ps 44 (45):10.
50. Cf. Ez 16:5.
51. Is 1:21.
52. Is 34:15, 13:22.
53. Ps 117 (118):6, 55:5 (56:4).
54. Ps 41:12 (42:11).
55. Ps 136 (137):9.
56. 1 Cor 10:4.

57. A reference to the period spent by Jerome in the Desert of Chalcis in Syria ad 374, 'Parched by the blazing heat of the sun' is a reminiscence of Sallust *Jugurtha* 19.6, which Jerome had probably read in the course of his youthful studies.

58. Sg 1:3–4.

59. 1 Tm 5:6.

60. 1 Tm 5:23.

61. Eph 5:18.

62. Rm 14:21.

63. Gn 9:20–21.

64. Ex 23:6.

65. Gn 19:30–38.

66. Dt 23:3.

67. 1 (3) Kgs 19:4–6.

68. 2 (4) Kgs 4:38–41.

69. Ex 15:23–5.

70. 2 (4) Kgs 6:22.

71. Dn 1.8; 17; Bel 33–39.

72. Dn 9:23.

73. Ps 83 (84):6.

74. Mt 4:2–3.

75. Ph 3:19.

76. Jb 2:3, 40:16.

77. Ps 131 (132):11.

78. Gn 46:26.

79. Gn 32:24–5.

80. Ex 12:11.

81. Jb 38:3.

82. Mt 3:4.

83. Lk 13:35.

84. Ez 16:4–6.

85. Jdg 13–16.

86. 2 Sm (2 Kgs) 11.

87. Ps 50 (51):4.

88. 1 (3) Kgs 4:33.

89. In the fourth century, when Jerome was writing, Solomon was commonly held to be the author of the Book of Wisdom.

90. 1 (3) Kgs 11:4.

91. 2 Sm (2 Kgs) 13:1–22.

92. Is 13:14.

93. Tt 1:15.

94. The Manichees believed evil to be inseparable from matter and therefore practiced a rigid asceticism.

95. Jr 3:3.

96. Romans of patrician family wore clothing with a broad purple stripe; those of plebeian family, clothing with a narrow purple stripe. Jerome appears to make a slight allowance for these ladies in view of

their exalted social origin, but by his day, the distinction between patrician and plebeian had little force.

97. The name *agapetae* (literally 'beloved ones') is Greek in origin, and was sometimes rendered by *subintroductae*. These women lived with unmarried men, allegedly as spiritual sisters, but often in reality as mistresses or concubines. They were therefore a source of scandal, and canons against the practice of the clergy keeping them were passed by the Councils of Ancyra (Canon 19, ad 314), Nicaea (Canon 3, 325), and Elvira (Canon 27, *c.* ad 386.).

98. Pr 6:26–8.

99. Mt 13:8.

100. Cf. Terence, *Phormio* 342, Horace *Sat.* 2.2, 27.

101. Cf. Sg 1:6.

102. Cf. Sg 1:6.

103. I.e., virgins are to invoke the aid of the martyrs in the privacy of their own room and are not to make expeditions to crowded shrines.

104. Eph 6:16.

105. Hos 7:4, 6.

106. Lk 24:32.

107. Ps 118 (119):140.

108. Sg 3:1.

109. Col 3:5.

110. Gal 2:20.

111. Ps 38 (39):6.

112. Ps 118 (119):83.

113. Ps 108 (109): 24, 101 (102):5.

114. The male grasshopper keeps up a strident and monotonous chant by day, which the ancients, particularly the Greeks, considered exquisitely beautiful. At night the insect is silent. Jerome appears to imply that Eustochium is to engage in perpetual prayer, (cf. 1 Th 5:17) and that her prayer will be pursued more effectively during the silence of the night.

115. Ps 6:7.

116. Ps 101:8 (102:7).

117. Cf. 1 Cor 14:15.

118. Ps 102 (103):2–4.

119. Ps 101:10 (102:9).

120. 2 (4) Kgs 2:13.

121. Gn 3:16.

122. Gn 2:17.

123. Gn 1:28.

124. Gn 3:18.

125. Mt 13:8ff.

126. Mt 19:11–12.

127. Si 3:5.

128. Mt 3:9.

129. Zch 9:16.

130. Jn 19:23.

131. Ps 114 (116):7.
132. Is 11:1.
133. Sg 2:6.
134. Dan 2:45.
135. Sg 2:6.
136. Gn 7:2.
137. Cf. Ex 3:5, Josh 5:16, Mt 10:10.
138. Is 23:24.
139. 1 Cor 7:25.
140. 1 Cor 7:7–9.
141. 1 Cor 9:5.
142. Is 31:9.
143. Is 54:1.
144. Ps 127 (128):3.
145. Ps 104 (105):37.
146. Is 56:3.
147. Cf. Lk 16:19–31.
148. Gn 25:1.
149. Gn 30:14–16.
150. The mandrake is a poisonous plant with narcotic and emetic qualities.
151. Gn 30:1–2.
152. 1–2 Kgs.
153. Jr 16:2.
154. Jr 1:5.
155. 1 Cor 7:26.
156. 1 Cor 7:29.
157. Jr 4:7.
158. Lam 4:4.
159. Is 7:14.
160. Is 9:6.
161. Jdth 13:4–10.
162. Est 7:10.
163. Mk 8:34.
164. Mt 8:20–22.
165. 1 Cor 7:3.
166. *De perpetua virginitate beatae Mariae liber in Helvidium* (PL 23: 193–216), esp. chapters 20–21 (213–216). For a translation, see Fremantle, pp. 334–346, esp. p. 344.
167. 1 Th 5:17.
168. 1 Cor 7:3.
169. 1 Cor 7:28.
170. This work has been lost. Jerome refers to it again in his treatise against Jovinian, a monk condemned, by synods at Rome in 386 and Milan in 393, for his unorthodox views. He denied that virginity as such was a higher state than marriage and that abstinence as such was better than thankful eating. He shared Helvidius' disbelief in the perpetual

virginity of Mary. For Jerome's treatise and his reference to Tertullian, see *Adversus*, Iovinianum (PL 23: 221–352), esp. ch. 13 (241). For a translation, see Fremantle, p. 336.
171. For the complete works of Pope Damasus, see PL 13:347–418.
172. Ambrose, *De virginibus ad Marcellinam sororem suam* (PL 16 197–244). He also wrote a general treatise, *De virginibus* (PL 16 279–316), *De institutione virginis ad Eusebium* (PL 16:319–334), *Exhortatio virginis* (PL 16:347–380), and *De lapsu virginis admonitio* (PL 16:379–406). See *Saint Ambrose on Virginity*, trans. Daniel Callam CSB (Toronto: Peregrina Press).
173. Mt 24:13.
174. Mt 20:16.
175. 2 Sm (2 Kgs) 6:6–7.
176. 2 Sm (2 Kgs) 6:6–7.
177. 2 (4) Kgs 20:10, 13.
178. Ex 25:11.
179. 1 (3) Kgs 8:9.
180. Mt 21:5, Ex 5, 13, Josh 1ff.
181. Mt 21:1–3.
182. Ex 7:16.
183. Mt 21:12.
184. Mt 26:12–12.
185. Mt 23:38.
186. Mt 23:38.
187. Lk 10:41–42.
188. Sg 3:4.
189. Sg 6:9, Gal 4:26.
190. Cf Gn 26:8.
191. Sg 5:2,4,8.
192. Sg 4:12.
193. Gn 34.
194. Sg 3:2.
195. Mt 4:17.
196. Sg 3:2, 5–6.
197. Sg 5:7.
198. St 5:2.
199. Sg 1:12 (13).
200. Sg 1:7.
201. Sg 1:8.
202. Pr 4:23.
203. Mt 25:33.
204. Is 26:20.
205. Mt 6:6.
206. Rv 3:20.
207. Sg 5:2–3.
208. Sg 5:6.
209. Si 10:4.
210. Dn 6:10.

211. Jr 9:21.
212. Jn 5:44.
213. Jr 9:24.
214. 1 Cor 1:31.
215. Gal 1:10.
216. Ps 43:9 (44:8).
217. Mt 6:3, 16–18.
218. Ps 130 (131).1.
219. Mt 6:16.
220. Ps 52 (53):6.
221. 1 Cor 11:24.
222. Jerome seems here to refer to Palestinian/Syriac ascetics. See Theodoret of Cyrrhus, *A History of the Monks of Syria*, Trans. R. M. Price (Kalamazoo, 1985).
223. 2 Tm 3:6–7.
224. Diomedes (Vergil, *Aeneid* 1, 752; Lucretius, *De rerum natura* 5.31), a bold and enterprising warrior in the Trojan War, who came to be worshipped as a hero in Greece and on the Adriatic coast of Italy, where in all probability, he became confused with local deities of horse-taming and navigation.
225. Gn 3:1.
226. 2 Cor 2:11.
227. 2 Cor 11:2.
228. Some manuscripts read *Cur mens adversa sit?* (Why should your thoughts be different?) but the reading *mensa*, adopted by Hilberg, appears to make better sense, because it brings out the contrast between the togetherness of mistress and servants at the Lord's Table and their separation at the ordinary dinner table.
229. 1 Cor 7:9.
230. 1 Cor 15:33.
231. 1 Tm 5:11–12.
232. 2 Cor 6:14–15.
233. Saint Paul and Cicero are contrasted here as great letter-writers.
234. Tt 1:15.
235. 1 Tm 4:4.
236. Mt 6:21.
237. Ps 6:5.
238. Lk 16:12.
239. Pr 13:8.
240. Mt 6:24.
241. Mt 13:7, 22, 6:25.
242. Mt 6:35.
243. Mt 6:25–6, cf. 6.28ff, 5:3,6.
244. 2 Cor 12:10.
245. 2 Cor 12:7.
246. Ps 96 (97):8.
247. Jb 1:21.
248. 1 Tm 6:7.

249. Mt 6:2.

250. The love-feast or *agape* was originally a common religious meal customarily held in the early Church in close relation to the Eucharist. 1 Cor 11:17–34, condemns the abuses which accompanied this common meal preceding the Eucharist. Probably it was the existence of these abuses which led to the separation of the *agape* from the Eucharist. By the time of Saint Cyprian (d.258), the agape was celebrated in the evening and the Eucharist early in the morning, fasting. As time went on, the *agape* developed into a kind of charity supper, as is obviously meant here.

251. Col 3:5.

252. 1 Tm 6:10.

253. Mt 6:33.

254. Ps 36 (37):25.

255. Cf. 1 (3) Kgs 17:4, 6.

256. 1 (3) Kgss 17:9–16.

257. Ac 3:6.

258. Gn 28:20–21.

259. Gn 32:5, 10.

260. Gn 32:5, 10.

261. The region of Nitria in Libya, to the West of the mouth of the Nile, was celebrated as a center of early christian monasticism. A large colony of hermits assembled there in the fourth century under the inspiration of Ammonius (or Ammoun). For a description of Nitria, see *The Lives of the Desert Fathers*, ed. Benedicta Ward, trans. Norman Russell (London-Oxford-Kalamazoo, 1987) pp. 105–107, 148, and, for further details, 111–112; and *The Sayings of the Desert Fathers*, trans. Benedicta Ward (Oxford-Kalamazoo, 1975) p. 27.

262. Mt 26:15.

263. For details of Macarius, Pambo, and Isidore, see Ward and Russell, *The Lives*, pp. 108–110, 148–149; Ward, *The Sayings*, pp. 105–116, 164–166, 82–83.

264. Ac 8:20.

265. From the Greek κοινὸς, common life.

266. Apparently an Egyptian word. It is not found elsewhere.

267. From the Greek ἀναχωρεῖν, to withdraw.

268. These people appear to correspond to the Sarabaites (mentioned by Cassian, *Conference* 18.7, and Benedict, *RB* 1.6–9), who lived in little groups. They were not under discipline, but followed their own inclinations. It is possible that they represented a survival of an earlier, pre-monastic asceticism.

269. This may refer to Dalmatia, Jerome's native land, but more probably to Syria, where he had tried to live the eremitical life in the Desert of Chalcis in the early 370s. See Paragraph 7 of this letter.

270. I.e., 3 pm.

271. Letter Fifty two.8 (not included in this selection; for a translation, see Fremantle, p. 93) contains a similar expression of approval for a preacher who has the ability to make his hearers weep.

272. Ps 54:7 (55:6).

273. Philo was a jewish writer living in Alexandria, *c.* 20 bc - ad 50. His principal achievement was to develop the allegorical interpretation of the Old Testament, and he therefore had a strong influence on the Alexandrian Christian interpretation of the Scriptures.

274. Saint Paul the Hermit, whose life is one of Jerome's three 'religious romances', the other two being the lives of Hilarion and Malchus. For particulars of texts and translation, see bibliography.

275. Saint Antony the Great, whose life was written in Greek by Saint Athanasius (PG 26:835–878). By the mid-fourth century at least two latin versions were circulating in the West, and thus influencing the development of western monasticism. For particulars of texts and translations, see the bibliography.

276. Lam 3:27, 28, 30, 31.

277. Lam 3:24; cf. Ps 72 (73):26.

278. 1 Th 5:17.

279. These times correspond to 9 am, 12 noon and 3 pm. In Jerome's day the seven canonical hours has not yet been fixed, but he mentions five here, which correspond to the later Lauds, Terce, Sext, None, Vespers, and adds the Night Office in the next sentence. See Letter 107.9, Letter 108.20, Letter 130.15.

280. Ps 49 (50):20.

281. Rm 14:6.

282. Is 58:5.

283. Is 58:3, 4.

284. Jerome appears to be quoting from memory, as he conflates two passages in the Epistles to Timothy. In 1 Tm 1:19–20, Hymenaeus and Alexander 'made shipwreck' of their faith, whereas in 2 Tm 1:15, Phygelus and Hermogenes 'turned away'.

285. 1 Sm (1 Kgs) 16:7.

286. 1 Cor 7:34.

287. Lk 1:28.

288. Is 8:1.

289. Jerome should have substituted 'prophet' for 'prophetess' here. Otherwise the quotation loses its force.

290. Is 8:3.

291. Is 26:18.

292. Mt 12:49.

293. Pr 7:3; Jer 26:33.

294. Josh 6:16–17.

295. Founder of the sect of the Manichaeans, to which Augustine at one time belonged. Manes (or Mani) was born *c.* 216 in Persia. He incurred the opposition of the Zoroastrians when he began teaching in 240. He was put to death in 276, by being flayed alive. The Manichaean system of beliefs was based on the idea of a primeval conflict between light and darkness. Since one of its most important principles was that all matter was inherently evil, the Manichaeans practiced a very rigid asceticism.

296. Cf. Qo 1:2–3.

297. Phl 3:8.

298. Rm 6:4, Gal 5:24.

299. Here Jerome, quoting from memory, makes an obvious slip of the tongue. The generally accepted latin reading is *latitudo et longitudo* (breadth and length) following the Greek Το πλάτος καὶ μῆκος, which makes far better sense.

300. Rm 8:35, 38–9; Eph 3:18–19.

301. An echo of the Nicene Creed.

302. Jerome was presumably speaking rhetorically. A single ms (Berolensis/18 lat) of the twelfth century reads *novem* (nine).

303. Cf. Ps 94 (95):4–5, Is 11:12.

304. Lk 2:51–2.

305. Ps 115 (116): 12–13, 15.

306. Gn 4:8, Mt 23:35.

307. Gn 20.

308. 1 Kgs 11:6ff.

309. Hb 12:6.

310. Cf. Mt 16:40.

311. Gn 29:20.

312. Gn 31:40.

313. Ps 37:3 (38:2).

314. Ps 119 (120):5.

315. Rm 8:18.

316. Rm 3:5.

317. 2 Cor 11:23–7.

318. 2 Tm 4:7–8.

319. Mt 11:12.

320. Lk 11:5–8.

321. 1 Cor 2:9.

322. Ex 15:20–21.

323. A legendary virgin, the heroine of the apocryphal *Acts of Paul and Thecla*. According to this story, Saint Paul preached on the benefits of chastity at Iconium and won Thecla over from Thamyris, her fiancé. Paul was charged by the authorities and beaten; Thecla was condemned to death, but miraculously saved.

324. Sg 2:10–11.

325. Sg 6:10.

326. Sg 6:9.

327. Gn 17–24, Lk 2:36.

328. Eustochium's natural mother was Paula (see Letter 108.4) and her spiritual mother, Marcella (see Letter One 127).

329. Mt 21:1–9.

330. Is 8:18.

331. Mt 21:9.

332. Rv 14:1–4.

333. Sg 8:6.

334. Sg 8:7.

DEMETRIAS
AN ASCETIC EXILE IN NORTH AFRICA

ETTER 130, to Demetrias, is a much more impressive production than Letter 128, which was written a year earlier. Jerome seems to have recovered from his personal losses and from his shock at the fall of Rome in 410; moreover the prospect of theological controversy, in this case with Pelagius, had probably done much to revive his spirits.

The general tone of the letter is rhetorical and, at times, fulsome, because Jerome was eager to make an impression on a distinguished family, which he did not know personally. He had never set eyes on Demetrias. Like many aristocratic Romans—she was a member of the Anicii—she had fled, together with her mother Juliana and her grandmother Proba, to North Africa after the fall of Rome. In North Africa she had come under the influence of Augustine and Alypius. Preparations had been made for a splendid marriage when she astonished everyone by dedicating herself to virginity in the presence of Bishop Aurelius of Carthage. Jerome professes to believe that Juliana and Proba were delighted, but whether this was really the case we do not know. At any rate her family were anxious that she should receive the best possible guidance in her new way of life and therefore consulted Jerome and Pelagius, whose letter is also still extant.[1]

Once he has paid what he thinks are appropriate compliments, Jerome gives his usual advice to virgins: Demetrias is to study the Bible, avoid the society of young men and married women, obey her mother and grandmother, work with her hands, and so on. He also suggests that she might try to use her fortune, when she has gained control of it, to help the sick and the poor and the religious communities. Indeed he appears to be dropping a hint that the two monasteries at Bethlehem, his own and the women's monastery founded by Paula, are in need of help.

In this letter Jerome draws attention to the dangers of Origenism, which at first seems strange, as this was not a menace in North Africa. His real object, however, is to warn Demetrias of the dangers of Pelagianism, which he believes to stem from Origenism, but he does not like to mention Pelagius or his doctrines by name, since Pelagius is a personal friend of her family, the Anicii.

This letter is often compared with Letter 22, but it is milder in tone. Fasting, for example, is to be conducted with moderation and helping the poor and the sick receives more emphasis. Some allowance must be made for the probability that Jerome had mellowed a little with advancing years, but the reason for the difference in tone is that the letter was written in a different set of circumstances from Letter 22, which, as we have already seen, formed part of a campaign in favor of asceticism. Though it is addressed to Eustochium, it was intended to be read by other people. Jerome is therefore giving directions which were not confined to the recipient of the letter, but were intended for general consumption. At the same time, since Jerome felt a sincere affection for Eustochium, whom he had known from childhood, he permitted himself some personal touches. Since, however, he had never seen Demetrias, Letter 130 is more detached and impersonal than Letter 22. Perhaps we should also bear in mind that Eustochium was living in Rome in 384, in her own home in comfortable circumstances, whereas Demetrias was in exile with her family, who had suffered a good deal personally as the result of their migration to North Africa. Jerome may have felt that Demetrias had suffered enough as it was and should not therefore be called upon to suffer austerities as severe as those which he had imposed upon Eustochium some thirty years earlier.

J. M. P.

To Demetrias (Letter 130)

AMONG ALL THE SUBJECTS upon which I have written from my you up to the present time either by my own hand or by the hands of secretaries, none is more difficult than my present work. I am going to write to Demetrias, a virgin of Christ and a lady who by birth and riches is second to none in the roman world. If I speak of her in words adequate to describe all her virtues, I shall be thought to flatter her; and if I suppress some details, lest they seem incredible, my reserve will not do justice to her merits. What am I to do then? I dare not deny what I am not able to describe completely. Her mother and her grandmother are both women of distinction, and they have alike authority to command, faith to seek, and perseverance to obtain what they require. It is not indeed anything very new or special that they ask of me; my wits have often been exercised on similar themes. What they wish for is that I should raise my voice and bear witness as strongly as I can to the virtues of one who—in the words of the famous orator—is to be praised less for what she is than for what she gives promise of being.[2] Although she is a young girl, she has a glowing faith beyond her years and has begun from a point at which others think it a sign of remarkable virtue to leave off.

Let disparagement stand aloof and envy depart; let no charge of self-seeking be brought against me. I write as a stranger to a stranger, at least so far as the personal appearance is concerned. For the inner person finds himself well-known by that knowledge whereby the apostle Paul knew the Colossians and many other believers, whom he had not previously seen.[3] How highly I think of this virgin, rather, indeed, what a miracle of virtue I esteem her, you may judge from the fact that being occupied in the explanation of Ezekiel's description of the temple[4] —the hardest job in the whole range of holy Scriptures—and finding myself in that part of the shrine, where the Holy of Holies and the altar of incense are,[5] I have chosen by way of a brief rest to pass from that altar to this, that on it I might consecrate to eternal chastity a living victim acceptable to God and free from all stain.[6] I know that the bishop has with words of prayer covered her holy head with the virgin's bridal veil, and has solemnly recited the words of the Apostle, *I wish to present you all as a chaste virgin to Christ,*[7] *when she stood as a queen at his right hand, in clothing wrought of gold and many different colors.*[8] Such was the coat, woven with many threads, that is, formed of many different virtues, in which Joseph was clad;[9] it was also the ordinary dress worn by the daughters of the kings of old. Thereupon the bride herself rejoices and says, *The king has brought me into his bed-chamber,* and the choir of her companions responds, *The king's daughter is all-glorious within.*[10] But my prayer will also bring some reward. The speed of racehorses is quickened by the applause of spectators; prize-fighters spurred on by the cries of their supporters, and the general's speech fires the soldiers ranged with drawn swords in the line of battle. So it is in your present work, your grandmother and mother have indeed planted, I will water and the Lord will give the increase.

It is the practice of the rhetoricians to embellish the subject of their praises by referring to his ancestors and forefathers and the past nobility of his race, so that a fertile root may make up for a barren branches and that you may admire in the stem what you have not got in the fruit. Thus I ought now to recall the distinguished names of the Probi and of the Olybrii and that illustrious Anician house,[11] the representatives of which have seldom or never been unworthy of the consulship. Or ought I to bring forward Olybrius, our virgin's father, whose premature death Rome has mourned. I fear to say more of him, lest I intensify the wound suffered by your saintly mother and lest the commemoration of his virtues become a renewal of her grief. He was a dutiful son, a loveable husband, a kind master, a courteous and friendly citizen. He was made consul while still a boy, but he was more illustrious as a senator, thorough the goodness of his character. He was happy in his death—for it saved him from seeing the ruin of his country— and happier still in his offspring—for the distinguished name of his great-grandmother Demetrias has made the nobility of his family even more distinguished, on account of the perpetual chastity of his daughter Demetrias.[12]

But what am I doing? Forgetful of my purpose and filled with admiration for this young man, I have been praising his worldly success, when I ought rather to have been praising his worldly success, when I ought rather to have been praising our virgin, because she has rejected all worldly advantages and has decided to regard herself not as an aristocratic and wealthy lady, but simply as a human being. Her strength of mind almost passes belief. In the midst of jewels and silks, and surrounded by crowds of eunuchs and young maid-servants, a bustling household of flattering and attentive domestics, and with access to the most exquisite meals that the abundance of a large house could supply, she sought the toil of fasting, rough clothing, and frugal living. For she had read the words of the Lord, who says, *Those who are clad in soft clothing are in kings' houses.*[13] She was filled with admiration for the manner of life followed by Elijah and by John the Baptist, both of whom confined and mortified their loins with girdles of skin;[14] while the second of them is said to have come in the spirit and power of Elijah as the forerunner of the Lord.[15] As such he prophesied while still in his mother's womb,[16] and before the day of judgement, won the commendation of the Judge.[17] She admired also the zeal of Anna, the daughter of Phanuel, who continued even to extreme old age to serve the Lord in the temple with prayers and fastings.[18] When she thought of the four virgins who were the daughters of Philip,[19] she longed to join their band and to be numbered with those, who, by their virginal purity, have attained the grace of prophecy. With these and similar meditations she fed her mind, dreading nothing so much as offending her grandmother and her mother. Although she was encouraged by their example, she was discouraged by their expressed wish and desire; not indeed that they disapproved of her holy purpose, but that the prize was so great that they did not venture to hope for it or to aspire to it. Thus this poor novice in Christ's service was sorely perplexed. She came to hate all her fine apparel, and with Esther addressed the Lord, *You know that I hate the sign of distinction on my head*, that is to say, the diadem which she wore as queen, *and I shall look upon it as being as unclean as if it were a rag worn by a menstruous woman.*[20] Among the holy and aristocratic ladies who have seen and known her, some have been driven by the tempest, which has swept over Africa from the shores of Gaul, to find refuge in the holy places. They tell me confidentially, night after night, though no one knew of it but the virgins dedicated to God in her mother's and grandmother's retinue, Demetrias never used linen sheets or the softness of a feather-bed, but spread a rug of goat's hair on the bare ground and watered her face with ceaseless tears. In her mind she used to cast herself down at her Saviour's knees, imploring him to accept her intention, fulfil her aspiration and often the hearts of her grandmother and mother.

Why do I delay in telling the rest of the story? When her wedding day was close at hand and when a marriage chamber was being prepared for the bride and bridegroom, secretly, without any witnesses and taking comfort from the darkness of the night, she is said to have nerved herself with such considerations as these: 'What is the matter with you, Demetrias? Why are you so fearful of defending your chastity? What you need is freedom and courage. If you are afraid in time of peace, what would you do if you were called on to undergo martyrdom? If you cannot bear so much as a frown from your own family, how would you steel yourself to face the tribunals of persecutors? If male examples leave you unmoved, at least let the blessed martyr Agnes[21] exhort you and make you brave. For it was she who conquered both youth and a tyrant and crowned the name of chastity by her martyrdom. You do not know, unhappy girl, you do not know to whom you owe your virginity. Not long ago you trembled in the hands of the barbarians and were covered by the folds of your grandmother's and your mother's cloaks. You have seen yourself a prisoner and your chastity not in your own power. You have shuddered at the fierce looks of your enemies; with secret agony you have seen the virgins of God ravished.[22] Your city, once the capital of the world, is now the grave of the roman people, and will you on the shores of Libya, yourself an exile, accept an exile for a husband? Whom will you have as brides-woman?[23] With what companions are you to be brought home? A harsh punic tongue will sing to you the wanton fescennine songs.[24] Away with all your hesitations! *Perfect love [of God] casts out fear.*[25] Put on the shield of faith, the breastplate of righteousness, and the helmet of salvation and advance to the battle.[26] The preservation of your chastity has a martyrdom of its own. Why do you fear your grandmother? Why do you dread your mother? Perhaps they may themselves wish for you a course which they do not think you wish for yourself.

When she had been roused to enthusiasm by these arguments, she flung away her bodily adornment and worldly attire as hindrances to her purpose. Her precious pearls, costly necklaces, and glowing gems were put back in their cases. She put on a coarse tunic and covered herself with a still coarser cloak. Coming in unexpectedly, she suddenly flung herself down at her grandmother's knees and, with tears and sobs, showed her what she really was. That staid and holy woman was amazed when she saw her granddaughter in so strange a dress, while her mother stood by in joyous astonishment. Neither of them could believe that what they had longed for had come true. Their voices stuck in their throats; what with blushing and turning pale, with fright and with joy, they were a prey to many conflicting emotions.

Here I must *give in* and not begin to describe what defies description. In the effort to explain the greatness of that joy past all belief, the river of Cicero's eloquence would run dry and the sentences poised and hurled by Demosthenes would become spent and fall short.[27]

We heard then of things being done that mind can conceive, things speech cannot interpret. Mother and child, grandmother and granddaughter eagerly kissed each other. The two elder women wept copiously for joy, they raised the prostrate girl, they embraced her trembling body. In her purpose they recognized their own mind, and congratulated each other that now a virgin was to make a noble house more noble still by her virginity. She had found, they said, a way to benefit her family and to lessen the calamity of the ruin of Rome. Good Jesus! what exaltation there was all through the house. Many virgins sprouted forth at the same time, as shoots from a fruitful stem, and the example set by their patroness and lady was followed by a host of both followers and servants. Virginity flourished in great numbers in every household, and although those who made profession of it were, as regards the flesh, of lower rank than Demetrias, they sought the same reward with her, the reward of chastity. My words are too weak. Every church in Africa danced for joy. The news reached not only the cities, towns, and villages, but even scattered huts. Every island between Africa and Italy was full of it; the glad tidings ran far and wide with unhindered foot. Then Italy put off her mourning and the ruined walls of Rome resumed in part their former splendor, for they believed the full conversion of their foster-child to be a sign of God's favor towards them. You would fancy that the band of Goths had been annihilated and that the concourse of deserters and slaves had been filled by a thunderbolt from, the Lord on high. There was less elation in Rome when Marcellus won his first success at Nola, after thousands of Romans had fallen at the Trebia, Lake Trasimene, and Cannae.[28] There was less joy among the noblemen cooped up in the capitol, on whom the future of Rome depended, when, after buying their lives with gold, they heard that the Gauls had at length been routed.[29] The news penetrated to the shores of the East, and this triumph of christian glory was heard of in remote cities in the interior. What christian virgin was not proud to have Demetrias as a companion? What mother, Juliana, did not call your womb blessed? Unbelievers may scoff at the doubtfulness of rewards to come. In the meantime, in becoming a virgin of Christ you have gained more than you have sacrificed. Had you become a man's bride, only one province would have known of you, while as a christian virgin, you are known to the whole world. Mothers who have only a little faith in Christ unhappily have the habit of dedicating to Christ only ugly and crippled daughters for whom they can find no suitable husbands. Glass beads, as the saying goes, are thought equal to pearls. Men who pride themselves on their religion give to their virgin daughters sums scarcely sufficient for their maintenance and bestow the bulk of their property on their children, of both sexes, who are living in the world. Quite recently in this city a wealthy presbyter left two of his daughters a mere pittance, while he provided his other children with ample means for self-indulgence and pleasure. The same thing has been done, I am sorry to say, to many women who have adopted the ascetic life. Would that such instances were rare, but unfortunately they are not. Yet the more frequent they are, the more blessed are those who refuse to follow an example which is set them by so many.

All Christians are loud in their praises of Christ's holy yoke-fellows,[30] because, when she professed herself a virgin, they gave to Demetrias the money which had been set apart as a dowry for her marriage. They would not wrong her heavenly Bridegroom; in fact they wished her to come to him with all her previous riches, that these might not be wasted on the things of this world, but relieve the distress of God's servants.

Who would believe it? They say that Proba, who of all persons of high rank and birth in the roman world bears the most illustrious name—whose holy life and universal charity have won for her esteem even among the barbarians who has made nothing of the regular consulships of her three sons, Probinus, Olybrius[31] and Probus—now that the houses of Rome had been seized and set on fire and prisoners taken in the city, is selling her ancestral prop-erties and making friends with the mammon of unrighteousness which will receive her into everlasting habitations. Well may the Church's ministers, whatever their status, and those monks who are monks only in name; blush for shame that they are buying estates while this noble lady is selling them.

Scarcely had she escaped from the hands of the barbarians and had stopped weeping for the virgins whom they had snatched from her arms, when she was suddenly struck by an intolerable bereavement—and one which she never had cause to fear—the death of her devoted son.[32] Yet as one who was to be the grandmother of a christian virgin, she bore up against this death-dealing wound, strong in hope of the future and proving true of herself the words of the lyric:

Should the round world in fragments burst, its fall
May strike the just, may slay, but not appal.[33]

We read in the book of Job how, while the first messenger of evil was yet speaking, there came also another messenger.[34] And in the same book it is written, *Is there not a temptation—or as the Hebrew better gives it*—a warfare to man upon earth?[35] It is for this end that we labor, it is for this end that we risk our lives in the warfare of this world, that we may be crowned in the world to come. That we should believe this to be true of men is nothing wonderful, for even the Lord himself was tempted,[36] and of Abraham Scripture bears witness that God tempted him.[37] It is for this reason that the Apostle says, *Rejoicing in tribulation and . . . knowing that tribulation works to bring patience; and patience the time of testing, and the time of testing hope; and hope does not throw us into confusion,*[38] and in another passage, *Who shall separate us from the love of Christ? Shall tribulation or poverty or persecution or famine or nakedness or peril or sword? As it is written, For your sake we are killed all the day long; we are regarded as sheep for the slaughter.*[39] The prophet Isaiah comforts those in a similar situation in these words, *You who have been weaned from milk, you who have been torn from the breasts, look for tribulation upon tribulation, but also for hope upon hope.*[40] *The sufferings of this present time are not worthy to be compared with the glory which shall be revealed in us.*[41] Why I have reflected on these passages the discourse which follows will make plain.

Proba, who from the midst of the sea had seen her native land going up in flames and had committed her own safety and that of those nearest to her to a fragile boat, found that the shores of Africa were even more cruel. For she was taken in by a man,[42] of whom one would not know whether to say that he was more covetous or more heatless, a man who cared for nothing but wine and money, and who under pretence of serving the mildest of emperors,[43] stood out as the most savage of all despots. If I may be allowed to quote a fable of the poets, [Heraclian] was like Orcus in Tartarus.[44] Like him too he had with him a Cerberus,[45] not three-headed but many-headed, ready to seize and rip apart everything within his reach. He tore betrothed daughters from their mothers' arms and sold young girls of noble birth in marriage to those greediest of men, the merchants of Syria. No plea of poverty induced him to spare either ward or widow or virgin dedicated to Christ. Indeed he looked more at the hands than at the faces of those who appealed to him. Such was the dread Charybdis and such the hound-girt Scylla,[46] which this lady encountered in fleeing from the barbarians, monsters who neither spared the shipwrecked nor heeded the cry of those made captive. Cruel wretch![47] At least imitate the enemy of the Roman Empire. The Brennus[48] of our day took only what he found, but you seek what you cannot find.

Virtue, indeed, is always exposed to envy, and envious persons may marvel at the secret agreement by which Proba purchased the chastity of her numerous companions. They may allege that the count, who could have taken everything, would not have been satisfied[49] with part, and that she could not have questioned his claim, since in spite of her rank, she was only a slave in his despotic hands. I perceive also that I am laying myself open to the attacks of enemies and that I may seem to be flattering a lady of the highest birth and distinction. Yet they will not be able to accuse me when they learn that until now I have said nothing about her. I have never in the lifetime of her husband or since his death praised her for the antiquity of her family or for the extent of her wealth and power, which other people might perhaps have praised in mercenary speeches. My purpose is to praise the grandmother of my virgin in a style appropriate to the Church and to thank her for having helped with her good will the good will of Demetrias. For the rest, my monastic cell, my coarse food, and my despicable clothing, and also my advanced age, already near death, and my resources for the short time to come, refute every infamous charge of flattery. In the remaining parts of my letter my discourse will be directed to the virgin herself, a virgin of noble birth—noble as much on grounds of holiness as of family. Of her it may be said that the higher she climbs, the more terrible will be her fall.

For the rest
This one thing, child of God, I lay on thee;
Yea before all, and urge it many times.[50]

Love to occupy your mind with the reading of Scripture. Do not in the good ground of your breast gather only a crop of darnel and wild oats. Do not let an enemy sow tares among the wheat when the householder is asleep,[51] that is, when the mind (which ever cleaves to God) is off its guard, but say always with the bride in the

Song of Songs, *By night I sought him whom my soul loves. Where do you feed and where do you lie down at noon?*[52] and with the psalmist, *my soul follows close behind you and your right hand holds me up*[53] and with Jeremiah, *I have not found it hard . . . to follow you,*[54] for *there is no grief in Jacob or toil in Israel*[55] When you were in the world, you loved the things that were of the world. You rubbed your cheeks with rouge and painted your face with white lead. You adorned your hair and built a tower on your head from hair that had belonged to other people. I shall say nothing of your costly earrings, your shining pearls from the depths of the Red Sea,[56] your bright green emeralds, your flashing onyxis, your blue-sea of sapphires—stones which turn the heads of married ladies and make them eager to possess them. For you have left the world, and since your baptismal vow you have taken a second vow; you have entered into a compact with your adversary, saying, 'I renounce you, O devil, and your world, your pomp and your works'. Keep the treaty that you have made therefore, and keep terms with your adversary while you are in the way of this world. Otherwise he may some day deliver you to the judge[57] and convince him that you have taken what is his, and then the judge will deliver you to his servant, who is at the same time your enemy and your avenger,[58] and you will be sent to prison and to the outer darkness[59] which surrounds us with greater horror in that it separates us from Christ, the one true light.[60] You will not emerge from there until you have paid the very last penny,[61] that is, until you have expiated your most trifling sins, for on the day of judgement we shall have to render an account of every idle word.[62]

In saying these things, I want, not to utter an ill-omened prophecy against you, but simply to warn you as an apprehensive and prudent counsellor who also, in your case, fears even what is safe. *If the spirit of the man who has power*, says Scripture, *rises up against you, do not leave your place.*[63] We stand always clad in our armor and drawn up in the line of battle for the fight. Our enemy wants to dislodge us from our place and to make us fall back; we must plant our feet firmly down and say with the psalmist, *He has set my feet upon a rock,*[64] and *The rocks are a refuge for conies.*[65]

For this last word, many people read 'hedgehogs'. The hedgehog is a small animal, very shy and weighed down with bristles. yet even so was Jesus çrowned with thorns for us and bore our sins and suffered pain for us, that the roses of virginity and the lilies of chastity might be born from the thorny tribulations of women, in respect of whom it is said, *In anxiety and sorrow you shall bring forth children and you shall turn to your husband and he shall rule over you.*[66] The Bridegroom *feeds among the lilies,*[67] that is, among those who have not defiled their garments, for they have remained virgins[68] and have listened to the saying of the Preacher, *Let your garments always be white.*[69] As the author and prince of virginity says boldly of himself, *I am the flower of the field and the lily of the valleys.*[70] *The rocks,* then, *are a refuge for conie, who when they are persecuted in one city, flee to another,*[71] and have no fear that the prophetic words, *Flight failed me,*[72] will be fulfilled in their case. *The mountains are for stags.*[73] Their food consists of serpents, which a little boy draws out from their holes, when the leopard and the kid take their rest together at the same time, and the ox and the lion eat straw[74] not, of course, that the ox may learn ferocity from the lion, but that the lion may be taught gentleness.

But let us turn back to the passage already quoted, *If the spirit of the ruler*[75] *rises up against you, do not leave your place,* a sentence which is followed by these words, *For administration causes very great sins to lie at rest.*[76] The meaning is: that if the serpent finds his way into your thoughts, guard your heart with all possible diligence[77] and sing with David, *Cleanse me from my secret faults, O Lord, and spare your servant from strange faults,* and you will never attain the *greatest transgression,* which is sin in your actions.[78] On the contrary, you will immediately slay the fires of vices while they are still only in your mind, and will dash the children of Babylon against the stones,[79] where the serpent can leave no trail.[80] Be wary and make a promise to the Lord, *If they shall have no dominion over me, then shall I be without stain and cleansed from the greatest offence.*[81] For elsewhere Scripture also testifies, *I will visit the sins of the fathers upon the children unto the third and fourth generation.*[82] That is to say, God will not punish our thoughts and resolves at once, but will send retribution on their offspring, that is, on the evil deeds and habits of sin which arise out of them. As he says by the mouth of Amos, *For three transgressions of such and such a city and for four, shall I not turn away the punishment thereof?*[83]

Let it be enough of a reminder for you to have plucked in passing, as it were, a few flowers from the fairest meadow of holy Scriptures, to the effect that you close the inner room in your breasts fortify your brow by making the sign of the cross frequently. Do this, so that the destroyer of Egypt may find no place to attack you and that the first-born of your soul may escape the fate of the first-born of the Egyptians (Ex 12:23, 29), and that with the prophet you may be able to say, *My heart is ready, O God, my heart is ready; I will sing and give praise. Awake, my glory; awake, lute and harp.*[84] Sin-stricken as she is, even Tyre is bidden to take up her harp[85] and to do penance; with Peter she is told to wash away the stains of her former foulness with bitter tears. But let us know nothing of penitence, lest the thought of it easily lead us into sin. Let it be a second plank for those unfortunate people who have been shipwrecked; but an inviolate virgin may hope to save the ship itself. It is one thing to look for what you have cast away and another to keep what you have never lost. Even the Apostle kept under his body and brought it into subjection, lest having preached to others he might himself become a castaway.[86] Heated with the passions of the human race, he spoke from his own experience, *O wretched man that I am, who will deliver me from the body of this death?,*[87] and again, *I know that nothing good lives in me, that is, in my flesh; for to will to do good lies nowhere within me. For the good that I would I do not, but the evil which I would not, that I do*[88] and once more, *They that are in the flesh cannot please God. But you are not in the flesh, but in the Spirit, if the Spirit of God dwells in you.*[89]

After you have paid very careful attention to your thoughts, you must then put on the armor of fasting and sing with David, *I have humbled my soul with fasting,*[90] and, *I have eaten ashes like bread,*[91] and, *As for me, when they troubled me, my clothing was sackcloth.*[92] Eve was expelled from paradise because she had eaten the forbidden fruit.[93] Elijah, on the other hand, after forty days of fasting, was carried in a fiery chariot into heaven.[94] For forty days and forty nights Moses lived by the intimate converse which he had with God,[95] thus proving in his own case the complete truth of the saying, *Man does not live by bread alone, but by every word that proceeds out of the mouth of God.*[96] The Saviour of the world, who in his virtues and his mode of life has left us an example to follow,[97] was, immediately after his baptism, taken up by the Spirit, that he might contend with the devil,[98] and after crushing and overthrowing him, might deliver him to his disciples to trample under foot. Thus the Apostle says, *God shall swiftly bruise Satan under your feet.*[99] Yet after Jesus had fasted forty days, it was through food that the old enemy laid a snare for him, saying, *If you are the Son of God, command that these stones be made bread.*[100] Under the law, in the seventh month after the blowing of trumpets and on the tenth day of the month, a fast was proclaimed for the whole jewish people, and the soul which on that day preferred self-indulgence to self-denial was cut off from among his people.[101] In Job it is written of the dragon, *His strength is in his loins and his courage is in the navel of his belly.*[102] He takes advantage of young men and girls through their youthful ardor and sets on fire the wheel of our birth.[103] He thus fulfills that saying of Hosea, *They are all adulterers; their hearts are like an oven,*[104] and are checked only by the mercy of God and the chill of fasting. These are the fiery darts of the devil,[105] which simultaneously both wound and set on fire and which were prepared by the king of Babylon for the three children. However, when he had built a furnace forty-nine cubits high,[106] he also turned to his own ruin[107] the seven weeks which the Lord had appointed for a time of salvation.[108] As a fourth man, having a form like a son of man, cooled the immense heat and, in the midst of the burning fiery furnace, taught the flames to lose their warmth—until on the one hand, they were threatening only to look at and, on the other, they rendered themselves possible to touch—[109] so it is that in the virginal soul, the flame of passion in a young girl is extinguished by the dew of heaven and by strict fasting, and the angelic way of life is brought about in a human body. Therefore the chosen vessel[110] declares that, concerning virgins, he has no commandment of the Lord.[111] You must act against nature, or rather above nature, if you are to forswear your natural function, to cut off your own root, to pluck no fruit but that of virginity, to be ignorant of the marriage bed, to shrink in horror from contact with men and, while in the body, to live as though out of it.

I do not, however, enjoin you to undertake excessive fasting or abnormal abstinence from food. These practices immediately cause delicate bodies to break down and cause people to become ill before the foundations of a holy way of life have been laid. It is, moreover, the opinion of philosophers that moderation is virtue and excess is vice: μεσότητας ἀρετας, ὑπερβολας κακίας εἶναι. In Latin this can mean that virtues are qualities of moderation and that those qualities which exceed the measure and limit are to be classed among the vices. It is in this sense that one of the Seven Sages propounds the famous aphorism quoted in the comedy, 'In nothing too much'.[112] You must not go on fasting until your heart begins to race and your breath to fail and you have to be supported or carried by others. You must keep up enough strength to read Scripture, to sing psalms, and to observe vigils. Fasting is not a complete virtue in itself, but only a foundation on which other virtues may be built. The same may be said of sanctification and of that chastity without which no man shall see God.[113] Each of these furnishes us with a step as we climb upwards, but if it is solitary, it cannot by itself obtain the virgin's crown. Let us read the gospel story of the wise and foolish virgins; some of them enter the bridegroom's marriage chamber, while others are shut out from it, because, not having the oil of good works, they cannot keep their lamps alight. On the subject of fasting, a wide field is opened up, in which I myself have often run about and about which many have written their own books. I send you to read these, to learn how good self-control is and on the contrary, how bad over-eating.

Imitate your Bridegroom,[114] be subject to your grandmother and to your mother. Do not look at men, particularly young men, unless you are with them. Do not be acquainted with a man whom they do not know. It is a maxim of the world that to like and dislike the same things is a firm basis for friendship.[115] The holy atmosphere of your home, as well as their examples, has taught you to strive for virginity, to know the teachings of Christ, and to know what is expedient for you and what you ought to choose. Do not consider that what is yours is yours alone; it also belongs to those ladies, who in you have expressed their chastity and their honorable marriages[116] and have brought you forth as the most precious flower of an undefiled marriage bed, a flower which will produce perfect fruit, if you will humble yourself under the mighty hand of God[117] and will remember what is written, *God resists the proud and gives grace to the humble.*[118] Now where there is grace, this is not given in return for works but is the free gift of the giver, so that the Apostle's words may be fulfilled, *It is not the property of the person who will sit or of the person who runs after it, but of God who shows mercy.*[119] Yet it is our job to will and not to will; and all the while the very liberty that is ours is ours only by the mercy of God.

Again, in selecting for yourself eunuchs and maids and young men-servants, pay more attention to their characters than to their good looks, for whatever their age or sex, and even if mutilation ensures in them a compulsory chastity, you must take account of their dispositions, for these cannot be operated on except through fear of Christ. When you are present, there is no place for buffoonery and loose talk. Never hear an improper word. If you do hear one, do not be angry. Men of abandoned mind often make use of a single light expression to test the barriers of chastity. Leave it to worldly people to laugh and be laughed at. A solemn demeanor is fitting for someone in your position. According to Lucilius,[120] Cato[121] —he I say, who was the Censor and in olden times a leading figure in your city and who in his last days did not blush at greek literature as censor nor despair as an old man in his study of it—and Marcus Crassus[122] too laughed only once in their lives. These men may have affected this grave air while seeking glory and notoriety for themselves. For so long as we dwell in the tabernacle of this body and are enveloped by this fragile flesh, we can regulate and govern our feelings and passions, but we cannot cut them right off. Knowing this, the psalmist says, *We are angry and we do not wish to sin,*[123] which the Apostle explains as, *Do not let the sun go down upon your wrath.*[124] For if to be angry is human, to put an end to one's anger is christian.

I think it superfluous to warn you against covetousness, since it is the practice of your family both to have riches and to despise them, and the Apostle too teaches us that covetousness is idolatry.[125] Moreover, to someone who asked him, *Good master, what good thing shall I do and have eternal life?* the Lord replied, *If you wish to be perfect, go and sell what you have and give to the poor, and then you shall have treasure in heaven; and come, follow me.*[126] Such is the climax of complete and apostolic virtue: to sell all that one has and to distribute to the poor[127] and, thus freed from all earthly encumbrance, to fly up to the heavenly realms with Christ. To us, indeed to you, a careful stewardship is entrusted, although in such matters full freedom of choice is left to every individual, whether old or young. Christ's words are, *If you wish to be perfect.* I do not compel you, he seems to say, I do not command you, but I set the palm before you, I show you the prize;[128] it is for you to choose whether you will enter the arena and win the crown. Let us consider how wisely Wisdom has spoken. *Sell what you have.* To whom is the command given? Was it not to him to whom it was said, *If you wish to be perfect.* The command was not 'Sell part of your goods', but 'Sell all that you have'. When you have sold them, what follows? *Give to the poor.* Not to the rich, not to your relatives, not to minister to self-indulgence, but to relieve need. It does not matter whether a man is a priest or a close relative or a connection; you are to consider nothing about him except his poverty. Let your praises come from the stomachs of the starving and not from those who belch at rich feasts. In the Acts of the Apostles, we read that, while our Lord's blood was still warm and believers were fervent in their newly-found faith, they all sold their possessions and laid the price of them at the apostles' feet—to show that money ought to be trampled under foot—and it was distributed individually to every person, according to his need.[129] But Ananias and Sapphira were timid, and what is more, deceitful stewards; therefore they brought condemnation upon themselves. For having made a vow, they offered their money to God as if it were their own and not his to whom they had vowed it. And keeping back for their own use a part of what belonged to another, through fear of famine—which true faith never fears—they abruptly drew down on themselves the avenging stroke which was meant, not in cruelty towards them, but as a warning to others.[130] In fact, the apostle Peter in no way called death down upon them, as Porphyry foolishly says.[131] He merely announced God's judgement by the spirit of prophecy, that the doom of two persons might be a lesson to many. From the time of your dedication to perpetual virginity, your property is yours no longer; or rather, it is now first truly yours, because it has come to be Christ's. Yet while your grandmother and mother are living, you must deal with it according to their wishes. If, however, they die and rest in the sleep of the saints—and I know that they desire that you should survive them—then when your years are riper and your will steadier, and your resolution stronger, you will do with your money what seems best to you, or rather what the Lord shall command, knowing as you shall that hereafter you will have nothing except what you have spent here on good works. Others may build churches, may adorn their walls, once built, with incrustations of marble, may procure massive columns, may deck the insensate capitals with gold and precious ornaments, may cover church doors with ivory and silver, and may adorn the altars with gold and gems. I do not blame those who do these things; I do not repudiate them.[132] Everyone must follow his own judgement,[133] and it is better to spend one's money this way than to hoard it up and brood over it. Your duty, however, is of a different kind. It is yours to clothe Christ in the poor, to visit him in the sick, to feed him in the hungry, to shelter him in the homeless, particularly such as are of the household of faith,[134] to support monasteries of virgins, to take care of God's servants, of those who are poor in spirit, who day and night serve the same Lord as you, who while they are on the earth live the angelic life and speak only of the praises of God. Having food and raiment,[135] they rejoice. They seek nothing more, if only they can persevere in their intention. For as soon as they begin to seek more, they are shown to be undeserving even of those things that are necessary.

The preceding counsels have been addressed to a virgin, who is wealthy and a lady of rank.

But what I am now going to say will be addressed to the virgin alone. I shall take into consideration, that is, not your circumstances, but yourself. In addition to the rule of psalmody and prayer, which you must always observe at the third, sixth, and ninth hours, at evening, at midnight and at dawn,[136] decide how many hours you ought to give to memorizing holy Scripture, and how much time you should spend in reading, not as a burden, but for the delight and instruction of your soul. When you have spent your allotted time in these studies, often kneeling down to pray—as care for your soul will impel you to do—have some wool always in your hands, and spinning out the threads of the weft with your thumb, attach them to the shuttle, and then throw this to weave a web; or wind into a ball the yarn which others have spun or prepare it to be woven. Examine what has been done, find fault with its defects, and arrange how much work is to be done. If you busy yourself with these numerous and varied occupations, you will never find your days long. However late the summer sun may be in setting, a day will always seem too short on which something remains undone. By observing these rules, you will save yourself and others, you will be the teacher of a holy way of living and you will put to your credit the chastity of many. For the Scripture says, *The soul of every idler is filled with desires*.[137] Nor must you cease from toil on the plea that God's bounty has left you in want of nothing. No; you must labor with everyone else, so that, being always busy, you may think only of the Lord's service. I shall speak quite plainly. Even supposing that you give all your property to the poor, Christ will value nothing more highly than what you have made with your own hands. You may work for yourself or to set an example to your virgins; or you may give presents to your mother and grandmother to draw from them larger sums for the relief of the poor.

I have almost passed over the most important point of all. While you were still quite small, bishop Anastasius of holy and blessed memory[138] ruled the roman Church. In his days a terrible storm of heresy came from the East and threatened first to corrupt and then to undermine that simple faith which the Apostle praises.[139] Yet the bishop, rich in poverty and in apostolic care for his flock, at once smote the noxious thing on the head and silenced the hydra's hissing. Now I have reason to fear—in fact a report has reached me to this effect—that the poisonous seedlings of this heresy still live and to this day sprout in the minds of some people.[140] I think therefore that I ought to forewarn you, in dutiful and affectionate love, to hold fast the faith of the saintly Innocent—[141] the successor of Anastasius in the apostolic see and his spiritual son—and not to receive any foreign doctrine, however wise and discerning you may take yourself to be. People of this type whisper in corners and pretend to enquire into the justice of God, 'Why,' they ask, 'was such and such a soul born in such and such a province? What is the reason that some are born of christian parents, and others among wild beasts and savage tribes who have no knowledge of God?' Whenever they strike the simple with their scorpion sting and raise an ulcer fitted to their purpose, they diffuse their venom. 'Is it for nothing, do you think,' for thus they argue, 'that a little child scarcely able to recognize its mother by a laugh or a look of joy, which has done nothing either good or evil, is seized by a devil or overwhelmed with jaundice or doomed to bear afflictions which godless men escape, while God's servants have to bear them?' Now if God's judgments, they say, are *true and justified in themselves*,[142] and if *There is no unrighteousness in him*,[143] we are compelled by reason to believe that our souls have pre-existed in heaven, that they are condemned to, and (if I may say so) buried in, human bodies because of some ancient sins, and that we are punished in this valley of weeping[144] for old misdeeds. According to them, this is the prophet's reason for saying, *Before I was afflicted, I went astray*[145] and again, *Bring my soul out of prison.*[146] In the same way they explain the disciples' question in the Gospel, *Who committed sin, this man or his parents, that he was born blind?*[147] and other similar passages.

This godless and wicked teaching formerly circulated in Egypt and the East. Now it circulates secretly, like a viper in its hole, among many persons in those parts, defiling the purity of the faith and gradually creeping along like an inherited disease till it has reached many. But I am sure that if you hear it, you will not accept it. For you have as teachers under God women whose faith is a rule of sound doctrine. You will understand what I mean, for God will give you understanding in all things.[148] You must not ask me on the spot to give you a refutation of this dreadful heresy and of others worse still; were I to do so, I should criticize where I ought to condemn, and my present object is not to refute heretics but to instruct a virgin. Besides, by God's help, I have overturned their misrepresentations and their cunning efforts to undermine the truth in another work[149] which, if you want to have it, I shall send to you promptly and with pleasure. I say, if you want to have it, for as the proverb says, wares proffered unasked are little esteemed, and a plentiful supply brings down prices, which are always highest where scarcity prevails.

People often discuss the comparative merits of life in solitude and life in community, and the preference is usually given to the first over the second.[150] Still for men, there is always the risk that, being withdrawn from the society of their fellows, they may become exposed to unclean and godless ideas, and in the fullness of their arrogance and disdain, may look down on everyone but themselves, and may arm their tongues for the purpose of disparaging the clergy or the other monks. Of them it is well said by the psalmist, *As for the children of men, their teeth are spears and arrows and their tongue a sharp sword.*[151] Now if all this is true of men, how much more does it apply to women, whose fickle and vacillating minds, if left to their own devices, soon slide down to something worse. I am myself acquainted with anchorites of both sexes who, by excessive fasting, have so impaired their faculties that they do not know what to do or where to turn, when to speak or when to act. Most frequently those who have been so affected have lived in solitary cells, cold and damp. What is more, if persons untrained in secular learning read the works of able church writers, they acquire from them only a wordy fluency and not, as they might do, a fuller knowledge of the Scriptures. The old law applies to them: having not the wit to speak, they

cannot remain silent.[152] They teach to others Scriptures they do
not understand themselves, and if they are fortunate enough to
convince them, they take the airs of the learned. They set up as
instructors of the inexperienced before having gone to school
themselves. It is a good thing therefore to defer to one's elders,
to obey those who are advanced, and to learn not only from the
Scriptures but from the example of others how one ought to order
one's life, and not to follow that worst of all teachers, one's own
self-confidence. Of women of this type, the Apostle says: they *are
carried about with every wind of doctrine,*[153] *always learning and
never able to come to the knowledge of the truth.*[154]

Avoid the company of married women who are devoted to
their husbands and to the world, so your mind does not become
unsettled by hearing what a husband says to his wife, or a wife to
her husband. Such conversations are filled with deadly venom. To
express his condemnation of them, the Apostle has taken a verse
from a profane writer and pressed it into the service of the Church.
It may be rendered literally, *Evil communications corrupt good
manners,*[155] but the latin translation cannot reproduce the iambic
metre.[156] Let serious women, particularly widows and virgin, be
chosen as your companions, women of a proven way of life, of
few words, and holy modesty. Shun the frivolity of girls who wear
hair ornaments, let their hair fall in a fringe over their forehead,
who use face-cream and cosmetics to improve their skins, and
who go in for tight sleeves, dresses without a crease, and slippers
with curled-up toes. By pretending to be virgins, they easily sell
themselves into destruction. Moreover the character and tastes of
a mistress are often indicated by the behavior of her attendants.
Regard as fair and loveable a woman who is unconscious of her
good looks and careless of her appearance, who does not expose
her breast and her throat out of doors to throw back her cloak
to reveal her neck, who veils her whole face, leaving scarcely an
opening for one eye—and that only from the need to find her way.

I hesitate about what I am going to say, but, as often happens,
whether I like it or not, it must be said—not that I have reason
to fear anything of the kind in your case, for probably you know
nothing of such things and have never even heard of them—but

in advising you, I may warn others. Let a virgin shun, as so many plagues and banes of chastity, young men with hair arranged in ringlets and curled with tongs and with skins scented with artificial musk. To them the words of Petronius Arbiter may well be applied,

'He does not smell good who always smells good'.[157] I need not speak of those who, by their persistent visits to virgins, bring discredit both on them and on themselves. Even if they do nothing wrong, no greater wrong can be imagined than to find oneself exposed to the calumnies and attacks of pagans. I do not speak of all, but only of those whom the Church itself rebukes, who it sometimes expels and against whom the censure of bishops and presbyters is not infrequently directed. As it is, it is almost more dangerous for frivolous girls to show themselves in the abodes of religion than to walk about in public. Women who live in monasteries and of whom large numbers are assembled together, should never go out by themselves or unaccompanied by their mother.[158] A hawk often singles out one of a flight of doves, pounces on it, and tears at it until it is gorged with its flesh and blood. Sick sheep stray from the flock and fall into the jaws of wolves. I know some saintly virgins who, on holy days, keep at home to avoid crowds and refuse to go out when they must either take a strong escort or altogether avoid all public places.

Some thirty years ago I published a treatise *On the preservation of virginity*,[159] in which I felt constrained to oppose certain vices and to lay bare the wiles of the devil for the instruction of the virgin to whom it was addressed. My language then gave offence to a great many, for everyone applied what I said to himself and, instead of welcoming my admonitions, turned away from me as an accuser. Was it any use, do you ask, to arm a host of remonstrants this way to show by my complaints the wounds which my conscience received? Yes, I answer, for while the people have passed away, my book still remains. I have also written short exhortations to several virgins and widows, and in these small works I have gathered everything there is to be said on the subject. I am reduced to the alternatives of repeating exhortations which seem superfluous or of omitting them to the serious injury of this treatise. The blessed Cyprian has left a noble work on virginity;[160] and many other writers, both Greek and Latin, have done the same. Indeed the virginal life has been praised both by tongue and pen among all nations and particularly among the churches.[161] Yet most of those who have written on the subject have addressed themselves to those who have not yet chosen virginity and who need help to enable them to choose aright. But I , and those to whom I write, have made our choice, and our one object is to remain constant to it. Therefore as our way lies among scorpions and adders, among snares and banes, let us go forward, staff in hand, our loins girded and our feet shod,[162] that so we may come to the sweet waters of the true Jordan, and enter the land of promise and go up to the house of God. Then shall we sing with the prophet, *Lord, I have loved the beauty of your house and the place where your glory dwells,*[163] and again, *One thing will I ask of the Lord, that I may dwell in the house of the Lord all the days of my life.*[164]

Happy is her conscience, happy her virginity in whose heart there is room for no other love than the love of Christ. In himself he is wisdom and chastity, patience and justice and every other virtue. Happy too is she who can recall a man's face without the least sigh of regret, and who has no desire to set eyes on someone whom, once she has seen him, she may find herself unwilling to give up. Some there are, however, who by their bad behavior, bring discredit on the holy profession of virginity and on the glory of the heavenly and angelic company who have made it. These must be frankly told either to marry if they cannot be continent, or to be continent if they do not wish to marry. It is a matter for laughter, or rather for tears, that when mistresses go out walking, they are preceded by maids better dressed than themselves; indeed this has become so usual that if you see two women, one less neat than the other, you take her for the mistress as the matter of course. Yet these maids are professed virgins. Not a few choose dwellings set apart and away from onlookers, in order to live more freely than they otherwise could do. They take baths, do what they please, and try as much as they can to escape notice. We see these things and put up with them, and, if we catch sight of the glitter of gold, we are ready to count them as good works.

I end as I began, not content to have given you only a single warning. Love the holy Scriptures, and wisdom will love you. Honor wisdom, and it will embrace you.[165] Let this be the jewels on your breast and in your ears. Let your tongue know no theme but Christ, let no sound pass your lips that is not holy, and let your words always reproduce that sweetness of which your grandmother and your mother set you the example. Imitate them, for they are models of virtue.

NOTES

1. Pl 30:16.
2. See Letter 28, n.1.
3. Col 2:1.
4. Ezk 41:22.
5. Jerome mistakenly takes 'the altar of wood' to mean 'the altar of incense'.
6. Rm 12:1.
7. 2 Cor 11:2.
8. Ps 44:10, 14–15 (45:9, 13–14).
9. Gn 37:3.
10. Ps 44:13 (45:14).
11. Demetrias was a member of the *gens Anicia*. The roman *gentes*, of which three of the most illustrious are mentioned here, were extended families, comparable to the ancient scottish clans. For details of their members in the late imperial period, see PLRE, where there is a *stemma* (family tree) of the Anicii in volume 1, p. 1133.
12. Anicius Hermogenianus Olybrius, the father of Demetrias, was made consul, together with his brother, in 395. He was 'happy in his death', because it occurred before the sack of Rome in 395.
13. Mt 11:8.
14. 4 (2) Kgs 1:8; Mt 3:4.
15. Mt 11:14, Lk 1:17.
16. Lk 2:36–7.
17. Ac 21:29.
18. Lk 2:36–7.
19. Ac 21:29.
20. Est 14:16.
21. There are various legends about Saint Agnes. Nothing definite is known about the date and manner of her death which occurred probably during the persecutions carried out in the reign of Diocletian (284–305). According to persecutions carried out in the reign of Diocletian (284–305).

According to tradition, she was a young roman girl of about thirteen, who preferred death to the betrayal of her faith and the loss of her virginity. The basilicas of Saint Agnes in Rome is believed to have been built *c.* 350, above her remains, and her name occurs in the Roman Canon of the Mass.

22. For the cruelties of Heraclian, count of Africa, see p. 227, and n. 42 below.

23. The *pronuba* was a married woman, who acted as the bride's principal attendant at a roman wedding.

24. Lascivious wedding songs, called after their place of origin, Fescennia in Etruria.

25. 1 Jn 4:18.

26. Eph 6:16, 14, 17.

27. Marcus Tullius Cicero (*c.* 106–43 bc) and Demosthenes (384–322 bc) are cited as the types of latin and greek eloquence. Cicero was a fluent speaker, both as a lawyer and as a politician, and left behind him a considerable body of speeches; some of these were actually delivered, but others were compiled later. He was the originator of the classic latin prose style, on which later writers modelled themselves. Many of his writings, both speeches and letters, survive and are still studied in schools and universities. Demosthenes, on the other hand, was not a natural orator, but took pains in curing himself of speech defects and in writing out his speeches in advance. Many of his speeches deal with the danger of the rising power of Philip of Macedon, which threatened the Athenian Empire. As in the case of Cicero, many of his speeches survive and are still standard texts for study.

28. The battle of Nola (216 bc), was the first roman victory in the Second Punic War, after defeats inflicted on roman forces by Hannibal at the river Trebia, Lake Trasimene and Cannae.

29. A reference to the siege of the capitol at Rome by the gallic chieftain Brennus in 390 bc.

30. I.e., Juliana and Proba, the mother and grandmother of Demetrias.

31. The husband of Juliana and father of Demetrias.

32. Olybrius.

33. Horace, *Odes* 3.3, 7–8.

34. Jb 1:16.

35. Jb 7:1.

36. Mt 4:11.

37. Gn 22:1.

38. Rm 5:3–5.

39. Rm 8:35–36, Ps 43 (44):22.

40. Is 27:9–10.

41. Rm 8:18.

42. Heraclian, notorious as the murderer of Stilicho at Ravenna in August 408. As a reward for this crime, he was given command of the armies of Africa later the same year. In the troubles of 409–410, he remained loyal to the Emperor Honorius against Priscus Attalus and sent him financial

help. As soon as he reached Africa, he killed Constans, whom Attalus had sent to succeed him. He then stopped all trade between Africa and Italy, to put pressure on Attalus. Although the chronicler reports that he made strenuous efforts to restore life in the roman world, he treated refugees from Rome harshly, as we see from this description of Proba's experiences. After invading Italy in 413, he was defeated at Utriculum and driven back to Carthage, where he was subsequently murdered in the same year. His consulship and acts were annulled. Sabinus may have been the son-in-law of Heraclian, described by Orosius as an able man, who would have been called wise, if he had devoted himself to quiet studies (Historiae 7.42.11). After the overthrow of Heraclian, Sabinus fled to Constantinople, but was handed over to the authorities of the Western Empire, who sent him into exile (Orosius, *Historiae* 7.42.14).

43. Honorius (b. 384) was emperor 393–423. He was the younger son of Theodosius I and Aelia Flavia Flaccilla, and married in succession the two daughters of Stilicho, Maria and Thermantia.

44. I.e., Pluto, king of the underworld.

45. Cerberus was the three-headed dog with hair of snakes, who acted as guardian of the underworld. He gave a friendly welcome, but would not allow anyone to leave. 'Cerberus' here stands for Sabinus, the son-in-law of Heraclian.

46. Scylla and Charybdis are, respectively, the female sea-monster and the whirlpool which the ancients believed to be situated at the Straits of Messina. They are described by Homer in *Odyssey* 11.85–110. Scylla barked like a dog and had twelve feet and six necks, on each of which was a head with three rows of teeth. If a ship came near, she grabbed a member of the crew with each of her heads. Evasive action taken to avoid Scylla could result in the ship being sucked down by the whirlpool Charybdis. Here Charybdis appears to represent Heraclian, and Scylla, Sabinianus, surrounded by his minions, who pursued their prey like hounds.

47. I.e., Heraclian.

48. For Brennus the Gaul, see note 29 above. 'Brennus' here stands for Alaric the Goth.

49. Hilberg (CSEL 56:185,6) reads *dignatus*, but Fremantle's emendation, *dedignatus*, makes better sense.

50. Vergil, *Aeneid* 3, 435.

51. Mt 13:25.

52. Sg 3:1, 1:7.

53. Ps 62:9 (63:8).

54. Jr 17:16.

55. Nb 23:21.

56. The Indian Ocean.

57. Mt 5:25.

58. Mt 22:13.

59. Mt 8:12.

60. Jn 8:12.

61. Mt 25:6.

62. Mt 12:36.
63. Si 10:4.
64. Ps 39:3 (40:2).
65. Ps 103 (104):18.
66. Gn 3:16.
67. Sg 2:16.
68. Rv 14:4.
69. Si 9:8.
70. Sg 2:1.
71. Mt 10:23.
72. Ps 141 (142):4.
73. Ps 103 (104):18.
74. Is 11:6–8.
75. Jerome here interprets 'the ruler' as the devil.
76. Si 10:4.
77. Pr 4:23.
78. Ps 18 (19) 12–14.
79. Ps 136 (137):9.
80. Cf. Pr 30:19.
81. Ps 18 (19):13.
82. Nb 14:18.
83. Am 1:3.
84. Ps 56:8–9 (57:7–8).
85. Is 23:15–16.
86. 1 Cor 9:27.
87. Rm 7:24.
88. Rm 7:18–19.
89. Rm 8:8–9.
90. Ps 68:11 (69:10).
91. Ps 101:10 (102:9).
92. Ps 34 (35):13.
93. Gn 3.
94. 3 (1) Kgs 19:8.
95. Ex 24:18, 34:28.
96. Dt 8:3, Mt 4:4.
97. Jn 13:15, 1 P 2:21.
98. Mt 4:1.
99. Rm 16:20.
100. Mt 4:3.
101. Lv 23:27, 29.
102. Jb 40:11.
103. Jm 3:6.
104. Hos 7:4.
105. Eph 6:16.
106. Dn 3:40.
107. Dn 4:16, 25, 32.
108. Lv 25:8.
109. Dn 3:25.

110. Ac 9:15.
111. 1 Cor 7:25.
112. Terence, *Andria* 61.
113. Hb 12:14.
114. Lk 2:51.
115. Sallist, *Catil.* 2.4.
116. Hb 13:1.
117. 1 P 5:6.
118. 1 P 5:5, Jm 4:6.
119. Rm 9:16.
120. Lucilius was a satirical poet, born c. 180 bc. Only fragments of his work remain, none of which contains this story.
121. Marcus Porcius Cato (234–168 bc) is famous as the embodiment of all the ancient roman virtues and as an ardent patriot who feared all innovations. After serving with distinction in the Second Punic War, he held numerous public offices, culminating in the consulship in 195 bc and the censorship in 184 bc. The duties of this office included both taking the census of the population and the general supervision of public morals. The statement that Cato became acquainted with greek literature in his old age is also made by the historian Livy (59 bc–ad 17) in his *Ab urbe condita libri*, bk 39.40, from which Jerome must have drawn his information. Jerome's text is corrupt here. Hilberg inserts a lacuna here, but the passage can make sense without it.
122. Marcus Porcius Crassus, who already possessed the epithet *Dives* on account of the wealth of his family, received the additional nickname of greek origin, father of the more famous Marcus Porcius Crassus Dives, who became consul with Pompey and who with the latter and Julius Caesar formed the so-called First Triumvirate in 60 bc.
123. Ps 4:5 (4).
124. Eph 4:26.
125. Eph 6:6.
126. Mt 19:16, 21.
127. Lk 18:22.
128. 2 Tm 2:5.
129. Ac 4:34–5.
130. Ac 5:1–10.
131. Porphyry (c. 232–303) was a neoplatonist philosopher. It is possible that he was once a Christian, but at any rate he was convinced of the principles of Neoplatonism by Plotinus (205–270), the founder of the system. Porphyry's work, *Against the Christians*, was condemned to be burned in 448 and survives mainly in fragments in works written to refute it. He seems to have observed in it a certain restraint in his treatment of Jesus Christ, but to have launched bitter attacks on the apostles.
132. But in Letter 52 (not included in this selection; for a translation, see Greenslade, *Early Latin Theology*, pp. 312–329, or Fremantle, pp. 89–96), Jerome passes severe judgement on the building of elaborate churches and stresses the desirability of purity and simplicity among Christians.
133. Rm 14:5.

134. Gal 6:10.
135. 1 Tm 6:8.
136. See Letter 22, n.39.
137. Pr 13:4.
138. Anastasius was pope 398–402.
139. Cf Rm 1:8.
140. The teaching of the Origenists: see Letter 127, notes 68, 71 (p. 121).
141. Pope Innocent I (402–417) made more substantial claims for the papacy than any of his predecessors and exercised authority in the East as well as in the West.
142. Ps 18:10 (19.9).
143. Ps 91 (92):15.
144. Ps 83:7 (84:6).
145. Ps 118 (119):67.
146. Ps 108: 8 (142:7).
147. Jn 9:2.
148. 2 Tm 2:7.
149. Apparently a reference to Letter 124 (not included in this selection; for a translation, see Fremantle, pp. 238–244), in which Jerome deals with Origen's treatise, *On first Principles*.
150. In Letter 125.9 (not included in this selection; see Fremantle, pp. 244–252), Jerome advises Rusticus not to become a solitary but to continue as a member of a community.
151. Ps 56:5 (57:4).
152. *quid loqui, quid tacere solent*: the manuscripts here vary between *facere* = to act (adopted by Hilberg) and *tacere* = to be silent (adopted by Fremantle). I have followed Fremantle, as this reading seems to provide a stronger contrast.
153. Eph 4:14.
154. 2 Tm 3:7.
155. 1 Cor 15:33.
156. This is a quotation from a lost play by the greek writer of comedies, Menander (342–290 bc).
157. This appears to be a slip of memory. The words appear not in the poems of the satirist, Petronius Arberter (d. ad 66), but in the *Epigrams* of Martial (*c.* 40–102) II.12,4.
158. 'Mother' is a technical term here, meaning the head of a community of women religious, but in the case of a domestic monastery, this lady might also be the natural mother of some of its members, as in the case of Paula and Eustochium.
159. Letter 22.
160. Cyprian; see Letter 22, n. 250, p.215.
161. Gregory of Nyssa also wrote on virginity.
162. Ex 12:11.
163. Ps 25 (26):8.
164. Ps 26 (27):4.
165. Pr 4:6, 8.

PAULA THE YOUNGER AND PACATULA
HOW TO RAISE YOUNG VIRGINS

To Laeta

LAETA, the recipient of Letter 107, was the daughter-in-law of Paula the Elder and the mother of Paula the Younger. Laeta belonged to the group of high-born roman ladies to whom Jerome acted as a spiritual director and whom he encouraged to practice a life of asceticism, whether at home or in a monastery. She was the daughter of a pagan, Albinus, but had married the Christian Toxotius, son of the elder Paula. She was also the cousin of Marcella, one of Jerome's closest friends.

While very little can be said of Laeta herself, her daughter Paula appears quite often in Jerome's correspondence. The present letter was successful in its plea that she should be sent to Bethlehem as a consecrated virgin, to be trained in the monastery of her grandmother Paula and her aunt Eustochium. But—or so it would seem—Laeta was too affectionate or too prudent a mother to send her there in infancy or early girlhood. There is no mention of the elder Paula ever seeing her, and the first evidence of her presence in Bethlehem comes from Letter 134 (written in 415–416), where Eustochium and Paula send their greetings through Jerome to Augustine, and where we hear of a presbyter, Firmus, who is travelling to Ravenna, Africa and Sicily *ob rem earum*, that is, presumably, on business concerning their estates. With Eustochium she went through the raids made by the pelagian party upon her monastery (Letters 134–137), and on her aunt's death in 418–419 she took charge of it, though still very

251

young. In one of Jerome's last letters, written in 419 to Augustine and his friend Alypius, she is described as *neptis vestra* (grand-daughter), spiritually, of course, but in contrast to Eustochium, *filia vestra*.

The date of her birth cannot be determined with absolute certainty, but when this letter was written she was still unweaned (¶13). The letter unquestionably precedes the death of the elder Paul in AD 404, and Cavallera argues reasonably enough that it also precedes her long illness of 402–403, which would otherwise have been mentioned in ¶13. He places it in 400, concluding from ¶2 that it antedates the destruction of the Temple of Marnas at Gaza in 401; though one might rather infer that Jerome is speaking rhetorically of an event which has recently occurred or at a time when the doom of the temple is known and imminent, and thus in 401 or 402.[1] Wright puts Paula's birth in 397 and the letter in 403, but without discussion.

With the substance of the letter we can compare Jerome's letter (128) to Gaudentius, on the education of his daughter. Written in AD 413, it is shorter, but similar. Jerome's ideas may then be compared with the almost contemporary tract of John Chrysostom, *On the Education of Children* (the Golden Book), whose authenticity seems now, after some questioning, to be generally admitted.[2] There is an amusing combination of the three documents in J. G. Davies, *Social Life of Early Christians*, Chapter 5, where it is justly pointed out that, whatever christian parents decided to do about sending their sons to the public schools, there were none for girls.

PACATULA is the subject of Letter 128, written from Palestine in 413, when Jerome, on his own admission, was feeling grief-stricken, old, and tired. He was about eighty-two years old, a very considerable age in the fourth century. The manuscripts differ as to the person to whom the letter was addressed; some read Pacatula and others Gaudentius. It appears that the latter, a personal friend, had written from Rome to ask Jerome's advice on the upbringing and education of his little daughter, Pacatula, who had been dedicated by her parents as a virgin from birth. The letter begins by playfully addressing Pacatula, in the hope that she will be able to read it later on, but Jerome, who admits in the last paragraph that he is dictating it 'in some confusion of speech', is unable to keep up his would-be playful style and at the end, he frankly apostrophizes Gaudentius.

This letter is briefer than Letter 107 instructing Laeta, the daughter-in-law of Paula, on the upbringing of her daughter, Paula the younger, another child-oblate. The advice given is very similar: young girls should be protected from worldly companions, and above all, from boys and worldly women; their lessons should be made interesting and pleasurable; they should learn the alphabet, spelling, latin grammar and syntax, and should receive some attractive little present as a reward. They are always to go about with their mothers and are not to frequent public places, particularly crowded churches, but should find their pleasure in their own rooms. Above all, their appearance is to be austere and unattractive. They are to wear dark clothing as an indication of their dedication to virginity; they are not to use make-up or adorn themselves with jewelry. On the other hand, there is not to be an ostentatious display of poverty and ugliness, lest people praise them for these qualities. Their diet is to be very simple; they are allowed a little wine and meat only while they are still growing. Spinning wool is to be encouraged as an occupation.

In the earlier letter, Jerome's instructions are more detailed: little Paula was to have as a plaything an alphabet made of box-wood or ivory; she is to begin to learn the greek letters at the same time as the latin. Paula was to have a male tutor of ripe years and scholarship, whereas Pacatula is to have a governess of plain and dowdy appearance.

This educational advice presents Jerome in a more human light, but, in point of fact, many of these pedagogical details are culled from Quintilian, whose works Jerome no doubt studied at the rhetorical stage of his education.

The style of this letter is diffuse. A long digression about male and female virginity and the rehearsal of the arguments for and against dressing child-oblates in dark clothes, combined with its generally pessimistic tone, suggest that age and infirmity were causing Jerome to begin to lose his grip.

J. M. P.

1. F. Cavallera, *Saint Jerome*, dates the destruction to 401 AD, without discussion. According to Mark the Deacon, it would be 402.
2. M. L. W. Laistner, *Christianity and Pagan Culture in the later Roman Empire* (1951) contains a translation of Chrysostom's tract.

To Laeta (*Letter 107*)

THE BLESSED APOSTLE PAUL, writing to the Corinthians and instructing in sacred discipline a church still untaught in Christ, has among other commandments also laid down this: *The woman who has a husband who does not believe, and if he is content to dwell with her, should not leave him. For the unbelieving husband is sanctified by the believing wife, and the unbelieving wife is sanctified by the brother; otherwise your children would be unclean, but now they are holy,*[1] Should any person have supposed hitherto that the bonds of discipline are too far relaxed and that too much indulgence is conceded by the teacher, let him look at the house of your father, a man of the highest rank and learning, but one still walking in darkness; and he will perceive, as the result of the Apostle's counsel, sweet fruit growing from a bitter stock and precious balsams exhaled from common canes. You yourself are the offspring of a mixed marriage; but you and my friend Toxotius are the parents of Paula. Who could have believed that to the *Pontifex*[2] Albinus a granddaughter should be born in answer to a mother's vows; that a delighted grandfather should hear from the child's faltering lips the song of *Alleluia*, and that in his old age he should nurse in his arms one of Christ's own virgins? Our expectations have been fully gratified. The one unbeliever is sanctified by his holy and believing family. For, when a man is surrounded by a believing crowd of children and grandchildren, he is a candidate for the faith. (I for my part think that, had he possessed such kinsfolk, even Jove himself might have come to believe in Christ!) For though he may spit on my letter and laugh at it, and though he may call me a fool or a madman, his son-in-law did the same before he came to believe. Christians are not born but made. For all its gilding the Capitol is beginning to look dingy. Every temple in Rome is covered with soot and cobwebs.[3] The city is shaken to its foundations and the people pour past their half-ruined shrines to visit the tombs of the martyrs. The faith which has not been accorded to knowledge may come to be extorted by very shame.

I speak thus to you, Laeta, my most devout daughter in Christ, to teach you not to despair of your father's salvation. My hope is that the same faith which has won you your daughter may win your father too, and that you may be able to rejoice over blessings bestowed on your entire family. You know the Lord's promise: *The things which are impossible with men are possible with God.*[4] It is never too late to mend. The robber passed from the cross to paradise. Nebuchadnezzar also, the King of Babylon, recovered his reason, even after he had been made like the beasts in body and in heart and had lived with the brutes in the wilderness.[5] And to pass over old stories which to unbelievers may well seem incredible, did not your own kinsman Gracchus, whose name betokens his patrician origin, when a few years back he held the Prefecture of the City, overthrow, break in pieces, and set on fire the grotto of Mithras and all the dreadful images therein? Those I mean by which the worshippers were initiated as Raven, Bridegroom, Soldier, Lion, Persian, Sun-runner, and Father? Did he not send them before him as hostages, to obtain for himself christian baptism?[6]

Even in Rome itself paganism is left in solitude. They who once were the gods of the nations remain under their lonely roofs with owls and birds of night. The standards of the military are emblazoned with the sign of the cross. The emperor's robes of purple and his diadem sparkling with jewels are ornamented with representations of the shameful yet saving gibbet. Already the Egyptian Serapis has been made a Christian, while at Gaza Marnas mourns in prison and every moment expects to see his temple overturned.[7] From India, from Persia, from Ethiopia we daily welcome monks in crowds. The Armenian bowman has laid aside his quiver, the Huns learn the psalter, the chilly Scythians are warmed with the glow of the faith. The Getae, ruddy and yellow-haired, carry tent-churches about with their armies:[8] and perhaps their success in fighting against us may be due to the fact that they believe in the same religion.

I have nearly wandered into a new subject, and while I have kept my wheel going, my hands have been molding a flagon when I meant to make a jug.[9] For, in answer to your prayers and those of the saintly Marcella, it was my intention to address you as a mother and to instruct you how to bring up our little Paula, who was consecrated to Christ before her birth, and vowed to his service before her conception. Thus in our own day we have seen repeated the story told us in the prophets, of Hannah, who though at first barren, afterwards became fruitful.[10] You have exchanged a fertility bound up with sorrow for offspring which shall never die. For I am confident that, having given the Lord your first-born, you will be the mother of sons. It is the first-born that is offered under the Law.[11] Samuel and Samson are both instances of this, as is also John the Baptist who, when Mary came in, leaped for joy. For he heard the Lord thundering by the mouth of the Virgin and desired to break from his mother's womb to meet him. As then Paula has been born in answer to a promise, her parents should give her a training suitable to her birth. Samuel, as you know, was nurtured in the temple, and John was trained in the wilderness. The first was venerated for his long hair, drank neither wine nor strong drink, and even in his childhood talked with God. The second shunned cities, wore a leathern girdle, and had for his food locusts and wild honey. Moreover, to typify repentance, he preached clothed in the spoils of the hump-backed camel.[12]

Thus must a soul be educated which is to be a temple of God. It must learn to hear nothing and to say nothing but what belongs to the fear of God. It must have no understanding of unclean words, and no knowledge of the world's songs. Its tongue must be steeped while still tender in the sweetness of the psalms. Boys with their wanton play must be kept far from Paula: even her maids and female attendants must be separated from worldly associates. For if they have learned some mischief, they may teach more. Get for her a set of letters made of boxwood or of ivory and called each by its proper name. Let her play with these, so that even her play may teach her something. And not only make her grasp the right order of the letters and remember their names by a rhyme, but constantly disarrange their order and put the last letters in the middle and the middle ones at the beginning, that she may know them all by sight as well as by sound. Moreover, as soon as she begins to use a stylus on wax, and her hand is still faltering, either guide her soft fingers by laying your hand over hers, or else have the character cut on a tablet, so that her efforts, confined within these limits, may keep to the lines traced out for her and not stray outside of them. Offer prizes for good spelling and draw her onwards with little gifts such as children her age delight in. And let her have companions in her lessons to excite emulation in her, that she may be stimulated when she sees them praised. You must not scold her if she is slow to learn, but must employ praise to excite her mind. Let her be glad when she excels others and sorry when she is excelled by them. Above all you must take care not to make her lessons distasteful to her, lest a dislike for them conceived in childhood may continue into her maturer years. The very words which she tries bit by bit to put together ought not to be chance ones, but names specially fixed on and heaped together for the purpose, those for example of the prophets or the apostles or the list of patriarchs from Adam downwards as it is given by Matthew and Luke.[13] In this way, while she is doing something else, her memory will be stocked for the future. Again, you must choose for her a master of approved years, life, and learning. A man of culture will not, I think, blush to do for a kinswoman or a highborn virgin what Aristotle did for Philip's son when, descending to the level of an usher, he consented to teach him his letters.[14] Things must not be despised as of small account if without them great results cannot be achieved. The very rudiments and first beginnings of knowledge sound differently in the mouths of an educated and of an uneducated person. Accordingly, you must see that the child is not led away by the silly coaxing of women to form a habit of shortening long words or of decking herself with gold and purple. One of these habits will spoil her conversation and the other her character. She must not therefore learn as a child what afterwards she will have to unlearn. The eloquence of the Gracchi is said to have been largely due to the way in which from their earliest years their mother spoke to them. Hortensia became an orator at her father's knee. Early impressions are hard to eradicate from the mind. Once wool has been dyed purple who can restore it to its previous whiteness? An unused jar long retains the taste and smell of what it is first filled with.[15] Grecian history tells us that the imperious Alexander who was lord of the whole world could not rid himself of the faults of manner and gait which in his childhood he had caught from his governor Leonides. We are always ready to imitate what is evil, and faults are quickly copied where virtues appear unattainable. Paula's nurse must not be intemperate, or loose, or given to gossip. Her nursemaid must be respectable, and her foster-father of grave demeanor. When she sees her grandfather, she must leap on his lap, put her arms round his neck, and, whether he likes it or not, sing *Alleluia* in his ears. She may be fondled by her grandmother, may smile at her father to show that she recognizes him,[16] and may so endear herself to everyone as to make the whole family rejoice in the possession of such a rosebud. She should be told at once whom she has for her other grandmother and whom for her aunt, who is her captain and for what army she is being trained as a recruit. Let her long to be with the absent ones and threaten to leave you for them.

Let her very dress and garb remind her to whom she is promised. Do not pierce her ears or paint her face, consecrated to Christ, with white lead or rouge. Do not hang gold or pearls around her neck or load her head with jewels, or by dyeing her hair red make it suggest the fires of hell. Let her pearls be of another kind and such that she may sell them hereafter and buy in their place the pearl that is *of great price*.[17] In bygone days a lady of rank, Praetextata by name, at the bidding of her husband Hymettius, the uncle of Eustochia, altered that virgin's dress and appearance and waved her neglected hair, desiring to overcome the resolution of the virgin herself and the wishes of her mother. But mark, in the same night an angel came to her in her dreams. With terrible looks he threatened punishment and broke silence with these words: 'Have you presumed to put your husband's commands before those of Christ? Have you presumed to lay sacrilegious hands upon the head of someone who is God's virgin? Those hands shall wither this very hour, that you may know by torment what you have done, and at the end of five months you shall be carried off to hell. And if you persist in your wickedness, you shall be bereaved both of your husband and of your children.' All of which came to pass in due time, a speedy death marking the unhappy woman's too long delayed repentance. So terribly does Christ punish those who violate his temple, and so jealously does he defend his precious jewels. I have related this story here not from any desire to exult over the misfortunes of the unhappy, but to warn you that you must with much fear and carefulness keep the vow which you have made to the Lord.

We read of Eli the priest that he became displeasing to God on account of the sins of his children.[18] And we are told that a man may not be made a bishop if his sons are loose and disorderly.[19] On the other hand it is written of the woman that *she shall be saved in childbearing, if they continue in faith and charity and holiness with chastity.*[20] If, then, parents are responsible for their children when they are of ripe age and independent, how much more must they be responsible for them when, still unweaned and weak, they cannot, in the Lord's words, *discern between their right hand and their left,*[21] when, that is to say, they cannot yet distinguish good from evil? If you take precautions to save your daughter from the bite of a viper, why are you not equally careful to shield her from *the hammer of the whole earth,*[22] to prevent her from drinking of the golden cup of Babylon, to keep her from going out with Dinah to see the daughters of a strange land,[23] to save her from the tripping dance and from the trailing robe? No one administers poison until he has rubbed the rim of the cup with honey;[24] so better to deceive us, vice puts on the smile and semblance of virtue. Why then, you will say, do we read: "the son shall not bear the iniquity of the father, neither shall the father bear the iniquity of the son," but *the soul that sins shall die?*[25] The passage, I answer, refers to those who have discretion, such as the fellow of whom his parents said in the Gospel: *He is of age, let him speak for himself.*[26] While the son is a child and thinks as a child, and until he comes to years of discretion to choose between the two roads to which the letter [Y] of Pythagoras points,[27] his parents are responsible for his actions, whether good or bad. But perhaps you imagine that, if they are not baptized, the children of Christians are liable for their own sins, and that no guilt attaches to parents who withhold from baptism those who by reason of their tender age can offer no objection to it. The truth is that, as baptism ensures the salvation of the child, this in turn brings advantage to the parents. Whether or not you would offer your child lay within your choice, but now that you have offered her, you neglect her at your peril. Though in your case you had no discretion, having vowed your child even before her conception. Someone who offers a victim that is lame or maimed or marked with any blemish is held guilty of sacrilege.[28] How much more then shall she be punished who gets ready for the embraces of the King a portion of her own body and the purity of a stainless soul, and then proves negligent of this her offering?

When she comes to be a little older and to increase like her Spouse in wisdom and stature and in favor with God and man,[29] let her go with her parents to the temple of her true Father, but let her not come out of the temple with them. Let them seek her upon the world's highway amid the crowds and the throng of their kinsfolk, and let them find her nowhere but in the shrine of the Scriptures, questioning the prophets and the apostles on the meaning of her spiritual marriage.[30] Let her imitate Mary, whom Gabriel found alone in her chamber and who was frightened, it would appear, by seeing a man there.[31] Let the child emulate her of whom it is written that *the king's daughter is all glorious within*.[32] Wounded with love's arrow let her say to her beloved: *The king has brought me into his chamber*.[33] At no time let her go abroad; lest the watchmen who go about the city find her, lest they smite and wound her and take away from her the veil of her chastity,[34] and leave her naked in her blood. Nay rather when someone knocks at her door let her say: *I am a wall and my breasts like towers*.[35] *I have washed my feet; I cannot defile them*.[36]

Let her not take her meals with others, that is, at her parents' guest-table, lest she see dishes she may long for. Some, I know, hold it a greater virtue to disdain a pleasure which is actually before them, but I think it a safer self-restraint not to know what would attract you. Once as a boy at school I met the words: 'It is ill blaming what you allow to become a habit.'[37] Let her learn

even now not to drink wine *wherein is excess*[38] But as, before
they come to their full strength, strict abstinence is dangerous
to young children, let her go to the baths if she must, and let
her take a little wine for her stomach's sake.[39] Let her also be
supported by a meat diet, lest her feet fail her before they begin
to run their course. But I say this by way of concession, not
by way of command;[40] because I am afraid of weakening her,
not because I want to teach her self-indulgence. Besides, why
should a Christian virgin not do wholly what others do in part? The
superstitious Jews reject certain animals and products as articles
of food, while among the Indians the Brahmans and among the
Egyptians the gymnosophists subsist entirely on porridge, rice and
fruit.[41] If mere glass is worth so much, is a pearl not worth more?[42]
Paula has been born in response to a vow. Let her life be as the
lives of those who were born under the same conditions. If the
grace accorded is in both cases the same, the pains bestowed
ought to be so too. Let her be deaf to the sound of the organ, and
not know even why the pipe, the lyre, and the harp are made.

And let it be her task daily to repeat to you a fixed portion of
Scripture. Let her learn by heart a number of verses in the Greek,
but let her be at once instructed in the Latin also. For, if the tender
lips are not from the first shaped to this, the tongue is spoiled by a
foreign accent and its native speech debased by alien elements.
You must yourself be her teacher, a model on which she may
form her childish conduct. Never let her see either in you or in
her father what she cannot imitate without sin. Remember that
you are the parents of a consecrated virgin, and that your example
will teach her more than your precepts. Flowers are quick to fade,
and a baleful wind soon withers the violet, the lily, and the crocus.
Let her never appear in public without you. Let her never visit a
church or a martyr's shrine except with her mother. Let no young
man, no dandy with curled hair, ogle her. If our little virgin goes
to keep solemn eves and all-night vigils, let her not stir a hair's
breadth from her mother's side. She must not single out one of
her maids to make her a special favorite or a confidante. What she
says to one all ought to know. Let her choose for a companion not
a handsome well-dressed girl, able to warble a song with liquid

tone, but one pale and serious, somberly attired and inclined
to melancholy. Let her take as her model some aged virgin of
approved faith, character, and chastity, who can instruct her by
word and by example to rise at night to recite prayers and psalms
to sing hymns in the morning, at the third, sixth, and ninth hours
to take her place in the line to do battle for Christ, to kindle her
lamp and offer her evening sacrifice.[43] In these occupations let
her pass the day, and when night comes, let it find her still engaged
in them. Let reading follow prayer and prayer again succeed to
reading. Time will seem short when employed on tasks so many
and so varied.

Let her also learn how to spin wool, to hold the distaff, to put
the basket in her lap, to turn the spinning wheel and to shape
the yarn with her thumb. Let her put away with disdain silken
fabrics, chinese fleeces, and gold brocades: the clothing which
she makes for herself should keep out the cold and not expose the
body which it professes to cover. Let her food be vegetables and
wheat bread with now and then one or two small fishes. And that
I may not waste more time in giving precepts for the regulation
of appetite (a subject I have treated more at length elsewhere,[44])
let her meals always leave her hungry and able on the moment
to begin reading or praying or chanting. I strongly disapprove—
especially for those of tender years—of long and immoderate
fasts in which week is added to week and even oil and fruit are
forbidden as food. I have learned by experience that the ass toiling
along the highway makes for an inn when it is weary. Leave that to
the worshippers of Isis and Cybele who gobble up pheasants and
turtle-doves piping hot, that their teeth may not violate the gifts of
Ceres![45] If an unbroken fast is intended, it must be so regulated
that those who have a long journey before them may hold out
through it all; and we must take care that we do not, after running
the first lap, fall halfway. However in Lent, as I have written before
now, those who practice self-denial should spread every stitch of
canvas, and the charioteer should for once slacken the reins and
increase the speed of his horses. Yet there will be one rule for
those who live in the world and another for virgins and monks.
The layman in Lent consumes the coats of his stomach, and, living

like a snail on his own juice,[46] gets his paunch ready for rich foods and feasting to come. But with the virgin and the monk the case is different; for, when they give rein to their steeds in Lent, they have to remember that for them the race has no intermission. An effort made only for a limited time may well be severe, but one that has no such limit must be more moderate. For whereas in the first case we can recover our breath when the race is over, in the latter we have to go on continually and without stopping.

When you go into the country, do not leave your daughter behind at home. Leave her no power or capacity of living without you, and let her feel frightened when she is left to herself. Let her not converse with people of the world or associate with virgins indifferent to their vows. Let her not be present at the weddings of your slaves and let her take no part in the noisy games of the household. As regards the use of the bath, I know that some are content with saying that a christian virgin should not bathe along with eunuchs or with married women—with the former because they are still men at heart, and with the latter because pregnant women are a revolting sight. For myself, however, I wholly disapprove of baths for a virgin of full age. Such a person should blush and feel overcome at the idea of seeing herself naked. By vigils and fasts she mortifies her body and brings it into subjection. By a cold chastity she seeks to put out the flame of lust and to quench the hot desires of youth. And by a deliberate squalor she makes haste to spoil her natural good looks. Why, then, should she add fuel to a sleeping fire by taking baths?

Let her treasures be not silks or gems but manuscripts of the holy scriptures, and in these let her think less of gilding, and baby-lonian parchment, and arabesque patterns, than of correctness and accurate punctuation. Let her begin by learning the Psalter and distract herself with these songs, and then let her gather rules of life out of the Proverbs of Solomon. From Ecclesiastes let her gain the habit of despising the world and its vanities.[47] Let her follow the example set in Job of virtue and of patience. Then let her pass on to the Gospels, never to be laid aside when once they have been taken in hand. Let her also drink in with a willing heart the Acts of the Apostles and the Epistles. As soon as she has enriched the storehouse of her mind with these treasures, let her commit to memory the Prophets, the Heptateuch, the books of Kings and of Chronicles, the rolls also of Ezra and Esther. When she has done all this, she may safely read the Song of Songs; but not before. For, were she to read it at the beginning, she would fail to perceive that, though it is written in fleshly words, it is a marriage song of a spiritual bridal. And not understanding this she would suffer harm from it. Let her avoid all apocryphal writings, and if she is led to read them not by the truth of the doctrines they contain but out of respect for the miracles contained in them, let her understand that they are not really written by those to whom they are ascribed, that many faulty elements have been introduced into them, and that it requires discretion to look for gold in the midst of dirt.[48] Cyprian's writings let her have always in her hands. The letters of Athanasius and the treatises of Hilary [of Poitiers] she may go through without fear of stumbling. Let her take pleasure in the works and wits of all writers in whose books a due regard for the faith is not neglected. But if she reads the works of others, let it be rather to judge them than to follow them.

You will answer: 'How shall I, a woman of the world, living at Rome, surrounded by a crowd, be able to observe all these injunctions?' In that case do not undertake a burden to which you are not equal. When you have weaned Paula as Isaac was weaned,[49] and when you have clothed her as Samuel was clothed,[50] send her to her grandmother and aunt; set this most precious of gems in Mary's chamber and put her in the cradle where Jesus cried. Let her be brought up in a monastery, let her be among companies of virgins, let her learn to avoid swearing, let her regard lying as sacrilege, let her be ignorant of the world, let her live like the angels. While in the flesh let her be without the flesh, and let her suppose that all human beings are like herself. To say nothing of its other advantages, this course will free you from the difficult task of minding her, and from the responsibility of guardianship. It is better for you to regret her absence than to be for ever trembling for her, watching what she says and to whom she says it, to whom she bows and whom she likes best to see. Hand her over to Eustochium while she is still but an infant and her every cry is a prayer for you. She will thus become her companion in holiness now as well as her successor hereafter. Let her gaze upon and love, let her 'from her earliest years admire',[51] someone whose language and gait and dress are an education in virtue. Let her grandmother take her on her lap and repeat to her grand-daughter the lessons that she once bestowed upon her own child. Long experience has shown her how to rear, instruct and watch over virgins; and daily inwoven in her crown is the mystic hundred[52] which betokens the highest chastity. O happy virgin! happy Paula, daughter of Toxotius, who through the virtues of her grandmother and aunt is nobler in holiness than she is in lineage! Yes, were it possible for you with your own eyes to see your mother-in-law and your sister and to realize the mighty souls which animate their small bodies, such is your innate chastity that I cannot doubt that you would go to them even before your daughter, and would exchange God's first decree[53] for his second law of the Gospel.[54] You would count as nothing your desire for other children and would offer yourself up to the service of God. But because *there is a time to embrace, and a time to refrain from embracing,*[55] *and because the wife has no power over her own body,*[56] *and because every man should abide in the same calling wherein he was called*[57] in the Lord, and because someone under the yoke ought so to run as not to leave his companion in the mire, pay back to the full in your offspring what meantime you defer paying in your own person. Once Hannah had offered in the tabernacle the son whom she had vowed to God, she never took him back; for she thought it unbecoming that someone who was to be a prophet should grow up in the same house with her who still desired to have other sons. Accordingly after she had conceived him and given him birth, she did not venture to come to the temple alone or to appear before the Lord empty, but first paid him what she owed, and then, when she had offered up that great sacrifice, she returned home; and because she had borne her first-born for God, she was given five children for herself.[58] Do you marvel at the happiness of that holy woman? Imitate her faith. Moreover, if you will only send Paula, I promise to be myself both a tutor and a foster-father to her. Old as I am, I will carry her on my shoulders and train her stammering lips; and my charge will be a far prouder one than that of the worldly philosopher. For while he only taught a King of Macedon who was one day to die of Babylonian poison,[59] I shall instruct the handmaid and bride of Christ who will one day be offered in the kingdom of heaven.

NOTES

1. 1 Cor 7:13–14.

2. *Pontifex*, one of the state priesthoods, indicative rather of social status than religion. The college of pontiffs advised the state on all matters of cultus.

3. This letter was written after the legislation of Theodosius against pagan worship. Jerome typically exaggerates.

4. Lk 18:27.

5. Dan 4.

6. Furius Maecius Gracchus is mentioned in the *Codex Theodosianus* as Prefect of Rome in ad 376 and 377. His destruction of the cave of Mithras is also alluded to by Prudentius, *Contra Symmachum* 1.562. Platner and Ashby, *Topographical Dictionary of Ancient Rome* (1929), list eight known Mithraea in Rome, with another doubtful. This passage is important for the seven degrees of initiation into Mithraism, but the text is not wholly certain. The Latin words are: *corax, nymphius, miles, leo, Perses, heliodromus, pater*; Hilberg substitutes *cryphius* for *nymphius* on the basis of inscriptions, but this is against the manuscripts.

7. The Serapeum at Alexandria was destroyed in 391. Marnas was the chief god of Gaza, sometimes said to be of syrian or philistine origin, sometimes to be equivalent to the cretan Zeus (cf. the name Minos). Jerome refers to him in *Vita Hilarionis* 20 and in his commentary on Isaiah (7.17). The full story of the destruction of the Marneion is told in Mark's *Life of Porphyry of Gaza*, who went to Constantinople, as bishop of Gaza, in 398 to get an order for the destruction of the temple. "He obtained it, but it was not enforced. He went again, and obtained a fresh decree early in 402. The temple took ten days to pull down in May 402. Mark's details cannot all be trusted, but the main facts seem secure. Jerome (*Isaiah*, as above) says that churches were built instead of the Serapeum and Marneion.

8. Cf. Ambrose, Letter 20.12, and note, *Early Latin Theology*, Ancient Christian Classics, p. 211.

9. Horace, *Ars poetica*, 21.

10. 1 Sm 1:1–20.

11. Num 3:13.

12. Mt 3:4, Mk 1:6. *Tortuosissimi animalis*, perhaps with a reference to the writhings of penitence. Fremantle, however, compares letter 79.3, *animal tortuosum*, the camel and the eye of the needle; that is, penitence is just as difficult.

13. Mt 1, Lk 3:23–38.

14. Alexander the Great. This and the following classical reminiscences are taken from Quintillian, *Institut. orat.* So is the advice about teaching letters.

15. Horace, *Epistles* I.2.70.

16. Vergil, *Georgics* 4.60.

17. Mt 13:46.

18. 1 Sm 2:22–36.

19. 1 Tm 3:4–5.

20. 1 Tm 2:15.

21. Jon 4:11.

22. Babylon, Jer. 50.23.

23. Gn 34.

24. Lucretius, *De rerum natura* I.936.

25. Ezk 18:20.

26. Jn 9:21.

27. The Greek *upsilon* (Y), the stem being the time of childhood; cf. Persius, *Sat.* 3.56.

28. Dt 15:21.

29. Lk 2:52.

30. Cf Lk 2:4–47.

31. Lk 1:29.

32. Ps 44/45:13.

33. Sg 1:4.

34. Sg 5:7.

35. Sg 8:10.

36. Sg 5:3.

37. Publilius Syrus, *Sententiae* 180.

38. Eph 5:18.

39. 1 Tm 5:23.

40. 1 Cor 7:6.

41. Cf. Tertullian, *Apology* 42: We [Christians] are not Brahmans or Indian gymnosophists, living in the woods, exiles from life . . . We repudiate no creature of God.'

42. Here, and in Letter 79.7, 130.9, from Tertullian, *Ad martyras* 4.

43. Six of the 'canonical' hours of prayer: Vigils/Nocturns, Matins, Terce, Sext, None, Vespers. Cf. Letters 22.37, 108.20, 130.15.

44. Letter 54.9–10, and *Contra Jovinianum* 2.

45. Having vowed not to eat bread, he means, they eat luxuries.

46. Platus, *Captivi* 80.

47. In the preface to his *Commentary on Ecclesiastes*, Jerome relates that he read the book at Rome with Blesilla, to induce her to despise the world.

48. In the 'Helmeted Preface' Jerome rejected all books outside the Hebrew Canon of the Old Testament as apocryphal, though he was inconsistent in his practice. he might be referring here to the so called 'New Testament Apocrypha', many of which books were gnostic.

49. Gn 21:8.
50. Cf 1 Sm 1:24.
51. Virgil, *Aeneid* 8.517.
52. The parable of the sower (Mt 13) was used to suggest that chastity in marriage is rewarded thirty-fold, faithful widowhood sixty-fold, virginity a hundredfold. Virginity is therefore *intrinsically* superior to marriage; cf. Letter 48 and Ambrose, Letter 63.7, 10.
53. Gen 1:28 (*Be fruitful and multiply*).
54. 1 Cor 7:1.
55. Qo 3:5.
56. 1 Cor 7:4.
57. 1 Cor 7:20.
58. 1 Sm 2.
59. Aristotle and Alexander the Great.

To Pacatula

his letter was written from Palestine in 413, when Jerome, on his own admission, was feeling grief-stricken, old, and tired. He was about eighty-two years old, which was a very considerable age in the fourth century. The manuscripts differ as to the person to whom the letter was addressed; some read Pacatula and others Gaudentius. It appears that the latter, a personal friend, had written from Rome to ask Jerome's advice on the upbringing and education of his little daughter, Pacatula, who had been dedicated by her parents as a virgin from birth. The letter begins by playfully addressing Pacatula, in the hope that she will be able to read it later on, but Jerome, who admits in the last paragraph that he is dictating it 'in some confusion of speech', is unable to keep up his would-be playful style and at the end, he frankly apostrophizes Gaudentius.

This letter is briefer than Letter 107 instructing Laeta, the daughter-in-law of Paula, on the upbringing of her daughter, Paula the Younger, another child-oblate. The advice given is very similar: young girls should be protected from worldly companions, and above all, from boys and worldly women; their lessons should be made interesting and pleasurable; they should learn the alphabet, spelling, latin grammar and syntax, and should receive some attractive little present as a reward. They are always to go about with their mothers and are not to frequent public places, particularly crowded churches, but should find their pleasure in

271

their own rooms. Above all, their appearance is to be austere and unattractive. They are to wear dark clothing as an indication of their dedication to virginity; they are not to use make-up or adorn themselves with jewelry. On the other hand, there is not to be an ostentatious display of poverty and ugliness, lest people praise them for these qualities. Their diet is to be very simple; they are allowed a little wine and meat only while they are still growing. Spinning wool is to be encouraged as an occupation.

In the earlier letter, Jerome's instructions are more detailed: little Paula was to have as a plaything an alphabet made of box-wood or ivory; she is to begin to learn the greek letters at the same time as the latin. Paula was to have a male tutor of ripe years and scholarship, whereas Pacatula is to have a governess of plain and dowdy appearance.

This educational advice presents Jerome in a more human light, but, in point of fact, many of these pedagogical details are culled from Quintilian, whose works Jerome no doubt studied at the rhetorical stage of his education.

The style of this letter is diffuse. A long digression about male and female virginity and the rehearsal of the arguments for and against dressing child-oblates in dark clothes, combined with its generally pessimistic tone, suggest that age and infirmity were causing Jerome to begin to lose his grip.

To Pacatula (*Letter 128*)

It is hard to write to a little girl who cannot understand what you say, of whose mind you know nothing and of whose inclinations it would be rash to prophesy. In the words of a famous orator, 'she is to be praised more for what she will be than for what she is'.[1] Are you to urge a child who longs for cakes, who prattles on her mother's knee in her chattering voice, and to whom honey is sweeter than words, to exercise self-control? Is someone whose whole delight is in nursery tales to listen to the deep things of the Apostle? Is she, whom her nurse can frighten with a frown, to perceive the mysteries of the prophets? Is she to grasp the majestic character of the Gospel, when its splendor dazzles all mortal intellects? Am I to urge someone who beats her laughing mother with her soft little hand, to obey her parents? For reasons like these, my dear Pacatula is to undertake to read this letter later on. In the meantime, let her learn the alphabet, spelling, grammar, and syntax. To induce her to repeat her lessons in her shrill little voice, let cakes and honey-water and sweets be held out to her as rewards. She will hasten to perform her task if she is to receive some pleasant-tasting sweet, some bright bunch of flowers, some glittering trinket, some enchanting doll.[2] Also in the meantime, let her attempt to spin, twisting the yarn with her tender thumb. Let her frequently break the threads so that, with practice, a day will come when she no longer breaks them.[3] After her work, let her have some recreation. Let her hang round her mother's neck or snatch kisses from her nearest and dearest. Let her receive a reward for singing psalms. Let her love what she is obliged to recite, so that it is not a task but a delight, something not compulsory but voluntary.

Some mothers, when they have vowed a daughter to virginity, make a habit of clothing her in a dark-colored tunic, wrapping her up in a somber cloak and taking away her linen garments and, what is really good advice, they do not allow her to wear any gold ornaments on her neck or head, lest she learn to possess, when she is of tender years, what she will afterwards be compelled to lay aside. To other people the contrary course seems the right one.

'What if she does not have such things, will she not see others in possession of them? It is a woman's nature to love finery and we know that there are many women, remarkable for their modesty who dress attractively, not for any man but for themselves. Rather let her have enough of her possessions and decide for herself that those other women who do not have possessions are the ones to be praised. It is better that she despise possessions, having had her fill of them, than that she should long for possessions by not having them.' Such was the plan which the Lord adopted for the children of Israel. When they longed for the fleshpots of Egypt, he sent them flights of quails and allowed them to gorge themselves until they were sick.[4] Many people who have once lived worldly lives can more easily do without the bodily pleasure they have experienced than can those who from childhood have never known lust. The former trample on what they have known; the latter seek what is unknown. While the former penitently shun the insidious snares of pleasure from which they have fled, the latter flirt with sensual allurements and, thinking them to be honey, discover they are deadly poison. Honey drops from the lips of a loose woman,[5] and at the time it is rich in the throats of those eating it, but it is afterwards found to be more bitter than gall.[6] For this reason, honey is not offered in the Lord's sacrifice and wax, which goes along with honey, is rejected;[7] oil, which is produced from the bitterness of the olive, is burned in the temple of God.[8] Moreover the passover is eaten with bitter herbs[9] and *with the unleavened bread of sincerity and truth.*[10] Someone who receives these will suffer persecution in the world. This is why the prophet mystically sings, *I sat alone, because I was filled with bitterness.*[11]

What then? Are young people to lead a life of self-indulgence, so that self-indulgence may subsequently be more forcefully rejected? Far from it, they say, *Let everyone remain in the vocation to which he has been called.*[12] Anyone who has been called, *having been circumcised* that is, as a virgin, *let him not become uncircumcised.*[13] This means that he is not to seek the marriage garment of skins with which Adam was clothed when he was thrown out of the paradise of virginity.[14] *Anyone who is called to be uncircumcised*, that is, the man who has a wife and is wrapped in the skin of matrimony, should not seek the nakedness of virginity[15] and of that eternal chastity which he has lost once for all, but let him *use his vessel in sanctification and honour.*[16] Let him drink from his own springs and not from the broken cisterns[17] of harlots, which cannot contain utterly pure waters of chastity.[18] The same Paul in the same chapter, when discussing the subjects of virginity and marriage, calls those who are married slaves of the flesh, but those not under the yoke of matrimony free men, who serve the Lord in complete freedom.[19]

What I say I do not say as universally applicable; my treatment of the subject is only partial. I speak only of some, not of all. My words are directed to both sexes and not only to *the weaker vessel.*[20] You are a virgin; why then do you take pleasure in the society of a woman? Why do you commit to the high seas your frail, patched boat and embark confidently on the great peril of an uncertain voyage? You do not know what you want, yet you cling to her as though you had either desired her before or—if I may put it as gently as possible—as though you might desire her in the future. 'But,' you will say, 'the female sex is better suited for service.' In that case, choose an old woman, choose a deformed woman, choose a woman whose continence is proven in the Lord. Why should you find pleasure in youth, beauty, and voluptuousness? You go about, looking ruddy with health, with your skin shining, you eat meat, you abound in wealth and are dressed in expensive clothes. Do you believe you can sleep safely beside a poisonous serpent? You may tell me that you do not live in the same house with her, at least not at night, but you spend whole days conversing with her this way. Why do you sit alone with her, and without witnesses? Although you may not sin yourself, you seem to others to do so, affording an example to other unhappy men who do wrong under the authority of your name. And you, whether virgin or widow, why do you allow a man to detain you in conversation so long? Why are you not afraid to be left alone with him? At least let the necessity of your bowels and bladder compel you to leave the room, that you may for this reason leave the man with whom you have behaved with more liberty than you would with your brother and with much more shamefacedness than you would with your husband. You say you are asking a question about the holy Scriptures. Ask it in public. Let your maids and your companions hear it. *Everything which is made manifest is light.*[21] Good conversation does not look for secret corners, but rather takes pleasure in its own praise and in the witness of many hearers. He must be a remarkable teacher who thinks little of men, despises his brethren and exerts himself in secretly instructing one feeble little woman.

I have strayed a little from my path on to other matters, and while I instruct, indeed nurture, little Pacatula, I have immediately drawn down on myself the hostility of many women who are by no means the daughters of peace.[22] I shall now return to my proper theme. The female sex should associate with its own sex. Let a girl be ignorant of boys and indeed dread playing with them. She should never know an immodest word and if, amid the bustle of the household, she should happen to hear some base utterance, she should not understand it. Her mother's nod should carry as much weight with her as her spoken word, and her advice should be as a command. She should love her as a parent, obey her as her mistress, and reverence her as her teacher. When she has reached her seventh year and is no longer an unformed and toothless little maiden, she will begin to blush, to know when to keep silence, and to hesitate over what she should say. Then let her commit the psalter to memory and, until she is grown up, she should make the books of Solomon, the Gospels, the apostles and the prophets the treasure of her heart. Let her not appear in public too freely or too frequently attend crowded churches. Let her find all her pleasures in her own room. Let her never look at young men, at dandies with curled hair who would wound her soul through her ears by the sweetness of their voices. Let lascivious young girls be shoved away from her. The more freedom of access allowed such people, the more difficult it is to avoid them, and what they have learned, they secretly teach and they harm our sequestered Danaë by the babble of the crowd.[23] Let her teacher be her companion, a governess not much given to wine and not, in the words of the Apostle, an idler and one given to tittle-tattle,[24] but someone who is sober, grave, and industrious in spinning wool, and whose words will form her childish mind to the practice of virtue.[25] As water follows a finger drawn through the sand, so someone of soft and tender years is pliable in both directions and can be drawn wherever you choose to guide her. Moreover, sportive and well-turned out young men have a habit of asking nurses for access for themselves to their charges by means of flattery, making themselves agreeable and giving little presents, and when they have gently effected their entry this way, they arouse the fires of passion from sparks and little by little, advance to the most shameless requests. It is quite impossible to check them, for in their case, the verse is proved true, 'It is ill to rebuke what you have allowed to become a habit.' It is shameful to say it, but it must nevertheless be said: aristocratic ladies about to have even more aristocratic suitors cohabit with men of the lowest class and with slaves. In the name of religion and under the protective shadow of continence they sometimes desert their husbands. Our Helens follow their Alexanders and do not fear their Menelauses.[26] Such women are seen and lamented, but not punished, because the number of the sinners obtains tolerance for the sin.

Alas! The world sinks into ruin and our sins within us do not sink along with it. The fabled city, the capital of the roman empire, is swallowed up by a single fire. There is no region which does not hold roman exiles. Churches once sacred have fallen into heaps of ash and glowing embers, and yet we have our minds set on the desire for gain. We live as though we are going to die tomorrow, yet we build as though we are going to live forever in this world. Our walls shine with gold, as do our ceilings and the capitals of our pillars; yet Christ dies outside our doors naked and hungry in the persons of his poor. The high priest, Aaron, we read, went to meet the raging flames and, having put fire in his censer, checked the wrath of God; the high priest stood between death and life and the fire did not dare to pass beyond his feet.[27] God spoke to Moses: *Let me alone and I will destroy this people.*[28] When God said, *Let me alone,* he showed that he was being held back from doing what he threatened. The prayers of his servant were hindering his power. Who is there now under heaven, do you think, who could encounter the wrath of God, who could go to meet the flames and could say in the words of the Apostle, *I wished to be accursed for the sake of my brethren?*[29] Flocks perish with their shepherds, for as a people is, so is the priest. Moses spoke with a sense of compassion: *If you forgive this people, then forgive them, but if not, blot me out of your book.*[30] He is willing to perish with those who perish and was not satisfied with his own salvation. Indeed, *In the multitude of the people is the king's honor.*[31]

In such times as these is Pacatula born, among such playthings does she pass the first years of her life. She is destined to know tears before laughter and to feel sorrow before joy. She has scarcely made her entrance when she makes her exit. She thinks the world has always been as it is now. She is ignorant of the past, she shuns the present, she longs for the future. I was dictating these words in some confusion of speech, and after the deaths of friends and my ceaseless grief, I have only recently recovered sufficiently to write as an old man to a child. My affection for you, brother Gaudentius,[32] has induced me to make the attempt. I have thought it better to say just a little than to make no response at all, when I have been asked to do so, since on the one hand, my will might be thought to be paralysed by grief, and on the other, my friendship to be insincere.

NOTES

1. Jerome claims to be addressing this letter to the little girl Pacatula, at present only a baby, for her to read when she is older, but in fact, he is replying to his friend Gaudentius, who has written to consult him about how to bring up his daughter, whom he has consecrated to virginity. The quotation is from Cicero, *De republica*, fragm. 5, which is repeated in letter 130, p. 225.
2. *Cf* Letter 107, pp. 257–8.
3. *Cf ibid.*, p. 263.
4. Nm 11:4, 18–20, 31–3.
5. Pr 5:3.
6. Rv 10:9–10.
7. Lv 2:11.
8. Ex 27:20.
9. Ex 12:8.
10. 1 Cor 5:8.
11. Jr 15:17.

12. 1 Cor 7:24.
13. 1 Co 7:18.
14. Gn 3:21.
15. Gn 3:25.
16. 1 Th 4:4.
17. Jr 2:13.
18. Pr 5:15.
19. 1 Cor 7:21–2.
20. 1 P 3:7.
21. Eph 5:13.
22. The latin term *male pacatae*, used by Jerome to describe the ladies whose hostility he has incurred, is a pun on the name Pacatula, which means 'Little Peace'.
23. Danaë was the daughter of Acrisius, king of Argos. An oracle had pronounced that she would give birth to a son who would kill his grandfather. Her father therefore kept her locked up in an underground room, but there she became the mother of Perseus, the slayer of the Gorgon, as the result of a visit from Zeus in the from of a shower of gold.
24. 1 Tm 5:13.
25. *Cf* Letter 107, p. 262.
26. Helen of Troy, who left her husband Menelaus. Alexander is another name for Paris.
27. Nm 16:46–48.
28. Ex 32:10.
29. Rm 9:3.
30. Ex 32:32.
31. Pr 14:28.
32. Jerome now gives up the claim to be addressing his letter to Pacatula. He has already remarked that he had dictated it 'in some confusion of speech'.

MELANIA
THE ELDER
&
MELANIA
THE YOUNGER:

ASCETIC MATRONS
IN EGYPT
&
JERUSALEM

INTRODUCTION

PALLADIUS AND THE LAUSIAC HISTORY

PALLADIUS, the author of the *Lausiac History* from which these accounts of Melania the Elder and Melania the Younger are taken, was born *c*. 364 in Galatia and appears to have received the normal classical education of his day. He became a monk *c*. 386 and lived in Palestine, where he passed three years on the Mount of Olives with a hermit called Innocent. During his stay there he made the acquaintance of Rufinus and Melania the Elder, and it was apparently on their advice that he decided to go to Egypt. His monastic career shows some striking parallels with that of Saint Antony the Great. First of all, like Antony, he stayed for a year in Alexandria, where he lived with a priest named Isidore, who seems to have introduced him to the egyptian ascetics' way of living. Then, again like Antony, he departed for the desert near Alexandria, where he lived under the spiritual direction of the hermit Dorotheus. Finally, to complete the parallel, he penetrated further into the desert when, in 390, he proceeded to Nitria and then made his way to the cells, where he lived for nine years. There seems also to have been a similarity in the spiritual life of the two ascetics: both found that the further they distanced themselves from the world, the greater was their spiritual progress. At the Cells Palladius lived with Macarius of Alexandria and then with Evagrius Ponticus, who exercised a profound spiritual influence over him and whom he always regarded as his spiritual master. Unfortunately he became ill in the same year in which Evagrius died (probably 399), and on medical advice, he left the desert for Bethlehem, where he lived for a year with an ascetic called Posidonius, whom he describes as gentle and innocent. Around 400 Palladius became bishop of Hellenopolis in Bithynia. We next

283

hear of him in 403 with Saint John Chrysostom at the Synod of the Oak. The Synod, held near Chalcedon, had been convened by Chrysostom's enemy and disappointed rival, Theophilus, patriarch of Alexandria who had hoped to become patriarch of Constantinople. Chrysostom was appointed to that office until in 398. Palladius' connection with Chrysostom involved him in the origenistic disputes at the Synod.

This connection continued. John Chrysostom's attempts at social and ecclesiastical reform in Constantinople caused him to incur the wrath not only of Theophilus but also of the emperor and, even more, of the empress, Eudoxia. As a result of the intrigues of Theophilus and his clique, he was condemned at the Synod. Palladius himself had to submit to cross-questioning about his own Origenism. For a time after the Synod he remained with his friend John Chrysostom, but he did not join him when he was sent into exile. Instead he made his way to Rome on his behalf to plead his cause with Pope Innocent I. It was on this visit that he was hospitably received by Melania the Younger. As soon as he returned to Constantinople in 406, he was at once arrested on the orders of the emperor Arcadius and sent into exile. He went once more to Egypt, where he lived first at Syene and then at Antinoë in the Thebaid.

When the opposition to John Chrysostom had come to an end, he left Egypt for his native Galatia, where he seems to have lived with a priest called Philoromos, but, according to the church historian Socrates, he soon became bishop of Aspuna. It was during this period of his life (419–420), when he was fifty-six years old, that he wrote the so-called *Lausiac History* at the request of Lausus, chamberlain of the emperor Theodosius II. Palladius died sometime between 420 and 431, for a man called Eusebius is designated as bishop of Aspuna in the list of bishops present at the Council of Ephesus in 431.

The *Lausiac History* is a curious and somewhat shapeless book, though a recent editor, G. J. M. Bartelink, has pointed out that its ground-plan, from which there are numerous digressions, is the life-story of Palladius himself. From the circumstances of his life he had acquired a wide knowledge of the monasteries of Egypt and Palestine; yet his work is not a systematic treatise but a picture of his own experience of monasticism. The style of the individual essays varies: some of them contain dialogues in direct speech and recall the *Apophthegmata patrum*; others are narratives, more reminiscent of Athanasius' life of Antony.

The passages chosen for translation in this book all fall into the narrative category. They have been selected because they deal with women leading the religious life. There are other such women in the pages of Palladius, but the accounts which I have omitted are of a more anecdotal character and do not throw light on the movement as a whole.

The first of the passages, which I have used as a general introduction, has been chosen because it refers to three women, who figure elsewhere in this book:[1] Paula, Eustochium, and Asella, and to another, Sabiniana, who is of interest as the kinswoman of one of the great Doctors of the Church, Saint John Chrysostom. Paula and Eustochium are representative of those able women who administered the earlier domestic monasteries, while Asella and Sabiniana are solitaries. This passage gives us an independent opinion of the characters of Paula, Eustochium, and Asella, whom we know chiefly from Jerome's letters, and of the relationship between Paula and Jerome.

Palladius may have come to know Jerome personally during the period when he lived with Posidonius at Bethlehem. At any rate he does not seem to have cared much for him, perhaps because of their differing views on Origenism, but more obviously because of Jerome's jealous disposition. Palladius refers to this characteristic in chapter 36.6 of the *Lausiac History*, where he writes that not even Jerome's superior education and cultural attainments can cover up this flaw. He also reports the holy man, Posidonius, as prophesying that Paula would die before Jerome and that only after her death will Jerome rid himself of this fault.

The second passage gives some idea of Palladius' understanding of the regime in a pachomian cenobite community.[2] Doubtless Palladius' ideas penetrated to the West, where they influenced later monastic rules.

The passage about Melania the Elder, combined with the letters and poems of Paulinus of Nola, provides the principal source for her story. It contains certain discrepancies and difficulties, which will be dealt with in the notes, but it is nevertheless historically valuable because Palladius must surely have obtained much of his information from Melania herself, when he was living on the Mount of Olives in the 380s. Palladius portrays a woman of strong character, whose assurance of manner does not appear to have depended on her vast wealth. Both Palladius and Gerontius, the author of the life of Saint Melania the Younger, provide interesting evidence of the extent of the enormous fortunes at the disposal of upper-class roman families in the fourth century. This material only serves to point out the contrast between Melania's life with her parents and with her husband in the years of her marriage, and the way of life which she subsequently adopted. We can recognize in her the kind of vigorous and capable woman who in the Middle Ages became abbess of a large monastery and in our own day is active in church life, politics, business, or the professions.

The last of the Palladian passages deals with Melania the Younger, and must also have been based on personal knowledge since, as we have already seen, Palladius stayed with her when he went to Rome to intercede with Pope Innocent I on behalf of John Chrysostom. The material is similar in character to that of the following life of Melania, the author of which, Gerontius, seems to have been acquainted with the *Lausiac History*.[3]

Palladius again gives us a glimpse of the vast fortunes of members of the roman aristocracy. Both Palladius and Gerontius are at pains to stress the contrast between the circumstances of her earlier and later life. The nearest equivalent to Melania in modern times would be one of the great american heiresses of the early years of the present century.

Melania the Younger was born, probably, in 383 and she died in 439. At the time when Palladius was writing (419–20), she must have been about thirty-seven years old. Thus she would have been about twenty-one when she entertained Palladius on his visit to Rome in 404/5, which accounts for his describing her as 'young in the flesh' in this passage. He was thinking of her not as the woman in early middle age, which she in fact was at the time he was writing, but as the young woman whom he had met fourteen and fifteen years previously. Palladius confines himself to what he knew from his personal contact with her and therefore describes only the events of her life which occurred before she left Italy. It is to the greek life by Gerontius, which follows, and to a latin life that we owe our knowledge of her travels and her subsequent activities.

I am well aware that the passages translated here are only a small and by no means typical selection of the *Lausiac History*, but I hope that readers will be encouraged to dip into one of the translations recommended on p. 435–441 in order to catch the full flavor of the writings of Palladius and to learn more of the ways of the Desert Fathers and other early ascetics.

My translation is based on the text to be found in *La storia lausiaca*, edited by G. J. M. Bartelink, Vite di santi 2 (Milan, 1974). My debt to Professor Bartelink's commentary and to the work of the late Abbot Cuthbert Butler OSB, is obvious and is gratefully acknowledged here.

THE LIFE OF MELANIA THE YOUNGER BY GERONTIUS

We make the acquaintance of Melania the Younger in the pages of Palladius, but our principal sources of information about her are two *Lives*, one in Greek, the other in Latin, which came to light in comparatively recent times and which have occasioned both ecclesiastical and academic controversy. We have already noted certain discrepancies between Palladius' account and that of Gerontius, the writer of the greek life. It is not necessary to weary the reader with controversial details, but a brief account of the history of the greek and latin texts may be of interest.

For many years Melania the Younger was almost forgotten in the West; she existed simply as a name in the liturgy until 1556, when a latin translation of her life, taken from the *Menologion* of Simeon Metaphrastes,[4] by Louis Lipomani, bishop of Vicenza, was published in Venice. This was subsequently incorporated in the *Roman Martyrology*, published on the orders of Pope Gregory XIII. The original greek text of Metaphrastes was not published until 1864, when it was included in Migne's *Patrologia graeca* 116: 753–794.

The text of Metaphrastes was not the original primitive greek text, but one which had been 'worked over' by him to conform to the taste of his day. It was not until the nineteenth century that the earlier texts, both greek and latin, were brought to light. By 1889 Père de Smedt was able to publish a more complete version of the latin life,[5] based on a combination of a manuscript found in the Bibliothèque Nationale, Paris,[6] and a fragment of a manuscript found at Chartres, which he discovered to be closely linked with the metaphrastic greek text. A little later the Bollandists found in the Barberini Library in Rome a manuscript containing the complete text of the pre-metaphrastic greek life. In the meantime the future Cardinal Rampolla, who in 1884 was papal nuncio in Madrid, had found in the Escorial Library a latin text of the life which was not only more complete than those already discovered,[7] but even surpassed the greek text of the Barberini manuscript.

In view of Rampolla's discovery the Bollandists abandoned their plans for producing a *corpus melanianum* and in 1903 simply published the text of the Barberini manuscript, with a brief introduction and notes drawing attention to the places where it differed from their own latin version of 1889 and the metaphrastic greek text in PG 116.[8] It was not until 1905 that Rampolla's monumental edition of the *Life* appeared.[9] It contains the greek text originally discovered by the Bollandists and now carefully collated by other scholars, together with his own edition of the latin text and much other interesting material. My own translation is made from the greek text published in Sources chrétiennes 90.[10] The question of the relationship between greek and latin texts is not yet fully determined, and this does not seem an appropriate place for discussing it, since this book is intended for readers who will be more interested in the subject matter of the *Life* than in the niceties of textual criticism.

The Authorship of the Life of Melania the Younger

Neither the greek nor the latin text supplies the name of its author, but from internal evidence, we conclude that he was a priest who was closely associated with Melania and an eye-witness of much that he describes. Dr Denys Groce, the editor of the greek text in Sources chrétiennes, detects 'a special coloring' in the narrative from chapter forty-nine onwards,[11] after the death of Pinianus, when 'the priest' plays a more prominent part in the story. He had evidently come to the Melania's link with the outside world and her principal assistant in directing the affairs of the monasteries. In the latter part of the *Life* stress is laid on theological and liturgical matters which would be of particular interest to the clerical narrator. His references to the humbleness of his own position may remind the modern reader of Uriah Heap in *David Copperfield*, but we need to remember both his very real gratitude to Melania for all that she had done for him—he apparently owed his conversion to her[12] —and the conventions of the age in which he lived: the *confessio humilitatis* was a common literary *topos* in Late Antiquity and the early Middle Ages. Père de Smedt long ago identified the author with the priest Gerontius, known from the writings of Cyril of Scythopolis, a sixth-century monk and hagiographer of the monastery of Saint Sabas in Jerusalem.[13] This attribution is now generally accepted.

The Personality of Melania

Gerontius was clearly no Athanasius or Gregory of Nyssa. His work lacks the spiritual framework apparent in the *Life of Saint Antony* and the *Life of Saint Macrina*, but it gives a convincing portrait of a real person, based on first-hand observation. It is, however, an external portrait. We are told that Melania persuaded her husband to live with her as her brother rather than as her husband and that she renounced her vast wealth, but we learn nothing of her interior feelings, nor do we feel that we have heard the whole story of her reasons for acting as she did. Were there other factors in addition to her obviously genuine sense of vocation? Was she a young girl genuinely frightened of the responsibilities of sex and marriage? Did the state of her health render it dangerous for her to have more children? Was it a relief to her to give up her fashionable clothing and luxurious style of living? It looks as though she found much less difficulty in renouncing the world than Pinianus did. This lack of information, or even of speculation, about Melania's inner feelings is not, however, surprising: Augustine is perhaps the only writer of this era who both practiced introspection and set down what he discovered.

Melania emerges as a personality comparable to her redoubtable grandmother, Melania the Elder. Like her, she was a woman of vast wealth who wished to give it all away. She seems to have had the same qualities of leadership and powers of organization and the same love of learning, but there was a humility and tenderness about her which were lacking in the older woman. We learn, for example, that she would not put herself in charge of the monastery for women that she had founded, but occupied herself in ministering to the members of the community as if she were a slave. When she believed that the superior was being too strict, she devoted herself to the bodily needs of the sisters and hid extra comforts in the cells of those who were in poor health.[14] This contrasts with the stern attitude of her grandmother, who upbraided the young deacon Jovinus for repeatedly washing his hands and face in cold water on an excessively hot day.[15] Pinianus gives the impression of being a less strong personality, content—after some inner conflict—to follow his wife's lead, but this impression may be partly due to the fact that Gerontius did not have much opportunity to observe him at close quarters. The conversion of the couple seems to have been a gradual process. They began by withdrawing from their home in the city to their villa on the outskirts of Rome, on the Appian Way, and at first, wisely, did not attempt too much, but adopted modest ascetic practices, such as wearing cheap simple clothes and giving up wine. Melania increased her period of fasting as time went on, until she took food only at intervals of five days. The practical difficulties and the opposition from highly-placed persons of senatorial status which they encountered when they decided to give away their vast wealth may require a little explanation for the modern reader. The highly-placed senators would include a number of their own relatives, who seem to have been a rapacious set, and giving away money and property was regarded in late fourth-century society as an insane act.[16]

Melania and Pinianus, as members of senatorial families, were subject to special laws and had to make special contributions to senatorial funds. At the time when they decided to enter 'the angelic life', moreover, they were both minors, who would have needed the permission of a guardian to dispose of their property. Even in that era of vast personal fortunes, Melania possessed remarkable wealth and Pinianus, too, was very well-endowed. The extent of their combined fortunes must have aggravated the problem. After the death of their children, the heir to the property would have been Severus, the younger brother of Pinianus, who certainly would not wish to be deprived of his inheritance. They also faced the difficulty of disposing of the slaves who formed part of their property and among whom Severus attempted to stir up trouble. As it was, he had a very good bargain when he took possession at a reduced price, of those who did not wish to be freed. One way round the difficulty of disposing of their property was to obtain from the emperor a dispensation known as a *venia aetatis*,[17] Such would enable them to act as though they had come of age. It appears from the text that the imperial family took the initiative towards helping the couple.[18] At this point Melania was under twenty-one years of age. The process of disposing of their estates must have been protracted and personally very painful for them.

In the world of Late Antiquity it was considered a great compliment to a woman to say that she resembled a man. Palladius, as we have seen,[19] recalls certain women, 'with masculine qualities, to whom God granted the grace to carry on struggles equal to those undertaken by men'. Gerontius wrote in the same tradition: in the Prologue to the life he asks rhetorically who would be able to give 'a worthy and clear account' of her 'truly masculine acts', he reports how the empress praised her for being in no way inferior to a man in her firmness of purpose: and finally, he praises her because she was received by the Desert Fathers as though she were a man. 'It can truthfully be said that she was a woman of more than average feminine ability and that she had acquired a masculine, or rather, a heavenly cast of thought'.[20] This is one of those places where it is most important not to judge the people of late Antiquity by the standards of the twentieth-century. The belief in the inferiority of women was so much ingrained that the only way of praising a woman was to say that she was like a man. Women like Melania were the pioneers in showing what hidden capacities women possess, and they are to be honored for doing so.

THE PLAN OF THE WORK

The ground-plan of the *Life* may in theory be described as geographical-chronological but the chronology is confused and the author introduces digressions, which contain valuable material but do not fit readily into the chronological framework. These are marked in the analytical table below.

Geographical background	*Chronological background*
Rome	1. *Liberation from wealth*
The Campania	1. Family disputes
	2. Struggles with the Senate Intervention of Serena
	3. The struggle against the Devil
Sicily	2. *Melania's travels*
Africa	1. In Africa
	*2. Melania's practices of fasting and Bible-study
	*3. Melania's life of contemplation
	*4. Melania's spiritual detachment
Alexandria, Jerusalem	5. Melania's journey to the Holy Places and first stay there
Nitria and the Cells	6. The Egyptian journey
Jerusalem	3. *On the Mount of Olives*
	1. Melania's first period as a recluse
	2. The death of Albina and the foundation of the women's monastery

A lack of precise dating in the *Life* and in other sources makes it difficult to arrange the events described in chronological order, but the following scheme is tentatively suggested:

383	Birth of Melania to Albina and Publicola
397	Marriage of Melania and Pinianus
c. 398–c. 403	Births and deaths of the two children
402	Visit of Melania the Elder to Rome
403	Death of Publicola and first attempts to dispose of property
c. 404–406	Departure to villa on Via Appia and the beginning of 'the angelic life' Interview with Serena

407	Departure to Sicily, visiting Paulinus at Nola en route
410	Alaric's attack on Rome: they depart from Sicily to Africa
410–417	Residence in Africa where they founded two monasteries, one for men and one for women
414	Arrival at Alexandria and meeting with Cyril
417–418	Arrival in Jerusalem where they register as 'poor pilgrims'. First stay in Jerusalem
418–419	Arrival of unexpected sum of money enables them to visit the Desert Fathers in Egypt
420	Death of Albina. Melania's first period as a recluse
	Foundation of women's monastery, where Melania lived for about eleven years
432	Death of Pinianus
432–436	Melania's second period as a recluse
	Foundation of men's monastery
436–437	Visit to Constantinople
c. 438	Visit of the empress Eudoxia
439	Death of Melania

From this work we learn something of the conditions of life and scale of values with which people in Melania's social circle lived. We also see the importance of the role played by clothes in the life of the early ascetics, when we read of the numerous silk garments which Melania gave to be cut up for altar hangings and of the angora cloak which Pinianus exchanged for rough peasant attire . The assumption of the monastic habit was regarded as a very significant step, as we see not only from the writings of Palladius and Paulinus of Nola and from Gregory the Great's life of Saint Benedict (*Dialogue* II), but also those of the Desert Fathers and last, but not least, from the present work.[21] It seems as though Melania adopted plain dress principally as a symbol of her consecrated life apart from the world, but also as an act of reparation for her earlier extravagances.

After this important *mutatio vestium* (change of attire) came the adoption of a rule of fasting and further acts of discipline. As we have already observed, the lack of precision shown by Gerontius in his writing, combined with his determination to concentrate on the period during which he was in personal contact with Melania, renders it difficult to trace the development of her ascetic practices. It appears that she began with a modest rule and then gradually increased her periods of fasting until she took food only on Saturdays and Sundays. In fact, until she was rebuked by her mother, she even fasted at Easter. It was her practice to read both the Old and the New Testaments right through three times a year. She was a great lover of the psalms, which she encouraged her sisters to learn by heart, and she had a great devotion to the shrines of the martyrs. Even when the time of her labor was drawing near she insisted on spending the eve of the feast of Saint Laurence by keeping vigil in her own chapel before going early next morning to his shrine.[22] On her way to Constantinople from Jerusalem, she spent a night in prayer at the shrine of Saint Leontius at Tripoli, and immediately before her arrival, she offered further prayers at the shrine of Saint Euphemia at Chalcedon.[23] When she went to meet the empress Eudotia at Sidon, she stayed at the shrine of Saint Phocas in that city.[24] On her return to Jerusalem, she accomplished a project near to her heart by building a chapel containing a small shrine, where the Eucharist could be celebrated in the women's monastery. Relics of Zachariah the prophet, Saint Stephen the protomartyr, the Forty Martyrs of Sebaste and others were deposited in this shrine.[25]

From various sources, and particularly from the *Life*, we can form some idea of the daily program at the women's monastery. At the night office, Melania did not wait until cock-crow, but woke up the virgins herself, before they had had their fill of sleep. They followed the roman practice of having three readings (rather than the longer egyptian practice of twelve psalms), after which there followed fifteen antiphons. On holy days it appears that there were five readings; Gerontius tells us that on the Feast of Saint Stephen these included a non-scriptural account of the finding of the saint's relics, read by a priest, and the series ended with the reading, by

Melania herself, of the account of his martyrdom in the Acts of the Apostles. During the day there were normally services at the third, sixth and ninth hours, and vespers took place at the time of the lighting of the lamps; in fact what is now the traditional monastic *khorarium* had already been established.[26]

The Holy Eucharist was celebrated in the chapel on Sundays, Fridays, and holy days,[27] but from the Latin life and from the life of Peter the Iberian we learn that Melania was a daily communicant, which suggests that there was a daily Mass, a practice which is attested elsewhere.[28]

What can we learn from Melania's spirituality? At first sight her life and practices seem remote from our own. We do not find appealing her views on cleanliness and her description of a saintly old man who held up the ideal of becoming like a statue, impervious to insults as the statue was impervious to kicks and blows. And yet we can learn some important lessons from her. In the first place, she teaches us the value of regularity, discipline, and obedience in the practice of our religion—a lesson fundamental to all members of religious communities and important for lay people. Secondly, we learn from her the importance of being good stewards of our resources, whether intellectual, material, or spiritual, and of practicing the virtue of detachment. Thirdly, she shows us the real value of fasting; she now saw it as a virtuous end in itself, but always as a means of deepening the spiritual life and of thus drawing nearer to god. Finally, she puts before us the importance of holding a balance in our lives. She saw nothing degrading in manual labor, and long before the time of Saint Benedict, she grasped that men and women needed to occupy themselves in both manual and intellectual labor and to hold both the Word of God and the sacraments of the Church in equal reverence.

I owe a considerable debt to the edition of the greek life in Sources Chrétiennes, by Dr Denys Gorce, which I gratefully acknowledge here. I also owe much to Cardinal Rampolla's seminal edition of the greek and latin lives.

NOTES

1. Above pp. 105, 123–218.

2. For the pachomian documents themselves, see Armand Veilleux ocso, *Pachomian Koinonia*, three volumes, CS 45, 46, 47 (Kalamazoo) p. 267. This passage will also be of interest for comparison with the description of a cenobite religious community given by Jerome in Letter 22, pp. 201f.

3. See Palladius, *HL*, ed. E. C. Butler (Cambridge, 1898–1904) vol. 2: xxxiii–xxxiv.

4. *Sanctorum priscorum patrum vitae* 5 (Venice, 1556). Saint Simeon Metaphrastes owes his fame to the compilation of this *Menologion*, an example of a type of liturgical book in the Eastern Church, which contains the lives of the saints arranged by months throughout the ecclesiastical year, beginning with September. The soubriquet Metaphrastes is a greek word meaning, 'one who works over' or 'the Reviser'. He is also sometimes known as Saint Simeion Logothetes, the latter being an official byzantine title.

5. C. de Smedt, ed. 'Vita S. Melaniae Iunioris', *Analecta Bollandiana* 8 (1889) 16–33.

6. BN nouvelle acq. 2178.

7. Escorial Lat. a II 9, which dates from the latter part of the tenth century and may perhaps have originated in Oviedo.

8. H. Delehaye, ed., 'S. Melaniae Iunioris acta graeca', *Analecta Bollandiana* 22 (1903) 5–50.

9. Mariano, Cardinal Rampolla del Tindaro, *Santa Maria Iuniore, senatrice romana* (Rome, 1905).

10. D. Gorce, ed., *Vie de sainte Melanie*, Sch 90 (Paris, 1962).

11. *Ibid.*, p. 55.

12. See below, prologue, p. 299.

13. See Gorce, SCh 90: 56 for details. See also Cyril of Scythopolis: *Lives of the Monks of Palestine*, Introduction 42, 14ff, translated by R. M. Price (Kalamazoo: Cistercian Publications, 1991) 38ff.

14. Below. p. 336.

15. P. 305.

16. As we learn from Jerome, p. 105.

17. For the *venia aetatis*, see *Codex Theodosianus* 2.17.1; *Codex Justinianus* 2.45.1–2. Even if this privilege were granted, their families would still have the right to impose upon them a guardian chosen from among their relatives, should they show any signs of mental disturbance or extravagance (Gaius, *Digest* 27.10.13; Ulpian, *Fragmenta* 12.2; Justinian, *Institutiones* 1.33.3).

18. Pp. 316–322

19. P. 299.

20. Pp. 334–335.

21. Chapters 4, 7, 8, 11, 18, 24 and 31. [These references are provided for those wishing to locate the passages in the original. In this translation, internal enumeration has not been indicated—ed.]

22. Chapter 5.
23. Chapter 52.
24. Chapter 58.
25. Chapter 48.
26. Chapter 47.
27. Chapter 40.
28. E.g., Cyprian, *De dominica oratione* 18 (CSEL 3.1:280–281; Ambrose, *In psalmos* 118.26, 8.28 (PL 15:1461–1462); Augustine, *Ep.* 54 (CSEL 3.1:160).

MELANIA THE ELDER
BY
PALLADIUS, BISHOP OF HELENOPOLIS

WE MUST ALSO RECALL in this book certain women with masculine qualities to whom God granted the grace to carry on struggles equal to those undertaken by men, in order that people might not make the excuse that women were too weak to practice virtue. I have seen many of them and I have met many women of noble character, both virgins and widows, among whom was the roman lady, Paula,[1] the mother of Toxotius.[2] She was of great nobility in the spiritual life. One Jerome,[3] a man from Dalmatia, became an obstacle to her. Paula, who was a very able woman, was able to fly higher than everyone else, but he hindered her progress through his personal jealousy, by drawing her into his own orbit. Her daughter is still alive and practices an ascetic life in Bethlehem. Her name is Eustochium.[4] I have not had the good fortune to meet her, but she is said to be a woman of the utmost wisdom and to be in charge of a community of fifty virgins. . . . At Antioch I have also encountered a very venerable lady who lives in communion with God. She is the deaconess Sabiniana,[5] the aunt of John [Chrysostom], bishop of Constantinople. I have also seen in Rome that fine woman Asella,[6] a virgin who has grown old in the monastic life. She is a woman of the utmost gentleness and is a pillar of the community.[7]

THE WOMEN'S MONASTERY IN THE DESERT

The monks of Tabennesis also have a monastery of about four hundred women, which has the same rules and the same way of life as their own, apart from the wearing of the *melota*.[8] The women's monastery is situated on the far side of the river, while the men's is opposite it. When a virgin dies, the other virgins, after preparing her body for burial, carry it and set it down on the bank of the river. Then the brothers cross the river by ferry and bring her to the other side. They carry little palm leaves and olive branches and sing psalms. They bury her in their own cemetery. Apart from the priest and the deacon—and this happens only on Sundays— no one crosses over the river to the women's monastery.[9]

THE REGIME AT A PACHOMIAN MONASTERY

The rules and mode of life of the men's monastery, which the women also followed, are reported to have been given to its founder, Pachomius, by an angel, and were incised on a bronze tablet. They were as follows:

> You shall allow each man to eat and drink according to his capacity. Entrust the monks with tasks proportionate to their appetites. Do not forbid anyone either to fast or to eat. In this way, entrust those who are stronger and who eat with the tasks requiring strength, and those who are weaker and more feeble with the light tasks. Build separate cells in the courtyard and let the monks live three to a cell, but let the food for everyone be served in the same room. Do not let them sleep lying down, but when they have constructed chairs that slope more than is usual, let them sleep on them in a sitting position. At night let them wear linen tunics[10] with girdles. Let each [monk] have a goatskin *melota* and not eat without it. When they come to Communion on Saturdays and Sundays, let them unfasten their *melotae* and enter wearing only the cowl.

He commanded that these cowls be without fleece, like children's cowls, and instructed that they be marked with a purple mark in the form of a cross. He also ordered that there should be twenty-four classes of monks and imposed a greek letter on each class: alpha, beta, gamma, delta, and so on. Thus, when the superior asked questions or was very fully occupied with so large a community of monks, he could say to his second-in-command, 'How is class alpha?' or 'How is class zeta?' or again, 'Greet the rhos', following a private code of meaning for each letter:[11] 'Upon the more simple and more pure-minded you shall impose the *iota*, but to the more intractable and more devious, you shall assign *xi*.' Thus he fitted a letter to each class, according to the nature of their dispositions, its and lives, and only the spiritual fathers knew what each letter symbolized. 'Let a guest from another monastery with a different rule not eat or drink with these monks, and let him not enter the monastery unless he is found to be on a journey.'

For a period of three years they do not allow someone who enters the monastery to dwell with them to go into the inmost sanctuary of the monastery, but he may do so when the three years are up and after he has performed tasks of a more laborious nature. The inscription continues:

'While they eat, let them cover their heads with their hoods, so that no brother may see another brother chewing. There is to be no talking while the monk eats, nor is he to let his eye stray beyond his plate on the table.'

It is laid down that they should recite twelve prayers throughout the day, twelve prayers at the evening office, when the lamps are lit, twelve during the night, and three at the ninth hour. When the community are about to eat, it is their rule to sing a psalm first. . . . [12]

The monks who are on duty for the day get up early in the morning; some work in the kitchen, others at the tables. They lay the tables within a fixed time, setting on each of them bread, charlock preserved in a dressing of salt and oil, olives, cheese made of cows' milk, and chopped-up green vegetables. There are some who come to eat at the sixth hour, others, at the seventh, eighth, ninth or eleventh or later in the evening; yet others come every two days. Each letter of the alphabet knows its appropriate time. The monks work at the following tasks: one works as a tiller of the soil, another in the garden, another in the forge, another in the bakery, another in the carpenter's shop, another in the fuller's shop; yet another weaves large baskets, another works in the tannery, another in the shoemaker's shop, another at calligraphy and another makes little baskets. They learn the whole of the Scriptures by heart.[13]

MELANIA THE ELDER

The thrice-blessed Melania was a Spaniard by race, that is, a Roman. She was the daughter of Marcellinus, a man of consular rank, and the wife of a man of distinction, but I have no precise recollection of him.[14] She herself was left a widow at the age of twenty-two and was considered worthy of God's favor. Without saying anything to anyone—for she was forbidden to do so during the reign of the emperor Vallens[15] —she caused a guardian to be appointed for her son and, taking all her moveable belongings, embarked on board ship and sailed rapidly to Alexandria, accompanied by certain men-servants and maids. She sold all her material possessions, exchanging them for gold pieces. She then went from Alexandria to the mountain of Nitria, where she fell in with such Fathers as Pambo, Arsisius, Sarapion the Great, Paphnutius of Scete, Isidore the confessor and bishop of Hermopolis, and Dioscorus. She stayed with them for six months, touring the desert and questioning all the saints.

After this, the prefect of Alexandria sent Isidore, Pisinius, Adelphius Paphnutius, and Pambo—and, in addition to them, Ammonius the One-Eared and twelve bishops and priests—into exile in the district around Diocaesaraea in Palestine.[16] Melania followed them and supported them from her own resources. Since they were forbidden to have servants, as they tell us (for I have met the saint Pisimius Paphnutius, and Ammonius), she used to put on a slave's hooded cloak in the evenings and bring them what they needed. When the consular governor of Palestine learned of this, he planned to blackmail her, because he wished to fill his own pockets. Not knowing her status as a married woman, he arrested her and threw her into prison, but she spoke plainly to him. 'I am the daughter of So-and-so and the wife of So-and-so,' she said to him, 'but I am also the servant of Christ. Do not despise me for my lowly appearance for I am able to make myself look grand, if I wish. For this reason you cannot frighten me or take anything away from me. I made this declaration to you, in order that you might not incur charges as the result of your ignorance; for one must display a hawk-like pride in the presence of dull-witted people.'

The judge then grasped the situation and apologized. He bowed to her and told her that she might meet the saints unhindered.

After these men had been recalled from exile, Melania founded a monastery in Jerusalem, where she lived for twenty-seven years in the company of fifty virgins.[17] A man called Rufinus,[18] who came from Aquileia in Italy, lived there too. He was of very good family, of character similar to her own, and very energetic; later he was thought worthy to become a priest. During thee twenty-seven years they welcomed people who visited Jerusalem for the sake of their vows—bishops, monks and deacons—and supported all their guests at their own expense. They settled the schism of Paulinus, which involved about four hundred monks, and together they won over all the heretics who denied the divinity of the Holy Spirit, and brought them into the Church.[19] Thus they lived out their lives without causing scandal to anyone.[20]

I have already given a superficial description of that wonderful, saintly woman, Melania, in this book; nonetheless, I should now like to reveal the rest of her story. It is not for me, but for the inhabitants of Persia,[21] to describe how much of her wealth she spent with God-given generosity, as though she were burning it in a fire. No one—East, West, North, or South—has failed to enjoy her benefactions. During the thirty-seven years[22] that she lived apart from the world, she helped churches, monasteries, refugees, and prisoners with her private fortune; her family, her son himself and his personal guardians also furnished her with means. Because she persisted so long in her life of separation from the world, she did not possess so much as a square yard of land,[23] nor was she distracted by desire for her son; her longing for her only son did not separate her from her love for Christ.

Through her prayers the young man achieved a high standard of education and character and made a distinguished marriage. He was to be found among the recipients of worldly honors and had two children. After a long time had passed, Melania heard about the situation of her grand-daughter, how she was married and had decided to separate herself from the world. As she was afraid that the couple might succumb to bad teaching or heresy or evil-living, Melania, through an elderly lady of sixty, embarked on board ship, set sail from Caesaraea, and reached Rome twenty days later.

There she met Apronianus,[24] a Greek, who was a very fortunate man and worthy of all possible respect. She gave him religious instruction and made him a Christian, having persuaded him to live in continence with his wife, who was her cousin and was called Avita. Then after having strengthened her grand-daughter Melania and her husband Pinianus in their resolve, and after having instructed her daughter-in-law Albina, the wife of her son, she persuaded all of them to sell their possessions. She took them away from Rome and led them to the haven of a consecrated and peaceful life. Thus she 'fought with beasts', that is, with the senators and their wives, who were preventing her from withdrawing the rest of her family from the world.[25] She spoke to them this way: 'Little children, it was written four hundred years ago that "the last hour has come". Why do you cling to your empty lives? Are you not afraid that the days of the Antichrist will overtake you and you may not enjoy your own or your inherited wealth?'

She set all these people free and brought them to monastic life. She gave religious instruction to her younger son Publicola and took him to Sicily. Having sold all her remaining property and received the money for it, she went on to Jerusalem. After distributing all her worldly goods, she fell asleep forty days later, at a fine old age and in the deepest peace.[26] She left behind a monastery in Jerusalem and the money for its endowment.

After all these people had left Rome, the barbarians stormed the city.[27] the forecast of their invasion had long lain concealed in the prophetic books. They did not spare the bronze statues which stood in the Forum, but ravaged everything in their barbaric fury and consigned it to destruction. The result was that Rome, which had been adorned with beauty for twelve hundred years, became a ruin. Then those who had received religious training from Melania and those who had ben opposed to such training from melania and those who had been opposed to such training both glorified God, who, by overturning the accepted order of things, won over the unbelievers. Of all the other people who had been taken prisoner, only those households were saved which had offered themselves as sacrifices to the Lord through the zeal of Melania.

We happened to be on a journey from Jerusalem to Egypt, escorting the holy woman Silvania, the sister-in-law of the ex-prefect Rufinus.[28] Among those who were with us was Jovinus, who was then a deacon, but is now bishop of the church at Ascalon, a devout and cultivated man.[29] We were suddenly overcome by the most intense heat, and when we were at Pelusium, it happened that Jovinus took a basin and washed his hands and feet repeatedly in very cold water. After he had washed, he revived himself by lying down on a skin rug which he had flung on the ground. Melania approached him, just as a wise mother would approach her real son, and teased him gently, saying: 'How dare you cosset your flesh in this way at your age, when you are still hot-blooded? Don't you see the dangers to which this gives rise? Trust me! Trust me! I have reached the sixtieth year of my life, but except for the tips of my fingers, neither my feet nor my face nor any of my limbs have touched water.[30] Although I have been stricken with various ailments and have been constrained by the doctors, I have never allowed myself the usual comforts of the flesh: I have neither rested on my bed nor travelled in a litter.'

She was a very learned lady, who loved the Word. She turned night into day and went carefully through all the works of the ancient commentators. Among these she read three million lines of Origen, two million five hundred thousand lines of Gregory, Stephen, Pierios, and Basil and two million of other very erudite authors. She did not read them once only or at random, but went laboriously through each book seven or eight times. She was therefore freed from pseudo-knowledge, and by the grace of their words, she was able to be borne on wings. With the support of good hopes, she made herself into a bird of the Spirit and was able to soar away on her journey towards Christ.[31]

NOTES

1. For details of Paula's life and her relationship with Jerome, see his *Ep.* 108, above pp. 126ff.

2. Toxotius was the name of Paula's husband and also of her son, who is mentioned here. We last heard of him in Letter 108 (p. 130) as a little boy, holding out his hands to his mother as the ship carried her away from Rome. It is possible that Palladius met him on his visit to Rome in 405.

3. This passage reveals Palladius' great hostility of Jerome. Cf. HL 36, where Palladius mentions Jerome's excessively jealous nature.

4. Eustochium: see above, pp. 169–70.

5. Nothing else is known of Sabiniana.

6. Asella: almost certainly identical with the lady to whom Jerome refers in Letters 24 (p. 106) and 45.

7. Palladius, *Historia Lausiaca* 41.1, *VSanti* 2.210–211; *Heraclidis Paradisus* 29; PL 74:314–315.

8. *Melota*: a sheepskin cloak worn by the monks.

9. HP 33; *VSanti* 2:160–161; HP 20; PL 74:298. See Veilleux's note in *Pachomian Koinonia* 2:135 (HL33:1).

10. The garment referred to here is the *lebiton* or sleeveless linen tunic.

11. See the letters of Saint Pachomius, *Pachomian Koinonia* 3:51–78.

12. HI 32.2–7, *VSanti* 2:152–157; HP 19; PL 74 296–297; Cf. *Pachomian Koinonia* 2:125–127.

13. HL 32.11; *VSanti* 2:158–161; HP 19, PL 74:298; in *Pachomian Koinonia* 2:128–129.

14. Presumably Melania's mother was of spanish origin. The name of her husband in unknown.

15. Presumably Melania had to suffer for her principles during the reign of the barbarous emperor Valens (364–378), who was an Arian.

16. The banishment of these men was due to the intrusion of Lucius, an Arian, into the see of Alexandria in May 373.

17. The reference here to 'twenty-seven years' appears to contradict what is said in Chapter 54, where Melania is described as having lived thirty-seven years apart from the world. The twenty-seven years can be explained as covering the whole period of her absence from Rome, to which she seems to have returned in 402, visiting her relative, Paulinus of Nola, en route (see his Letter 29). Probably Palladius is regarding the whole span of her ascetic life as thirty-seven years, rather than the period between her departure from Rome, aged twenty-two, and her return at the age of sixty, since she lived for a further twelve years. Otherwise, to make the figures fit, we have to postulate a sojourn of ten years in Egypt, which seems unlikely.

18. This is Tyrannius Rufinus, once the friend and later the implacable enemy of Jerome, owing to the dispute about Origenism. Palladius, with

his obvious personal dislike of Jerome, writes favorably about Rufinus here.

19. There are two possibilities as to the identity of this schism: (1) The Antiochene schism, in which Paulinus, the candidate favored by the followers of Eustathius (bishop of Antioch, *c.* 324–30), was regarded by Catholics as the rightful bishop of Antioch; (2) The schism that arose between the monks of the Bethlehem monasteries and Bishop John of Jerusalem, consequent on the ordination of Jerome's brother, Paulinianus (whose name is wrongly given here as Paulinus) by Bishop Epiphanius without the sanction of the diocesan, Bishop John. The balance seems to be in favor of (2); it would be easy for the scribe to write the more common name in place of the more unusual name.

20. HL 46, *VSanti* 2:220–225; HP 36; PL 74:318–320.

21. There is no clear reason why the Persians are included. It may simply be a rhetorical flourish to mention them, in order to indicate the vast scope of melania's benefactions.

22. See note 46 above.

23. The Greek word used here literally means 'a span', but I have altered this to a 'square yard', as this has more significance for the English-speaking reader.

24. Apronianus, Avita and their daughter, Eunomia, are mentioned in HL 21 as people whom Palladius met on his visit to Rome in 405. Paulinus of Nola, writing in 406, mentions them along with Albina, Pinianus and Melania the Younger in his Carmen 21.205–9, as *mancipia Christi, nobiles terrae prius* (bond-servants of Christ, once landed nobility).

25. The most powerful and influential senators, from whom the opposition came, undoubtedly included Melania's own relatives, who would not care for the idea of her vast fortune passing out of the family. There would have been many legal difficulties. For a discussion of this problem, in connection with the similar opposition encountered by Melania the Younger and Pinianus, see p. 290. Giving-away property was regarded by late fourth-century society as an insane act, as we learn from Jerome's Letter 23 (p. 105).

26. The death of Melania the Elder probably occurred in 398.

27. The Goths under the leadership of Alaric sacked Rome in 410.

28. This is not the Rufinus referred to in n. 13) above, but a prefect of the praetorian guard. There is no evidence for assuming, as some authorities do, that his sister-in-law, Silvania, was the author of the *Peregrinatio* (*Egeria's Travels*), to which reference is made elsewhere in this book.

29. A bishop called Jovinus is mentioned by Augustine as having taken part in the Council of Diospolis in 415, and may well be identical with this man, as Mansi believed.

30. We have already seen in the Introduction that Christians in late Antiquity regarded baths and bathing as undesirable. It has been suggested that Melania kept the tips of her fingers clean because she receive the consecrated Host with them, but according to Cyril of Jerusalem, the normal practice was to receive the sacrament on the palm of the hand.

31. HL 55; *VSanti* 2:250–253; HP 42; PL 74:327–329.

MELANIA THE YOUNGER

SINCE I PROMISED EARLIER in this book to give an account of the grand-daughter of Melania,[1] I must pay my debt, as is proper. it is not right to despise her for being young in the flesh and to let so much virtue lie hidden and uncommemorated—that great spiritual virtue in which she really far surpassed those who were advanced both in years and in fervor. Her parents constrained her to marry one of the leading men in Rome, but she was always influenced by descriptions of her grandmother and [eventually] suffered so many pricks of conscience that she was no longer able to submit herself to the demands of marriage. After she had borne two sons and both of them had died, she developed so great an aversion to marriage that she said to her husband, Pinianus, the son of Severianus and a man of prefectorial rank, 'If you choose to live an ascetic life with me, according to the principle of chastity, then I shall recognize you as my master and as the lord of my life. If, however, this seems a burden to you, because you are still a young man, take all my goods and set my body free, so that I may fulfil my desire, which comes from God, to become the inheritor of the zealous spirit of my grandmother, whose name I bear. If God had wished us to produce children, he would not have taken my offspring from me before their time.'

After the couple had quarrelled a good deal, God finally took pity on the young man and implanted in him too the desire for withdrawal from the world, so as to fulfil the Scripture, *Wife, how do you know whether you will save your husband?*[2] Melania was married when she was thirteen years old and lived with her husband for seven years, but in her twentieth year, she renounced the world. Then, first of all, she gave away her short silk outer-wear tunics for the altar. The saint Olypias has done the same. She cut up her remaining silk garments and made them into different kinds of church ornaments.[3]

She entrusted her gold and silver to a priest called Paul, who was a monk of Dalmatia. She dispatched overseas ten thousand *denarii* to Egypt and the Thebaid in the East, another ten thousand to Antioch and its dependencies, fifteen thousand to Palestine, ten thousand to the churches on the islands and those in exile beyond the frontiers, and personally allotted a similar sum to the churches of the West. All these riches—and four times as much again—she succeeded in snatching (if one may use such a word in the presence of God) 'from the lion's mouth', that is, from Alaric, through her faith. She liberated eight thousand slaves who wished for their freedom; the rest did not wish to be liberated, but chose to be her brother's slaves. She allowed him to receive them for three *denarii* each. She sold her possessions in Spain, Aquitaine, and Gaul, and kept for herself only those in Sicily, Campania, and Africa, and these she used for the upkeep of monasteries.[4] This was the wisdom that she displayed in connection with her burden of wealth. Her ascetic discipline was as follows: she ate every other day at the beginning she ate at five days interval—and shared the daily routine with her serving women, whom she had made her companions in the ascetic life. In addition, she had her mother, Albina, living with her. She too had adopted the ascetic life and had privately distributed her wealth. They lived in the country, first in Sicily and then in Campania, with fifteen eunuchs and sixty virgins, both slaves and free women. Her husband, Pinianus, lived in a similar way with thirty monks and occupied his time in reading, gardening, and conversations with serious people. When we were on our way to Rome, though we were a large party, they received us with the greatest possible respect, on account of the holy bishop John,[5] and refreshed us with their hospitality and their most generous provision for our journey. By means of the tasks that God had given them to do and by the perfection of their way of living, they cultivated the fruit of eternal life.[6]

NOTES

1. For a fuller account of Melania the Younger, see pp. 283ff.
2. 1 Cor 7:16.
3. This was a normal gesture for wealthy ladies upon entering the religious life. Presumably Melania's tunics and 'her remaining silk garments' were cut up to make altar cloths. Special vestments for the Eucharist were probably unknown at this date.
4. This contradicts the statement in Gerontius' life of Melania the Younger (pp. 322, 324) that Pinianus and Melania had sold all their

properties in the neighborhood of Rome, in Italy, in Spain, and in the Campania. Palladius is almost certainly wrong here. On leaving Rome in c. 410, they went to Sicily and then to Africa and Egypt. They settled in Palestine in 414 and never returned to Europe. One can only conclude that Palladius had such a vivid impression of their italian household in his mind that he continued to picture them as living there in the place where they had entertained him, even when the facts were against him. We have already noticed his habit of visualizing people and places as they were in the past.

5. Bishop John is the famous patriarch of Constantinople, Saint John Chrysostom, on whose behalf Palladius travelled to Rome in 405 to plead his cause with Pope Innocent I, after he had been sent into exile through the plotting of Theophilus, patriarch of Alexandria.

6. HL 61; *VSanti* 2; 264–269; HP 49; PL 74:332–334.

THE LIFE OF THE HOLY MELANIA
BY
GERONTIUS

PROLOGUE

... Bless me, Father.[1]

Blessed be God, who has aroused your honored person, O holy priest,[2] to ask my humble self[3] for an account of the life of our saintly mother, the roman lady Melania, who now dwells with the angels—my humble self, who passed along time with her and has a vague knowledge both of the history of her illustrious family and of how she entered on the angelic life, trampling underfoot the vain glory of this world. But since I was well aware of my own clumsiness and I did not think that I could adequately describe such mighty contests, I decided to take the safer decision of refusing your request, in the belief that it was better to praise the noble handmaid of God through silence than to treat her outstanding virtues with disrespect through the awkwardness of my words. But when you once again promised to help me with your holy prayers, O holy priest, I took courage, by the power of the Holy Spirit, and prepared to reach out into the boundless sea of narrative, looking to a heavenly reward for my obedience. It is not surprising if I, clumsy and slow of speech as I am, am numbed at such a prospect. I believe that not even those who are excessively learned in philosophy would be likely to presume to undertake so great a task. Who would be able to give a worthy and clear account of the truly masculine acts of this blessed lady? I mean her absolute renunciation of the affairs of this life, her zeal, burning with more heat than fire itself, for the orthodox faith, her unsurpassed practical kindness, her tireless energy, her consistent practice of sleeping on the ground, her harsh treatment of herself, her ceaseless ascetic discipline of soul and body, her gentleness, her self-control in her struggles with incorporeal powers, her poverty-stricken appearance, and, with all this, her humility, the mother of all other virtues. For each one of three, her virtues, furnishes me with, as it were, a boundless sea of thought, and the pretext for writing a complete book, which would be too much for my strength. This is why, when I look upon the interminable length of my narrative, I shall try to be like the fishermen, who though they realize that they will not be able to catch all the fish, nevertheless do not give up, but bring to land what comes their way each man according to his strength. Again, I shall try to be like those people, who on entering a meadow where there are all kinds of flowers with varied scents, even if they have not the strength to gather everything in the meadow, at any rate go away, taking what each of them considers enough. Making use of this figure of speech and encouraged by the prayers of Your Holiness, I shall come into the spiritual meadow formed by the deeds of our blessed mother Melania. There I shall gather what comes to hand and I shall lay it before my attentive audience, to arouse in them a zeal for virtue and to benefit them greatly, when they wish to dedicate their souls to God, the Saviour of all.

Where shall I—clumsy and slow of speech as I am, as I have already said—begin my description of the mighty contests, or with what eulogies shall I praise Melania, who is praised in heaven? What shall I bring to her who has endured so much in the hope of my salvation, other than my call for her holy prayers to help me? For they contributed much to my salvation when she was still in the flesh. I still call upon her after her falling asleep, in order that, remembering her holy instructions, I may set aside all delay, forgetfulness, blindness, double-mindedness, and disobedience, and that I may be able to reveal in part her very great virtues, which she herself, in accordance with the teaching of the Gospel, was eager to conceal. Yet the voice of the Lord himself says, *That is why all that you have heard with your ears shall be proclaimed on the housetops,*[4] virtues of the saints cannot be hidden. Even if they would prefer all their good actions to be concealed, God—whose intention is the salvation and edification of the many—will reveal their very great virtues not only for the benefit of those who hear about them, as I have said, but also for the glory of those who have fought for him until death. Therefore out of many events I have written down an account of all those which I have witnessed personally or of which I have gained an exact knowledge by asking other people. I shall leave the rest for your curiosity to discover, as it is written, *Give a wise man the opportunity, and he will become even wiser.*[5]

LIBERATION FROM WEALTH

Family Disputes

The blessed lady Melania was the first roman lady of senatorial rank who from her early youth longed for Christ and, after receiving the wound of love, desired bodily chastity. Her parents, who were distinguished members of the roman senatorial order, hoped however, to ensure the continuation of their family through her. They therefore compelled her to be joined in marriage with that holy man, her husband Pinianus, who was of consular rank. She was then in her fourteenth year and her partner was about seventeen years old.[6] After she had made trial of marriage, she finally came to hate the world and piteously addressed to her husband the following plea:

> If you wish, my lord, [she said,] to practice a life of chastity with me and to live with me in accordance with the principle of continence, then I choose you as master and lord of my life—but if this seems a burden to you, and if you are not strong enough to endure a young man's fiery desires, here are all my goods, which I lay before you. From now on take them and use them as you wish; I ask only that you set my body free, that I may present my soul to Christ without stain on the dread day [of judgement]. In this way I shall fulfil my desire in accordance with God's will.

At first, he neither agreed to her proposition nor, on the contrary, did he deflect her completely from her intention. Instead he replied to her in the following terms: 'When, by God's will, we have acquired two children as heirs to our property, we will renounce the world together.'

By the will of Providence, a daughter was born to them, whom they immediately dedicated to God in a life of virginity.

Melania's heart burned still more with divine fire. Whenever she was sent to the baths by her parents, as was the custom, she betook herself there unwillingly. Entering the warm-air chamber, she washed her face, as proof of her obedience to her promise, and then wiped it with her clothes.[7] She gave money to those who accompanied her, to prevent them from telling anyone what she had done. This way the blessed lady Melania kept the fear of God before her eyes by every possible means.

She frequently begged her young husband, who was still attracted by worldly glory, to keep his body chaste, but he did not give in to her, saying that he still wanted one more child.

The saint then tried to run away and to leave him all her possessions. She consulted holy men about this question. They advised her to wait for a little while, so that by her patient endurance, she might fulfil the words of the Apostle: *Wife, do you know whether you will save your husband?*[8] She began to wear a coarse woolen garment under her silk clothing. When her aunt discovered this, she asked her not to clothe herself in this garment without giving this matter some thought. Melania was very much upset that she had not been able to escape notice and begged her aunt not to reveal this practice to her parents.

When at last the saint's prayers were answered and the time approached for her to give birth to her second child, the commemoration of Saint Laurence intervened. She took no rest at all, but spent the whole night in vigils and prostrations in her chapel. She rose early next morning with her own mother and went to the martyr's shrine. There she entreated God with many tears that, freed from the world, she might pass the remainder of her life in solitude; this was what she had wanted from the beginning. After she had returned from the shrine, she had an extremely difficult labor and gave birth to a premature baby. It was a boy, and after he had been baptized, he departed to the Lord.

At last her holy husband saw that she was deeply disturbed and was losing the will to live. He became faint-hearted and took a risk himself. He ran to the altar and in tears, cried aloud to God, begging that his wife's life be spared. Here is what the saint revealed to him as he sat by the altar: 'If you want me to go on living, give me your word here in the presence of God that we shall pass the rest of our lives in chastity. Then you will see the power of Christ.'

Very much afraid that he might no longer see her alive in the flesh, he made this promise joyfully. Then, partly as the result of grace from on high and partly as the result of her young husband's declaration, she began to recover. Once she was quite well, she gave up wearing all her silk clothing, pleading the death of her baby as an excuse.

At the same time her daughter, who had been dedicated to virginity, also died. From then on the couple were eager to fulfil their promises to God, but they did not obtain the permission of their own parents to do so. They fell into such a state of grief that they refused to eat unless their parents would agree to regard them as fit to be released from their obligation to them. Their purpose was to renounce worldly dignities and to adopt the values of the angels and of heaven. The aforesaid parents, however, fearing that other people would reproach them, did not give in to their children's desire. Melania and Pinianus suffered grievously when, because of violent parental opposition, they could not freely take up the yoke of Christ. Accordingly they planned together to retreat into solitude and to flee from the city. While they were deliberating these matters—as the holy woman has told us for our benefit—evening suddenly fell and over them drifted a heavenly scent[9] which changed the shadow of their grief into unspeakable joy. Giving thanks to God, they took courage against the wiles of the enemy.

In the course of time, Melania's father was stricken with a terminal illness As he was a devoted lover of Christ, he summoned the holy pair to his side and said:

> Forgive me, children. Because through my excessive folly,
> I have fallen into great sin. Because I was afraid of the
> reproaches of blasphemers, I distressed you by hindering
> you from your vocation. But now, you see me on my

journey towards Christ. From now onwards, be your own
masters and follow your desire, in accordance with God's
will, as you have already chosen to do. One thing I ask,
on my behalf: appease God who is master of all.

They heard these words with great joy, and after he had fallen
asleep in the Lord, they immediately took heart and left the great
city of Rome. They lingered at leisure on its outskirts, where they
trained themselves to practice the virtues. They clearly recognized
that it would be impossible for them to offer pure worship to God
unless they were to withdraw themselves form the turmoil of life
as it is written, *Listen, my daughter, behold and incline your ear;
leave your people and your father's house and the king shall desire
your beauty.*[10]

*Struggles with the Senate: The Intervention of the Empress
Serena*

When they began to lead the angelic life,[11] the blessed lady
Melania was twenty years old and Pinianus, who was from then
on to be her brother in the Lord, was twenty-four. For the moment,
owing to the delicacy of their upbringing in their youth, they were
not able to practice a severe form of asceticism, but they made
it their business to adopt a cheap style of dress. The blessed lady
dressed herself in a cloak which was worth very little and was
of old-fashioned design at that. Thus attired, she tried to make
less of her youthful beauty. Pinianus, when he turned away once
and for all from his magnificent and luxurious life style, clothed
himself in cilician garments. The blessed lady saw by this that he
had not yet come completely to despise elegance of dress. She
was deeply distressed, but she was afraid to rebuke him openly,
because he still secretly possessed the normal feelings of a young
man at his time of life; she realized that he was at the height of
his physical powers. She therefore dissembled her own feelings
and said to him: 'From the time we began to fulfil our promise to
God, has your heart not been open to the thought of desiring me'?

The holy man Pinianus, with an exact understanding of the
purity of her thoughts, affirmed in the presence of the Lord: 'From

the time we gave our word to God and began our life of purity, I have not looked upon you any differently from your holy mother, Albina.'

Melania replied to him with a word of encouragement: 'Then obey me, as your mother and spiritual sister, and give up your cilician clothes, for it is not suitable for a man who has given up worldly vanities for God's sake, to wear such things'.

Pinianus saw that she was speaking to him for his good, and immediately obeyed her excellent advice. After thinking it over, he realized that it was advantageous to both of them for their salvation. Laying aside his garments of cilician cloth, he put on clothing of the antiochian type, of a natural color.[12] It was worth only a single coin.

When by God's grace, they had succeeded in achieving this kind of virtue, they turned afresh to one another and wisely reflected on the question of discipline together.

> If we undertake a form of ascetic discipline beyond our strength, our bodies will be unable to endure such harsh treatment, owing to the softness of our earlier way of life, and will become completely enfeebled, in the end, we shall give ourselves over to pampering ourselves.

For this reason, they chose the following course for themselves. They made the rounds of all the sick people without exception, visiting them and giving them treatment. They entertained visiting foreigners and sent them on their way rejoicing, through their generous supplies of provisions and money. They gave unsparing help to the needy and to beggars. Going round the prisons, places of exile, and the mines, they freed those detained for debt by providing them with money. Following the example of Job, the blessed servant of the Lord, they left their door open to all who were in some kind of need. Then they began to sell their possessions, thinking of the saying which the Lord addressed to the rich man: *If you wish to be perfect, sell what belongs to you and give the money to the poor and you will have treasure in heaven; and take up your cross and follow me.*

At the same time as they were forming these plans, the devil, the enemy of truth, prepared an extreme test for them. Envious of the young people's ardor for God, he made a suggestion to Severus, the brother of the holy Pinianus, and persuaded their slaves to say, 'No, we are not for sale, but if anyone forces us to the point of allowing ourselves to be put on sale, your brother Severus is our master and it is he who has bought us.'[13] After this, Pinianus and Melania were deeply distressed when on the outskirts of Rome they saw their slaves in a state of rebellion.

The pious empress Serena,[14] who perfectly well understood the brilliance of the saintly Melania's life at this period and had heard of the great heights of virtue to which she had attained and of her conversion from earthly vanity to the fear of God, very much wanted to see her. She was thinking of the saying of the Psalmist, *This is the change in the right hand of the Most High.*[15] But Melania, who despised worldly glory, had declined to see her. When their slaves on the outskirts of the city rebelled, however, she said to her holy partner: 'Perhaps this is the occasion for seeing the Empress; for if the servants who are near us revolt in this way, what do you think that those in distant foreign cities are going to do to us? Indeed I am speaking of those in Spain and Campania and Sicily and Africa and Brittany and the other countries.' This, therefore, is why they felt obliged to pay a visit to the most pious empress. This took place through the mediation of some holy bishops.

As we have thought it extremely desirable to give a few details regarding their visit—details which Melania herself very frequently described for our edification—I will write them down as truthfully as I can for the benefit of those who may happen to come across them. Many people were saying, as she herself told us, that during her audience, she should uncover her head, in accordance with the custom of senatorial society in Rome. With noble courage, however, she affirmed that she would neither change her tunic—for it was written, *I have put on my clothes; how shall I take them off?*[16] —nor uncover her head. Her reason was the Apostle's words: *The woman must not pray without covering her head.*[17]

'Not even if I am destined to lose all my goods, for it is more fitting for me not to neglect to dot the i's and cross the t's of

Scripture nor to stifle my conscience in the sight of God than it is for me to gain the whole world.'

Her clothes were the garments of salvation and she looked on everything in her life as a prayer. Therefore she would not tolerate the uncovering of her head, even for a moment, so that she might not grieve the angels who were with her.

She took ornaments of no small value and crystal drinking-cups as presents for the most pious empress. In addition, she brought other adornments—rings, silverware and silk clothing—to offer to the loyal eunuchs and officers. She arrived at the palace, and after they had been announced, they were bidden to enter. At once the pious empress most joyfully came to meet them at the entry to the portico. When she saw the holy woman in this humble attire, she became stricken with great compunction. Having received her, she installed her on her own golden throne. She summoned all those who served her in the palace and began to speak to them in the following words:

> Come here and look at this lady, whom we saw four years ago, when she was glorying in her health and strength and was splendidly adorned; but now she has grown old in heavenly wisdom. Let us learn from her how godly thoughts triumph over all the pleasures of the body. Here she is, having trampled underfoot her gentle upbringing, her vast wealth, her weight of honors, in short, all the pleasant things of life. She fears neither weakness of the flesh nor voluntary poverty nor any of the things which cause us to shudder, but having placed restraints on herself, according to her nature, she has devoted herself to dying daily. By her actions she has shown everyone that when its purpose is firm, the female sex in no way falls behind the male, where the practice of virtue according to God's will is concerned.

After she had heard this, this true servant of the Lord, Melania, was not puffed up by these eulogies, on the contrary, the more the empress praised her, the more she humbled herself, thus fulfilling the words of prophecy, *The whole glory of man is as the flower of grass*.[18] When she was embraced by the empress, she cast her eyes down and again described to those present how much she had suffered at the time of their withdrawal from the world, and how they were pursued by her father and were prevented from either completely attaching themselves to the saints or hearing the world of salvation relating to the way of God. The devil had brought her aforesaid father, virtuous man though he was, to such a pitch of wickedness as to commit a great sin on the pretext of doing good. The reason why he was eager to deflect Pinianus and Melania from their heavenly designs, as we have already described, was that he was suspected of wishing to take their property and to distribute it among his other children. The empress gave them her blessing, and told them how much suffering they would endure, as they were being plotted against by Severus, brother of Lord Pinianus, who wished to take over all their possession sand properties, which were both numerous and large. She also told how each of their kinsmen—people of senatorial rank—was conspiring to secure their goods, wishing to acquire riches from them. The empress then said to them:

'Do you want me to arrange for Severus to be punished and for him, once he has gained wisdom, to learn to take no more advantage of those who have consecrated their souls to the Lord?'

The saints replied to the empress in these words:

Christ has commanded us to suffer injustice but not to perform unjust acts, to be slapped on the right cheek and to turn the other, to travel two miles with those who press us into accompanying them for one mile, and to give our cloak to the man who takes our tunic.[19] It is therefore improper for us to render evil for evil, especially when those who are trying to take advantage of us happen to be our relatives. We have come to trust in Christ that through his help and through the patronage of your pious majesty, even our modest resources will be well spent.

On hearing these words, the empress was much edified. She immediately indicated to her most truly pious brother, the friend of Christ, the emperor Honorius,[20] that he should decree that in each province, their goods should be sold at the risk of the governors and magistrates and that, still at the risk of these persons, the price should be restored to them. The emperor, the friend of Christ, did this so eagerly and joyfully that they were no sooner sitting down than the decrees, along with the deeds of execution, were given to them.

Astounded at the liberality of the most pious rulers, Melania and Pinianus gave glory to God, the Saviour of humankind, and brought out the ornaments, along with the crystal drinking-cups, and offered them to their most pious majesties, saying, 'Please receive from us these small offerings, as Christ received the two small coins from the widow'.

The empress smiled kindly at these words and made the following reply: 'The Lord will be convinced of your reverence of him. So I think that anyone, apart from the saints or the poor, who takes any of your possessions, commits sacrilege and will heap upon himself the fire of eternal damnation, because he has taken things which have been consecrated to God.'

The empress then commanded the chief officer of the household and two other distinguished eunuchs to escort them back with every honor and made them swear by the safety of her most pious brother, the emperor, that neither they nor anyone else in the palace would receive even one coin from them. The servants of the imperial pair, the friends of Christ, who were themselves also friends of Christ, carried out with complete joy and readiness what they had been ordered to do.

The saints departed full of happiness, having gained spiritually. For they had as a pledge the words of Christ, who said, *Well done, good servant. You were faithful over a few things; I will set you over many. Enter into the joy of your Lord.*[21]

They were expecting to scatter over the earth those things which they believed they had brought together as an inviolable treasure in heaven. When they reached their lodging, they planned to make some thank-offering to the empress, who had provided so much for them. Since none of the senators in Rome had found means to buy the house belonging to the holy man Pinianus, they pointed this out to the aforesaid empress through the mediation of some holy bishops, so that she might buy it. The empress, as she did not wish to buy it, said to the intermediaries, 'I do not think I can buy this house at its proper price'. They begged her at any rate to accept some very valuable marbles from it as a keepsake from the saints. She consented with difficulty, as she did not wish to cause them further distress. The holy pair were unable to sell the house; after the incursion of the barbarians, when it was burned, they gave it away for less than nothing.

The Struggle against the Devil

As to their fortune, I will pass lightly over what I heard from the mouth of the holy man, Pinianus. He told me that he possessed an annual income of 120,000 pieces of gold, more or less, apart from the wealth accruing from his wife. Their movable property was so great that it could not be measured. At once they began eagerly to distribute these goods, putting the ministry of the distribution of alms into the hands of holy men. They dispatched money to different countries, to one 40,000 [gold pieces], to another 30,000, to another 20,000, to another 10,000, and so on, as the Lord moved them. The saint herself said to her holy partner and brother: 'The burden of life is too heavy for us, and we are not strong enough in our present situation to take upon ourselves the light yoke of Christ. Let us therefore quickly rid ourselves of our goods, that we may gain Christ'.

Pinianus received the blessed lady's admonitions as though they came from God, and they flung away their property with generous hands.

Once she was invited by us in the strongest terms to tell us how they were able to descend from such an exalted position to one so humble. She began to speak:

'At the beginning we underwent numerous trials and assaults on the part of the enemy, who hates all that is good. This lasted until we were able to strip ourselves free from so great a mass of possessions. We were angry and sore, because we were wrestling not with flesh and blood, but, as the Apostle says, with principalities and the powers of darkness of this age. One night we fell asleep in great distress. We both saw ourselves passing through a very narrow crack in a wall. We were aching so hard all over on account of its narrowness, that there seemed nothing else for us to do but to give up the ghost. When with great difficulty,' she said, 'we emerged from our pain. We found that we had achieved a wide and deep sense of relief and repose and an unspeakable joy. God revealed this to us, comforting our feeble spirits, that we might look with courage to the rest that we would receive after so much trouble. Now one day, 'as this noble and large-hearted servant of Christ told us, 'we had brought together a vast and untold quantity of gold, so as to be able to send 45,000 pieces for the service of the poor and of the saints. I entered the dining-room, and as the result of the devil's activity, I imagined the house lit up, as if by fire, from the abundance of riches, and the enemy was saying to me, as I reflected, "Whence comes this kingdom of heaven, that it is bought with so much money?" Since I found it hard to stand up to the Devil,' she said, 'I immediately ran, fasting, to the unconquerable means of help, and kneeling down, I begged the Lord to take the adversary away from me. After this prayer, I became calm and said to myself, "Those are purchases made with things which are corruptible, concerning which the Scripture says, *Eye has not seen nor ear heard nor the human heart understood the things which God has prepared for those who love him.'* "[22]

She said that she had had the same experience a second time, when she was teaching us about the enemy's artful methods, how souls who wish to please the Lord must always keep awake and never live entirely free from care.

'We had,' she said, 'a much admired property, and on that property a swimming pool surpassing in its splendor all others in the world. On one side lay the sea, on the other, a wood containing all kinds of trees, in which wild boar, stags, deer, and other kinds of game made their home while bathing there, one could watch, on one side, boats sailing in the wind, and on the other, the wild creatures in the wood. The devil once more found a favorable pretext in this,' she went on, 'and placed before my eyes the variegated splendor of the marbles and the untold end of the income which came to me from the village—for it contained sixty-two dwellings round about the pool.'

But the blessed lady again lifted up her eyes to God in devout meditation and drove the devil off saying:

> You shall not check my course, you devil. What are these things—things here today and tomorrow perhaps destroyed by either barbarians or fire or time or some other misfortune—in relation to those eternal goods which are always the same, which extend into infinity, and which are bought by means of these perishable goods?

The enemy, realizing that in fighting with her, he was not getting the better of her, that instead, when he had been defeated, he would win greater crowns for her, became ashamed and confused and dared plague her no longer.

For the rest, having bravely disposed of what remained of their possessions in Rome, Melania and Pinianus went to the help of the whole world, so to speak. What city or what country has not had its share of their enormous benefactions? Shall we speak of Syria, the whole of Palestine, and parts of Egypt and the Pentapolis? In short, the whole of the West and the whole of the East have had a share of their bounty. Of course, when I travelled along the route to Constantinople, I heard for myself many old men giving thanks to the saintly pair and in particular, to the lord Tigrios, the priest of Constantinople. Having had the good fortune to acquire numerous islands, they presented them to holy men. Having similarly acquired hermitages both of monks and of perpetual virgins, they presented them to their inhabitants, providing a sufficient sum of gold to each place. In addition, they gave away all their silk garments, which were numerous and of great value, for the altars of both churches and monasteries.[23] Cutting their silver, which was vast in quantity, up into pieces, they made altars and church treasures and many other offerings to God.

Having sold their properties in the neighborhood of Rome, in Italy, in Spain, and in the Campania,[24] they sailed to Africa. Immediately afterwards Alaric descended on the properties the holy pair had sold, and everyone glorified the Master of all things, saying, 'Happy are they who anticipated events and sold their goods before the barbarian invasion'.

When they had left Rome, the prefect of the city, who was deeply imbued with the ideas of greek paganism, plotted with the entire Senate to ensure that all their goods became public property. He was eager to carry this plan out early in the morning, when, by the Providence of God, the whole population rose against him because of their lack of bread. They wounded and killed him in the middle of the city and the rest of the population was freed from fear and remained quiet.

MELANIA'S TRAVELS

In Africa

While they were sailing from Sicily to visit the most holy bishop Paulinus,[25] to whose house they withdrew at the beginning, contrary winds blew, in accordance with God's plan, and hindered their journey. A great storm arose. The ship was crowded and the water supply failed, and for a short time,t hey were all in danger. The sailors said that this was the wrath of God, but the blessed lady replied, 'It is quite contrary to God's will that we leave for the place where we intended to go. Therefore commit the ship to the prevailing wind and do not struggle against the winds.' The sailors, just as they had been commanded by the saint, spread the sails and made their way to an island[26] of which the barbarians had gained control, having dragged off the principal citizens along with the women and children. The barbarians asked them for a conspicuously large sum of money. If they gave it, the captives would be released; otherwise they would themselves be killed and the city would be set on fire by the barbarians. When the saintly pair disembarked from the ship, the bishop, who had heard of their arrival, came with other people to meet them. They fell on their knees before them, saying, 'We have as much gold as the barbarians are demanding, except for 2,500 pieces'. By readily supplying these, the saints freed all the people of the city from the barbarians. They gladly gave them another 500 pieces and also some bread and provisions from what they had brought with them and rescued those who had suffered distress from starvation and oppression. Not only that: By providing 500 pieces of gold they also ransomed from among the islanders a distinguished lady who had been seized by the barbarians.[27]

Then they sailed away from the island towards Africa, as we have already said. When they had arrived there, they immediately sold their possessions in Numidia, Mauretania, and Africa itself and divided the proceeds. Some of this money they sent to the service of the poor and some to ransom prisoners. Scattering their money generously this way, they rejoiced in fulfilling the Scripture by their action: *He has dispersed; he has given to the poor, his righteousness will endure for ever and ever.*[28]

Once the holy pair had decided to sell all their own possessions, the great and most holy bishops in Africa—indeed I am speaking of the holy Augustine, his brother bishop Alypius, and Aurelius of Carthage[29] —gave them the following advice: 'The money you now provide for monasteries will be spent in a short time, but if you want to have a memorial that will not be forgotten in heaven on earth, present each monastery with a house and an income'.

Melania and Pinianus eagerly accepted the excellent counsel of the saints, and acted exactly as they had been advised. They themselves made progress towards perfection and strove to accustom themselves to every kind of frugality, both in their place of residence and in their diet.

The city of the most holy bishop Alypius, which is called Thagaste, was small and very poor. The holy pair chose it for their residence, especially on account of the fortunate chance that the aforesaid Alypius was its bishop, for he was most skilled in arriving at the truth of holy Scripture by discussion. Our blessed mother Melania—lover of learning that she was—held him in affection. Indeed she trained herself so well in this respect that the Bible never left her holy hands. She gave so great an endowment to the church of this holy personage, both in money and in offerings of gold, silver and precious stones, that the envy of the other bishops of that province was aroused against him. Melania and Pinianus founded two monasteries, providing each of them with an adequate income. One of them was inhabited by eighty holy men, the other by three hundred virgins.

Melania's Practices of Fasting and Bible-study

As the saint made progress in the practice of the virtues, she saw that she had found a little relief from the weight of her wealth and that she had fulfilled the work of Martha. She then began also to imitate Mary, who is praised in the Gospel as having chosen the good part.[30] Now, to begin with, she tasted only a few drops of oil towards evening and took a little liquid. Even when she was in the world, she had never used wine, because the children of roman senators were brought up to do without it. Finally she began to discipline her body by severe fasting. At first, she took food without oil every two days, then every three days and then every five days; that is to say, only on Saturdays and Sundays did she eat some coarse bread. She was eager to surpass everyone else in asceticism.

She wrote elegantly and faultlessly in little notebooks. She mentally decided how much she should write each day, how much in the Canonical Books [of Scripture] she should read, and how much in the collections of homilies. After she had had her fill of these writings, she went through the lives of the Fathers as if she were eating a cake. Then she slept for an interval of about two hours. As soon as she awoke, she aroused her fellow-ascetics, saying:

> Just as the blessed Abel and each of the saints used to offer the first fruits to God, so we too will spend the first hours of the night in the praise of God. We ought to spend every hour in watch and prayer, as it is written, because we do not know at what hour the thief will come.[31]

She gave strict rules to her sisters who were living with her, that neither useless words nor immoderate laughter might issue from their mouths. She even enquired carefully into the use of their minds and did not allow the slightest impure thought to dwell in them.

She herself, as we have said, fasted from holy Pentecost until the weeks of Easter, taking no oil at all. And, as so many of those with an exact understanding of the situation testify, she never slept without her coarse garment of sackcloth nor did she eat on Saturdays before completing her entire office.

Having followed this ascetic practice for many years, she now began to fast even through the holy feast of the Lord's resurrection. Her holy mother, who imitated the lives of the saintly women of earlier times, was deeply grieved at this. (Her virtuous life is in need of another author. In her regard, I need only say that the tree is known by its fruit and that sound fruit comes from a good root.) She spoke to her daughter on these lines:

'It is not right for a Christian to fast on the day of the resurrection of our Lord Jesus Christ; on the contrary, one should enjoy physical food as well as spiritual.'

But with these words she succeeded only in persuading her daughter, that blessed lady, to partake of oil during the three days of the festival and then to return once more to her customary way of life, hastening to her work like an excellent farmer who owns a fertile field.

The blessed lady used to read the Old Testament and then the New Testament three or four times a year. She made a fair copy of what was sufficient for her needs and provided the saints with copies which she had written herself. When she had finished the Office with the virgins who lived with her, she recited the remaining psalms by heart in private. She read the Scriptures so completely that no book she could find escaped her notice. Some books she owned, others she borrowed; she read them so earnestly that no utterance or idea escaped her. Because of her extraordinary love of learning, when she read in Latin, she seemed to everyone not to know any Greek, and again, when she read in Greek, she was not to understand Latin.

Melania's Life of Contemplation

Towards those who practiced philosophy Melania possessed a gentleness which it is impossible to describe. She had such zeal for the name of our Lord Jesus Christ and for the orthodox faith that if ever she heard, even at the bare mention of his name, that anyone was a heretic, she would have nothing to do with him unless he accepted her advice to repent and turn to better ways—if he did not accept her advice, she did not allow herself to receive any contribution from him even for the service of the poor. I was offering up in the holy *anaphora* the name of a lady of the highest rank, who had departed from this life while on pilgrimage to the Holy Places, along with the names of the saints who had died—for we make this our custom, in order that in that dread hour, they may act as intercessors for us. When this lady, who was in communion with us, the orthodox, was reported to us by certain people to be a heretic, the blessed lady Melania was so angry that she spoke very frankly to me on the spot: 'Long live the Lord! If you name her, I shall no longer communicate when you offer the Holy Sacrifice.'

When I gave my word on the holy altar that I would no longer name her, she said, 'Once is too much. Since you have named her, I will not communicate with you.' She considered it a sin against the orthodox faith to mention the names of heretics in the holy *anaphora*.

She had such an extraordinary longing for chastity that by means of her presents and her suggestions she persuaded many young men and women to renounce an intemperate and immodest way of life by giving teaching along the following lines to those whom she came across:

> Our present life is short and is no different than a dream. Why therefore do we destroy our bodies which, as the apostle of God proclaims, are temples of the Lord?[32] Why also do we exchange corrupt acts which last but a moment, and sordid pleasures for the purity in which Christ commands us to dwell? The dignity of virginity is so truly great that our Lord Jesus Christ was thought worthy to be born of a virgin.

On hearing such words as these, many people conceived a passionate desire for purity and, so to speak, took flying leaps in the athletic grounds for virtue. How many saints' feet has Melania herself washed? Sometimes through her gifts, sometimes through her messages of comfort, for how many servants of God has she not performed services? How many Samaritans and Greeks and heretics has she not brought to God by persuading them with her gifts and exhortations? He alone knows, who is the Lord of all things and through whom she carried forward so many great conflicts to the end.

Melania's Spiritual Detachment

Melania successfully practiced almsgiving, as one who expected to obtain mercy only by her own efforts, as the Lord said, *Blessed are the merciful, for they shall obtain mercy.*[33] In addition to all this, she so loved poverty that a little while before she departed to the Lord, she assured us that she no longer possessed any property of her own except for a sum of gold for the oblation, amounting to about fifty pieces, which she sent to a very saintly bishop, saying, 'I do not wish to possess even what comes from our patrimony'. Not only did she offer God what she had, but she trained others to do the same. This is why many lovers of Christ handed over their wealth to her as to a faithful and wise steward, and she arranged for it to be distributed faithfully and prudently, in accordance with the requests of the donors.

She made herself a cloak, veil, and cowl of horsehair, and—so great was her burning desire for God—from the holy feast of Pentecost until the fifth day of the holy feast of Easter, she did not take them off either by night or by day although she had been delicately nurtured, as befitted a lady of so great a senatorial family. Those who knew the exact details of her upbringing as a child used to say that when she was wearing worldly dress, the embroidery on the valuable drapery that she was wearing, happened to touch her skin one day and caused an inflammation because her skin was extremely sensitive. But the Lord who said, *Ask and it shall be given you, see and you shall find, knock and it shall be opened to you*[34] granted her power from on high when she asked for it.

When she had received the wound of God's love, she did not tolerate the idea of remaining always in the same way of life, but prepared herself to struggle forward to greater conflicts. She decided to shut herself up in her cell and not to meet anyone at all, but to spend her time in continuous prayer and fasting. This was impossible, however, because many people were helped by her godly teaching. For its sake, she was importuned on all sides. She did not therefore carry out this resolution completely, but arranged for herself fixed hours in which she helped those who approached her, with her wise conversation. During the remaining hours she conversed with God and accomplished her spiritual work through prayer. She furnished herself with a chest, the dimensions of which were such that when she was lying in it, she could turn neither to the right nor to the left nor was she any longer able to stretch out her body. Though she possessed such great virtues, she was never puffed up by her own righteousness, but always lamented her wretchedness and called herself an unprofitable servant.[35]

If it sometimes happened that her mother was stirred by pity for her daughter to enter her cell when she was occupied in writing or reading, Melania did not even look at her or speak to her until she had fulfilled her customary quota of work. Then she said only what was necessary. At this point, her mother would embrace her, and as she wept, she would speak to her in words such as these: 'My child, I am confident that I too have a share in your sufferings. For if the mother of the seven sons of the Maccabees, after she had seen in one hour the tortures that they had undergone, found that she possessed eternal happiness with them, how much more should I receive, tortured as I am every day more than she was, seeing you waste away and give yourself no rest from such great toil? Then she used to add, 'I thank God that, unworthy as I am, I received such a daughter from the Lord'.

Melania's Journey to the Holy Places and Her First Stay There

Melania and Pinianus spent seven years in Africa. Then they laid aside the entire burden of their wealth and at last hastened on to Jerusalem. A longing to venerate the Holy Places came over them. They set sail from Africa towards the East and reached Alexandria. There the very saintly bishop Cyril received them in a manner appropriate to his sanctity. At that moment, the saintly Abba Nesteros, a man who possessed charismatic gifts, happened to be in the city, for it was the saint's custom to go into the city once a year for the purpose of healing the sick. He had received the gift of healing from the Lord, and those who came to him he released from different diseases by providing them with oil which had been blessed. When the holy pair, who were great lovers of sanctity, heard about him, they hurried at once to talk with him, in order to obtain spiritual comfort. Owing to the extraordinarily large crowd that was approaching him, they became separated from each other. Melania's most holy brother was the first to enter among the never-ending throng of people. He hurried forward to receive a blessing, so he could leave. The holy man, however, gazed upon Pinianus with the eyes of the spirit and recognized the beauty of his soul. He seized hold of him and set him beside himself. Then Melania, the servant of Christ, entered, after a great crowd. The holy man, as he gazed about him, recognized her with his inner eye and held her in his sight with the other two. As a third person, he saw her holy mother. After he had dismissed the crowd, the holy man Nesteros began to describe Melania, her brother and her holy mother and to tell the crowd, by encouraging and prophetic words, how many afflictions Melania and Pinianus had variously endured in renouncing the world. Warning them as if they were his own children, he urged them not to be faint-hearted, because the end of afflictions brings unspeakable joy.

'For the sufferings of the present time,' he said, 'are not worthy to be compared with the glory that will be revealed to us.'[36]

They were therefore immensely encouraged, and praised God more and more as they set sail for Jerusalem, the goal to which they were hastening. They lodged at the church of the Holy Resurrection and, not wishing to distribute with their own hands the gold which remained to them, they passed it on to the people who were entrusted with the administration of poor relief, for they did not want anyone to see them engaged in good works. They went so far in stripping themselves of their possessions that the holy woman affirmed to us, 'At the beginning of our stay here, we decided to be enrolled in the church register and to receive official rations with the poor'.

Thus they descended to the lowest depths of poverty, because our Lord was poor for our sakes and took the form of a servant. It happened that Melania was taken ill when they first arrived in Jerusalem, and since she had nowhere to sleep except on a bed of sacks, a virgin from among the nobly-born presented her with a pillow. When she was well again, she devoted herself to reading and prayer, offering genuine service to God.

She made her home alone with her mother and was in no hurry to meet anyone—except for saintly and distinguished bishops, particularly those who were famous for their learning—so that she might spend even the time of her conversation with them in questioning them about divine sayings. As we have already mentioned, she used to write in little notebooks and to fast during the week. In the evenings, after the closing of the church of the Holy Resurrection, she remained by the cross until the arrival of the psalm-singers. Then she departed and rested for a little while in her cell.

Since she was not able to dispose of all her lands, owing to the barbarian invasion, she had left some of them unsold. However, a faithful Christian, whose heart God had touched with compunction, was able to put on sale part of them which lay in those regions of Spain that were at peace. He was able to collect a little gold as the result of the sale, and brought it to the holy pair in Jerusalem. Melania, having snatched it from the lion's mouth, so to speak, consecrated it to God and said to her spiritual brother Pinianus, 'Let us go to Egypt and consult the holy men there'. Indefatigable where such good works were concerned, Pinianus listened joyfully to her, as to a teacher of really noble character. When Melania was about to depart on this spiritual enterprise, she encouraged her saintly mother to build for herself in the neighborhood of the Mount of Olives a cell with interior walls of wood, so that she might rest in it quietly for a definite period.

The Egyptian Journey

After Melania and Pinianus had arrived in Egypt, they toured round the cells of the holy monks and of the intensely faithful virgins. They behaved like truly wise stewards in accordance with what Scripture says, ministering to them according to their needs. While they were doing this, they reached the cell of a saintly man, Abba Hephaistion, as he was called, and begged him to receive a little gold from their hands. But he declared vehemently that he would have none of it. The blessed lady then went round the saint's cell, examining his belongings, and discovered that he possessed nothing on earth except a little rush mat, a round basket containing a few dry biscuits, and a little basket of salt. As her compunction was thoroughly aroused by the saint's ineffable and heavenly riches, she hid the gold in the salt and rapidly departed, for fear the old man might discover what she had done. When they had asked him for a prayer, they hastily left, but they failed to escape his notice. They had just crossed the river, when the man of God ran after them, clutching the gold and shouting, 'What do I want with this?' The blessed lady Melania then said to him, 'It is for you to give to those in need'. He solemnly swore that he would neither keep it nor give it away, particularly because the place was a desert and no needy person could be present there. He became more and more obstinate in his argument, but he could not persuade them to take the gold back from him. Finally the saint threw it into the river himself. Many other holy hermits and devout virgins were also unwilling to accept gold. The blessed lady therefore left it in their cells, by means of a spiritual subterfuge. She considered that it was a very considerable spiritual gain and a great advantage to the soul to give comfort to the saints in this way.

After Melania and Pinianus had completed their tour, they returned once more to Alexandria, where they had the privilege of meeting a number of holy men. Among them they encountered the superior of the Tabennesiots and the most holy Abba Victor, as well as the most godly fathers and superiors called the Zeugetes, and another holy priest, Elias by name, and many others whose names it is unnecessary to mention because of their number. The holy woman took care to receive the fruit of his personal help and blessing from each holy man, and to share his virtue. Leaving Alexandria, Melania and Pinianus came to Mount Nitria and to the place called The Cells, where the saintly fathers received Melania as though she were a man. It can truthfully be said that she was a woman of more than the average feminine ability and that she had acquired a masculine, or rather, a heavenly cast of thought. They were therefore at one with the holy fathers, and having received their blessing, they stayed with them and then departed, escorted on their way by all of them, with great contentment.

ON THE MOUNT OF OLIVES

Melania's First Period as a Recluse

The holy pair returned to Jerusalem, bringing with them a full cargo of godliness, so to speak. Having accomplished the work of serving our Lord Jesus Christ with great zeal, they both became ill on account of the unhealthy climate. The blessed lady found that the cell on the Mount of Olives had already been completed by her saintly mother. There, after the feast-day of the holy Epiphany, she enclosed herself and settled down in sackcloth and ashes. She met nobody except, on certain days, her most saintly mother and her spiritual brother. Her cousin, the holy virgin Paula, also saw her. She it was whom the saint had directed towards the commandments of God and had brought down from an attitude of great pride and a typically roman outlook to the depths of humility. Melania also had as a servant a single virgin, who frequently assured us, 'At the season of holy Easter, when the blessed lady used to leave the narrow confines of her cell, we used to shake the sack which she had under her, and out of it fell enormous worms'. She led an ascetic life this way for fourteen years.

The Death of Albina and the Foundation of the Women's Monastery

The Lord called her holy mother, and she departed to receive the good things promised to his saints. After they had accompanied her remains and buried them on the Mount of Olives with great honor and with the singing of psalms, Melania remained there in her dark cell, not wishing to live in the city any longer. She completed that year in great sorrow and austerity of life and in very strict fasting. She invited her brother to bring together a few virgins to join her. She had a community of about ninety virgins, whom from the beginning she instructed never to encounter a man. When she had created a water-supply for them inside the monastery and had provided for all their bodily needs, she said, 'I shall minister to you in every respect as if I were a slave and I shall not let you lack any necessity. Only be on your guard against meeting men.' Urging the women away from places with a bad reputation, she offered them as a sacrifice to God; she knew what was written in the Scriptures: *If you take away what is precious from what is base, you shall be as my mouth.*[37]

She never ceased to address them on the subject of their own salvation. She was so excessively humble that she did not wish to be regarded as their Superior, but entrusted this office to another woman who was both spiritual and afire with a desire for God. When the Superior was a little too strict, Melania vigorously devoted herself to supplying their bodily needs. She took such care of the more delicate sisters that she hid whatever they needed and carefully put it in each one's cell, under the straw on the floor. When they cam in, they found everything she had prepared for their comfort, without their Mother knowing about it. The sisters usually recognized that it was the blessed lady who had done this for them. They attached themselves to her above all others and devoted themselves to obeying her in everything, for they knew that her sympathy was boundless.

Melania's Ascetic Teaching

I find it impossible to speak of the unceasing and inspired teaching which Melania gave the sisters, but I shall try to discuss it a little from certain aspects. Her entire attention was always devoted to teaching them about spiritual works and virtues, so that they might present their virginity of soul and body without stain to Christ their heavenly bridegroom and master. She taught them first about the necessity of remaining resolutely awake during the night office, and of not allowing their attention to wander, but of concentrating their minds on the chanting of the psalms. She used to say:

'Consider, my sisters, how those subject to corruptible and earthly rulers stand in their presence in total fear and vigilance.

Consider also with what great fear and trembling we ought to accomplish our duty and service as we stand in the presence of our dread heavenly King. Recollect that neither the angels nor the whole spiritual and celestial creation can worthily glorify the Lord, who lacks nothing and is higher than all glory. If therefore the incorporeal powers, far surpassing our human nature, are yet deficient in the worthy praise of the God of all things, as we have already remarked, how much more ought we, his unprofitable servants, to sing his praise in utter fear and trembling, in order not to bring judgement on ourselves, instead of reward and benefit, as the result of our indifferent attitude in glorifying our Master.

We ought to guard with all possible care our pure love for him and for each other, as we have been taught by Holy Scripture, recognizing that without spiritual love, every ascetic practice and every virtue is vain. For the devil can imitate all the righteous acts which we appear to do, but he is splendidly defeated by love and humility. This is what I am telling you. We fast, but he eats absolutely nothing. We keep watch, but he does not sleep at all. Let us therefore hate pride because, through it, he fell from heaven, and again because, through it, he wants to drag us down with him. Let us also shun the vainglory of the present age, which is transient, like the flower of grass. Above all, let us steadfastly guard our holy and orthodox faith, for this is the groundwork and foundation of our whole life in the Lord. Let us love the consecration of our souls and bodies, because without it, no one will see the Lord.'

Since she was afraid that any one of them might fall through excessive ascetic practices, she used to say that fasting was the last of all the virtues, and that 'Just as a bride decked out in full finery cannot wear black sandals, but adorns her feet in the same way as her body, so the soul needs fasting, accompanied by all the other virtues. If anyone is eager to practice fasting apart from the other virtues, she is like a bride whose body is naked, and who adorns only her feet.'

She often used to exhort the sisters about obedience to God, speaking in such terms as these: 'Not even the affairs of this world can be organized without obedience. Worldly rulers, too, are submissive and obedient to one another. If you speak of the man who wears the crown, in the majority—and most urgent—of cases, he cannot command anything of his own accord, unless he first obtains the opinion of the Senate. Again, in worldly households, if that great possession, which is obedience, is removed all order is taken away. When there is no order, our peaceful world totters. We must therefore render obedience to one another. Obedience to one another. Obedience consists of doing what you do not want to do, for the purpose of satisfying the person who gives you orders, and of compelling yourself to obey, on account of the saying of Jesus, *The kingdom of heaven suffers violence and violent men take it by force.*[38]

She used to quote the saying of a saintly old man, to the effect that anyone who lives in the midst of men must endure everything that is likely to happen to a person in his situation.

'Someone who wished to learn from him,' she used to say, 'approached a saintly old man. The old man said to him, "Are you able to obey me in every respect, for the Lord's sake?" The other man replied, "Everything that you command I will do with the greatest willingness." "Take a whip, then," said the old man, "set out from here and beat and kick that statue over there." The man carried out his orders with alacrity and then came back; whereupon the old man said to him, "While the statue was being beaten and kicked, did it protest or reply to you?" The other man replied, "Not at all". "Go away then," said the Father, "strike it a second time and do it some further injuries." When he had done the same thing a third time, in accordance with the Father's orders, and the statue had not replied—indeed how could it, for it was made of stone?—then the saintly old man finally said to him, "If you are able to become like that statue, letting yourself be insulted without offering an insult in return, and beaten without answering back, you will also be able to be saved and to stay with me." Let us therefore imitate this man and bear everything— insults, reproaches, and contempt—so that we may inherit the kingdom of heaven.'

As regards perseverance in fasting, she used to repeat this saying of the Apostle: *Not grudgingly nor from compulsion, for*

God loves a cheerful giver,[39] and she left the duty of fasting to the discretion of each individual. But as regards goodness, humility, gentleness, and the remaining virtues, she used to say, 'It is not possible for anyone to impute blame to his stomach or any other part of his body, but every person who fails to carry out the commandments of the Lord is answerable for his failure. I urge you therefore to carry on the struggle in patience and long-suffering, for it is by the narrow gate that the saints enter into eternal life. The labor itself is small, but the rest is vast and eternal. Wait a little while, so you may put on the crown of righteousness.'

The Liturgy at the Women's Monastery

During the nighthours, she woke the sisters for the prayer of praise, because of the words of the prophet, *I anticipated the dawn and I cried aloud,*[40] and again, *At midnight I awoke to confess you.*[41] She used to say, 'We should not get up for the night office after we have had our fill of sleep. On the contrary we should do violence to ourselves, so we may obtain the reward for this violence in the age to come.' After they had completed the customary canon, she caused them to sleep a little, thus giving them a rest from the weariness of the vigil and for renewing their bodies for the daily recital of the psalms.

The night office consisted of three psalms sung antiphonally, three readings, and fifteen antiphons at daybreak. They used to sing Psalms at the third hour of the day, 'because at that hour,' Melania said, 'the Holy Spirit descended upon the Apostles', at the sixth hour, because at that hour the patriarch Abraham was thought worthy of receive the Lord; at the ninth hour, in accordance with the tradition of the holy apostles, for at that hour, the apostles Peter and John, going up to the temple at the hour of prayer (the ninth) healed the lame man.[42] She used to cite other examples from Holy Scripture which were consistent with this idea. She spoke about the most holy prophet Daniel, telling how he prayed three times a day on bended knee,[43] and about the parable in the holy Gospel where it is said that the master of the house went out at about the third hour and about the ninth hour to pay the workmen in his vineyard.[44]

We ought to discharge the evening office with great zeal,'
she said, 'not only because we have passed through the
space of one day in peace, but also because at that very
hour, Cleopas and his companion were thought worthy to
accompany the Lord on the road after his resurrection.[45]

She used to exhort the sisters to be especially eager on Sundays
and the other great feast days to employ themselves in the earnest
singing of the psalms, saying, 'If it is good not to be negligent in the
daily office, we ought with even more reason to sing the psalms
a little more on Sundays and on the other feast days than in our
normal office.'

By speaking this way, she so encouraged them in their enthusiasm by her sound teaching that if ever the blessed lady wished to
spare them in their vigils on account of their great weariness, they
themselves would not agree to it, saying, 'Just as you continually
consider our bodily needs day after day, so much the more should
we not let anything drop out of our daily office, where spiritual
matters are concerned.' The blessed lady rejoiced greatly when
she saw their generous decision in the Lord. She was very eager
to build a chapel in the monastery and to place an altar in it, so
that they might have the honor of participating continually in the
holy mysteries. She arranged for two *anaphoras* to be celebrated
for them every week, apart from feastdays: one on Fridays, the
other on Sundays. She deposited relics of the holy martyrs there,
that is to say, of Zachariah the prophet, Stephen the protomartyr,
and the Forty Martyrs of Sebaste, as well as of others whose names
are known only to God.

*The Death of Pinianus and Melania's Second Period as a
Recluse*

While our saintly mother Melania was thus doing battle, her
most holy brother fulfilled the allotted span of his life in the flesh.
He had fought the good fight and gained his crown,[46] as the result
of his voluntary poverty and his obedience to divine precepts.
He therefore departed joyfully to the God of the Universe eight
years before Melania herself fell asleep. Surely God ordered all
things for his good purpose, that through still greater contests, the

blessed lady might render her conduct more glorious in the sight of the Lord. After her brother had fallen asleep in the Lord, she remained in the Apostoleion which she had herself established a little earlier, and in which she deposited the remains of her blessed husband. There she remained for about four years and became excessively thin, being wasted away through fasting, vigils, and incessant mourning.

The Foundation of the Men's Monastery

After this, she was moved by divine fervor, and longed to establish a monastery of holy men, so that they might achieve continuous singing of the psalms, by night and day, in the place of the Ascension and in the cave where the Saviour used to talk with his disciples about the end of the age. Some people, however, opposed this excellent project, saying that she would not be in a position to carry out so great a task, on account of her excessive poverty. But the Lord, whose riches are infinite, fulfilled the desires of this saintly soul by putting it into the mind of a man who was a lover of Christ to offer her two hundred pieces of gold. She received them with joy, and summoning the priest who was with her and whom she had taken out of the world and offered as a sacrifice to God—he was my pitiable self—she said to him, 'Trust that you will receive the reward of your labors from the Lord in the age to come. Take these few gold pieces and buy stones for us, so we may begin building the men's monastery in the name of our Lord Jesus Christ. Thus, while I am still in the flesh, I shall be able to see a church where a perpetual round of services is carried on and where the bones of my mother and my brother will be at rest, thanks to the singing of the psalms.'

Once she began the project in the name of the Lord God—who worked with her in all her schemes—she completed such an undertaking that everyone was amazed to learn that it really was through an impulse from on high that the work had been accomplished. She installed these men, who were holy and friends of God and who performed the liturgy joyfully, both in the Church of the Ascension of Christ and in the Apostoleion, where her blessed mother and brother lie buried.

AMONG THE GREAT

The Journey to Constantinople

Suddenly other combats, which surpassed their predecessors, afflicted her. She had scarcely begun to draw a little breath after she had completed the foundation of the monastery, when a letter arrived from her uncle Volusianus, ex-prefect of the great city of Rome, to say that he was coming to Constantinople on a embassy of the most pious empress Eudoxia, who had been granted in marriage to our most Christian emperor Valentinian.[47] A desire to see her uncle gradually stole over her. By the grace of prompting from on high, she longed to see him, so she might save his soul by taking great trouble, for he still remained a pagan. She was in great anxiety, lest she act in a way contrary to the purpose of God. She shared the problem with all the holy men and asked them to pray fervently that her journey might be in accordance with the will of God. Then, having entrusted the monastery to the Lord, she departed from Jerusalem.

Once she had begun her journey, the holy men in every city and country district—I mean by this the bishops and clergy—paid her extraordinary respect and honor. Both monks who were very dear to God and devout virgins, once they saw that the lady about whom they had long heard shone with her many virtues, could tear themselves away from her only in floods of tears.

I do not think it safe to pass over in silence the miracle which the Lord performed through her in Tripoli, because as the Scripture says, *It is good to keep secret the mystery of the king, but it is glorious to reveal the works of the Lord*. When we entered that town, we stayed at the shrine of Saint Leontius, where numerous miracles have been performed. Since many of us who were travelling with her were without special tickets, the official displayed excessive strictness in the matter of delivering the animals to us. The blessed lady was extremely distressed by this. She remained in prayer and vigil by the relics of Saint Leontius from evening until the time the animals arrived. We had journeyed a little less than seven miles after leaving the town, when the official followed hard upon us. He was very upset and asked us, 'Where is the priest?'

As I was an inexperienced traveller, I was afraid that he had come to ask to have the animals back. I got down and enquired of him the reason why he was upset. He replied, 'I am anxious to have the honor of seeing the great lady'. When he had seen her, he fell down, and seizing her feet, he began to speak, weeping copiously and saying, 'Forgive me, servant of Christ, that I, being ignorant of your great sanctity, was slow in handing over the animals.' When she answered, 'God will bless you, my son, because you have all the same handed over the animals, even if you were slow in doing so,' he immediately took out the three gold coins which I had given him as a gratuity and begged me to take them from him:

'All night long, my wife, your servant, and I were tested by the holy martyr Leontius; for that reason, as soon as we got up, we both ran to the shrine. As we did not find you there, my wife went back because she cannot run far, but I overtook you, and now I beg Your Holiness to pray for us both, that the God of all things may be favorable to us.'

When we heard these words, we sent the official on his way, rejoicing and in peace. All the company were struck with amazement at what had happened, whereupon the blessed lady said, 'Be of good courage! Our journey is in accordance with God's will'. When we all clearly demanded to know the reason for this, the saint replied, 'All night I entreated the holy martyr Leontius to show us a good omen for our journey and now, unworthy though I am, I have obtained what I asked.' We went rejoicing on our way and were welcomed on all sides.

When we finally arrived at Constantinople, the city that loves Christ, the saint was filled with anxiety. She had emerged from a long period of asceticism and solitude and was now about to enter a royal city of vast size. We arrived at the shrine of Saint Euphemia at Chalcedon; there she who had gained the prize comforted the saint, giving her much fragrance and consolation. From there, she took courage in the Lord and entered Constantinople.

At Constantinople

The Lord Lausus, the chamberlain, received her as befitted a man of such high character.[48] She also found her uncle who, by divine providence, had fallen ill. When he saw her wearing her poor and extremely simple clothing, he, who was always proudly dressed in the splendor of worldly fashion, began to speak to my humble self, seeping copiously:

'Do you not know, reverend sir, how delicately my niece was brought up—more so than all the rest of our family? And now to what a degree of austerity and poverty she has surrendered herself!'

The blessed lady took the opportunity to reply to him thus: 'You have learned from me, my Lord, that it is on account of the future eternal blessings—which the author and creator of the world grants to those who genuinely believe in him—that I have despised glory and riches and all ease in this life. Come now, I beg you, to the laver of immortality, so that at the same time you flee temporal blessings, you may obtain eternal blessings. Free yourself from the error of the demons, who will burn in the everlasting fire, along with those who obey them.'

When her uncle perceived that Melania was planning to refer the matter to the imperial rulers, he was overcome by compunction and said: 'I beg Your Holiness not to take from me the gift of free will, with which God has honored human beings from the beginning. I am ready and I pray that the stain of my many sins may be washed away. But if I do this in accordance with imperial instructions, I shall find myself acting as if compelled by force and I shall lose the reward of my decision.'

Melania did not resign herself to being silent, but made a submission on this subject, through certain men of high distinction, to the most holy bishop Proclus.[49] He arrived to see her uncle and gave him considerable help, by discussing numerous matters regarding his salvation. Her uncle had great powers of penetration and perceived that if the archbishop had arrived to see him, it was at the suggestion of the blessed lady. Indeed he declared to her: 'If we had three men in Rome such as the Lord Proclus, no one there could be called a pagan.'

The devil was there just then and was disturbing the souls of simple people through the corrupt doctrines of Nestorius.[50] Many of the wives of the senators and other distinguished men came to our holy mother and discussed questions relating to the orthodox faith with her. She in whom the Holy Spirit had his dwelling never ceased from morn to night from speaking of God. Those who had been deceived she converted to the orthodox faith and those who had doubts she supported. In a word, she helped everyone she met by her teaching, which was inspired by God. For this reason, the enemy of truth, the devil, became extremely jealous, on the one hand, of her building-up of the people who came to see her, on the other, of the salvation of her uncle. He therefore changed himself into the form of a young black man, who approached her and spoke to her in the following manner:

'How long are you going to destroy my hopes through your words? Note well that if I can harden the hearts of Lausus and the emperors . . . If not, I shall inflict such tortures on your body that your life itself will be at risk, and you will be silent against your will.'[51]

Melania caused him to disappear by invoking our Lord Jesus Christ. Then she sent for my humble self and described the black man's threats to me. She had not finished speaking to me, when she began to feel a pain in her hip. So great was the pain that suddenly came over her that she remained unable to speak for three hours. After we had made an offering of prayer on her behalf, she scarcely recovered consciousness. She spent six days in unspeakable pain and felt a greater sense of revulsion than when she saw the black man.

When on the seventh day we were expecting her to depart this present life, a messenger arrived from her uncle to tell us that he ran the risk of dying as a catechumen.

The grief caused by this news was worse than her suffering and pains. She said to us, 'Take me to him before I die'. We were afraid even to touch her, because her foot was like dry wood, but she insisted, saying, 'Carry me to my uncle. If you do not, I shall be in worse danger because of this affliction.' In obedience to her orders, they brought a litter and deposited her upon it very carefully. I went on ahead to the palace and asked how the

ex-prefect was. Some important people there replied, 'Yesterday
he asked for the blessed lady, and when he learned that she was
very ill indeed, he summoned the nurse of the most religious
empress Eudoxia,[52] the lady Eleutheria, and was, by God's grace,
enlightened.'[53] As soon as I heard these words, I rejoiced in the
Lord and dispatched a horseman at top speed to announce this
good news to the blessed lady. Once Melania had heard that her
uncle had been baptized, she cheerfully moved her foot without
pain. The devil was ashamed and retreated at that very hour; all
the pains he had inflicted departed with him from the blessed
lady, so that she who had been unable to be carried, climbed
up all the steps by herself and entered through the portico of the
palace into the home of the Emperor Eudoxia, who was dear to
Christ. All the onlookers were amazed and gave glory to God on
the defeat of our enemy. Melania sat all night by her uncle's bed
and encouraged him with such words as these:

> You are truly blessed, sir, because at the present time
> you have been appropriately glorified, and in the time
> to come, you will advance towards the Lord, justified be-
> cause you have been cleansed in the laver of immortality.

Having caused him to share three times in the holy Mysteries—
it was the feast of the holy Epiphany—she said farewell to him
and sent him in peace to the Lord.

Everyone gave thanks to him who had accomplished such great
marvels. The blessed lady praised God's ineffable love for her
uncle: 'How much does he in his goodness care for even one
soul! He summoned Volusianus here from Rome and caused us
to move from Jerusalem, so that a single soul which had lived its
whole appointed time-span in ignorance might be saved!'

She remained in Constantinople until she had completed her
forty-days' stay, as she had vowed, and gave an extraordinary
amount of help to the people there, especially the imperial ladies
who loved Christ. She strengthened the most religious emperor
Theodosius in character. She asked him to let his wife go to the
Holy Places, since she longed to go there, and we left Constantinople at the end of February.

The Return to Jerusalem

At that moment the winter weather became so intensely cold that the bishops of Cappadocia and Galatia solemnly declared that they had never seen a winter like it. We ourselves were covered with snow all day, but we continued our journey without giving in. We saw neither the land nor the mountains, but only the inns in which we spent our nights. Melania was like steel. She never completely gave up her fast, saying, 'Now more than ever must we endure hardship and give thanks to God, the master of all things, for the marvels that he has brought about for us. By persevering in ceaseless prayer, she let neither herself nor us suffer anything painful in that very harsh cold weather. She showed us that the prayer of a righteous person, which avails much in its working and prevails over the elements themselves, is a very powerful weapon.[54] When all the saints tried to detain us on our journey, she did not let herself be persuaded by any of them. She had only one desire: to celebrate the Passion of the Lord in Jerusalem. This God granted to her, in accordance with the promise of his most holy prophet, which says, *He will do the will of them that fear him and will listen to their prayer.*[55]

We arrived at the Holy Places on the third day of the week, before the saving Passion. After she had celebrated the Passover and the holy Resurrection spiritually and very joyfully with her own sisters, she once again followed her usual custom by occupying herself with the two monasteries. Having observed how well-ordered was the singing of the psalms in church by the monks, who were very dear to God, she was overcome by another divine longing; she decided to establish a small shrine. She then spoke to my humble self in words such as these:

'This is the place on which the feet of the Lord stood.[56] Let us therefore build a holy chapel here, that the Holy Sacrifice may be continuously offered in this place, after my departure from this world to the Lord, as well for my soul as for those of my masters. As her wishes and her intentions completely satisfied the God of all things, the work was finished in a few days. She again collected together other holy men and installed them there.

The Travels of Eudocia

When this had been done, news came that the most religious empress[57] had already reached the city of Antioch and would soon be arriving in Jerusalem. Melania therefore turned over in her mind the question of what she should do both to glorify God and to benefit other people. She said: 'If I go to meet her, I am afraid that I may be blamed for travelling through all the cities in my humble attire. If, on the other hand, I stay here, I am afraid that this course of action my be interpreted as pride on my part.' After reasoning with herself in this religious manner, she decided to leave, saying, 'It is fitting for strong people like ourselves, who "have taken up the yoke of Christ", to carry such a faithful empress on our own shoulders, which rejoice in the power of the Lord, because he has set over us an empress who is such a lover of Christ.'

Melania therefore met the empress in Sidon and returned thanks for the surpassing love which she had shown her in Constantinople. She stayed at the shrine of Saint Phocas, where it is said that the faithful Canaanite woman lived, who said to the Lord in the holy Gospel, *Yes, Lord, but the dogs eat from the crumbs which fall from their masters' table*.[58] Thus the blessed lady used to be eager to please the Lord, in her home, in her conversation, and in every other activity. When the empress, who was dear to God, saw her, she welcomed her with all possible respect as her true spiritual mother, and rightly so, for it was a glory to the empress to honor her who truly glorified the King of Heaven. The saint, accepting her faith and appreciating the toils of her journey, encouraged her to make even more progress in well-doing. The godly empress replied to her in these memorable words: 'I have discharged a two-fold vow to the Lord; to venerate the Holy Places and to see my mother, for I wished to have the honor of seeing Your Holiness, while you are still serving the Lord in the flesh.' Because of her surpassing spiritual love for Melania, the empress hastened to reach the saint's monastery. After she had entered it, she looked upon the virgins as her own sisters. Much refreshed by her visit, she wanted also to visit the men's monastery and to receive a blessing there.

The deposition of the holy relics in the shrine that Melania had recently built was about to take place, as we have stated above. The empress asked that the festival should be held in her presence.

The enemy of the good was once again envious of such great spiritual devotion, and prepared at the very moment of the deposition of the holy relics to crouch down on the empress' foot and to cause an extraordinary groaning as a result. No doubt this all happened to test the saint's faith. After she had escorted the empress to the church of the holy Resurrection, she herself settled down at the same time by the relics of the holy martyrs. She remained apart with her virgins in unceasing prayer, in fasting, and in mourning, until the empress sent for her. Her pain had now gone.

When the empress' pain had been cured, the blessed lady did not give up her battle with the devil, who wanted to make mischief between them. After Melania had spent a few days with the empress and had given her considerable help, she escorted her as far as Caesaraea. They were scarcely able to tear themselves away from each other, for they were bound very closely together by the tie of spiritual love. The saint returned once more to her ascetic way of life, praying that the godly Empress might be kept safe right up to the end of her journey and might be restored in good health to her husband. The God of all things granted her this wish.

Miracles and Humility

I shall try to recall a few of the many miracles which God performed through Melania. I am not capable of describing all of them, partly on account of their number and partly on account of my own uncouthness.

One day a young woman was seized by an extremely evil spirit. She closed her mouth tightly for some days and was completely unable to speak or eat, with the result that she was soon in danger of starvation. Many physicians employed numerous drugs in her case, but were unable to cause her even to move her lips slightly. When it was shown that the art of medicine was unable to defeat the demon, she was finally carried to the saint, followed by her parents. The blessed lady, rejecting human praise, said to them, 'Sinner that I am, I cannot bring about a cure, but let us carry her off to the holy martyrs' shrine and may the God who loves humankind heal her through their free conversation with Him.'

When they arrived there, the saint unceasingly invoked the Master of all things and taking the oil, which had been consecrated by the relics of the holy martyrs, she touched the mouth of the sick woman with it three times and said in a clear voice, 'In the name of our Lord Jesus Christ, open your mouth.' Immediately after the invocation of the Lord, the demon, ashamed, or rather frightened, withdrew, and the woman opened her mouth. The saint gave her something to eat. All the onlookers glorified God, and the woman who had been healed, was filled with joy and gave thanks to the Lord.

In the same way, the Lord restored to health through Melania another woman possessed by a similar affliction.

On yet another occasion a woman had had a very difficult labor. The fetus had died in its mother's womb and the unhappy woman could neither live nor die. When she heard this, Melania, the true servant of the Lord, suffered deeply as a result of her sympathy for the woman and felt pity for her. She therefore said to the virgins who were with her, 'Let us go to visit this woman who lies dangerously ill, that we may see the pains of those who live in the world and thus realize the extent of the miseries from which God has removed us.' When they reached the house where the woman lay dangerously ill, Melania said a prayer. Thereupon the sick woman said to the saint with difficulty and in a weak voice, 'Have mercy on me.' Melania stood for some time, importuning God on her behalf; then, undoing the girdle from around her waist, she placed it on her, saying, 'I have this as a blessing from a great man and I have faith that his prayers will swiftly heal her.' The dead body of the baby then immediately emerged. When she had fed the woman, Melania went home at once and God was glorified in the customary way. Melania humbled herself and said, 'The girdle belongs to a holy man and his prayers have cured this woman whose life was in danger.' So it was, she always attributed her own successes to the saints.

Once one of the virgins who were with her enquired whether she, having reached such a high pitch of ascetic discipline and virtue, was not tormented by the demon of vainglory and pride. She then began to speak in the following words, to strengthen us all:

'I myself am totally unconscious of anything good in myself, but if I were to see the enemy sowing proud thoughts in me, making fasting the pretext, I should answer him like this: "What is there remarkable about it, if I fast for a week, when other people do not eat for forty whole days? Or if I refrain from taking oil, when others do not quench their thirst even with water?" If the enemy were to put proud thoughts on the subject of my poverty into my mind, I should trust boldly in the power of God and oppose his unspeakable depravity in this way: "How many prisoners, captured by the barbarians, have been deprived of their freedom! How many people, incurring imperial anger, have been deprived of their property and their lives! How many people have been abandoned in poverty by their parents, while others, falling into the hands of false accusers or robbers, suddenly exchange riches for poverty?" It is therefore nothing wonderful if we despised earthly goods for the sake of what is pure and incorruptible. When, again, I saw the evil one making vainglorious suggestions to me, for example that instead of fine linen underclothes and a variety of silk garments, I now wore hair-cloth, I used to make myself very miserable; but I pictured in my imagination those who lie naked inn the market-place on nothing but a little rush mat and freeze in the chill air. In this way God drove the devil out of me.'

She used to say that the plots of the enemy were obvious: 'It was very often people with the outward appearance of holiness who inflicted harder troubles on me than the enemy, for when they saw me genuinely and earnestly putting into practice the saying of our Lord to the rich man, *If you want to be perfect, sell your goods and give the money to the poor and take up your cross and follow me*,[59] they used to say to me, "Certainly a man is allowed to be poor and to practice ascetic discipline for the

Lord's sake, but in moderation." Then I used to think of those who were serving as soldiers in this world, under mortal rules, and how in their search for greater glories, they risk their lives to the point of death. If they undergo such hardships for the sake of the flower of the grass[60] —for that is what earthly glory is—how much more should I seriously exert myself to obtain greater glory in the heavenly places.'

These were her teachings, which benefited the soul and were filled with the Spirit. She attained to such a high degree of gentleness and calm that if ever a sister who had distressed her asked for her pardon—which in all probability was a normal happening—the saint used to say to her such words as these: 'The Lord knows that as I am an unworthy woman, I do not judge myself to be good, even by the world's standards; but I confidently believe that the enemy will not accuse me on the day of judgement of going to sleep bearing a grudge against another.'[61]

THE DEATH OF MELANIA

Melania's Last Feast-days

After a time, Melania, like the best of runners who has run the course and desires the prize,[62] was in haste to be set free and to be with Christ. She also sighed with longing to be clothed outwardly in the habitation which comes from heaven, as the Apostle says. When the feast-day of our Saviour's birth was approaching, she said to her cousin, the lady Paula, 'Let us go to the holy city of Bethlehem, for I do not know whether I shall ever again see this feast-day in my flesh.' They arrived therefore and having completed the vigil, they took part in the awe-inspiring mysteries at dawn. Finally the saint, as if she had received an answer from God, said to her cousin: 'Pray for me, for from now on you will celebrate the Lord's birthday alone. In a very short time the term of my life in the flesh will be completed.' On hearing these words, her cousin was much distressed. They returned from the holy city of Bethlehem to the monastery, whereupon the saint, taking not the slightest notice of the fatigue caused by the vigil and the journey, went out into the cave and prayed without ceasing.

The next day we left for the shrine of the protomartyr, Saint Stephen—for the commemoration of his falling asleep had already arrived[63] —and held a service there, after which we returned to the monastery. In the course of the vigil, I was the first to read, then three sisters read, and last of all Melania read the account of the falling-asleep of Saint Stephen from the book of Acts.[64] When the fixed portion of the reading was over, all the sisters said to the saint, 'May you have good health for many years and celebrate many saints' days.' But she, as one who had received full assurance from on high, replied to them, 'May you too have good health, but you will no longer hear me read.'

At these words, they all suffered deep distress. They did not believe she had spoken prophetically. As she was already passing over from this world to the Lord,[65] she left them a spiritual testament, she spoke to them in these words: 'Take care, I beg you, after I am gone, to recite your office with fear and in a sober spirit, because it is written, *Doubly accursed is the person who performs the Lord's work carelessly.*[66] If I am separated from you in the flesh a little later on and am no longer with you, the eternal God, who fulfills all things, is always with you and knows the depths of each person's heart. Keep him therefore perpetually before your eyes and guard your souls in love and purity until the end, recognizing that you will all stand before his dread tribunal and that each of you will receive either reward for her labors or judgement for her sins.'

As they were all deeply lamenting because they were about to lose so good a guide and a teacher inspired by God, she left them and said to my humble self, 'Let us go to the shrine in the men's monastery, so we may pray there; for the remains of Stephen are there.' With great sorrow, I did what the saint had ordered and followed her. When we were inside the shrine, she prayed with many tears, as though she were already the companion of the holy martyrs. She spoke thus:

> Lord God of the holy martyrs, who knows all things before they come into being, you have understood my decision from the beginning, that I have loved you with my whole

heart and that from fear of you, my bones cling to my flesh. To you who formed me in my mother's womb I consecrate my soul and body. It is you who have held me by my right hand and helped me by your counsel. But as I am human, I have often sinned against you in word and deed, against you, who alone are pure and free from sin. Receive therefore my prayer, which I offer to you with these, my many tears, through the mediation of your victorious saints. Purge me, your servant, that when I come to you, my soul may not falter in its steps, and that the evil demons in the air may not have control over me, but that I may pass on towards you, spotless, guided by your holy angels, and that I may be found worthy of your bridal chamber in heaven, hearing the words of blessing which you will then say to those who are pleasing to you: *Come, you blessed of my father, inherit the kingdom which has been prepared for you from the creation of the world.*[67] *To you belong unspeakable pity and the multitude of mercies, and you save all those who hope in you.*[68]

Then she addressed the holy martyrs, saying,

Athletes of the Lord, you pour out of your precious blood to confess him, have mercy on the humility of your servant, who has always venerated your holy relics; and as you have always listened to me, do you, who have power, even at the present time, to speak freely to him, act as my ambassadors to God who loves humankind, that he may receive my soul in peace and keep the monasteries in his holy fear until the end.

She had scarcely finished her prayer when her flesh immediately began to tremble. We returned to the virgin's monastery and found the sisters going through the psalms. When I could no longer remain standing, because of the pain which encompassed me and pressed upon me, I withdrew a little, to take a rest.

Melania, however, went back again to the service. When the sisters noticed that she was growing increasingly feeble, they encouraged her by saying, 'Take a rest for a little while, since you have not the strength to stand.' But she did not assent to them, saying, 'Not until we have completed the psalms for Matins.' After they had completed the whole liturgy, she went away and lay down. She was then seized with a pain in her side and became very weak indeed.

Melania's Farewells and Commendations

Melania sent for me, humble as I am, and for all her sisters and then began to say to me, 'Behold, I am setting out on my journey to the Lord. Therefore pray for me.' I was even more heart-broken on hearing these words.

Then she again spoke to the virgins in the following terms: 'I beg you to pray for me because I have never wished anything evil for any of you. And if I have ever spoken harshly to any one of you, I have done so out of my spiritual love for you. Regard yourselves therefore as real servants of Christ. Spend the time of your lives that remains in the acquisition of perfect knowledge, that you may have your lamps burning for that great day and that you may thus please your heavenly bridegroom. See then, I entrust you to God who is able to watch over your souls and bodies. I entrust you to our lord the priest, and I beg you not to grieve him in any way, but to submit yourselves to him in complete humility, realizing that he too carries your burden for God's sake, and that she who opposes him and does not obey him, causes God pain.'

After saying these words, she wanted to be placed in the chapel and said, 'Carry me nearer to the holy martyrs.'

Then as her pains grew still greater, she said to us, 'My day is fulfilled.' Everyone lamented sorely, but the virgins were particularly grieved, as they were about to be bereft of a mother who truly loved them tenderly. When the blessed lady saw that my heart too was full of sorrow, she said to me on the fifth day of her weakness, on the day she died, 'My child, you are achieving nothing by all your prayers and tears, for I have heard a voice saying in my heart that in accordance with the command of God, I must be completely free from the fetters of my body and must be on my way to the Lord.'

As the Lord's day was dawning, she said to me before sunrise, 'Be kind enough to celebrate the holy *Anaphora* for us.' While I was making the offering, I could not speak loudly because of my grief. When she did not hear the *epiclesis*,[69] she very anxiously said to me, as I stood at the altar, 'Speak up, so I can hear the *epiclesis*.'

When she had received the Holy Mysteries, the bishop, who was very dear to God, arrived with his clergy, and when they had spoken sufficiently about the salvation of her soul, the blessed lady finally said to him, 'Receive in trust the priest and the monasteries, and in imitation of your own Master, take care of everyone inn them, like a good shepherd who tends sheep capable of reasoning. The bishop, since he perceived how much goodness was about to depart from this world, was extremely distressed, but the saint, having asked him also to give her Holy Communion, let him go in peace.

Then there entered the monks of her monastery, who were most dear to God. To them she said, 'I commend myself to you as I am about to depart this transitory life and I beg you, satisfy the priest in everything, in the knowledge that in this way you satisfy the God of the universe. This is because he himself, being free of all ties, has made himself your servant for Christ's sake, and though he is not under any compulsion, is bearing your burden.'

Then there entered the other monastic communities and numerous people from the city. Although cruel pains were laying hold of her body, Melania, true aristocrat that she was, flinched not at all, but commended herself to them all in singleness of heart and with great forbearance, as was fitting. After this, her cousin, the lady Paula, came in with all her household. She exhorted them all, but she addressed special words of comfort to Melania, who was extremely sad at being parted from her. Then, with many blessings and prayers, she went on her way.

Last of all, Melania addressed to my humble self the following words: 'It is superfluous for me to exhort the man who is the friend of God to take care of the monasteries. Of course, as long as I was alive, you were the one who carried the entire burden of care and helped me in every way with your support. That is why

I now entrust the monasteries to you, and I beg you as strongly as I can, to undertake the work on their behalf after I am gone. God will reward you for this in the life to come.' When she was commending herself to us in peace, she said, 'Make prayer for me.' Then she dismissed us all, saying, 'Leave me now to rest.'

About the ninth hour, she began to lose consciousness. Assuming that she had already died, we tried to stretch out her legs, but she recovered slightly and in a feeble voice said to me—insignificant though I am: 'My hour has not yet come.' I was unable to bear the pain which engulfed me, but I replied, 'When your hour does come, will you tell us?' She said, 'Yes'. She spoke this way, I believe, to signify that her body did not require people to lay it out until after she was dead. Some holy men remained there with me, for it was always her wish that she should give up the ghost in the presence of holy people.

The bishop, who was most dear to God, came back again, and with him the most holy anchorites living around Eleutheropolis, who were very holy men. They said to the blessed lady, 'You have fought the good fight on earth, you depart joyfully to the Lord, and all the angels rejoice. We, however, are utterly dismayed at the prospect of losing your helpful and spiritual conversation.' To this she replied with these final words, 'As it seemed good to the Lord, so has it happened,' and immediately she gave up her life to her Master, gently and quietly, in joy and exaltation, on the evening of the Lord's holy day, so that even in this matter, her great love for the Lord and his holy resurrection might be manifest.

Melania's Funeral and Her Heavenly Glory

No one was needed to lay out her holy remains, for her legs were stretched out, her two hands clasped on her breast, and her eyelids closed naturally. Then, as she had ordered, the holy fathers, who had been gathered together from different places, passed the whole night joyfully in psalm-singing and readings and then buried her.

Her grave-clothes were appropriate to her sanctity. I thought it necessary to say what they were, for the benefit of those who encounter my writings. She had the tunic of one holy man, the veil of another handmaid of God, a piece of a sleeveless tunic which had belonged to another holy man, the girdle of a third (with which she always girt herself when alive), the cowl of a fourth, and, as a pillow, the haircloth cowl of a fifth—from it we made a cushion and placed it beneath her honored head. It was fitting that she should be buried in the garments of those whose virtues she had acquired in her lifetime.[70] She did not receive any linen clothing, except for the shroud in which we wrapped her, over her clothes.

The saint received the fruit of her prayers and departed to heaven, clad in her virtues, as in a cloak. The powers of the enemy did not disturb her, for they could not find any of their personal qualities in her. The holy angels rejoiced as they received her, for she imitated in her corruptible body their own impassibility.

Likewise the holy prophets and apostles, whose lives and teachings she had fulfilled in her deeds, received her with great joy into their own choir. The holy martyrs, whose tombs she used to hold in honor and whose struggles she used to support of her own free will, came happily to meet her. So it was that she shared in heaven in those things *Which eye has not seen nor ear heard nor the heart of man conceived, which God has prepared for those whom he loves.*[71] To him be glory and power for ever and ever. Amen.

NOTES

1. This introductory formula, the equivalent of the latin *Iube, Domne, benedicere*, indicates that the *Life* was intended for liturgical reading. Before reading a Lesson, the reader asks the President of the assembly for a blessing.

2. This implies that the request for the *Life* to be written came from a bishop, The formula is the equivalent of the latin *sacerdos Dei sanctissime*, which is used of a bishop.

3. On this *confessio humilitatis*, see p. 289 above.

4. Lk 12:3.

5. Prov 9:9.

6. Gerontius and Palladius, though in substantial agreement over the subject matter of this section, disagree on some small points. According to Gerontius, Melania was thirteen when she was married, and she gave birth to a son and a daughter. Palladius, however, says that she was

fourteen and that she had two sons (above, p. 313). Probably Gerontius is the more reliable source, since he was closely associated with Melania over a long period.

7. We have already noticed the reasons for this aversion to bathing. See above, p. 28.

8. 1 Cor 7:16.

9. The 'odor of sanctity' is a frequent *topos* in the lives of the saints.

10. Ps 44:11.

11. For other references to 'the angelic life', see above, Jerome, *Ep.* 22 (p. 186) and 107 (p. 265).

12. This reference is puzzling, as elsewhere in classical and patristic literature, Cilician clothing is rough and harsh, whereas Antiochian clothing is smooth and elegant. The term *cilicina vestis* or *cilicium* is used in the Bible and the writings of the Fathers to denote the garment of penitence, generally made of camel's or goat's hair. Rampolla points out that in the Middle Ages, the hair of the long-haired Cilician goat was woven in to a type of Angora cloth for military cloaks, and suggests that this is possibly an early example of this luxurious material. He goes on to suggest that the Antiochian clothing meant here is the rough clothing of the peasants living around Antioch.

13. See pp. 289–90 above for an explanation of the situation described in this section.

14. Serena was the niece of the emperor Theodosius the Great (408–450) and was married to Stilicho, a Vandal officer whom he had raised to high office. Stilicho seems to have acted as regent to Honorius, the younger son of Theodosius, who succeeded his father as Emperor of the West at the age of ten, when his elder brother, Arcadius, became Emperor of the East. Serena was therefore a member of the imperial family, but was not, strictly speaking, the empress. Various explanations of this error have been offered, but on the whole, it seems probable that Gerontius was either writing carelessly or was misinformed about the various relationships of the imperial family in the West.

15. Ps 77 (76):11.

16. Sg 5:3.

17. 1 Cor 11:5.

18. 1 P 1:24.

19. Mt 5:38–42, Lk 6:28–31.

20. Honorius was Serena's cousin, not her brother. His first wife was Maria, daughter of Stilicho and Serena. The word 'brother' was often used loosely to mean 'kinsman'.

21. Mt. 25:21.

22. 1 Cor 2:9.

23. See p. 307 n. 25.

24. Palladius tells us the opposite, that these were the only properties that they had *not* sold; but as we have seen in n. 16 above, Gerontius is likely to be the more reliable informant.

25. Presumably Paulinus of Nola (*c.* 353–431).

26. This is presumably one of the Lipari Islands, but we have no evidence elsewhere for the presence of a bishop there, as stated later in this chapter.

27. The ransoming of captives by the holy man is a frequent *topos* in the lives of the saints.

28. Ps 111 (112):9.

29. Saint Augustine of Hippo, his childhood friend Alypius, who followed him into the priesthood and the episcopate, and Aurelius, of whom little is known.

30. Lk 10:42.

31. Gn 4:4, Heb 11:4, Mt 24:43, Lk 12:39.

32. 1 Cor 6:19.

33. Mt 5:7.

34. Mt 7:7.

35. Cf Lk 17:10.

36. Rm 8:18.

37. Jr 15:19.

38. Mt 11:12.

39. 2 Cor 9:7.

40. Ps 119(118):147.

41. Ps 119(118):62.

42. Ac 3:1–7.

43. Dn 6:10.

44. Mt 20.

45. Lk 24:13–39.

46. Cf. 2 Tm 4:7.

47. Valentinian III, emperor of the west from 425–455. Eudoxia was the daughter of the eastern Emperor Theodosius II and Eudocia.

48. Lausus was a high official at the courts of the emperors Arcadius (395–408) and Theodosius II (408–450). It is to him that Palladius dedicated, indeed named after him, his *Lausiac History*. He is known to have been a supporter of the anti-Nestorian faction at Constantinople.

49. Proclus was patriarch of Constantinople 434–446. He is famous for the sermon that he preached in 428 in the presence of the then patriarch, Nestorius, against the latter's heretical doctrines. However, he was a man of eirenic disposition, who refused to condemn dead bishops for heresy.

50. Nestorius (d. 451) was a Syrian who entered a monastery in Antioch, where he became thoroughly imbued with the teaching of the antiochene school. He became patriarch of Constantinople in 428 and soon became involved in the great controversy over the meaning of the term *Theotokos*. He was condemned by the Council of Ephesus in 421 for holding the view that Christ had two natures, human and divine, and consisted of two persons, man and God. His principal opponent was Cyril, patriarch of Alexandria, as we have already seen in n. 16.

51. There is a break here in the text, for which two explanations may be offered: (1) there is a lacuna in the manuscript; (2) there is an ellipsis similar to others found in the text. Gorce, the editor of the Sources

Chrétiennes edition, suggests that the Devil, 'good theologian as he is', is alluding to one of the great themes of theological reality (e.g., in Ex 7:3), that God is said to 'harden the heart of Pharaoh'. The meaning of this phrase had been debated in the controversy relating to Origenism and Pelagianism, which had taken place in Constantinople a little earlier and was still fresh in people's minds.

52. The daughter of Theodosius II and Eudocia, and the wife of Valentinian III.

53. A classic expression used in Late Antiquity to denote baptism.

54. Jm 5:16–18.

55. The writer has in mind 2 Cor 5:2, where the Christian is represented as longing to be clothed with his habitation from heaven. The same greek word, meaning 'habitation' or 'dwelling', is used here. It is not a reference to the monastic habit.

56. Ps 132:7.

57. The empress Eudocia, wife of Theodosius II and mother of Eudoxia.

58. Mt 15:27.

59. Mt 19:21.

60. Jm 1:10.

61. Cf. Cph 4:26–27.

62. Cf. 1 Cor 9:24.

63. 26 December.

64. Ac 7.

65. Cf. Jn 12:1.

66. Jer 48:10.

67. Mt 25:34.

68. Cf. Dan 9:9.

69. The invocation of the Holy Spirit.

70. The practice of handing on items of clothing worn by holy persons was common in the early Church.

71. 1 Cor 2:9.

RADEGUNDE:

A
ROYAL
FOUNDRESS
IN
GAUL

INTRODUCTION

THE THREE PRINCIPAL SOURCES for the life of Saint Radegunde are the *Vita* arranged by Bruno Krusch, the editor of MGH SRM 2 in two books, the first, *Vita I*^a, by Venantius Fortunatus and the second, *Vita II*^a, by the nun Baudonivia; the poem, *De excidio, Thuringiae*, once thought to be spurious, but now believed to have been composed by Venantius Fortunatus from material supplied by Radegunde herself; and chapters 104–106 of the *Liber in gloria confessorum* of Gregory of Tours. It is the first and third of these items which are translated in this work.

The incidence of the fourteen-hundredth anniversary of Radegunde's death in 1987 caused a revival of interest in her, particularly in France, whilst among English-speaking people, the evidence for her ordination as deacon has been brought forward as a contribution to the current debate in the Anglican Church on the ordination of women.

We have already seen that the late antique and early medieval *vitae* of saints are not biographies in the modern sense of the term. The life of Saint Radegunde is offered here as an example of this *genre* of hagiographical writing. We find in it many of those *topoi* which will become more and more familiar as the Middle Ages advance: the beauty of the heroine, who is noble by birth, but even more noble in character, and whose mind is enriched through a careful programme of sacred study; the call to chastity, overridden at first by the obligation to marry, but finally triumphant; the power

365

over birds and animals which is a recognized characteristic of the holy man or woman; and above all the power of the saint, whether living or dead, to work miracles.

Since the aim of our authors was the edification of what would probably have been a largely monastic audience, they did not trouble themselves unduly about dating their work or providing a chronological framework for their narratives. From internal evidence it appears that the life by Venantius Fortunatus was written at some date between 587, when Radegunde herself died, and 607, when Venantius Fortunatus died. A wandering italian poet, Venatius finally came to rest at Poitiers, took Holy Orders, and became its bishop in *c.* 590, after the death of Radegunde. The life of Baudonivia appears to have been written slightly later, since she refers to Leifastus as bishop of Autun (Augustudunum), and we know from other sources that his predecessor, Syagrius, died sometime after 599. Gregory the Great refers to him in a letter dated 602 as being *reverendae memoriae*. Thus it would appear that Leifastus succeeded him round about 600, to which approximate date we may assign the *Vita.*[1] The recollections of Venantius Fortunatus therefore belong to a period relatively soon after the death of his subject, whereas the narrative of Baudonivia embodies the memories of an elderly lady living some years after the events she describes.

THE *VITA PRIMA*

Venantius Fortunatus announces that his aim is to bring before a wider public details of Radegunde's life which are already known to an intimate circle. He gives information about her background and upbringing, which he must have learned from conversations with her, though he does his best to bring them into line with recognized hagiographical practice. He is anxious to stress for his readers the contrast between her royal origins and background and the simple devout and industrious character of her personal life, first as a queen and then as a religious.

The first twenty chapters of the *Vita I*[a] consist of an account of the years Radegunde passed as the wife of King Chlothar I.

From these it appears that she married him when she was about eighteen, in 538, and that she left him in about 550. The narrative suggests that she at first attempted to escape marriage: we are told that when the king wished to receive her at Vitry, she slipped away by night, and that when she finally married him at Soissons, she shunned royal display. Her life as queen must have imposed a considerable strain upon her, owing to the contrast between the regal splendor that was expected of her and the works of mercy that she performed at the country house at Athies-sur-Somme, combined with her rigorous personal austerities and her personal expenditure on the redemption of captives. We can understand the complaint of her husband that he had married not a queen but a nun. Radegunde, unlike other holy persons in late antique and early medieval hagiography, appears to have consummated her marriage, but she had no children.

The discovery that her brother had been put to death on her husband's orders brought to an end what must have been a frustrating and disappointing way of life. In *c.* 550 she fled to Noyon, where she demanded of the bishop, Medard, that he should consecrate her as a nun. He at first demurred, quoting the words of Saint Paul, *If a woman is bound to her husband, let her not seek to be loosed* (1 Cor 7:27), but so importunate was she that in the end, he made her a *diacona*. Until recently the meaning of this term and the exact status of Radegunde immediately on parting from her husband have received little attention. Indeed it seems to have been assumed that *diacona* simply meant 'a woman religious', but with the revived interest in the diaconate in the Roman Catholic Church and the granting of it to women in the Anglican Church, its significance has been examined more carefully. Sister Teresa, CSA, herself an anglican deacon, points out that a decree of the Second Council of Orleans (533) forbade the consecration of women as deacons, which implies that women must have been functioning as such in the early years of the sixth century. She adds that 1) Radegunde was already leading a life of service to others which was diaconal in character; 2) through her contacts with Eastern Christendom she would already have been aware of Justinian's legislation, which provided for the death of a man who assaulted a woman deacon or nun.[2] The latter does not seem a very strong argument for consecrating Radegunde as deacon rather than nun, since the legislation applied both to nuns and to women deacons. An interesting and more tenable explanation is offered by Michel Rouche, who examines the connection between Radegunde's marital status and her consecration as deacon in the light of canon law, though he admits that this was still in its infancy.[3] He also considers the significance of Radegunde's terrible austerities. He shows convincingly that Radegunde was not a concubine (*publicana*) but a woman who had been validly and publicly married (*publica*). The interference of the chieftains at Noyan, when she asked Medard to clothe her as a nun, (¶ 12) is thus explained, for this might have been possible, had she not been married legally to Chlothar. This also explains her possession of property (the house at Saix) and of treasure, of which it was her practice to give away a tenth. This would be her *Morgengabe*, which in accordance with germanic custom, was a present from the bridegroom to the bride after their wedding night, a thank-offering for the gift of her virginity. A further obstacle to the clothing of Radegunde as a nun was her age; if she was born *c.* 520 and had parted from her husband *c.* 550, she would not yet have reached forty, the lowest permissible age for consecration as a nun. Since a provision of the Council of Agde (506) allowed the consecration of married people to the diaconate, provided that the husband agreed and the couple separated, this probably seemed to Medard to be the most practical solution.[4] We know from Fortunatus that Radegunde went to Medard, *directa a rege*, which implies his consent. Perhaps her situation was so painful that Medard felt justified in defying the decree of the Council of Orleans by making her a deacon.

The expression *mutata veste*,[5] used by Gregory of Tours, implies that Radegunde ultimately took the habit of a religious, but it is not clear when this occurred. Fortunatus tells us that after she had been consecrated as deacon, she made a pilgrimage to Tours and to Candes, following in the steps of Saint Martin. She then settled on a country estate that belonged to her, at Saix in the region of Poitou, where she lived for an unknown period, perhaps two or three years, and devoted herself to austere living and to good works.

Rouche has made a detailed examination of her programme of austerities in the light of information supplied by H. Platelle in an important article in *Sacris erudiri*.[6] Now we know from Fortunatus that Radegunde was much preoccupied with the question of martyrdom, even as a child. Martyrdom had so long been presented to Christians as the highest good that after the Peace of the Church, when opportunities for it in Western Europe became infrequent, substitutes for it had to be devised. The most important of these was the monastic life itself, particularly when accompanied by a programme of severe fasting and penance. Fortunatus obviously regarded Radegunde's severe regime of fasting and penance, particularly during Lent, as the equivalent of martyrdom. Not only did she wear a hair-shirt, but she also lay on a bed of ashes covered with a hair-cloth. During Lent she bound three broad iron circlets round her neck and arms and implanted chains round her body. She also burned her body with a heated metal plate, shaped like a cross. Rouche believes that she lived at Saix as a penitent to expiate certain sins, pointing out that her austerities were examples of a form of discipline commonly adopted by such people: in particular, the metal circlets which she wore round her neck and arms during Lent were of a type commonly worn by penitent parricides. Radegunde may well have felt responsible for her brother's death, since she had persuaded him to remain in the kingdom of the Franks rather than join their cousin, Amalafrid, in Constantinople. The crime of parricide included responsibility for the deaths of near relatives. Radegunde may also have been performing an act of repentance for failure to keep a vow. It is possible that she had taken a secret vow of celibacy as a young girl but was pressured into marriage. The fact that she tried to escape marriage with Chlothar by fleeing at night supports this theory. She may have felt that she must expiate the two-fold sin of fratricide and failure to keep a vow, by leading a life of penitence at Saix.

Fortunatus implies that Bishop Germanus of Paris, who played an important part in persuading Chlothar that his wife did not wish to return to him, was instrumental in bringing their marriage to an end. Thus Radegunde would be free to take the vows of religion at the time of the foundation of the monastery at Poitiers. The sum of money granted by Chlothar for this purpose would then represent the final settlement on the termination of the marriage.

The transition in *Vita I*ᵃ from Radegunde's life of good works at Saix to her establishment as a recluse, presumably in a cell at Poitiers, is somewhat abrupt. This may be because Fortunatus' readers already knew something of Radegunde's subsequent history. There would be no need for example, to describe the events connected with her request for a relic of thee True Cross and with its subsequent arrival at Poitiers. On the other hand, these people might not know the details of Radegunde's earlier life or of her daily life at the monastery, including her diet and her personal austerities. These Fortunatus could have gathered only from personal observation or from his conversations with Radegunde and members of her community.

The *Vita I*ᵃ closes with an account of various miracles Radegunde performed. Some of these were achieved at a distance, through her prayers or through invocation of her name, but many of them are reported to have been performed by her personally. This follows the tradition of Eastern Christendom, rather than that of the West, where it is the dead saint who is often the miracle-worker. A number of these miracle stories have literary parallels or precedents in the writings of Sulpicius Severus, Gregory the Great, and Gregory of Tours, which suggests that Fortunatus was following the practices of the hagiographers rather than those of the historian.

THE VITA IIᵃ

As Jean Leclercq has pointed out,[7] had we only the references in the writings of Gregory of Tours and the poems and life by Venantius Fortunatus, Radegunde would emerge simply as a strong-minded and devout woman who was capable and energetic in carrying out works of mercy and who could not only perform acts of self-sacrifice in daily life, but also endure horrifying feats of self-torture. It is from Baudonivia that we learn of her participation in the contemporary political scene, of her pastoral relationship with her community, and above all of the character of her own spirituality. As Leclercq observes, the *Vita II^a* has not always received the attention it deserves, perhaps because it is the work of an obscure author written in a somewhat rustic Latin. Moreover Baudonivia has attached to Radegunde extracts from the life of Saint Caesarius of Arles (written by Cyprian of Toulon and others), and from at least two other lives by Fortunatus, in accordance with the custom of medieval hagiographers. This, however, need not mean that *Vita II^a* is without value as an historical source or as a portrait of Radegunde. Baudonivia explicitly states that she has not included any incident which has already been described by Fortunatus; furthermore, she brings to our notice aspects of Radegunde's character that are not revealed elsewhere.

In the first place, she shows us Radegunde as a participant in the political scene, who was always anxious for the peace and salvation of her country. The only incident she describes in Radegunde's pre-monastic life concerns a policy pursued by Saint Martin, as reported by Sulpicius Severus:[8] she instigated the destruction of a pagan temple. Her steadfast conduct, as she sat motionless on her horse while a number of Franks attempted to defend the shrine with swords and clubs, induced the tribes, which were at variance, to make peace with one another. Radegunde was also capable of playing a more active political role; when, as a religious, she observed the coming of bitterness and strife, presumably the outbreak of the revolt of Childebert and Chramn in 561, she wrote to the rulers concerned, begging them to make peace with one another, and her plea succeeded.

Radegunde's intervention to prevent the coming of civil war, her practice of praying for her persecutors and urging others to do the same, and her nocturnal prayers for the safety of the monastery are all evidence of her gift for intercessory prayer. Baudonivia describes her as 'she who alone bore·everyone's pains'.

The Rule of Saint Caesarius of Arles (*Regula sanctarum virginum*) was undoubtedly the basis of the daily prayer life of

Radegunde and her community, but the date of its adoption is uncertain. This is one of the many chronological difficulties connected with Radegunde's early years at Poitiers. If we accept that a letter to Radegunde from Caesaria the Younger (the abbess of the women's monastery at Arles) was written in the early days of the monastery at Poitiers, *c.* 552–557, as its wording and general tone suggests, we come into conflict with the statement of Gregory of Tours that Radegunde and the abbess went on a journey to Arles in 567/568, as the result of a dispute with Maroveus, bishop of Poitiers, concerning the relic of the True Cross, and that it was after this visit that the Rule of Arles was adopted, *c.* 570. But if the decision to adopt the Rule was made only at this date, why did not Radegunde and the abbess take a copy home with them? What would be the sense of the statement in the letter, 'I did what you bade me; I have forwarded copies of the Rule'? It looks as though Gregory of Tours who, although normally a serious and careful historian, sometimes makes errors of fact, has done so here. Both chronology and common-sense support the view that the Rule was adopted early in the monastery's history, but assumed a new importance after the visit to Arles in *c.* 570.[9]

Be that as it may, the framework of the Rule of Arles, which provided for the recital of eighteen psalms during the night office, six psalms during each of the day offices, and Scripture readings during vigils, would afford Radegunde many opportunities for reflective prayer; in Baudonivia's *Life*, she appears to have been a contemplative and a mystic. We learn that her prayer was continuous, particularly at night, and that she was, on one occasion at least, so rapt that she was unaware of what was going on around her. As Saint Teresa was to do later, Radegunde combined intense practicality—she habitually performed the most menial domestic tasks in the monastery—with the life of a visionary and mystic. Baudonivia affords us glimpses of two of her visions. What strikes the modern reader is the severity of the physical discipline, indeed the tortures, which Radegunde inflicted on herself, particularly during Lent. This is not the austerity which marked the lives of the Desert Fathers, but something far more painful, not far removed from masochism. The tortures which the fifth-century monks of

Syria inflicted on themselves, and which are described in detail by Theodoret in his *Historia religiosa*,[10] seem already to have made their way to western Europe by the end of the sixth century—though there is more evidence for their use from the mid to late ninth century.[11]

The dispute with Maroveus, bishop of Poitiers, of which more will be said later, meant that for some years, *c.* 569–587, there was probably no one available to give spiritual direction or instruction to the community; in other words, there was no one who stood in the same relationship to them as Caesarius did to the community at Arles. For most of this time Fortunatus was still a layman, who acted as Radegunde's secretary and liaison with the outside world. Radegunde undoubtedly had a talent for pastoral care and spiritual direction, however. We learn from Baudonivia that she applied herself daily to study and preaching as well as to prayer, and from Fortunatus that she had some knowledge of the writings of the Fathers.[12] As both the teacher and the loving mother of her community, she probably also expounded the Scriptures from her own experience. Always ready to learn from others she likely derived spiritual nourishment from outside contacts. From her early married days she enjoyed the company of holy men, particularly bishops, and liked to consult hermits. We know from Baudonivia that she was in the habit of receiving holy men at the monastery. From them she would 'pluck little flowers, from which to display the fruit of good works to herself and her followers'.

The cult of the relics of the saints played an important part in the spiritual life of Radegunde; her devotion followed similar lines to that of Victricius of Rouen, to whom Saint Ambrose in 396 gave relics to consecrate Rouen Cathedral.[13] She venerated the relics, which she had been collecting for many years, in the belief that they linked her with the saints in continuous meditation. Through concentration of mind and spirit and through fervent prayer, according to Baudonivia, she beheld the Lord in contemplation—she would have asked him to descend from heaven to live on earth in visible form, had that been possible—and this desire led her to apply for a relic of the True Cross. In spite of her years of seclusion, she had not forgotten royal protocol; her request to the emperor Justin II for the relic, which was granted in 567/568, was made through the agency of King Sigebert.

Owing to the hostility of Maroveus, bishop of Poitiers, there was some difficulty over an appropriate reception for the precious relic.[14] We can only conjecture the reasons for the hostile attitude. Possibly he was afraid that Radegunde was trying to establish the monastery as a 'peculiar', independent of episcopal jurisdiction, for which papal provision had been made at the women's community at Arles;[15] or he may have been angry at the request for the relic being made through King Sigebert, without consulting him, and jealous lest the monastery might become a more popular and lucrative place of pilgrimage than his cathedral, which lacked a focus of devotion comparable to the tomb of Saint Martin at Tours. The relic was lodged temporarily in the men's monastery at Tours (also founded by Radegunde) and was eventually brought from Tours to Poitiers by Euphronius, bishop of Tours with much ceremony and amid scenes of great rejoicing. Venantius Fortunatus wrote the famous processional hymns, *Vexilla regis*, and *Pange, lingua, gloriosi*, in honor of the occasion.[16] For the subsequent history of the relic, see the Appendix, pp. 433–34.

It is to Baudonivia and Gregory of Tours that we owe a moving description of Radegunde's deatha nd burial. We do not know the actual cause of her death, but Baudonivia tells us that until her last day, she never reduced the time given to the performance of her office and that her holy little body had endured protracted martyrdom for love of the Lord. As the end approached, the whole community gathered round her bed, weeping and beting their breasts. According to Baudonivia whenever Radegunde wished to do anything important, she chose to do it on the day of the week on which the birth of Christ occurred. By a fortunate chance, she died on Wednesday, the Ides (or 13th) of August.

Both Baudonivia and Gregory of Tours tell us that Maroveus was not available at the time of Radegunde's death, because he was visiting remote, rural parts of his diocese. A messenger was dispatched to Gregory of Tours, who travelled as quickly as possible from Tours to Poitiers to comfort the sisters. Baudonivia tells us that when he saw Radegunde's body, he was seized with a fit of trembling and said that he had seen a human being with the face of an angel.

Gregory brings vividly before us the scene on 13 August, when the sisters realize that their beloved mother has been taken from them, and enable us to visualize the solemn procession wending its way from the women's monastery to the church of Saint Mary (now known as the church of Saint Radegunde), where the burial took place. Under roman law, which evidently still prevailed at Poitiers, Radegunde could not be buried at the monastery, because it was within the city walls. Owing to the strict observance of the Rule of Arles as regards enclosure, however, the sisters could not leave the monastery to follow Radegunde to the grave because Saint Mary's church was outside their enclosure. They had to content themselves with watching the procession from the towers and ramparts of the city wall, into which the women's monastery was built.

The death of Radegunde did not bring any immediate improvement in the relationship between the community and bishop Maroveus, who was visiting the rural areas of his diocese at the time. After waiting in vain for three days for him to come, Gregory of Tours, who had come to the sisters at once on hearing the news, consecrated the tomb and conducted the funeral service, but left it to Maroveus to place the cover on the tomb and to complete the ceremonies.

CONCLUSION

The distinguishing virtue of Radegunde was undoubtedly her great humility. It is difficult for us to grasp what it must have cost her to perform the lowliest domestic tasks at the monastery, such as no free-born lady ever carried out in those days. Her humility is also evident from the status she assumed in the community. Reference has already been made to a journey undertaken by Radegunde 'and the abbess'. She appointed one of the nuns to act as abbess and administrator, whilst she herself took charge as 'mother' of the spiritual and educational needs of the sisters. There is some doubt as to who was abbess in the earlier years;

Caesaria in her letter refers to her as Richildis, but it is evident from the poems of Fortunatus that the abbess was called Agnes. Various solutions of this difficulty have been suggested: the most drastic asserts that the letter is spurious; more probable is the explanation, offered by Père Adalbert de Vogüé in his edition of the monastic works of Caesarius of Arles, that as Agnes must have been very young at the time of the foundation of the monastery and appears to have been consecrated by Germanus of Paris round about 570, whilst the hostile Maroveus was still bishop of Poitiers, there was likely an earlier abbess, whose name presumably was Richeldix.[17]

The existence of a colleague would have helped to ease Radegunde's sense of isolation. Her days were no doubt solaced by the friendship of Venantius Fortunatus, but saddened at the end by disputes among the sisters, though these do not seem to have developed into active rebellion until after her death.

The two lives of Radegunde afford us evidence of her holiness, which does not need the support of the miracle-stories which were an essential proof of sanctity in the Middle Ages. The lives also tell us something of her administrative and pastoral ability, in which she foreshadows the great medieval abbesses and the foundresses of congregations in later times.

NOTES

1. Gregory the Great's reference to Syagrius, bishop of Autun, as *reverendae memoriae* appears in *Reg.* 13.11; MGH Epp 2: 277. We know that *Vita Iᵃ* was already finished when Baudonivia began writing, because she tells us that she will not deal with anything already mentioned by Venantius Fortunatus.

2. For a study of Radegunde's ordination as a deacon, see Sister Teresa, CSA, 'Women in the Diaconate,' *Distinctive Diaconate*, Study 23, fasc. 4 (April 1985) 110–116 (obtainable from the Community of St Andrew, 2 Tavistock Road, London W11 1BA). For the canons of the Council of Orleans (533) relating to women deacons (17–18), see *Concilia Galliae* 511–695, ed. C. de Clercq, CCSL 148A (Turnholt, 1963) 101.

3. M. Rouche, 'Marriage et célibat consacré,' *La riche personnalité de sainte Radegonde: conférences et homélies proncées à Poitiers à l'occasion du XIVe centennaire de sa mort (587–1987)* (Poitiers, 1988) 79–98.

4. Council of Agde (506), canon 16, C. J. Hefele and H. Leclercq, *Histoire des counciles* 22 (Paris, 1908) 988.
5. LH 3.7, MGH SRM 1, 105; see also Rouche, 85–87.
6. H. Platelle, 'La violence et ses remèdes en Flandre au XIe siècle,' *Sacris erudiri* 20 (1971) 101–169, esp. 145–146, 152–154.
7. J. Leclercq, 'La sainte Radegonde de Venance Fortunat et de Baudonivie: essai d'hagiographie comparée,' *Fructus centesimi: mélanges offerts à Gerard J. M. Bartelink*, ed. A. A. R. Bastiaensen et al. (Steenbrugge, 1989) 207–216.
8. See *Vita* II.ᵃ, 2, p. 425, n. 11.
9. For the full history of the adoption of the Rule of Arles, see A. de Vogüé's commentary to Césaire d'Arles, *Oeuvres monastiques* 1, SCh 345 (Paris, 1988) 443–460; Y. Labande-Mailfert, 'Les débuts de sainte Croix,' *Histoire de sainte Croix de Poitiers*, Mémoires de la Société des Antiquaires de l'Quest, 4e serie, t.19 (Poitiers, 1986–1987) 41–45.
10. *Historia religiosa*; ed. P. Canivet and A. Leroy-Molinghem, *Histoire des moines de Syrie*, SCh 234, 257 (Paris, 1977–79); English translation by R. M. Price, *A History of the Monks of Syria*, Cistercian Studies Series 88 (Kalamazoo, 1985).
11. See H. Platelle, 'La pénitence des parricides', *Sacris erudiri* 20 (1971) 145–161.
12. *Carmina* 8.1, 53–61, MGH AA 4/1: 179–180; Radegunde may have read in *florilegia* portions of the authors mentioned: Gregory of Nazianzus, Basil, Athanasius, Hilary of Poitiers, Ambrose, Augustine, and Caesarius of Arles; but as the greek authors in this list were available in latin translations, it is possible that she was able to study texts of all of them.
13. *De laude sanctorum* 3; PL 20:445; see also E. W. Kemp, *Canonisation and Authority in the early Church* (London, 1948) 4–5.
14. Gregory of Tours, *Liber historiarum* 9.40 (MGH SSRM 1(i): 464–465); Baudonivia, *Vita IIᵃ*.16 (MGH SSRM 3:337). These passages give the impression that Maroveus was not at first ill-disposed towards the reception of the relic, but was worked upon by some of the inhabitants of Poitiers.
15. For permission to establish a 'peculiar', see Hormisdas, *Epistola* 2, in A. de Vogüé's edition, Césaire d'Arles, *Oeuvres monastiques* 1, SCh 345 (Paris, 1988) 354–355.
16. *Liber historiarum* 9.40, 464; *Vita IIᵃ*.16, 388–389. For the hymns by Venantius Fortunatus, see *Carmina* 3.3. *Pange, lingua, gloriosi* (MGH AA 4 [i]: 28) and 3.6 (*Vexilla regis, ibid.* 34). Both are familiar to English-speaking Christians in the nineteenth-century translations by J. M. Neale (*Hymns Ancient and Modern*, Standard edition, 96, 97; *English Hymnal*, 94, 95, 96; *New English Hymnal* 78, 79, 517), *The Hymnal 1982* 165–166, 161–162.
17. See A. de Vogüé in *Césaire d'Arles, Oeuvres monastiques* 1: 443–460, for a full discussion of the identity of the abbess.

PRINCIPAL EVENTS OF THE LIFE OF ST RADEGUNDE*

c. 520	Birth in Thuringia
c. 531	Capture by the Franks and installation in Chlothar I's country house at Athies-sur-Somme
c. 538	Chlothar's first attempt to marry her at the royal house at Vitry-en-Artois and her escape by night
c. 538–550	Married life of Radegunde and Chlothar. Period of 'double life', when Radegunde performed works of mercy and underwent a program of severe personal austerities
c. 550	Assassination of Radegunde's brother and break-up of her marriage Consecration of Radegunde as deacon by Medard, bishop of Noyon Pilgrimage to Tours and Candes in the footsteps of Saint Martin
c. 550–552	Life as a penitent in her country house at Saix Consultation with the hermit John of Chinon Vision of a man shaped like a ship
c. 552–559	At a date within these years, foundation of the women's monastery at Poitiers at the expense of Chlothar, perhaps as a final settlement on the dissolution of their marriage
c. 558	Adoption of the Rule of Arles
567–568	Arrival of the relic of the True Cross at Poitiers
c. 570	Journey of Radegunde and the abbess to Arles to the abbess of Saint John's
c. 585	Radegunde's letter to all the bishops
c. 586	Radegunde's vision of Christ as a young man
c. 587	13 August: Death of Radegunde. Funeral conducted by Gregory of Tours three days later.

*Based on the scheme adopted by Yvonne Labande-Mailfert in the first two chapters of *Histoire de l'abbaye de Sainte-Crois de Poitiers*, Mémoires de la Société des Antiquaires de l'Quest, 4e série, t. 19. Poitiers, 1986–1987.

TRANSLATOR'S NOTE

My translation of the two lives of Saint Radegunde, the first by Venantius Fortunatus and the second by the nun Baudonivia, is, so far as I am aware, the first English version of these works. It is based on the texts edited by Bruno Krusch in MGH AA 4 (2), since these are likely to be the most accessible to those of my readers who wish to refer to the original. It has been pointed out to me by Mme Yvonne Labande-Mailfert that there are two manuscripts in the Bibliothèque Muncipale at Poitiers, dating from the thirteenth century, which contain superior readings in certain cases, but were apparently unknown to the editors of the MGH: ms 253 (8 bis), ff.41^r-62^v and 252(8), which is incomplete. She has based her own admirable french translation of *Vita II^a* on these manuscripts. It is to be found in *Lettre de Ligugé* 239 (1987) 9–32.

Our two authors use certain expressions of which it is difficult to give an exact rendering in English. One of these is *villa*, a word which has acquired during the nineteenth and twentieth centuries a number of associations quite alien to life in the sixth century. 'Ranch' might convey the idea, if it were not so much associated by English-speaking people with cowboys. On the whole, 'country house' or 'country estate' seemed to convey the meaning without unfortunate overtones. I have translated *monasterium* by 'monastery', irrespective of the sex of the inmates, since the word 'convent' for houses of women religious is of recent date and is not used by either of our authors.

My thanks are due to Mme Yvonne Labande-Mailfert for her help and kindness, not least for taking me on an interesting tour of the places in Poitiers connected with Saint Radegunde, to Mère Hildegarde Camus, OSB, former abbess of Sainte-Croix de Poitiers, for showing me the relic of the True Cross, and to Dr Paul Fouracre, of Goldsmiths' College, University of London, for help in elucidating some linguistic problems in *Vita II^a*.

J. M. P.

THE LIFE OF SAINT RADEGUNDE

BOOK ONE
By Venatius Fortunatus

THE BOUNTY OF OUR REDEEMER is so rich that he uses the female sex for the celebration of brave victories and makes renowned for their intellectual distinction those women who are delicate in body. Those who are born with tender hearts, Christ makes strong in faith, so that those women who seem week are rewarded according to their merits and win for themselves the praise of the Creator who made them by holding the treasures of heaven concealed in earthen vessels. He who dwells in their wombs with his own riches is Christ the King. These women render themselves dead to worldly life; they despise earthly society and have been cleansed from the contagion of the world. They put no trust in what is transient and are unshaken by any fall. Seeking to live with God, they are wedded to Paradise for the glory of their Redeemer. Among them there is numbered the lady, the course of whose powerful life, though it has been described in private, we are now attempting to bring before the public. Our purpose in doing so is to make sure that the glorious memory of the lady, whose life is with Christ, may be honored in the world.

The most blessed Radegunde came of a barbarian tribe in the region of Thuringia. Her grandfather was King Bessinus, her uncle was Hermenfred, and her father was King Berthaire.[1] She attained a very lofty worldly position, sprung as she was from a royal stem, but although she was of noble birth, she was far more noble in her actions. When she had remained only a short time with her high-born parents, the storm of barbarian invasions broke, and the territory of the Thuringians was laid waste as a result of the victory of the Franks.[2] After the manner of the Israelites,

381

she departed and became an emigrant from her native land.[3] Then strife broke out among the conquerors themselves over the captive, as to whose booty the young princess was, and if she had not been given away by lot, a struggle would have ensued, and the chieftains would have made war upon each other. She fell to the lot of the most high King Chlothar. Having been brought to Athies-on-the-Somme,[4] in the region of Peronne, she was handed over to guardians to be brought up in the royal palace there. The young girl was taught her letters as well as other subjects appropriate to her sex. She talked frequently with the children,[5] saying that if destiny were to bestow such an opportunity on her, she would wish to become a martyr. Thus while still young, she indicated the reward which she wanted to gain in her old age. To some extent she gained what she sought. While the Church was flourishing in time of peace, she herself patiently endured persecution from members of her household. This is what she did when she was still a little girl: she collected the little children together, washed their faces one by one and set out little stools for them. Fetching water for their hands, she offered them whatever she had left over at table and waited on them. She also anticipated the future when she play-acted with Samuel, a little clerk. Having made a wooden cross, she followed him as he preceded her with it.[6] At this same time, the little children used to hurry to the chapel, singing psalms with the solemnity of grown-ups, and she herself used to collect with a cloth the dust which lay around the altar and bury it reverently outside, rather than throw it away. When, after making preparations, the aforesaid king wished to receive her at Vitry,[7] she slipped away from Athies through Beralcha by night.[8] Then when he directed her to go to Soissons, that he might raise her up as his queen, she avoided royal display, lest she grow in worldliness, but human glory was unchanged for him to whom it was due.

So it was she married an earthly prince. Yet she was not separated form her heavenly prince, and during the time worldly power had come her way, her will inclined her towards him more than her position would allow. She was always subject to God, she followed the advice of priests and she behaved as a woman who participated in the life of Christ, rather than as one joined in wedlock. At this moment, we are trying to reveal a few of the many things she did. So it was she was united with the prince, and fearing lest she sink lower in the sight of God as she advanced in worldly position, she devoted herself vigorously to almsgiving. If anything from the tribute-money fell to her share, she gave away a tenth of whatever had accrued to her even before she received it. Then she distributed what was left over to the monasteries and, having handed over her gift, travelled around where she could not go on foot. Not even a hermit could rid himself from her generosity. In this way she paid out what she had received, that she might not be weighted down by a burden. In her presence no poor man's voice rang out in vain, nor did she herself pass by, deaf to it. She often made gifts of clothing, for she believed that she was concealing the limbs of Christ beneath the garments of a poor man. In her opinion, she herself was the loser when she had not made a gift to the poor.

With her mind still intent on works of mercy,[9] she built a house at Athies, where she carefully made up beds and collected poverty-stricken women. She herself washed them in baths and tended their festering wounds. She washed the men's heads and performed the office of a servant, with her own hands waiting on those whom she had previously washed, so that the drinks which they took from her might revive them, wearied as they were with sweating. Thus this devoted lady, a queen by both birth and marriage, and mistress of a royal palace, served the poor as a handmaid.

At table a dish of vegetables was set before her secretly, so no one might happen to notice it; at royal banquets, in the manner of the Three Children,[10] she made an enjoyable meal of beans and lentils. She regularly sang grace; even if she were sitting at a meal, she made some excuse to the king and withdrew herself from the feast to render God what was due him. After she had slipped out, she would sing a psalm to the Lord and carefully enquire with what foot the poor outside had been refreshed.

When she was lying in bed at night with the king, she would ask his permission to rise to fulfil the call of nature and would then get up and leave the bedroom. She would fling aside her garment of haircloth and would prostrate in secret for such a long time in prayer that, warmed only by her breath, she lay frozen, with her whole body numb. With her whole mind intent upon Paradise, she did not worry about bodily torture. She made light of what she was bearing, so as not to become worthless to Christ.

Then she would return to the bedroom and could scarcely warm herself either by the fire or in bed. It was said of her that the king considered that he had married a nun rather than a queen. He was irritated by the prickliest good works, but she partly soothed him and partly endured the disputes inflicted by her husband.

It is enough to know how during the forty days of the lenten season, she clothed herself beneath her royal robes in an exceedingly penitential manner. As the time of fasting approached, she sent word to a religious, a nun called Pia. She with holy counsel respectfully directed the queen to wear a garment of haircloth, adorned with a girdle. Clothing her body in this, the saint wore it cheerfully as a burden beneath her royal robes throughout the forty days. When the days had passed, she sent back the haircloth, similarly adorned. But had the king not been present, would anyone believe how she [would have] poured herself out in prayer, how she would bind herself to the feet of Christ, as though he were present, and how content she was to keep the long fast in tears, as though she were replete with delicious food? She despised bodily food; Christ was her complete refreshment, and she hungered only for him.

How conscientiously she carried out this task, as she continually tended candles made with her own hands, that they might light up the chapels and churches all through the night! At this time, when she was told late in the evening that the king was inviting her to his table, and when she was fully occupied with the things of God, he would hear such complaints from his wife that he would make reparation to her with gifts because he had offended her with his tongue.

In one person's opinion, if any of the servants of God, either of his own accord or as the result of a summons, had seen to come to meet her, she would think she had attained the bliss of heaven.

When night fell again, she would make her way to him through mud, snow, or dust. Having heated some water, she would wash and dry the feet of the holy man, and without any resistance from the servant of God, she would give him a drink from a bowl. On the following day, she would entrust the care of her house to her steward and devote herself entirely to the holy man's words; she would pass the day in studying the rules for salvation and in discussing the means of achieving the heavenly life. If a bishop came, she was delighted to see him and, when she had cheered him with a present, would return regretfully to her own affairs.

Another matter: how wisely she made complete provision to achieve her own salvation! Whenever she wore a new linen scarf, like a cloak, decked with gold and jewels after the barbarians' custom, and was praised by the young girls of her entourage for being very beautiful, she judged herself unworthy to be adorned with such a garment and soon divested herself of this clothing. She would arrange that it be taken to whatever church was nearest and laid over the holy altar for a covering.

How the most saintly queen nearly died of torture if anyone guilty of a criminal offence were condemned by the king to be killed as is customary! She was afraid that the condemned man would die by the sword. How she went round among the faithful servants of the royal household and the nobles and by their flatteries softened the heart of the prince, until the word of reprieve flowed from the royal wrath from which had issued the death sentence.

The mercy of God carried Radegunde so far forward, occupied as she was in these blessed deeds that, while she was still living in the palace, they were declared to be miracles, for the Lord was generous to her. Once when the ever-saintly queen was walking after dinner in the garden at her country house in Péronne,[11] some men, who had been confined on a criminal charge, cried out to her loudly from their prison to come to their aid. She asked what was going on. Her servants lied to her, telling her that a crowd of beggars was asking for alms. Believing this, she handed over what was needed to relieve their need. In the meantime, the men, who were shackled by the feet, were constrained by the judge to be silent, but once night had fallen, and while she was saying her office to herself, the chains broke, and the men freed ran from their prison to meet the saint. When this became known, the servants who had lied to the blessed lady saw themselves as prisoners, whereas those who had been prisoners were released from their chains.

Since, by divine favor, an opportunity often occurs whereby a chance event becomes a means of salvation, her brother was killed, that she might live the religious life more fully.[12] She came at the king's direction to the blessed Medard, bishop of Noyon, and immediately implored him to consecrate her to the Lord once she had changed out of her secular clothes.[13] But he recalled the words of the Apostle, *If a woman is bound to her husband, let her not seek to be loosed,*[14] and put off the queen from being clothed as a nun. Then the nobles threw the blessed bishop into confusion and violently pulled him from the altar, lest he veil the royal spouse, and lest it seem good to him as a priest to arrange for her to be taken away from the king not as the publicly married queen of the kingdom, but as a concubine. When the ever-saintly queen learned this, she entered the sanctuary, dressed in the robes of a nun, and advanced to the altar. She addressed the very blessed Medard in these words: 'If you put off my consecration and fear man more than God, may the soul of a sheep, O shepherd, be missing from your flock.[15] Thunderstruck by this, the bishop laid his hands on her and consecrated her as a deacon.[16]

The queen immediately divested herself of the grand clothing in which she was accustomed to parade at the most important festivals, when she was attended by an entourage, and laid it on the altar. So it was she loaded the table of God's glory with purple cloth, jewels, and ornaments—so many gifts—as a sacrifice. She broke up a heavy golden girdle and gave it for the needs of the poor. Similarly she approached the cell of Saint Iumeris one day, when she gladly adorned herself as queen, and having made a speech (wearing what I shall call a barbarian headdress) with future benefit to herself, she transferred to the holy altar linen shirts, gloves, headdresses, and brooches, all of them adorned with gold and some with jewels in the form of a crown. Then, on a day when she had to be adorned with particular worldly distinction, with whatever a wealthy woman could wear, she proceeded to the cell of the holy man Daddo but after rewarding the abbot, she gave it all to the monastery. Again, when she had made her way to the place of retreat of Saint Gundulf, after he had become bishop of Metz,[17] she made his monastery famous with no less effort on her part.

Then she landed at Tours after a favorable voyage. With what eloquence can I fully described how much courtesy and how much munificence she displayed? Or how she behaved around the forecourts, sanctuaries, and basilica of Saint Martin, when she wept, but could not cry hard enough, as she lay by herself on their thresholds? There, when Mass was over, she laid the holy altar the clothing and ornaments she was accustomed to wear with great distinction and elegance at the palace. When the handmaid of the Lord arrived at the village of Candes, where the glorious hero Martin, the counsellor close to Christ, departed from the life of this world,[18] she gave gifts not inferior to these, for she was growing in the Lord's grace.

When, after a favorable journey, she approached in a fitting manner the country estate of Saix,[19] which lies near to the aforesaid village, who is to count up, from an infinite number, every individual example to illustrate what her conduct was like? For example, at table, she clandestinely ate rye bread and barley bread, hidden under a flat cake, so no one would notice.[20] From the time blessed Medard consecrated her and she took the veil[21] until her last illness, she ate nothing but pulses and vegetables— no fruit, fish, eggs or anything else. She drank no beverage but water mixed with honey, and pear juice. She touched neither pure wine nor brewed mead nor fermented beer.

In the manner of Saint Germanus,[22] she ordered a supply of salted grain to be brought to her very secretly, and throughout Lent, she continually distributed at the holy shrines as much as was required for four days' refreshment, making the offerings with her own hands. In the presence of the saint no less mercy was bestowed than was needed for the numerous crowd of people. Those who were seeking therefore did not lack, neither did what she gave run short, so it was cause for wonder that all were satisfied. Whence came so many treasures to an exile and such great riches to a foreign woman?

How much she paid out in daily redemption she alone knew, who carried down the money to her petitioners.[23] For beyond the daily meal with which she restored those on her poor-register, on two days of the week, the fifth and then seventh, she always prepared a bath and girt with a towel, herself washed the bodies of the poor. She rubbed thoroughly what was there, without feeling disgust at hard skin, mange, lice or pus. She sometimes even pulled out worms and cleaned up festering skin sores. She used to comb one by one of the heads which she herself had washed. For ulcers resulting from wounds—which loose skin had covered or nails had made worse by scratching—she soothed the infection of the disease in accordance with the Gospel.[24] by pouring in oil. She herself washed with soap from head to foot the limbs of the women, as they went down in turn into the bath. Then when they came out, if she saw any of them wearing worn-out clothes, she took away what had offended her and, supplying new clothes, she caused those who had previously been clad in rags, but were now tidily dressed, to come to a meal. When the people had been gathered together, preparations were made to serve them. She herself offered water and a towel to each in turn and personally wiped both the faces and the hands of the sick. Then three dishes were brought in, full of delicious food; she stood fasting before those who were dining, and in the presence of the guests, cut up the bread and meat, whatever was set before them. She did not cease offering food to the weak and the blind in a spoon; two women were present at this time, but she alone served the food, and like a new Martha,[25] busied herself until her brothers and sisters had joyfully drunk their fill at the feast. Then she withdrew from the place to wash her hands, completely satisfied with the well-served feast. If she heard the guests murmuring, she ordered them to sit down until they wanted to rise from the table. Every Sunday, that honored day, she made it her rule, both in summer and winter, once the poor had been assembled, to offer a drink of sweet wine to their leader. Afterwards she entrusted the wine to a young girl, that she might serve a drink to all of them, because she herself would hurry off to go to prayers, both to complete her daily round and to go to meet the priests whom she had invited to her table. At this time, in accordance with royal custom, she would not let them leave without a present, when they returned to their own homes. With what gentleness she used to perform an intimidating task! When lepers came and presented themselves, at a given signal, she would order her assistant to ask with respectful care whence they came and how many of them there were. When this information had been relayed to her, a meal was prepared, and during the resulting interval, she had a serving dish, spoons, knives, drinking-straws, a drink, and cups sent in secretly, so no one would notice. She herself grasped in her embrace women bearing various marks of leprosy and even kissed their faces, for she loved them with her whole heart. Then when the table had been set up, she brought warm water and washed their faces and hands and cleaned their nails and ulcers and again served them herself, feeding them one by one. As they went away, she presented them with little presents of gold or clothing, when hardly anyone was looking. Her servant, however, took it on herself to address her thus, in respectful terms: 'Most holy mistress, who is going to kiss you, when you embrace lepers in this way?' Radegunde kindly replied, 'If you don't kiss me, that does not worry me at all'.[26]

With God's help, she was conspicuous for different kinds of miracles. If anyone despaired of a blister or wound, her assistant offered the saint a vine leaf, declaring falsely that this was what she needed. The saint immediately made the sign of the cross, carried the leaf to the despairing sufferer, and placed it on the wound, after which healing took place. Again, if anyone came to her shivering or in a feeble state, and said that he had seen in a dream that he should approach the saint for the sake of his health, she offered a candle to one of her servants; through it, after it had burned through the night, the disease itself received death and the sick man, health. How often, when she had noticed someone lying in bed, she brought imported fruits which were both sweet and warm at the same time, and refreshed the sick person. An invalid who, even on the tenth day of his illness had been unconscious, received both food and health when she administered nourishment, but she herself commanded that no one should tell the story of this, to make it known.[27]

What a great gathering of people was present on the day the saint decided to become a recluse! It was so great that those for whom there was no room in the streets climbed up and filled the roof-tops. To what a degree of fasting, charity, toil, and torture did the ever saintly lady fervently attain! If anyone were to rehearse all her miracles, he would described her equally as both confessor and martyr. Indeed for that ever dedicated lady, every day, except Sunday, that honored day, was a fast day; her meal of lentils and green vegetables was almost a fast; she ate neither poultry nor fish nor fruit nor eggs. Her favorite delicacy was rye-bread or barley-bread, which she ate hidden under a flat cake, so that no one would notice.[28] Her drink was water mixed with honey, or pear-juice, poured out in a moderate quantity, just enough to quench her thirst.

Until the first Lent was over, after she had become a recluse in her cell, she took no nourishment except on Sundays, and then only the roots of vegetables and the green leaves of mallow, prepared without a drop of oil and without salt.[29] Throughout the entire fast, she did not drink even two *sestaria* of water.[30] Consequently she struggled so much with thirst that her throat dried up and in her parched condition, she could scarcely say a psalm. She wore a hair-shirt on her body instead of linen and spent the night-vigils continuously repeating the cycle of the psalms. A layer of ashes was spread before her, over which a hair-cloth was flung; this she used instead of a bed.[31] Rest itself wearied her, for whom too small a bed seemed to support her little body.

While all the nuns were still asleep, she cleaned and oiled their shoes and carried them back to each one individually. At other seasons she used to spend the fifth day of the week in a more relaxed manner, and subsequently, Sunday. In the time that remained to her, except for the days of Easter and of the great festivals, she always led an austere life in sack-cloth and ashes, as long as her feeble state permitted; she rose to chant the psalms before the community got up. As regards her monastic duties, nothing pleased her except to be the first to serve, and she punished herself if she performed a good deed after another sister had done one.

She took her turn in sweeping both the passages and the nooks and crannies of the monastery, cleaning whatever was dirty. Piling it up in front of her, she did not shrink from carrying away what others shrank from seeing. She did not even shrink from cleaning the privy, but busied herself with it, and carrying the smell of dung away from it, she formed a poorer opinion of herself, if she did not ennoble herself by the base and servile character of her work. She brought in firewood in her arms and encouraged the fire by blowing and with the tongs. She fell, and picking herself up unhurt, she served the sick over and above her normal weekly duties. She herself cooked their food and washed the invalid's heads. She herself used to visit the people whom she cherished; she offered them hot meals, but returned to her cell fasting.

Who is to explain how it was that she was stirred by such great enthusiasm and used to run to and fro from the kitchen, when she performed her week of duties? Not one of the nuns used to bring from the out-house in a bundle as much wood as was needed; she used to carry more of the wood that was needed than anyone else. She drew water from the well and distributed it in small vessels. She cleaned the greens, she washed the vegetables, she brought the fire to life by blowing on it and she became overheated as she bustled about cooking the food. She lifted the pots from the fire herself, washed the dishes and brought them in. When the meal was finished, she herself washed up and cleaned the kitchen until it shone; she brought to the highest state of cleanliness whatever was filthy. She then made her way to the sink; she went in no lukewarm spirit, and before she received the Rule of Arles,[32] after an adequate performance of her week of duties, she made herself full of warmth towards everyone. The ever saintly lady washed and kissed their feet with humility, and while prostrate before them all, asked pardon for her acts of negligence.

Even he who speaks shrinks with horror at the punishments she inflicted on herself after so much suffering. On one occasion, after she had bound three broad circlets round her neck and arms the days of Lent, and after she had implanted chains around her body, by binding herself so tightly that her tender flesh became swollen from being enclosed the hard iron. After the fast was over, when she wished to extract the chains enclosed beneath her skin, she could not do so; her flesh over her back and breast was cut in circles above the iron chains, so that her blood poured out and her small body was drained to the last extremity.[33]

On another occasion, she ordered that a brass plate be made in the shape of the cross of Christ, this she put to the flame in her cell and then applied quite deeply to places of her body. The flesh was completely roasted. In the blazing power of her spirit, she caused her flesh to burn. One day in Lent, thinking to torment herself more grievously—in addition to the austerity of her fast and the torture of her parched thirst, and while the file-like surface of her hair-cloth garment was destroying her tender limbs—she ordered that a wash-hand basin, full of burning charcoal, be brought to her. When those who had remained left her, her spirit was equipped for punishment, while her limbs trembled. She acted this way because these were not times of persecution, when she might become a martyr.[34] In the meantime, to cool so fervent a spirit, she decided to set her body on fire. She applied the white-hot metal to it, and her burning limbs creaked. Her skin was burned up, and wherever the heat reached there was a deep furrow. Silently she covered the open wounds in punishment, but the putrefying blood revealed what her voice failed to proclaim in penance. So it was the lady freely accepted bitter wounds in exchange for the sweetness of Christ, and it came about that her miracles were not silent about what she herself had concealed.

A married woman, the daughter of the nobleman Gislaadus, was called Bella [Beautiful], but was extremely wretched, because she had long been blind. She asked that she be brought from the Duchy of Francia to Poitiers in a spirit of devotion, into the presence of the saint. Although the request was made at a late hour, a meeting was arranged in the silence of the sinister, dark night. Bella prostrated herself at the knees of the saint and immediately beseeched her to deign to sign her eyes with the cross. Radegunde soon impressed the sign of the cross on them in the name of Christ. At once the blindness fled, her sight returned and, in the night season, the day gave light to her who had long been deprived of it, and she who had been brought by a guide, departed without anyone leading her.[35]

Again, a girl named Fraifledis, wretchedly tortured at the instigation of the enemy, without delay obtained healing at the saint's hands at Saix. Let us not pass over the time that remained to the blessed lady. A certain woman in the countryside called Leubila was seriously troubled by the Enemy. On the following day, while the saint was praying, by Christ's renewed care, the skin of the lady's shoulder cracked and a worm came out. She was healed publicly, and stamping on the worm with her foot, she left, freed from her infirmity.

Let what was done in secret be proclaimed to the people. A certain nun was frozen with cold in the daytime for a whole year, but by night she was ablaze with fire; she did not move even one step, but lay lifeless. Another sister told the saint of her infirmity. Since she was unconscious, the saint ordered that she be warmed, and caused the sick woman herself to be carried to her in her cell and to be laid in a warm bath. The saint told all those present to take themselves off, and the sick woman remained at the same time alone with her healer for almost two hours.[36] She bore her weak limbs with the frame of her body, as far as it stretched from head to heel. Wherever Radegunde's hands reached, the pain fled from the feeble woman, and she whom two women had placed in the warm bath emerged from it in good health. She who would not even sniff the scent of wine, received it, drank it, and was restored. What else is there to tell? On the following day, when she was expected to depart from the world, she walked out in public and in good health.

Let there be added to the praise of Radegunde an item which deserves not to perish. When a certain woman was struggling with an invasion of the enemy and when, with difficulty, they were able to bring the rebellious enemy to the saint, she commanded the Adversary to lie down in fear on the paved floor. He immediately flung himself down on the ground in accordance with the blessed lady's words, and he who was feared became himself filled with fear. When the saint, full of faith, had trodden on the woman's neck, he came out in a motion of the bowels.[37] Even in the slightest matters, the glory of the Creator is there. When therefore a ball of thread which the saint had spun happened to be hanging up in the chamber, a bat came to touch it, but before it could cut the thread, it hung dead in the act of biting it.

Let this wonderful story be included in this work. A certain man, Floreius by name, was busy at sea, going fishing on behalf of the same saint, when a whirlwind blew up and a great mass of waves arose. As the sailors bailed out, water poured over the boat. When it was full of water and was sinking, he cried out in his extreme distress, 'Holy Radegunde, so long as we obey you, do not let us sink in shipwreck, but obtain from God the granting of our request, that we may be freed from the mass of water.' When he had thus spoken, the storm-cloud was put to flight, calm returned, the waves fell, and the prow of the ship rose.[38]

Goda was a young woman in secular life, who afterwards became God's servant as a nun. She lay on her bed of sickness for a long time and grew weaker, although many remedies had been tried on her. Then a candle was made to correspond with the measure of her own height. The Lord took pity on her in the name of the saint; at the time when the chill of death was expected, its light burned and held, and by her goodness, the chill had been put to flight before the candle was burned out.

If we pass over a good deal for the sake of brevity, we make a serious mistake. Let us be swiftly purged of what remains and a cure put forth. The wife of a certain carpenter suffered torments for several days from an unclean spirit. The honored abbess said jokingly to the saint, 'Believe me, mother, I shall excommunicate you, if within three days, this woman is not purged of the enemy and has not recovered'. She spoke openly, but she caused the holy woman secretly to regret the time set for the woman's recovery. In order that we may not delay over what was actually done: on the second day, when the saint prayed, the adversary emerged, roaring, through the woman's ear and abandoned the vessel whom he had invaded. The woman returned with her husband to her lodging, safe and sound. Nor let an action, which is very similar, be passed over. The ever blessed lady asked that a strong bay tree be pulled up from its own place and transferred to her cell for her delight. This was done, but the transplanted tree did not take root, and its leaves withered completely. The abbess charged the saint in jest that if she did not pray that the tree cling to the earth, she would deprive her temporarily of food. She did not speak in vain, for at the intercession of the saint, the bay tree came to life in its leaves, branches and root.[39]

One of the nuns, who was on quite intimate terms with her, had her eye covered with blood from a discharge. The saint took a blade of wormwood, which she kept on her breast to refresh her, and laid it on the eye. The pain and blood departed, and a pure light burst forth from the green herb.[40] Let us call to mind something which can scarcely be passed over in silence. Anderedus was the steward of the same ever blessed lady. When sons were born to him, he lost them the moment he saw them, and the mourning mother was planning their burial while she gave them birth. The weeping parents laid their lifeless baby on the saint's haircloth.[41] The moment he came into contact with that most health-giving garment of noble cloth, the child returned from death to perform the functions of life, and his pallor, close to the pallor of death, turned to a ruddy color as a result of his contact with the covering.

Who can count the wonders which the mercy and pity of Christ achieve? The nun Animia lay stretched out, so swollen with the disease of dropsy that nothing could be done to save her, and her sisters were charged to watch for the moment when she would breathe her last. She seemed to be asleep, when the honored abbess, blessed Radegunde, ordered her to step down naked into an empty bath. Then the sick woman was seen to have oil poured over her head by the hand of the blessed lady and to be clothed in a new garment. When this mysterious act had been performed, she awoke from sleep without any sign of the disease about her; she had not even sweated and her water had been consumed internally. As the result of this new miracle, the disease did not even leave a trace in her womb. She who everyone believed was to be carried straight to her grave, rose from her death-bed to walk; the scent of the oil, which was present on her head, and the absence of disease in her abdomen were proof of her recovery.

Let there be proclaimed in our midst something at which the neighborhood rejoiced. As twilight was turning into darkness, there was by some chance a good deal of noisy singing interspersed with the sound of flutes and lyres, by lay people around the monastery, and the saint, as two of the sisters will testify, had been speaking from some time, when a certain nun said to her in jest, 'Lady, I recognized one of my songs being publicly performed by the dancers.' The saint replied, 'It is extraordinary that hearing a hint of worldly life delights you, who have been bound by the obligations of religion.' Then the sister spoke as follows: 'Lady, I have really heard here only two or three of my songs, which I know by heart.'

The saint replied, 'As God is my witness, I have not even heard a worldly song.' From this it is clear that though in her flesh she was in the world, in her mind she was in heaven.

Let a miracle of an ancient type, after the fashion of the miracles of Saint Martin, be proclaimed in praise of Christ at the present day.[42] When the blessed lady was enclosed in her cell, she heard the sound of weeping coming from a nun, and having given a signal, she asked her, when she came, what had happened. She announced that a sister who was still a small child was dead and that the cold water which had been prepared so she could be washed, was now warm. The saint expressed her sympathy and then ordered the body of the child herself to be brought into her own cell. When the body had been conveyed to her, she received it with her own hands; she immediately shut the door after her and told those who had brought the body to go farther away, so that no one should perceive what she was doing. Yet she was unable to conceal her secret deed. In the meantime, while preparations were being made for the dead girl's funeral, she worked for nearly seven hours over her dead body. But Christ, seeing her faith, could deny her nothing, and the girl's health was immediately restored. One rose from prayer, the other from death; the old lady raised herself up at the same time as the little girl revived. Having again given a signal, she returned a living girl to her whom she had received in tears.

Let the following noble deed be remembered. On the day when the holy woman departed from this world and when he was feeling very weak as the result of a fit of choking, a tax-official, whose name was Domolenus, seemed to himself to see in a dream the saint approaching a village in a dignified manner. He ran up to her, greeted her and asked what the blessed lady needed. She said that she had arrived there to see him; and because it was the wish of the people to establish a shrine for Saint Martin, the ever blessed lady grasped the official's hand, saying, 'In this place the relics of the confessor are to be venerated; in this place build a church to bring him the most fitting worship.'

How mysterious is God! A foundation and a pavement were found, where the basilica was built. While he was still in the same deep sleep, she drew her hand over his throat and outlining his gullet for some time, she said in addition, 'I come that better health may be bestowed on you by God'. She appeared to make the following request: 'Through my life, free on my account those whom you hold in prison'. When he woke up, the official recalled what he had seen and said to his wife, 'I really believe that at the hour the saint departed from this life'. He made his way to the city, to learn by this means the truth and he went over to the prison to free the seven prisoners confined there, as he had been advised. When he returned, he reported that the righteous woman had migrated from the world at that hour; and in three mysterious happenings—the opening of the prison, the official restored to health, and the building of the church—the saint's prophecy became true.[43]

Let a brief account of the blessed lady's miracles suffice, lest it prove irritating, but let it not be too short, when its richness can be recognized in a few miracles, showing with what religious devotion, mercy, affection, sweetness, humility, integrity, faith, and fervor she lived, so that after her death, the wonders of her glorious passage through this world may still accompany her.

NOTES

1. See also Gregory of Tours, LH 2.12; MGH SRM 1, ed. B. Krusch and W. Levison, 2nd ed. (Hanover, 1951) 61–62.

2. See Venantius Fortunatus, *Carmina* pp. 3.31; MGH AA 4(1): 378–279.

3. See Gregory of Tours (n.1) 61–62.

4. *Adteias* in Latin.

5. Venantius Fortunatus assumes that the identity of these children was known to his readers. Very probably they were the children of Chlothar by his previous unions. His matrimonial affairs are somewhat confused but it appears that his partners were (1) Ingunde, by whom he had five sons and one daughter; (2) Aregunde, her sister, by whom he had one son; (3) Chunsina, by whom he had one son; (4) Guntheuc, the widow of his brother Chlodomir. It is likely that Ingunde and Guntheuc were the sole official wives and the rest concubines.

6. This refers to the relic of the True Cross which, through the help of King Sigebert, was sent to Radegunde by the emperor Justin II and was received at the monastery at Poitiers in 568/9.

7. *Victoriacon* in Latin.

8. The meaning of the phrase 'through Beralcha' is obscure. Beralcha may have been either the name of a place through which Radegunde passed or that of a servant who helped her to slip away.

9. It is possible that *animus tendens ad opus misericordiae* and *mens intenta ad Christum* (*Vita II*ᵃ.2; MGH SRM 2: 380) are latin versions of the name Radegunde.

10. This biblical allusion combines two separate stories. The writer of 2 Samuel (2 Kings) 17:28 refers to three men who feasted on beans and lentils, but they were plainly not *pueri* (the latin word used by Fortunatus, meaning children or slaves), but important personages. Venantius is conflating this story with that of the Three Holy Children (*pueri*) who had no meat in Babylon to offer (Dan 3:15–17).

11. Presumably this was the garden of the house at Athies-sur-Somme, which was in the district of Péronne.

12. See Venantius Fortunatus, *De exicidio Thuringiae* 124 (MGH AA 4(1): App. 1:247); Gregory of Tours, LH 3.7 (MGH SRM 1:105).

13. The importance attached to the assumption of the religious habit has already been noted, see above p. 294.

14. 1 Cor 7:27.

15. See Gen 9:5.

16. For a full discussion of Radegunde's ordination as deacon, see Sister Theresa, CSA, 'Women in the diaconate', *Distinctive Diaconate*, Study 23, faxc. 4 (April, 1985) 110–116; and Michael Rouche, 'Le mariage et le célibat consacré de sainte Radegonde,' *La riche personnalité de sainte Radegonde*, Conférences et homélies du xivᵉ centennaire, Poitiers 1987 (Poitiers, 1988).

17. Gundulf, bishop of Metz, is not mentioned elsewhere, nor are Iumeris and Daddo.

18. Cf. Gregory of Tours, LH 10.31 (MGH SRM 1:527). The latin name of this place is *vi cus Condatensis*.

19. The village near Candes in which the country estate give to Radegunde by Chlothar was situated.

20. The *flado* seems to have been a flat cake, something like the modern greek pita bread, and to have been considered a delicacy. Radegunde apparently held it in front of her mouth, using it to conceal the coarse bread that she was in fact eating.

21. This implies that Radegunde became a nun at the same time she became a deacon, but this is unlikely. For a full discussion of this question, see Rouche (article cited in n.16).

22. See Constantius, *Vita S. Germani Autissiodensis 3*, SRM 3; MGH SRM 7; 252. Mola has two meanings: (1) a mill; (2) salted grain. Constantius gives us to understand that Germanus ground the corn himself, presumably with a little hand-mill, but the passage relating to Radegunde makes better sense if we adopt the second meaning. This, however, makes *more Germani* difficult to translate. The description of Germanus' character and austerities in ch. 2–3 (pp. 252–253) recalls those of Radegunde. Fortunatus may be applying the well-known technique of the hagiographer here, since the *vita* of Germanus was written c. 480, but it is likely that there were traditional forms of discipline which were common to ascetics and penitents.

23. *Redemption* may apply either to expenditure on resuscitating the poor or to ransoms paid in order to free captives, a favorite *topos* of the hagiographers, e.g., Cyprian of Roulon *et al.*, *Vita S. Caesarii Arelatensis* 1.20 (p. 464), 32 (p. 469).

24. Lk 10:34.

25. Lk 10:40.

26. Radegunde evidently had a sense of humor.

27. See Venantius Fortunatus, *Vita S. Martini* 1.361 (GH MA 4(1):308).

28. See n.20 above.

29. For a similar lenten fast, see *Vita S. Germani Autissiodensis* 4, p. 252. We have already met the practice of giving up oil in Lent in the life of Melania the Younger, *Vita S. Melaniae Iunioris*, p. 328 above.

30. We do not know what quantity this represents.

31. Cf. *Vita S. Germani Autissiodensis* 4, p. 253.

32. Gregory of Tours (*Liber historiarum* 10.40; MGH SRM 1; 404) tells us that since Maroveus, bishop of Poitiers, gave Radegunde and her community no help, Radegunde and the abbess were obliged to turn to the community of Saint John at Arles. For a description of the rule of Arles, see Historical Introduction, p. 37, n. 56; for a full discussion of the question of the dates when the rule was given to the community and Radegunde and the abbess made their journey to Arles, see p. 366. The domestic duties of the moanstery would have been divided in such a way that all took their turn at the menial work, no matter what their status had been before they entered.

33. See H. Platelle, 'La violence et ses remèdes en flandre au xie siècle,' *Sacris erudiri* 20 (1971) 101–169, esp. 145–146, 152–154.

34. From the earliest times martyrdom had been held up to Christians as the highest good, but after the Peace of the church in 315, when opportunities for martyrdom became fewer, substitutes had to be found. See J. M. Petersen, *The Dialogues of Gregory the Great in their Late Antique Cultural Background*, Studies and Texts 69 (Toronto, 1984) 73; F. Graus, *Volk, Herrscher und Heiliger im Reich der Merowinger* (Prague, 1965). Radegunde may have given her desire to imitate the martyrs as an explanation of her austerities to Fortunatus, but it seems likely that she was also performing a penance.

35. The story of the healing of the blind by means of the sign of the cross has many hagiographical precedents, e.g., Gregory the Great, *Dial.* 1.10; *Les Dialogues de Grégoire le Grand*, ed. A. de Vogüé, 3 vols, SCh 251, 260, 265 (Paris, 1978–1980) vol. 2: 92/3–94/5.

36. Possibly it was the application of the principles of hygiene which cured this patient.

37. Cf. Sulpicius Severus, *Vita S. Martini*, 17; vol. 1:290/1.

38. Stories of saints coming to the rescue of travellers, on the invocation of their names, are a commonplace of hagiography. e.g., *Vita sancti Martini* 1.2 (MGH SRM 2:588); 9 (pp. 593–594); Sulpicius Severus, *Dialogues* 3.14 (*Opera* ed. C. Halm, CSEL 1, [Vienna, 1866] p. 212).

39. This story is probably linked with a story of Sulpicius Severus, told by Gregory of Tours, LGC 49–50, MGH SRN 2, pp. 327–328.

40. Gregory of Tours tells how the holy woman Monegunde used leaves in her work of healing (VP 9(3) [MGH SRM 2:289], LGC 24 [p. 343]) and this may have been the inspiration of Fortunatus here.

41. Hair-cloths and other textiles were often considered efficacious for healing: e.g., Sulpicius Severus, *Vita S. Martini* 18.3 (vol. 1: 292/3), *Dialogues* 2(3). 9 (*Opera*, p. 207). There seems to be a contradiction in terms here, as Baudonivia lays great stress on the fact that Radegunde did not become abbess herself, but selected another for the post. We can only assume that either a zealous copyist, not grasping this, has inserted an explanatory note, or that the word *et* has dropped out.

42. *Vita S. Caesarii Arelatensis* 2. 12 (MGH SRM 3:488); 9 (p. 487); 13 (p. 489). Cf. Sulpicius Severus, *Vita S. Martini* 7 (vol. 1: 268/9–270/1); 1 (3) Kgs 17:21; 2 (Kgs 4:34–35; Mt 9: 25. For two similar stories, see *Vita S. Caesarii Arelatensis* 1.39–40

43. There are many stories of saints appearing to individuals at the time of their deaths, e.g., Gregory of Tours, *Liber in gloria confessorum* 20 (MGH SRM 2; p. 259); Gregory the Great, *Dialogues* 4.12–14 (vol. 3; 48/9–58/9), but the only example that I have so far been able to trace of a saint appearing to an individual at the time of his or her own death, is that of Saint John the Almsgiver; see Leontius of Neapoli's, *Vita S. Iohannis Eleemosynarii* 46 (ed. H. Gelzer, Freiburg i/B—Leipzig, 1903) pp. 260–261; *ET Three Byzantine Saints*, trans. Elizabeth Dawes and Norman H. Baynes (London 1948–Crestwood, NY 1977) 260.

THE LIFE OF SAINT RADEGUNDE

BOOK TWO
By the Nun Baudonivia

BAUDONIVIA, the humblest of all, to the holy ladies, adorned by the grace of their merits, Dedimia the abbess and the whole community of the glorious lady Radegunde.[1]

You enjoin me to accomplish a task which it would be no less impossible for me to achieve *than it would be for me to touch the sky with my finger;*[2] that is, that we should venture to say something about the life of the saintly lady, Radegunde, whom you knew very well. This task ought to be laid upon those people *who possess within themselves a spring of eloquence from which any task laid upon them flows out quite fully in a poem like a well-watered stream. On the other hand, those people who are of only narrow intelligence and have no flow of eloquence through which to refresh others and relieve the poverty of their own dryness, are not only eager to refrain from saying anything, but also filled with terror if any task requiring eloquence is laid upon them*[3] I recognize this characteristic in myself; I am timid and I have little eloquence and power of discernment. *It is as useful for learned people to speak as it is for unlearned people to remain silent. The former know how to derive important principles from small pieces of evidence, whereas the latter do not know how to deduce small pieces of evidence form important principles. That is why what some people seek is feared by others.*[4] Since I am the lowliest of all the very lowly, *the person whom from her cradle the lady Radegunde lovingly brought up as her personal little servant and kept in her presence,*[5] I will narrate briefly, in recognition of this great privilege, *not fully, in part, what I have been able to grasp about her outstanding work,*[6] in order that I may be able to proclaim her glorious life to the ears of her flock with an eloquence which is not worthy of her but is nevertheless full of devotion. In obedience I submit myself to your most kindly will, but I ask for the help of your prayers. The less is my learning, the greater my devotion. We do not repeat what the apostolic man, Bishop Fortunatus, has written in his life of the blessed lady, but only what he has passed over because he did not wish to prolong his narrative; as he indeed explains in his own book, when he says, 'Let a slight account of the blessed lady's miracles suffice, so that a wealth of material may not be wearisome, and let our account not incur reproaches for being very brief, when the wide scope of her miracles can be recognized from a very few examples.'[7]

We are trying, therefore, under the inspiration of the divine power which Radegunde was eager to please in this world and with which she now reigns in the world to come, and using speech which is rustic and lacking in elegance,[8] to comprehend a little about her deeds and to take in a little about her many miracles.

HERE ENDS THE PROLOGUE

1

As regards the life of the blessed lady Radegunde, an account of her royal origin and dignity is contained in Book One. Everyone therefore knows what her actions were while she was living with an earthly prince, her royal husband, King Chlothar. From the royal stem there sprang a noble shoot, and what she received from her own race she made more illustrious through her faith. She was a noble queen married to an earthly prince, and she herself belonged more to heaven than to earth. During the short period of her union, she so conducted herself as a wife that she served Christ with greater devotion, and as a laywoman she lived in the manner she longed to imitate. Her religious practices anticipated her approaching conversion to her future way of life. Beneath her secular clothing she was forming the model of her life as a religious. She was confined by no worldly fetters, but was bound by obedience to the servants of God. She showed anxious care for the ransoming of prisoners[9] and was generous to the needy. She believed that a poor man should regard as his own whatever he received from her.

While she was with the king and was still clad in worldly attire, her mind was directed to Christ[10]—and this I say with God as my witness, to whom, while the lips are silent, hearts are open, and from whom, even if the tongue is silent, no secret is hidden,[11] because we tell him what we have heard and we testify to what we have seen. While she was on a journey and was attended with much worldly pomp, she was invited to dinner at the house of married lady called Ausifrid. She had travelled a long way. Now a temple where the ranks used to worship lay very near the blessed queen's route—about a mile from it. When the queen heard that a temple where the Franks worshipped stood there, she ordered her household servants to set fire to it, for she believed that it was wrong to despise the God of heaven and to honor the devices of the devil.[12] When the Franks heard this news, a whole crowd of them tried to defend the shrine with swords and clubs, making diabolical noises. But the holy queen remained steadfast and motionless, carrying Christ in her heart, and did not stir on her horse, on which she was sitting at the forefront, until not only had the temple been burned down but, yielding to her request, the tribes had made peace between them. When this had taken place, everyone broke into admiration of the queen's steadfastness and courage and blessed God.

After the queen, through the operation of divine grace, had left her earthly king—something for which she used to ask in her prayers—she settled at Saix in a country house which the king had given her. In the first year of her conversion to the religious life she saw in a vision a ship, shaped like a man.[13] There were people sitting on all his limbs; she herself was sitting on his knee. He said to her, 'At present you are sitting on my knee, but you shall have a seat in my heart.' So it was that the grace which she would enjoy in the future was revealed to her. Earnestly entreating them to keep the matter secret, she described this vision to her faithful friends. She begged that no one should know this story in her lifetime. How cautious she was in speech and how fervent in her actions! In prosperity and in adversity, in joy and in sorrow, she was always the same. She never broke down under misfortune nor became too much elated by prosperity.

While she was still at this country house, there was a rumor to the effect that the king wanted to taker her back. He grieved, saying he was suffering a heavy loss for allowing a queen of such quality and greatness to depart from his side; if he could not have her back, he wished from the bottom of his heart not to go on living. When the ever blessed lady heard this, she became extremely frightened. To torment herself further, she obtained a very rough hairshirt and clothed her tender body in it. Moreover, she imposed the torture of fasting on herself; she passed the night in vigils and poured herself out in prayer She turned her eyes away from her home in her country, overcame the pleasures of married life, rejected worldly love, and chose to become an exile, in order that she might not journey far from Christ. Among her royal treasures she still possessed a cup decorated with gold, jewels, and pearls, which was worth a thousand gold *solidi*. This she sent through the nun Fridovigia, who was very close to her, and with an escort of faithful friends, to the holy hermit, Master

John, who lived in the fortress of Chinon, to ask him to pray for her, that she might not return to life in the world, and to send her a hairshirt with which she might, so to speak, rasp her body. He sent her a rugged hairshirt, which served her as both under and outer clothing. Furthermore, if the aforesaid man should learn anything of the matter about which she was fearful, through the guidance of the Holy Spirit, he was to let her know. If it was the king's wish that she return to him, she would choose to end her life before being yoked once again to an earthly king, because she had already embraced the King of heaven and was united with him in marriage. So the man of God passed a whole night in vigils and prayers. Under the inspiration of divine power, he told her the next day that it was the king's wish that she return to him, but that God would not allow it; the king would be punished by God's judgement before taking her back as his wife.

After this, the aforesaid lady Radegunde, her mind turned towards Christ,[14] with God as her inspiration and co-worker, built a monastery for herself at Poitiers, in accordance with the directions of King Chlothar. The apostolic man, Bishop Pientius, and the Duke Astrapius had the building put up quickly in accordance with the Lord's plan. The holy queen, rejecting the world's false blandishments, joyfully entered this monastery, where she sought the embellishments of perfection and brought a large community of young girls to Christ. There an abbess was elected and installed, and Radegunde, substituting the abbess' power for her own, handed over to her both herself and her possessions.[15] She kept none of her own rights for herself, so that she might be able to run swiftly in the footsteps of Christ and might grow in heaven in proportion to what she had given up on earth. Soon her holy life began to glow with the practice of humility, in the richness of its charity, in the shining light of its chastity, and in the abundance of its fasting. She handed herself over to her Bridegroom with such complete devotion that she embraced God with a pure heart and felt that Christ was dwelling in her.

But the enemy, who is covetous of everything that is good in the human race, and whose will she shrank from doing, even when she was in the world, did not stop persecuting her. Exactly as she had already learned from the messengers who went back and forth, something which she feared was coming to pass: the most high King Chlothar had come to Tours with his son, the most eminent Sigebert, on the pretext of devotion, so that they could reach Poitiers easily to receive the queen.

Having learned this, Radegunde directed a letter to him, written on oak. In it she bore witness to God's opposition to such a plan. She caused it to be sent under a solemn pledge to the apostolic man, Germanus, bishop of Paris, who was then at the king's court. She dispatched the letter together with gifts and blessings, secretly through her agent, Proculus. When Germanus, a man filled with the spirit of God, had read the letter, he flung himself down weeping at the feet of the king, before the tomb of Saint Martin, with the solemn pledge, as had been indicated to him in the letter, that the king should not approach the city of Poitiers. Then, though filled with bitterness—for he recognized that the petition came from the blessed lady, the queen—the king was brought to repentance. He reproached his evil counsellors and deemed himself unworthy to have had for so long such a queen. He too flung himself down on the threshold of Saint Martin's, at the feet of the apostolic man Germanus, and asked him to seek forgiveness on his behalf from the blessed lady Radegunde, that she might grant him her pardon, because he had sinned against her through his evil counsellors. Thereupon divine vengeance immediately struck these people; just as Arius,[16] who strove against the catholic faith, lost all his intestines in the privy, so it happened to those men, who acted against the blessed lady, the queen. Then the king, fearing the judgement of God because his queen had done God's will rather than her own during the time she had lived with him, asked Germanus to come there quickly. The apostolic man, the lord Germanus, therefore came to Poitiers and, having entered the monastery, flung himself down at the feet of the holy queen in the chapel, dedicated in the name of our Lady Mary, and asked for her pardon on behalf of the king. Since she truly rejoiced that she had been snatched from the yawning gulf of worldly life, she graciously granted it and bound herself to the service of God.[17] She now prepared to follow Christ, whom she had always loved, wherever he should go,[18] and hastened to him with a devoted heart. Intent on such matters, she added to her duties the order of vigils, keeping guard by night, as if she had made a prison of her body. Although she was merciful to others, she acted as a judge over herself; she paid dutiful respect to others, but was strict with herself as regards abstinence; she was generous to everyone, but exercised restrictions on herself, so that it was not enough for her to become immersed in fasting, unless she also triumphed over her own body.

2

Since she was devoted to these pursuits in all kinds of ways, as has been indicated in Book One, Radegunde soon could be at the disposal of God alone. At this time, having clothed herself in stronger armor, she gave herself unceasingly to prayer, vigils, and the meditative study of holy scripture. She herself served meals to visiting strangers at her table and with her own hands washed and wiped the feet of the sick. She did not allow her maid to offer her the comfort of her help when she hastened to do her a service. Indeed, so far as her lack of strength permitted, she enclosed herself in so tight a straitjacket of abstinence that with her mind intent, as it was, on God, she did not now require earthly food. After she had assumed the habit of a religious, she made a penitential bed for herself; at no time did soft feathers support her or dazzling white linen cover the bed of the lady, who subdued her body with sackcloth and ashes instead of a complete set of clothing. The previous book has taught us a good deal about the strictness of her abstinence and her attitude of service. So greatly did she impoverish herself for the sake of God that she provided an example to others. She had no gloves with gauntlets to put on her arms, except for a leather pair which she made herself, but she practiced poverty in such a way that not even the abbess was aware of it. *Who would be able to describe her patience, her charity, her fervor of spirit, her kindness, her holy zeal and her perpetual meditation on the law of the Lord by night and by day? When she appeared to pause in her meditation or recitation of*

*the psalms, the reader before her, one of the nuns, continued to
read.*[19] So far was the praise of God from departing from her heart
or from her lips that when she happened to see the portress of
the monastery, whose name was Eodegunde, passing by and she
wished to summon her, she called out 'Alleluia' instead of her
name. She did this thousands of times. There never proceeded
from her mouth any slander, any lie, or any curse on any person
whatsoever, and not only did she not speak evil against anyone,
but she would not listen patiently to anyone else speaking evil.
She always prayed for her persecutors and instructed others to
pray for them.[20] So much did she love the community which she,
filled with the desire for God, had collected together in the name
of the Lord, that she did not even remember that she also had
had parents and a king as husband. When she was addressing us,
she used frequently to say, 'I have chosen you as my daughters.
You are my lights; you are my life; you are my rest and my entire
happiness. I have planted you afresh. Conduct yourselves with
me in this life in such a way that we may rejoice in the life to
come. Let us serve the Lord in full faith, in the full affection of
our hearts. Let us seek him in fear and simplicity of heart, so that
we may say to him with confidence, "Grant, Lord, what you have
promised, for we have done what you commanded.'"

She never imposed on anyone else what she had not previously
undertaken herself. From wherever a servant of God came, she
carefully enquired in what way he would serve God. If she learned
from him something new, which she did not herself do, she at
once first eagerly applied herself to it and then afterwards showed
the community how to do it, as much by her word as by her
example. When the responsory chanting of the psalms had come
to an end in her presence, the reading of scripture did not cease
either by day or night, not even for a minute while she refreshed
her little body. While the readying was going on, she used to carry
out the cure of our souls with holy and dutiful care. She used to
say, 'If you do not understand what is being read, is that because
you do not carefully look into the mirror of your souls?' But if one
dared respectfully to question her all the same she did not cease
to expound, with her holy and dutiful care and motherly affection

for the salvation of one's soul, what the reading meant. Just as the bee assembles different kinds of flowers from which it gathers honey, so was she eager to pluck from those spiritually-minded men whom she invited little flowers from which to display the fruit of good works both to herself and to her followers. At night, when she seemed to snatch barely an hour's sleep, the reading of scripture always continued. She used to think that what she read, when she felt the languor of sleep on her, gave her a little rest. When the reading had ceased, Radegunde (her mind intent upon God),[20] just as if she were saying, *I sleep and my heart is awake*[21] used to remark, 'Why are you silent? Go on reading; do not give up'. But when midnight brought the time for rising, although she had previously completed her office and had not so far even felt sleep, she was ready and rose joyfully from her couch to serve the Lord, so that she might say with confidence, *At midnight I rose up to acknowledge you, O Lord.*[22] Frequently she seemed to chant the psalms in her sleep, so that she might rightly and truly say, *The meditation of my heart is truly in your sight.*[23] Who could ever imitate the blazing warmth of the love with which she loved all mankind? Each and every virtue shone forth in her: discretion with modesty; wisdom with simplicity; strictness with mercy; learning with humility. Her life was without stain, irreproachable and always uniform in character.

So much did she alienate herself from her own property that if she wished to give a drink of pure wine to one of the sisters, she did not presume to touch her own cellar herself. Since this was known, the honored abbess gave her a little barrel holding two hundred-eighty litres, the distribution of which she handed over to the blessed Felicitas, the steward of the cellar. From one grape-harvest to the next, this sister distributed it every day, whenever the saint ordered her to do it. The contents of the barrel never went down, but always remained the same. When the new wine which filled the cellar arrived, the little barrel believed that it had satisfied the saint. The wine jars and casks were empty before this little barrel, which had done the saints' will in every respect.[24] The Lord fed five thousand people from five loaves and a pair of fishes;[25] and his handmaid provided refreshment from his small quantity of wine wherever she saw that there was need for a whole year. She was always anxious for peace and devoted to the salvation of her country whenever anything was stirring between the kingdoms. Since she loved all the kings,[26] she used to pray for the lives of all of them and taught us to pray without ceasing for their stability. When she heard that bitterness was rising among them, she used to tremble all over and directed similar letters to one as to another, that they might employ neither war nor arms between themselves, but establish a firm peace, so that their country might not perish. Similarly she directed their chief counsellors that they should administer to their most high kings advice that would bring safety, so that as long as they reigned, their peoples and their country should be rendered more wholesome. She ordered her community to keep constant vigils and taught them, in tears, to pray ceaselessly for the kings. Who could describe in words what great tortures she inflicted on herself? At her intercession there was peace between the kings, the war died down, the country was saved. Knowing what she had obtained for them, they praised the blessed name of the Lord. Whatever the victory she secured with the help of the king of heaven in bringing about peace among the kings, she applied herself the more promptly to her devotion to God and made herself over to the service of all.[27] She did not care what kind of act of obedience she undertook, for she was eager to fulfil her service with all her strength. She washed everyone's feet with her own hands, wiping them with a towel and kissing them, and if it was permitted, she strove, like Mary, to wipe them with her flowing hair.[28] It was for this reason that in exchange for such immeasurable acts of kindness, the Lord, who generously grants miraculous powers, made for her quite famous for her miracles in the ducy of Francia, where, while she seemed to be reigning there, she prepared for herself a kingdom which was heavenly rather than earthly. She had a chapel made for herself, where as often as she withdrew herself from the king, she might always invoke the Lord of heaven. There, where her prayer was frequent, God's goodness was available to her when his name was invoked.

After she had enclosed herself in the monastery, a married woman called Mammezo was seriously injured while on a journey, because a little piece of dirt had entered her eye. At that moment, the same voice, the same pain and the same cry were present day and night, in order that the Lord might proclaim the faith of his servant. Although the saint was not present there in the body, she granted her kindly spirit at the invocation of her name. The Lord put it into the mind of Mammezo that she should make her way to the saint's chapel and should believe that she would be saved when she invoked her name. The woman, who was racked by pain and supported by the hands of her servants, could scarcely be led to the chapel. Enduring very intense pain, she flung herself on to the paved floor and began to cry out, 'Lady Radegunde, I believe that you are filled with the miraculous power of God, whose will you have done, rather than the will of man. Kind lady, you are full of holiness and loving care, have pity on me, help me, an unhappy woman, pray for me that my eye may be restored, for my soul is afflicted with grievous torment and pain.' She who bore alone everyone's pains while she was in the body, until she could heal them, kindly listened when her name was invoked. The Lord took pity on Mammezo. Through his intervention, the pain took flight, health returned, and she who alone felt the pain, received back in a sound condition, the eye which she believed that she had lost. The woman, who for so many days had neither taken food nor seen daylight, returned safely to her home on her own feet, without anyone supporting her, and giving thanks to the Lord—which she continues to do up to the present day.

Let another miracle be added in praise of Christ, who makes his people anxious for others. Vinoberga was one of Radegunde's household-serving women; with rash daring she presumed to sit on the throne of the blessed queen after her death. After she had done this, she was stricken by the judgement of God and blazed with such fire that everyone saw smoke advancing upwards from her, and she herself cried out in the presence of all the people, confessing that she had sinned: therefore she was on fire, because she had sat in the seat of the blessed lady. For three days and three nights she endured the same fire and cried out in a loud voice, 'Lady Radegunde, I have sinned and done wrong. Grant me pardon and cool my limbs, which have been burned in cruel torment. Your mercy is wide; you are glorious in your good works. Do you, who have mercy on all, have mercy upon me.' All the people who saw her in such great torment prayed on her behalf, as if Radegunde had been there, since she is present wherever she is invoked in faith. They said, 'Lady, of your kindness spare her, that she may not unhappily perish from such great torture.' So the most blessed lady graciously acceded to the prayers of all the people and quelled the blazing fire. Vinoberga returned safe and sound to her home. Her punishment made them all cautious and devout.

While she was at her country estate at Saix, Radegunde (her mind turned to Christ)[29] longed in her devout and faithful spirit and with complete devotion to possess relics of all the saints. While she was praying, a holy man, the priest Magnus, arrived, bringing with him relics of the lord Andrew and of as many other saints as possible. When the relics had been placed on the altar, she kept vigil devoutly by night and prostrated herself in prayer beyond what was necessary. A light sleep came over her, during which the Lord declared to her that her wish had been fulfilled. He said to her, 'Know, O Lady, blessed by God, that not only those relics which the priest Magnus has brought, but also those which you have collected together at your country house at Athies, are assembled together here.' When she opened her eyes, she beheld a man of very magnificent appearance, who told her this, and she rejoiced and blessed the Lord.

After she had entered the monastery, what a multitude of saints she assembled together by her even faithful prayers! The East bears witness to this, the North, South, and West proclaim that she personally obtained for herself, as much by gifts as by her prayers, precious jewels from every quarter, hidden in heaven and possessed by Paradise. She believed that she was linked to these saints in continuous meditation and that she was singing hymns and psalms with them.[30] One day news reached her of the lord Mammas the martyr,[31] that his holy limbs were resting in Jerusalem. When she heard this news, she drank it in like someone suffering hunger and thirst. Like a person suffering from dropsy, whose thirst increases in proportion to the quantity of water he drinks at the spring, she glowed with the warmer devotion, the more she was watered by the dew of God. She dispatched an honored man and priest called Reoval, who was then a layman and is still alive, to the Patriarch of Jerusalem, to ask for a relic of the blessed Mammas. This errand the man of God graciously undertook. While seeking the will of God, he made his prayers known to the people. On the third day, after mass had been celebrated, he approached the blessed martyr's tomb with all the people. There, in a loud voice and full of faith, he spoke in public as follows, saying, 'I beseech you, confessor and martyr of God, if the blessed Radegunde is the true handmaid of God, let your power become known among the nations. Grant that her faithful soul may receive what she asks from your relics.' When he had finished the prayer, all the people responded 'Amen'. He came to the holy tomb, continuously proclaiming the faith of the blessed lady, and touched the saint's limbs, which the most holy saint [Mammas] ordered him to do at the request of the lady Radegunde. He touched the fingers of the saint's right hand, one by one; when he came to the little finger, he carried it off with a gentle touch of his own hand, that he might satisfy the desire of the blessed queen and fulfil her wish. The apostolic man dispatched this finger to the blessed Radegunde with appropriate dignity. From Jerusalem to Poitiers the praise of God rang out ceaselessly in honor of it. Can you imagine how she awaited with her heart afire and with faithful devotion the prize of so great a relic and how she gave herself over to abstinence? But when the blessed queen had received this heavenly gift, she rejoiced with all her eagerness and strength. For a whole week she devoted herself in company with her entire community to vigils and fasting; she blessed the Lord that he had thought her worthy to receive such a gift. Thus God does not refuse his faithful what they ask. Frequently and gently she used to say, as it were in a figure of speech, so that no one could understand, 'Anyone who has the care of souls ought to have a strong fear of universal praise'. Nevertheless, the more the saint wished to avoid praise, so much more was the generous Dispenser of virtues eager to declare to her that she was faithful in all things, so that whenever a sick person invoked her, no matter what malady afflicted him, he was restored to health.

A distinguished man called Leo was summoned to the Council of the Synod[32] by the apostolic men, bishops Leontius and Eusebius. While he was on his way, his eye was enveloped by a heavy darkness, having been covered by a dense clot of blood. If he had not been supported by his servants, he could not have gone any further, for he could not see the road. He entered the blessed lady's monastery, where, being a devout man, he handed over his daughters to serve the Lord, and went into the chapel dedicated to the name of our Lady Mary. After he had said a prayer, being full of faith, he prostrated himself on the saint's haircloth and invoked her vehemently. He lay on the haircloth for a long time, until the pain had left him, the darkness had left him, the blood had clotted and the veins were performing their function. Then he went on his way. The man who had been led in, returned home with shining eyes, restored to health. He received his sight from the blessed lady's haircloth; he walked cheerfully and safely to the Synod, where he began to speak. After this, he told his story himself, and the whole Synod listened. When he returned from it, he told us the story with his own lips. His very devotion to the saint caused him to strike the foundation of the basilica of the lady Radegunde and he also provided a hundred *solidi* for the building itself. *Who could count how many sick people have been restored to health upon the invocation of her name? Who is there who ever saw her and believed that she was a human being belonging to this earth? By the God of heaven, I faithfully and truthfully state that her countenance, together with her soul, always so shone in the eyes of all that what was carried within her was deservedly made visible to the outer world.*[33]

After she had collected the relics of the saints, she would have asked the Lord himself to descend from his seat of majesty and to dwell here in visible form if it had been possible. Although her bodily eye did not see him, her mind and spirit, concentrating on frequent prayers, beheld him in contemplation. But since *the Lord will not deprive of good things those who walk in innocence,*[34] and who seek him with all their heart and all their soul and all their mind,[35] as this blessed lady did, the divine mercy displayed itself graciously towards her, and he in whose heart she reposed day and night put it into her mind that she should act as Saint Helena did. The blessed Helena, who was imbued with wisdom, filled with the fear of the Lord, and renowned for her good works, was searching for the saving wood on which the price of the world had been paid for our salvation, to snatch us from the power of the devil. When it had been found, she clapped her hands and bending her knee to the ground, she worshipped the Lord. She recognized that it was the Lord's very cross because a man rose from the dead after it had been laid upon him. She said, 'Truly, you are Christ the Son of God, who came into the world and redeemed your captive people with your precious blood.'[36] The blessed Radegunde did in Gaul what Saint Helena had done in an eastern country.

Since while she was in this world, Radegunde did not wish to act without consultation, she sent a letter to the most eminent lord, King Sigebert, by whose rule her country was being governed, petitioning him that for the sake of the salvation of the whole country and the stability of his realm, he allow her to ask the Emperor for wood from the Lord's cross. The king very graciously signified his assent to the holy queen's petition. Full of devotion and aflame with longing, she—who had made herself poor for God's sake—dispatched to the emperor not gifts, but her own messengers, with a prayer and with the help of the company of saints whom she ceaselessly invoked. She obtained the fulfillment of her wishes. She was able to rejoice proudly that she had in the very place where she lived the blessed wood of the Lord's cross, adorned with gold and jewels, and many relics of saints which the East had preserved. At the saint's request, the emperor sent his envoys with gospel-books, decorated with gold and jewels. When the wood, on which the Savior of the world had hung, arrived at the city of Poitiers, escorted by the company of saints, the bishop of the place, along with all the people, wished to receive it with devotion; but the enemy of the human race acted through his minions to repel the ransom of the world and to refuse to receive it into the city.[37] Such were the trials to which the blessed Radegunde submitted, while trading one thing for another, after the custom of the Jews, went on! However, it is not for us to discuss this question, but for others to look into it; the Lord knows his own. Radegunde was fervent in spirit and in a fighting mood; she again sent a message to the most gracious king to the effect that the bishop and people of Poitiers did not wish to receive their Salvation into their city. In the meantime, while she awaited the return of her messengers from the king, she entrusted the Lord's cross and the relics of the saints, accompanied by a choir of singing-psalm priests, to the men's monastery which she had founded at Tours for the salvation of the king himself. The holy cross suffered injury through envy no less than the Lord, called through his faithful forerunner and recalled before magistrates and judges, patiently bore every kind of cruelty so that his creation might not perish. In what great torment did her whole community place itself—in fasting, in vigils, in abundance of tears, in grief and mourning—every day until the Lord, who put it into the heart of the king to give judgement and do justice in the midst of the people,[38] looked on the lowliness of his handmaiden.[39] By one of his loyal supporters, the illustrious count Justin, the pious king dispatched to the apostolic man Euphronius, lord bishop of the city of Tours, the order to place the glorious cross of the Lord and the relics of the saints in the lady Radegunde's monastery with appropriate honor.[40] This was done. The saint, with all her household, rejoiced with great joy[41] and brought this good and perfect gift[42] from heaven to the community which she had collected together for the Lord's service. She felt in her spirit that after her passing, her community might have little influence, although she might be reigning with the King of heaven, and could from there help them.[43] So that she might never abandon her flock, excellent provider and good ruler as she was, she therefore set apart in her monastery, for the honor of the place and the salvation of the people, the price of the world, pledged by Christ, which she had sought from a distant region. There in that monastery, with the cooperation of God's miracle and with the ministration of the power of heaven, the eyes of the blind receive their sight, the ears of the deaf are opened, the lame walk and the demons are put to flight. What more is there to say? Anyone, no matter with what disease he is afflicted, who has come in faith to the monastery returns home whole by virtue of the holy cross. Who could say how great a gift and what kind of a gift she conferred on this city? It is for this reason that anyone who lives by faith calls down blessing on her name. She commended her monastery, calling on God as her witness, to the most eminent lords, the kings, and to the most serene lady, the queen Brunhild, all of whom she loved with dear affection, and also to the holy churches and their bishops.

After she had received this heavenly gift, the blessed lady sent her messengers—the aforementioned priest, accompanied by others—to the emperor, to thank him, with [a gift of] a simple article of clothing. On their return journey, the sea began to rise in great waves. There they suffered many dangers: storms and tempests, the like of which they said they had never seen. For forty days and forty nights their ship was subjected to great dangers on the open sea. Now despairing of their lives, they kept death before their eyes and made their peace with one another, because the sea was longing to swallow them up. Seeing themselves in such great danger, they raised their voices to heaven, crying out and saying, 'Lady Radegunde, come to the help of your servants. As long as we obey you, do not let us perish by drowning; free us from danger of drowning, for the sea is ready to swallow us up alive. Whenever you have been called on in faith, you have been merciful. Have mercy now on your people, and help them, that they may not perish.'

At these words a dove arrived in the midst of the sea and circled round their ship three times. The third time, when it flew, the queen's servant named Banisaios stretched out his hand in the name of the Trinity, which the blessed lady always loved in her heart, and brought away three feathers from its tail. When he dipped these in the sea, the storm was held in check, and at the invocation of the name of the blessed Radegunde, the dove which appeared brought back her servants to life from the gate of death. A great calm[44] then occurred in the midst of the sea. They cried aloud at the tops of their voices and said, 'You have come, gracious mistress, full of holy goodness, to snatch away your captives, that they may not be submerged by the waves.' At the invocation of her name, not only her servants but all of the people on the ship were freed by the miraculous power of the lady Radegunde herself. Those who had been freed from death brought the actual feathers here and devoutly distributed artificial feathers throughout the holy places. Whenever she was invoked, she listened kindly. If anyone were feverish or had a boil or suffered any kind of illness, no matter what, and could not come to her for reasons of distance, a candle burned in her name drove off every fever. Who could say how much her community loved her? It would not be possible to describe this, not even if a plectrum could strike the tongue and multiply the sound a hundredfold. *She introduced the custom that while they were taking meals, a lesson was always read, so that not only did their mouths receive food but their ears also heard the word of God.* Whatever she taught others to do, she did herself. She did everything for God's sake. Whatever she forbade to be done, or avoided doing, she acted from her zeal for God. She neither cooked nor tasted meat. Since she wished never to be at leisure from doing the work of God, she applied herself to prayer, reading, almsgiving, and preaching, daily and ceaselessly so that no member of the community could make excuses for herself on the grounds of ignorance.

Finally, by the generous grace of God, she received so great a gift in herself that in imitation of the Lord, the master of humility, who came down to earth from his throne in heaven, she followed him in spirit and went wherever he went.[45] After the community had lain down to rest, she passed the whole night in prayer and used to keep the monastery safe by making the sign of the cross with her holy right hand. On one occasion, when the blessed lady was making that sign, one of the sisters saw a million demons, appearing as goats, standing on the wall; but when the blessed saint raised her blessed hand in the sign of the cross, the multitude of demons was put to flight and never reappeared.

Similarly, when she was standing in front of her cell one night, continuously chanting her office in her heart and with her lips— for the praise of God always rang out secretly in the mysterious places of her heart—a night bird, which is always displeasing to people, made a disturbance by hooting on a tree in the middle of the monastery. One of the sisters, standing near Radegunde, said to her, 'Blessed lady, if you order me to do so, I will throw the bird out as soon as you say the word.' Radegunde replied, 'If the bird is harmful, go in the name of the Lord, but nevertheless make the sign of the cross over her.' The sister walked off and said to the bird, 'In the name of our Lord Jesus Christ, the lady Radegunde orders you, if you have not come to us from God's side, to depart from this place and not dare to sing here ever again.' Just as if the bird had heard the words issue from the mouth of God, she took flight and never reappeared. Birds and beasts rightly obeyed Radegunde, for she never neglected to obey the teaching of the Lord.[46] If sometimes, when she was feeling unwell, she would have liked to rest, her spirit remained alert and she would say, as if to recall the admonition of the psalmist, 'Act, speak.' there is no doubt that she was chanting the psalms in spirit with the saints or that sleep was really failing to overcome her. With her mind intent on Christ, it frequently happened that while she had been asleep, she had been pronouncing exhortations about future judgement and eternal reward, then, on waking up, she would say to us, *'Pick up, the Lord's grain of wheat, because I tell you in truth that you will not have a long time in which to pick it up. Take note of what I say! Pick it up, for you will be looking for the time to do it. Truly, truly, you will be searching for those days and you will greatly miss them.'* But if in our sloth, we then receive these words in a lukewarm spirit, we now prove that what she has said has come to pass. The prophecy has been fulfilled in us: 'I shall send you a famine in the land; a famine,' she said, 'not a famine of bread nor a thirst for water, but a famine of hearing the Word of God.'[47] Although the teachings which she established are read aloud,[48] *nevertheless her unceasing flow of words,* her counsels that we longed to hear and her sweet affection *have all come to an end. Who, O God, the good Creator, can ever described what kind of countenance or expression or personality she had?*[49] Even to recall them is a punishment. *We,* her humble sisters, *miss the teaching, the appearance, the countenance, the personality, the knowledge,* the holiness, the kindness *and the* sweetness of her whom God set specially apart from the rest of humankind.[50]

Her life was as holy as her appearance was pure and sweet.[51] A year before her death, she saw in a vision the place prepared for her. There came to her a young man who was very richly dressed and a very handsome and in age almost a child. When he addressed her, touching her gently and speaking to her pleasantly, she in her eagerness to maintain her virtue, repelled his flattering advances. He then said to her, 'Why are you aflame with desire, when you make requests to me with so many tears? Why do you seek me with sighs? Why do you pour out your prayers when you make supplication to me? Why do you afflict yourself with such great torment for me, when I am always standing at your side? You shall know, precious jewel, that you are the first jewel in my diadem.'[52] There is not doubt that her visitor was he, to whom she committed herself with full devotion while she was alive in the body, and that he revealed to her the glory she would enjoy in the future. She described this vision secretly to two faithful friends, with the earnest entreaty that they tell nobody in her lifetime. There is still much material of some importance which we have passed over in order to avoid a long and tedious narrative and in order that our prolixity might not weary our audience rather than enlighten them. How much do we recall of her love, her nurture, her charity, her preaching and, to sum it all up, of her totally sanctified way of life![53] We suffer torment and with eyes swollen with grief, look for similar great holiness, but we do not find what we have lost. What a cruel situation has come on us, unhappy as we are! O most holy lady, would that you had obtained from the Lord of heaven the right to send on ahead of you the sheep which you had collected together! You, following the Good Shepherd, would have handed your flock over to the Lord.

Now we come to her glorious passing, of which I cannot speak without weeping profusely. Our tears flow from the innermost parts of our being and our groans break forth, but as we mourn, they find no place of consolation anywhere. The less we speak of her faithful devotion, the more we sin. Up to the day of her death, she never reduced the time spent in the performance of her office, and what she had begun, she retained in her heart, since it is not he who begins, but *he who will have persevered to the end who will be saved.*[54] When her holy little body, which had endured a protracted martyrdom for love of the Lord, now came to the end of its life, the whole community of blessed ladies gathered together. Weeping and howling, they mourned around her couch and, striking their breasts with their hard fists and with stones, they raised their voices to heaven, crying out and saying, 'Lord, do not allow us to suffer so grievous a loss. You have given us light; why therefore do you leave us?' It is a fact that whenever she wished to do something very important, she chose to do it on the day of the week on which the Lord's birth occurred. By a fortunate chance, her glorious passing occurred early in the morning of the fourth day of the week, the Ides of August, which same is the thirteenth day of the month, when her eyes were closed and our eyes were darkened.

Woe to us! Because we have sinned, our hearts are afflicted with grief. We weep and mourn, because we have not deserved to keep you with us longer. On the very morning when this great misfortune befell us, when a single voice, a single lamentation, and single cry from us all reached the heavens, the stone-cutters, who were working on the hill, heard an angel speaking in the air. One of them said to the others, 'What are you doing? Bring her back down here.' Because these words reached the ears of the Lord, the angels who were carrying her said in reply, 'It has already been done'. What shall we do? Paradise has received her. There she is in glory with the Lord, the angels who were carrying her said in reply, 'It has already been done'. What shall we do? Paradise has received her; there she is in glory with the Lord. We believe that she does not separate herself from us, and that she wished to please him with whom she reigns. Such a person as she must not be mourned by us with tears, but regarded with holy awe. We have indeed lost a mistress and a mother in our present life, but we have sent her ahead to the kingdom of Christ as our intercessor. *In heaven she has caused marvelous joy, but on earth she has left us intolerable sorrow.*[55]

When her holy soul migrated from this world to Christ, the bishop of the place was not there. A messenger went on foot to the apostolic man, Gregory, lord bishop of the city of Tours, and he came. He included in the Book of Miracles he composed[56] as many of her miracles as he, being present, saw with his own eyes before he buried her. When he came to the place where her sacred body lay—he afterwards said weeping and confirmed by oath that he had seen the countenance of an angel in the form of a human being, for her face was resplendent like the rose and the lily—this very devout man, filled with God, was seized with a fit of trembling and stricken with fear, as if he were standing in the presence of the blessed Mother of the Lord. We waited for the bishop of the place, so that they might bury her with appropriate dignity. The whole community stood around her bier, singing psalms. When the singing died down just a little, an unbearable wailing broke out. We waited for the bishop for three days, because he was going round the villages, but when he did not arrive, the aforesaid apostolic man was faithful in his love, *for perfect love casts out fear.*[57] He buried her with appropriate dignity in the basilica founded in the name of Saint Mary, where the sacred bodies of the virgins of her own monastery are buried.[58]

Since she had ordered that no living sister should go beyond the monastery gate the whole community on the wall lamenting, her holy body, accompanied by a choir of psalm-singers, was being carried below the wall as their cries of mourning overcame the choir itself. *They rendered tears instead of psalms. Groans instead of the change, and sighs instead of the alleluias.*[59] As they painfully endured her absence, they asked from overhead that the bier on which the blessed lady was being carried might halt below their tower.[60] Then, that the Lord might proclaim her faithfulness in the midst of the people, he gave sight to a blind man while the bier was halted there. This man, who had not seen the light of day for many years, received the enlightenment of his eyes; he who had been led by the hand to follow the bier was able to see, and without anyone supporting him he departed to the saint's tomb, just as if he had not had any trouble with his eyes. He sees clearly to this day.

Let us not pass over yet another miracle. When the aforesaid bishop buried her, he did not put the cover on the tomb, pending the arrival of the bishop of the place. The free women who carried candles before her all stood in a circle round the tomb. Each of them had her name written in the candle; all of them handed the candles over to one of the servants, according to directions. A quarrel broke out among the people: some were saying that the candles ought to be deposited in her holy tomb; others, that they ought not to be. While this was going on, one of the candles escaped from the arms of a young servant who was carrying them all. It leaped over everyone and placed itself in the holy tomb, at the feet of the blessed lady. This put an end to all hesitation. When they looked to see whose name was on the candle, they found that it was Calva's. When the bishop and all the people saw this, they marvelled at blessed Radegunde's miracle and blessed the Lord. Who could count how many miracles were done there after her passing, how many people were freed from demoniac possession and how many people, suffering from fever, were restored to health?

An abbot called Abbo came from Burgundy with the apostolic man, bishop Leifastus. While he was in the city of Poitiers, he was stricken with a severe toothache. Day and night the same cry went up from him and he suffered the same pain. He longed for death, that he might be freed from such intense pain. This man, inspired by the mercy of God, asked that he be taken to the saint's basilica. Having entered it, he flung himself on the ground in faith before the holy tomb, keeping death before his eyes. Then he bit hard on the pall placed over the holy tomb. For seven days he had been unable either to take food or be refreshed by sleep, but when he thus bit, sleep returned to him, pain left him, and he went back to his lodging in good health. Afterwards he spoke about it himself, and a number of people understood what he meant, when he told them that he had been recalled from the gate of death through the power of the lady Radegunde.

It is the custom on the feast of Saint Hilary[61] for the other neighboring monasteries in the area to come to the basilica to celebrate vigils until midnight. After midnight, each abbot, with his brothers, returns to his own monastery to celebrate the office. On one occasion, while they were keeping vigil in the basilica of the blessed bishop, those possessed by evil spirits cried all night long. Among them were two women whom the enemy grievously tormented. One of them, especially, was in such a frenzy that the whole basilica trembled at her roaring. After the venerable man, Arnegisselus, abbot of the basilica of the blessed queen, departed with his monks, he went to his own basilica to complete his office, that office which the saint had loved. They heard the women, who had followed them, making a great commotion. Once they had entered the basilica, still making a racket, they begged the lady Radegunde to spare them. One of them was much tormented, having already been possessed by the evil spirit for fifteen years. Then, when Matins was being said, the fierce enemy left the vessel which he had invaded. The other woman was freed at Terce before the door of the basilica, and from then on the ever wicked Enemy could do her no further harm. How wide and how rich is the mercy of God, which causes his people to fear him! He himself, the generous giver and dispenser of miracles, seeks places where he can show his power through his faithful people. Some of those who were freed were directed to the basilica of the saintly man [Hilary], others to the basilica of the lady Radegunde, so that just as they were equal in grace, so they might be shown to be equal in miraculous power.

Who, suffering from an illness, although he might despair of life, would not be cured in the following manner? If the guardian of the tomb of the same lady [Radegunde] dipped the hem of its pall into a chalice of water and gave a cup of it to drink to a person suffering from fever, did sleep not come on that person and disease retreat from him almost as soon as he drank, lying before her tomb? By the bounty of Christ, every day many miracles occur there in the place from which she has gone, in the name of Jesus Christ. We too with faithful devotion and with the constant attention due her, venerate on earth her, in whose soul we trust, rejoice in her, and glorify her, because she is resplendent in heaven in his presence, who with the Father and the Holy Spirit, lives and reigns for ever and ever.

NOTES

1. The *prooemium* and indeed the whole of the prologue to *Vita II*[a] is an example of the *confessio humilitatis*, a topos of the medieval hagiographer; see e.g., Caesarius of Arles, *Epistola ad moniales* 1 (*Césaire d'Arles, Oeuvres monastiques* 1, ed. A. de Vogüé, SCh 345 [Paris, 1988 294/295–298/299). But Baudonivia seems to have been humble in fact.

2. See Venantius Fortunatus, *Vita S. Hilarii Pict.* 2 (MGH AA 4 (2): 2–3).

3. *Idem, Vita S. Marcelli* 1 (NGH AA 4 (2): 49.

4. *Ibid.*

5. Venantius Fortunatus; *Vita S. Hilarii Pict. 1* (p. 1).

6. *Ibid.*

7. See pp. 397.

8. An apology for the poor quality of the writer's Latin was also part of the *confessio humilitatis* (cf. Gregory of Tours, LH, praef.; MGH SRM 1 (1): 1), but Baudonivia's Latin is certainly not very elegant.

9. See *Vita I*[a], p. 385.

10. See above pp. 382f.

11. Cf. Sulpicius Severus, *Vita S. Martini* 14 (Sulpice Sévère, *Vie de saint Martin*, ed. J. Fontaine, 3 vols. SCh 133–135, vol. 1: 282/283–286/287) for the practice of destroying pagan temples. These stories of temple-destruction appear to be based on the Old Testament (e.g., 2 Chr 23: 16). Radegunde's action seems to be in accordance with general sixth-century papal policy; see, e.g., Gregory the Great, *Reg.* 11.37 (MGH Epp 2: 308–310); R. A. Markus, 'The *Registrum* of Gregory the Great and Bede,' *RBen* 18 (1970) 162–182.

12. This vision appears to signify that Radegunde was still at the beginning of her spiritual development, but would ultimately reach the profoundest depths of the spiritual life, perhaps what later mystics were to call the unitive way or prayer of union.

13. See n. 7 above.

14. There is some controversy as to the identity of the abbess, which is linked with the chronological problems of the life of Radegunde. According to Venantius Fortunatus (*Carm.* 11, 3, 9; MGH 4(2):25g, etc.), her name was Agnes, but in the letter of Caesaria the Younger (Césaire d'Arles, *Oeuvres monastiques* 1, ed. A, de Vogüé, pp. 476–477), it is given as Richildis, who is otherwise unknown. Vogüé suggests that Agnes may have succeeded Richildis *c.* 570, after the latter's return with Radegunde from their journey to Arles. For a fuller discussion of this question, see Vogüé, pp. 442–460.

15. For the fate of Arius, see Gregory of Tours, LH 2.23 (MGH SRM 1(1): p. 68).

16. This paragraph probably represents the culmination of negotiations to bring about the permanent separation of Chlothar and Radegunde, in which Germanus, bishop of Paris, may have played a prominent part and presumably refers to the consecration of Radegunde as a nun.

17. Mt 8:19.

18. This and subsequent passages in italics have been 'lifted' by Baudonivia from the *vita* of Caesarius of Arles (by Cyprian of Toulon *et al.*) with appropriate changes of gender where necessary. This was a common late antique and early medieaval practice, because it was generally believed that holiness was indivisible and that what could be said of one holy person could well be applied to another. Cf. *Vita S. Caesarii Arelat*. 1. 45 (MGH SRM 3: 474).

19. Mt 5:44.

20. See n. 10 above.

21. Sg 5:2.

22. Ps 118 (119):62.

23. Ps 18 (19):15.

24. The story of the vessel containing wine or oil which never needs to be replenished is a *topos* of hagiography. For other examples, see J. M. Petersen, *The Dialogues of Gregory the Great in their late antique cultural background*, Studies and Texts 69 (Toronto, 1984) pp. 388–41.

25. Mt 14:21.

26. She had probably known them as children at the country estate at Athies-sur-Somme. See p. 371.

27. For Radegunde as peacemaker, see E.-R. Labande, 'Radegonde, reine, moniale et pacificatrice,' *La riche personnalité de sainte Radegonde: conférences et homélies du xiv^e^centennaire (587–1987)* (Poitiers, 1988) pp. 37–38.

28. Lk 7:38.

29. See n. 10 above.

30. For further details of Radegunde's devotion to relics, see Gregory of Tours, LGM 5 (MGH SRM 1 (2): 39–42). For the cult of relics in sixth-century Gaul in general, see Petersen, pp. 122–124.

31. Saint Mammas is in all probability identical with Saint Mamas or Mammes, mentioned by Basil (*Hom*. 23; PG 31 589) and Gregory of Nazianzus (*In ix dominicam, or*. 44, PG 36:620).

32. The Council of Poitiers, ad 590. See Gregory of Tours, *Liber historiarum* 10.15–17; MGH ssrm 1²; ed. B. Krusch and W. Levison (Hanover, 1951, rpt. 1965) 503. The identity of the persons is unknown.

33. Cf. *Vita S. Caesarii Arelat* 2.35 (pp. 496–497).

34. *Ibid.*, 1.46 (pp. 474–475). Ps 83(84):13.

35. Mt 22:37, Mk 12:30, Lk 10:27.

36. For the story of Helena, see Socrates, *Hist. trip*. 11.18 (CSEL 71, rev. ed. [Vienna, 1952] pp. 114–115).

37. We can only conjecture the reasons for the dispute between Maroveus, bishop of Poitiers, and Radegunde. Possibly he was resentful because she had applied through King Sigebert and not through himself to Justin II for a relic of the True Cross, and jealous because the monastery, rather than his cathedral, was likely to become a place of pilgrimage, on account of the relic's presence. There was no focus of devotion there, comparable to the tomb of Saint Martin at Tours. Radegunde may even have been planning to make the monastery a 'peculiar', independent of episcopal jurisdiction. So far as the monastery at Arles

was concerned, provision was made for this in a letter of Pope Hormisdas (d.523), *Ep.* 2 (Césaire d'Arles, *Oeuvres monastiques* 1: pp. 354/355).

38. 1 (3) Kgs 10:19.

39. Lk 1:28.

40. Venantius Fortunatus composed for the occasion the famous processional hymns *Pange, lingua* (*Carm* 2.2., MGH AA 4(1), p. 28) and *Vexilla regis* (*Ibid.* 6, p. 34), which are familiar to English-speaking Christians in the nineteenth-century translations of J. M. Neale: *Sing, my tongue* and *The royal banners forward go.*

41. Lk 1:44.

42. Jm 1:17.

43. Radegunde evidently had fears—which in the event proved justified—for the future of her community. Gregory of Tours (LH 9.40–43; MGH SRM 1(1): 464–475) tells us about a rebellion of nuns, which seems to have been smoldering in her lifetime and which came to a head after her death. No doubt this group of two hundred women, largely of aristocratic origin and autocratic in their ways, was not easy to handle. Radegunde's letter to the bishops (now generally accepted as genuine) is a concrete expression of her fears. For its text, see Gregory of Tours, LH 9.42, pp. 470–474.

44. Mt 8:26.

45. Rev 14:4.

46. The power of the holy man or woman over living creatures is a *topos* of hagiography. Other examples, contemporary with Radegunde or a little later, are Columbanus (Jonas, *Vita Columbani abbatis* 1.17 (MGH SRM 4; p. 83).

47. Am 8:19.

48. Cf. *Vita s. Caesarii* 2.32 (495–496), 35 (496–497).

49. *Ibid.*, 2.35 (496).

50. *Ibid.*, (497).

51. *Ibid.*

52. This vision is in the classic mystical tradition. Later women mystics would see Jesus Christ in the guise of a young man, as their heavenly bridegroom; e.g., Gertrud of Helfta, Catherine of Siena.

53. Cf. *Vita S. Caesarii Arelat.* 2.37 (p. 497).

54. Mt 10:22.

55. *Vita S. Caesari*, 2.49 (500).

56. Gregory of Tours, LGM 5 (MGH SRM 1(2): 39–40).

57. 1 Jn 4:18.

58. The church at Poitiers, now dedicated to Saint Radegunde, was then the church of the men's monastery. Because it was situated outside the walls, it could be used for burials. The interment of a corpse within the walls of a city was forbidden by Roman law (*Codex Theodosianus* 9.17.7, *Theodosiani libri xvi cum constitutionibus sirmondianis et leges novellae . . .*, ed. Th. Mommsen and P. M. Meyer, 2 vols in 3 [Berlin, 1954] vol. 1(2): 466.

59. Cf. *Vita S. Caearii Arelat.* 2.47 (p. 500), where the writer is describing the death and funeral of Caesaria the Elder, but we have independent

confirmation by Gregory of Tours (LGC 104; pp. 364–366) of the moving character of the funeral of Radegunde.

60. The women's monastery was built along the city wall; hence the references to towers and ramparts by both Baudonivia and Gregory of Tours (LGC 104, p. 365). The first sentence of ¶ 24 indicates the strict application of the rule of enclosure to the community at Poitiers, presumably on account of the provisions of the Rule of Arles (*Reg. Virg.*, 1; Césaire d'Arles, *Oeuvres monastiques* 1: 180/181.

61. January 14.

THE DEATH AND
FUNERAL OF RADEGUNDE
BY GREGORY OF TOURS

HE BLESSED LADY RADEGUNDE, whose origin we have recalled in our book of martyrs,[1] departed from this world after her life's work was completed. When we received news of her death, we made our way to the monastery which she herself had founded in the city of Poitiers. We found her lying on a bier, and her holy face shone so that it made the beauty of roses and lilies seem something worthy to be despised. Around the bier stood a great throng of nuns, about two hundred in number, who had been converted through her preaching and were leading holy lives. According to the standards of the secular world, they were not only from senatorial families, but also, in some cases, from royal stock itself. They flourished in this form of religious life. Now they stood, beating their breasts and saying, 'To whom, holy mother, will you leave us orphans? To whom do you commend us, desolate as we are? We have left our parents, our properties, and our country and have followed you. To what will you leave us, other than to perpetual tears and never-ending grief? Behold, until now, this monastery has been more important to us than spacious country houses or cities. Wherever we have gone, there we found gold, there we found silver, as we contemplated your glorious countenance. There we beheld with admiration the leafy vine and the ripening crops; there we saw meadows verdant with various kinds of flowers. We plucked violets from you; you were for us a glowing red rose and a lily of dazzling whiteness. Your words were for us like the sun in their splendor and lit for us the clear lamp of truth like the moon in the darkness of our consciousness. Now, however, the whole earth has been darkened for us, confined in the precincts of this place, when we are no longer thought worthy to behold your face. Alas for us, deserted by our holy mother! Happy are those of our sisters who departed from this world while you survived. We know of course that you are linked with the choir of virgins and with the Paradise of God, but though we take comfort from this, it is a lamentable thing for us that we cannot look on you with our physical eyes.'

While they were giving vent to these and other lamentations, we were unable to restrain our tears. I turned to the abbess and said, 'Stop crying for a little while. It is better to carry on with the things that are necessary. Look, our brother bishop Maroveus is not here, on the pretext that his visits to parishes have kept him from us. Let us make a plan, so that her holy little body may come to no harm and that the grace that God has provided for her blessed limbs may not be taken away if the time of her burial is deferred. Make haste with the obsequies due to her, so that she may be yielded up for burial with honor.'

To this, the abbess replied, 'What shall we do, if the bishop of our city does not arrive, since the place where she ought to be buried has not been hallowed by an episcopal consecration?'

Then the citizens and other important men who had assembled for the funeral of the blessed lady, the queen, made a request to me, humble as I am, saying, 'Presume on the charity of your brother bishop and consecrate the altar. We trust in his good will, since what you will do would not cause him trouble, but instead would bring grace. Act thus presumptuously, we beg you, so that her holy flesh may be given burial.'

When we moved her holy body and began to carry it down, singing psalms, those possessed by evil spirits howled and, confessing her to be a saint of God, said that they were being tormented by her. While we were passing below the wall, the crowd of virgins again began to raise their voices through the windows in the towers and also through the very bastions of the wall, and to make lamentations from above, so that between the sound of weeping and the beating of their breasts with their hands, no one could restrain his tears. And the clerks themselves, whose function it was to chant the psalms, could scarcely chant the antiphons between their sobs and their tears. Then we approached the tomb. Providentially the abbess had had a wooden chest made, in which she had enclosed the body, which was laid there upon spices, to preserve it. On account of this, the tomb was wider than was normal, so that when one side had been taken away from each of a pair of tombs, the chest holding the holy limbs could be placed in them. Then, when the funeral oration had been delivered, we departed. We reserved for the bishop of the city the duty of closing the tomb with the cover after he had celebrated Mass. We returned to the monastery, and the abbess, with her virgins, led us to each of the places where the holy woman had been accustomed to read or to pray. The abbess said to us, as she mourned, 'See, we enter the cell, and we do not find our lost mother! Here is the stall where she used to kneel down and beg with tears for the mercy of Almighty God, but we do not see her here. Here is the book which she was reading, but her voice, seasoned with spiritual salt, does not strike our ears. Here are the spindles with which she was accustomed to spin during the long fasts, but her fingers, with their kindly dignity, are no longer to be seen.'

As she said these words, her tears were renewed, her sighs issued forth, and her very organs dissolved into tears from the emotion of weeping. So great a grief assailed my heart that I should have continued to weep, had I not known that the blessed lady Radegunde had been borne away from the monastery in her body, but not in the power of her spirit, and that having been taken from this world, she had been placed in heaven.

NOTE

1. Gregory of Tours, LGC 104; MGH SRM 2: 364–366.

APPENDIX

THE SISTERS OF SAINTE-CROIX DE POITIERS

The benedictine sisters of Sainte-Croix de Poitiers are the direct spiritual descendants of the community founded by Saint Radegunde. The date of her foundation is uncertain, but it cannot have been earlier than 552 or later than 557. It had therefore been in existence for a least ten years before the arrival of the relic of the True Cross in 567–568. In Radegunde's time the Rule of Saint Caesarius of Arles for nuns was adopted by the community, probably in the early days of the monastery, c. 552–557. The Rule of Saint Benedict was probably substituted for it c. 817, when Benedict of Aniane, the great reformer and systematizer of the Rule, is known to have been in the district and may have visited the monastery. To this Rule the sisters adhere to this day.

Unlike other religious communities in France, the sisters of Sainte-Croix de Poitiers have a continuous history, unbroken by the French Revolution. Certainly the sisters were required by the civil authorities to leave their buildings, which were subsequently demolished, but by sheer determination, inspired perhaps by their sense of responsibility as guardians of the relic, they survived by staying in the houses of friends or relatives and meeting together to say their office in little groups. Some of them even suffered a term of imprisonment, but after the Concordat between Church and State in 1801, they were able to settle down in an old house near the Cathedral, the former deanery of Poitiers. For many years subsequently they led a precarious and poverty-stricken existence, but they were able to re-establish the rhythm of the monastic life. Not even the tragic events of two World Wars has been able to interrupt it. Immense care has been taken to preserve

433

the relic, which during the Second World War, the abbess wore always next to her heart.

As time passed, it became clear that the city of Poitiers was no longer a suitable place for an enclosed religious community. The quarter in which the monastery was situated was becoming increasingly crowded and noisy, and there was little garden space. After much thought and prayer, the community decided to follow the example of other communities of nuns and to move from the city out into the country. The present home of the sisters is a large country house, called La Cossonnière, which was formerly occupied by the Jesuits. It is set in extensive grounds, away from the nearest village, Saint Benoît sur Quinçay, which afford quiet and peaceful surroundings. The removal was completed in 1964. Here the Sisters carry on their work of prayer and praise, as well as the manual work and study enjoined by the benedictine Rule, and receive guests. They have wide ecumenical interests and are in contact with other benedictine communities, both Anglican and Roman Catholic, in different parts of the world.

SUGGESTIONS FOR FURTHER READING

GENERAL BACKGROUND

Bynum, C. W. *Jesus as Mother: Studies in the Spirituality of the High Middle Ages*. Berkeley, Los Angeles and London 1982.

———. *Gender and Religion*. Boston 1986.

Clark, E. A. *Women in the Early Church*. Message of the Fathers of the Church 13. Wilmington, Delaware, 1982.

———. *Ascetic Piety and Women's Faith: Essay on late antique Christianity*. Studies in women and religion, 20. Lewiston, N.Y., 1986.

Hampson, D. *Theology and Feminism*. Oxford 1990.

Lanzoni, F. 'Il sogno presago della madre incinto nella letteratura medievale e antica', *Analecta Bollandiana* 45 (1927) 225–261.

Loades, A., ed. *Theology: A Feminist Reader*. London 1990.

Marrou, H. I. 'La patrie de Jean Cassien', *Orientalia Christiana Periodica* 13 (1947) 588–596.

Platelle, H. 'La penitence des parricides', *Sacris erudiri* 20 (1971) 135–161.

Rousseau, P. *Ascetics, Authority and the Church in the Age of Jerome and Cassian*. Oxford 1978.

Schüsler Fiorenza, E. *In Memory of Her: A Feminist Theological Reconstruction of Christian Origins*. London 1983.

Witherington, B. *Women in the earliest churches*. Society for New Testament Studies, biog. ser., 59. Cambridge 1988.

Zelzer, K. 'Cassianus natione Scytha, ein Südgallier', *Wiener Studien* 104 (1991) 161–168.

Apophthegmata patrum (Sayings of the Desert Fathers)

1. Texts: Greek

   Apophthegmata patrum [*Alphabetical collection*] PG 65: 71–412.

   Histoire de solitaires égyptiens. [*Anonymous collection*]. Edited by F. Nau. *Revue de l'Orient chrétien* 12 (1907); 13 (1908); 14 (1909); 17 (1912); 18 (1913).

2. Texts: Latin

   Verba seniorum 1–18 [=*Vitae patrum 5*], translated by Pelagius. PL 73: 85–992.

   Verba seniorum 1–43 [=*Vitae patrum 6*], translated by John: PL 73:991–1024.

   Verba seniorum. [=*Vitae patrum 7*], translated by Paschasius. PL 73:1025–1066.

   Aegyptiorum patrum sententiae [=*Appendix ad Vitas patrum*], translated by Martin of Dume. PL 74:381–394.

3. Translations from the Greek

   The Sayings of the Desert Fathers: The Alphabetical Collection (PG 65:71–90) Translated by Benedicta Ward, SLG. Introduction by Anthony Bloom. Kalamazoo-London 1975.

   The Sayings of the Desert Fathers: The Apophthegmata patrum [*Anonymous series*]. Introduction by Anthony Bloom. Translated [from Nau's text] by Benedicta Ward, SLG. Oxford 1975.

   The Wisdom of the Desert Fathers: The Apophthegmata patrum [*Anonymous series*] Introduction by Anthony Bloom. Translated [from Nau's text] by Bendicta Ward, SLG. Oxford 1975.

4. Translations from the Latin

   The Sayings of the Fathers [=*Verba seniorum 1–17*], with selections from 18–21. PL 73:855–1022. Edited and translated by Owen Chadwick. Library of Christian Classics 12:37–189. London 1958.

   Waddell, Helen. *The Desert Fathers* [selections, with some material from *Historia monachorum in Aegypto*; Palladius, *Heraclidis paradisus*; and John Moschus, *Pratum spirituale*]. London 1936.

5. Translations into French

Les sentences des pères du désert: Les apotegmes des pères (recension de Pélage et Jean). Introduction by L. Régnault. Translated by J. Bion and G. Oury. Solesmes 1966.

Les sentences des pères du désert: nouveau recueil apotegmes inédits our peu connus. Edited by L. Régnault. Translated by the monks of Solesmes. Solesmes 1970.

Les sentences des pères du désert: troisième recueil et tables. Edited by L. Régnault. Translated by the monks of Solesmes. Solesmes 1976.

Athanasius, Saint, Patriarch of Alexandria. [*Vita Antonii*] *Vita di Antonio* Introduction by Christine Mohrmann. Edited by G. J. M. Bartelink. Italian translation [of earliest Latin version] by P. Citati and S. Lilla. Vite dei Santi 1. Milan 1974.

———. *Life of St Antony.* Translated by Robert T. Meyer. Ancient Christian Writers 10. Westminster, Md, 1950.

———. *Life of Antony.* Edited and translated by R. Gregg. Classics of Western Spirituality series.

Egeria's Travels [*Peregrinatio Aetheriae*], edited and translated by J. Wilkinson. London 1971.

Historia monachorum in Aegypto. Greek text. Edited by A. J. Festugière. *Subsidia hagiographica* 34. Brussels 1961.

———. Latin text, by Rufinus, PL 21:387–462.

———. Translation by R. M. Price, *The Lives of The Desert Fathers.* Kalamazoo 1980.

John Moschus. *Pratum spirituale.* J.-P. Migne, *Patrologia Graeca* 87:2851–3116 = Jean Baptiste Cotelier, *Ecclesiae Graecae monumenta* 2:341–456. Paris 1681.

———. *The Spiritual Meadow of John Moschus.* Translated by John Wortley. Kalamazoo 1992.

MACRINA

Pfister, J. F. 'The brothers and sisters of St Gregory of Nyssa', *Vigiliae Christianae* 18 (1964) 108–113.

TEXTS

Gregory, Saint, Bishop of Nyssa. *The Life of St Macrina*. Translated by W. K. Lowther Clarke. London 1916.

Vita Sanctae Macrinae. Edited by V. Woods Callahan in Werner Jaeger, J.-P. Cavarnos, V. Woods Callahan, *Gregorii Nysseni Opera Ascetica*, 347–414. Leiden 1952.

Grégoire de Nysse. Vie de sainte Macrine. Introduction and French translation by P. Maraval. SCh 178. Paris 1971.

The Life of St. Macrina by Gregory of Nyssa. Translated by Kevin Corrigan. Saskatoon [Toronto] 1987.

———. *From Glory to Glory: Texts from Gregory of Nyssa's Mystical Writings*; selected and with an introduction by Jean Daniélou, SJ. Translated and edited by Herbert Musurillo, SJ. London 1962.

SAINT JEROME AND ASCETIC WOMEN

Clark, E. A. *Jerome, Chrysostom and Friends*. New York 1979.

Kelly, J. N. D. *Jerome: His Life, Writings and Controversies*. London 1975.

TEXTS

Jerome [Hieronymus], Saint. Selected letters. Translated by W. H. Fremantle in H. Wace and P. Schaff, *A select library of Nicene and Post-Nicene Fathers*, series 2, vol. 6. 1893.

———. *Epistolae*. Edited by I. Hilberg, CSEL 54–56. Vienna 1910–1918.

———. *Select Letters*. Translated by F. A. Wright. Loeb Classical Library. London and New York, 1933.

———. *Lettres* . . . . Text and French translation by J. Labourt. Editions Guillaume Budé. Paris 1949–63.

———. *Selected Letters* in *Early Latin Theology*. Edited and translated by S. L. Greenslade. Ancient Christian Classics 5: 279–384. London 1956.

———. *The Letters of St Jerome*. Translated by C. Mierow. Introduction and notes by T. C. Lawlor. Ancient Christian Writers 33. London and Westminster, Maryland 1963.

MELANIA THE ELDER AND MELANIA THE YOUNGER

Clark, E. A. *The Life of Melania the Younger* [including text of the Life by Gerontius of Jerusalem]. New York 1986.

Gerontius of Jerusalem. *Sanctae Melaniae Iunioris acta Graeca*, edited by H. Delehaye, *Analecta Bollandiana* 22 (1903) 5–50.

———. *Santa Melania Giuniore, senatrice romana*. [The Latin and Greek lives]. Edited with [Italian] translation [of the Greek life] by Cardinal M. Rampolla del Tindaro. Vatican City 1905.

———. [*The Life of Saint Melania*] *Vie de saint Melanie*. Edited with [French] translation by D. Gorce. SCh 90. Paris 1962.

Palladius, successively Bishop of Heliopolis and of Aspona. *The Lausiac History of Palladius 1–2*. Ed. E. C. Butler, Texts and Studies 5–6. Cambridge 1898–1904. See also E. C. Butler, 'Palladiana', *Journal of Theological Studies* 22 (1921) 31–35; 138–155; 222–238.

———. *The Lausiac History of Palladius*. Translated by W. K. Lowther Clarke. London and New York 1917.

———. *La storia Lausiaca*. Introduction by Christine Mohrmann. Text and commentary by G. J. M. Bartelink. [Italian] translated by M. Barchesi. Vite dei Santi 2. Milan 1974.

RADEGONDE

Aigrain, R. 'Le voyage de sainte Radegonde à Arles', *Bulletin historique et philogique, comitécide travaille historique et scientifique* (1926) 119–127.

———. *Sainte Radegonde*; new, revised and corrected edition. Poitiers 1952.

Bradshaw, H. *The lyfe of saynt Radegunde* [attributed to H. Bradshaw]; edited from the copy in Jesus College library by F. Brittain. Cambridge 1926.

Briand, E. *Histoire de sainte Radegonde, reine de France, et des sanctuaires et pèlerinages en son honneur*. Poitiers-Paris 1898.

Brittain, F. *Saint Radegund, Patroness of Jesus College, Cambridge*. Cambridge 1925.

Fleury, E. de. *Histoire de sainte Radegonde, reine de France au vi^e siècle et patronne de Poitiers*. 2 ed. Poitiers 1847.

Kirshner, J. *Women of the Medieval World*. Oxford 1985.

Kleinmann, D. 'Sainte Radegonde, le roi Clotaire et la politique en Gaule mérovingiene', *Bulletin des Amis de vieux Chinon* 8[10] (1986) 1383–1401.

Nanteuil, J. *Sainte Radegonde, princesse barbare et reine de France*. Paris 1938.

Radegunde. La riche personnalité de sainte Radegonde: conférences et homélies prononcées à Poitiers à l'occasion du xive centennaire de sa mort (587–1987). Poitiers 1988.

Scheibelreiter, C. 'Königstöchter im Klöster. Radegund (+587) und der Nonnenaufstand um Poitiers (589)', *Mitteilungen des Instituts für Oesterreichische Geschichtsforschung* 87 (1979) 1–37.

Societé des Antiquaires de l'Quest. *Histoire de l'Abbaye de sainte Croix de Poitiers. Mémoires de la Société des Antiquaires de l'Quest*, 4e série, 19 (1986/87) 25–75. [The history fills the whole of vol. 19]

Wallace-Hadrill, J. M. *The Frankish Church*. Oxford 1938.

TEXTS

Fortunatus, Venantius. *Vita prima sanctae Radegundis*. Edited by B. Krusch. MGH AA 4/2 (1885) 38–48; MGH SRM 2 (1888, rpt 1956) 364–377.

Baudonivia. *Vita secunda sanctae Radegundis*. Edited by B. Krusch, MGH SRM 2, 3ed. (1956) 377–395.

———. *Vie de Sainte Radegonde* [French] translated by Y. Labande-Mailfert, *Lettre de Ligugé* 239 (1987) 9–32.

Caesarius, Saint, Bishop of Arles. *Regula sanctarum virginum*. Edited by G. Morin, *Caesarii opera* 2. Maredsous 1942.

———. *[Regula sanctarum virginum] The rule of nuns of St Caesarius of Arles*. A translation by M. C. McCarthy. Catholic University of America, Studies in Mediaeval History, n.s. 16, Washington, D.C. 1960.

———. *Regula sanctarum virginum. Œuvres monastiques* 1, *Œuvres pour les moniales*. Introduction, critical edition of text, translation and notes by A. de Vogüé and J. Courreau. SCh 345. Paris 1988.

Fortunatus, Venantius. *Carmina*. Edited by F. Leo. MGH AA 4/1. 1881.

Gregory, Saint, Bishop of Tours. *Liber historiarum*. Edited by B. Krusch and W. Levison. MGH SRM 1/1, n. ed. 1951.

———. *Opera minora*. Edited by B. Krusch. MGH SRM 1/2. 1882, rpt 1969.